FOREWORD

The Jewish Publication Society takes pleasure in presenting herewith the third volume of a series of commentaries on the books of the Bible. The first volume, the Book of Micah with commentary, by Max L. Margolis, was published in 1908. The second volume, the Book of Deuteronomy with commentary, by Joseph Reider, was published in 1937. It is planned to issue additional volumes of the commentaries series in the future.

The series is intended for the teacher, the interested pupil and the general reader, and the commentaries are therefore written in as simple and popular a form as is consistent with clearness and accuracy.

Moreover being intended for the Jewish reader, it emphasizes the Jewish point of view and draws more largely than do the general commentaries on the traditional interpretations found in the classical Jewish literature of medieval and modern times.

The recent discoveries, linguistic, literary and archaeological are taken account of.

The translation follows the English version of the Jewish Publication Society.

PREFACE

So much has been written on the Bible throughout the ages that no new commentary on any one of its books can be expected to offer much that is novel or original. The value of any new commentary on a book of the Bible will consist chiefly in the point of view assumed and in the sources utilized. Careful and painstaking study may reveal to an author something that may have been overlooked by his predecessors and direct his attention to a line of investigation that remained unplumbed by the long array of distinguished scholars who dealt with the subject. His main work, however, is necessarily eclectic, the sifting of the large mass of material on hand, and the weighing of the various opinions expressed in the light of their intrinsic worth and in the light of the purpose which he sets for himself in the preparation of his work.

The present commentary on the Book of Numbers, published in the series of "The Holy Scriptures With Commentary", projected by the Jewish Publication Society of America, has the avowed purpose of furnishing a clear and concise interpretation of the book "for the teacher, the interested pupil and the general reader". This aim was held uppermost in the mind of the author, although he is not aware of any instance when simplicity and directness have been achieved at the expense of thorough investigation and full study. The classic Hebrew exegetes of the middle ages have been uniformly consulted and are frequently quoted. The more recent productions of Bible interpreters, whether Jews or non-Jews, have been carefully studied and their opinions, when cogent and in harmony with the aim of the author, were

adopted. Nor have the rabbinic legal and homiletic con-
structions given to some of the texts in the book been
neglected. Laws and institutions referred to in this book
have been traced also in their later development in the
post-biblical period, even unto the present day. Since
the book is intended primarily for Jewish readers, the
Jewish point of view and the Jewish attitude toward the
ideas, laws and legends were given special emphasis and
illumination. It is the fervent hope of the author that
this work, the result of many years of reverent study and
research, will prove stimulating and helpful to the student
who is anxious to understand not merely the text and the
ideas behind it, but also the manner in which these were
understood and regarded by the successive ages of outstanding Jewish personalities and their followers. A
partial bibliography of books used in the course of preparation will be found at the end of the Introduction.

I wish to record here my gratitude to the late Professor
Max L. Margolis who gave me the encouragement to
proceed with the work and offered many suggestions as
to treatment and plan. His untimely death deprived me
of his further counsel which would surely have been of
great benefit to me. Dr. Joseph Reider read the entire
manuscript and was of great assistance in the numerous
suggestions which he offered, most of which were adopted
and incorporated in the commentary. I am greatly be-
holden to him for his courteous interest and help. I also
wish to express my deep gratitude to my friend, Rabbi
Max D. Klein, for his uniform helpfulness in the reading
of the text and in the numerous suggestions and emendations, both in style and subject-matter, which proved of
great value to me.

Julius H. Greenstone

Philadelphia, 1938.

TABLE OF CONTENTS

MAPS:

1. CANAAN BEFORE THE CONQUEST.

2. EGYPT AND THE PENINSULA OF SINAI, WITH THE PROBABLE ROUTE OF THE ISRAELITES IN THE WILDERNESS.

INTRODUCTION

1. NAME

The Book of Numbers is the fourth book of the Pentateuch or Torah. The name is derived from the Latin *Numeri*, which is a translation of the Greek *Arithmoi*, the name by which the book was designated in the early manuscripts of the Greek version. This name has reference to the first few chapters (1.1–4.26), in which the census of the Israelites is recorded. The Hebrew name of the book is במדבר (*Bemidbar*), the fifth word of the first verse of the book. Although not intended originally to convey this idea, the name *Bemidbar* (in the wilderness of Sinai) fits well with the contents of the book. It was also known as וידבר, *Vayedabber*, after the first word of the book (see Jerome and ibn Ezra's introductory couplet), and as חמש הפקודים *Homesh ha-Pekudim* (that fifth part of the Torah which deals with the counted), which is similar in meaning to the Greek title (Yoma 7.1; Men. 4.3; Sotah 36b).

The book consists of 36 chapters, divided into 1288 verses. In the Masoretic version it consists of 158 sections, of which 92 are open (ending at the end of a line, פתוחות) and 66 are closed (ending in the middle of a line, סתומות). It is divided into ten portions (*Parashiyyot* or *Sidrot*), according to the usage of the reading from the Torah in the synagogue on Sabbath mornings. In the triennial system of Torah readings it is divided into thirty-two portions.

2. SCOPE

The book may well be divided into three grand divisions, namely chapters 1.1–10.10, dealing with the period of the stay of the Israelites in the Wilderness of Sinai; chapters 10.11–22.1, containing the narrative of events that occurred during the period of their wandering between the Wilderness of Sinai and the Plains of Moab; chapters 22.2–36.13, recounting incidents and laws promulgated during their stay in the Plains of Moab. The first section is intended to cover a period of nineteen days, from the first day of the second month of the second year of the Exodus to the twentieth day of the same month and year; the second section extends over a period of approximately thirty-eight years; the last section deals with events that occurred at the close of the journey, a period of approximately five months.

In Exodus 19.1 it is recorded that the Israelites reached the Wilderness of Sinai in the third month after their departure from Egypt, and in Numbers 10.11, 12, the departure of the Israelites from the Wilderness of Sinai is given as having occurred on the twentieth day of the second month of the second year after the Exodus. Thus, during the intervening eleven months, while they were encamped in the Wilderness of Sinai, the events recorded in Exodus, such as the Revelation at Mt. Sinai and the construction of the Tabernacle, the giving of the various laws of sacrifices contained in the Book of Leviticus and the taking of the census, the arrangement of the camp and the giving of the laws recorded in the first ten chapters of the Book of Numbers are assumed to have occurred. The first section of this book is thus closely related to the last section of the Book of Exodus. The Book of Leviticus, containing mainly laws pertaining to the sanctuary, fits in well after the narrative regarding the construction of the Tabernacle at the end of the Book of Exodus.

The second section, 10.11–22.1, tells of the departure of the Israelites from Mt. Sinai, journeying northward with a view of entering Canaan from the south. On reaching Kadesh, the people sent spies to investigate the land. The unfavorable report which they brought back led to a rebellion among the people. The decree was then passed upon them that they should remain in the wilderness for thirty-eight years more until the generation of the Exodus will have entirely passed away. During this long and wearisome period but few incidents are recorded to have occurred. The narrative simply indicates the very difficult problem that faced Moses, their leader, to keep the people pacified under trying circumstances; and also the methods which he used, by the direction of God, in quelling the various uprisings, the most serious of which was the rebellion of Korah and his followers. Several laws and regulations, mainly of an ecclesiastical character, interspersed through the narrative, are recorded to have been promulgated during that period. The narrative in this second section brings us down to the conclusion of the period of wandering when the Israelites had reached the confines of Moab, having scored victories over some of the Canaanite tribes, particularly the Amorites under Sihon and under Og, king of Bashan, and having appropriated their territories.

The last section, 22.2–36.13, begins with the Balaam and Balak episode, which the book records as having occurred when the Israelites reached the Plains of Moab, ready to take possession of the land promised to their ancestors. They did not attack the Moabites; but another tribe, the Midianites, represented as most hostile to Israel, was entirely exterminated in a punitive, religious expedition, because they had enticed the Israelites into idolatry. Some of the Israelitish tribes were then permitted to settle permanently in the conquered territory east of the Jordan, on condition that they participate actively with the other tribes in the conquest of Canaan. In the certain anticipation of its conquest, the boundaries of the land of Canaan are given in detail and princes are appointed for the tribes to aid Joshua and Eleazar in the work of allotting the land to each tribe. Special provision is made for the Levites, to whom no definite territory was to be assigned. The work of Moses is now completed and Joshua is appointed to succeed him and to lead the Israelites into Canaan. The narrative of the death of Moses is deferred to the end of the Book of Deuteronomy, the book devoted to the farewell addresses of the lawgiver. This section also contains several laws and regulations, some of an ecclesiastical nature and others of a civic character, intended to function in the life of the nation after its settlement in the land of Canaan.

3. Contents by Chapters

First Section 1.1–10.10.

1. The numbering of the Israelites.

2. The arrangement of the camp.

3. The sons of Aaron and the duties of the tribe of Levi; the number of the Levites; the number of the first-born among the Israelites; the substitution of the Levites for the first-born.

4. The duties of the several Levitical families in relation to the sanctuary.

5–6. Collection of Laws:

5.1–4. Unclean persons to be excluded from the camp.

5–10. Penalties prescribed for certain offences committed by individuals. These are to be given to the priests.

11–31. The case of the woman suspected by her husband of infidelity.

6.1–21. The law of the Nazirite.

22–27. The priestly benediction.

7. The offerings brought by the princes of the tribes at the dedication of the sanctuary.

stays the decree of utter destruction; instead, all the adults
that came out of Egypt, with the exception of Joshua and
Caleb, are condemned to die in the wilderness; the spies
die in a plague; the people attempt a passage to Canaan,
but are repulsed at Hormah.

18.1–7. The duties of the priests and the Levites.

8–20. The offerings due to the priests from the Israelites.

21–24. The offerings due to the Levites from the Israelites.

25–32. The offerings due to the priests from the Levites.

19. The laws of ritual purification by means of the ashes of the red heifer.

20.1–13. Arrival at the wilderness of Zin; death of Miriam; Israelites murmuring on account of lack of water; sin of Moses and Aaron at Meribah and the punishment decreed upon them.

14–21. Moses asks permission of the king of Edom to pass through his land, but his request is refused.

22–29. Death of Aaron.

21.1–3. The Israelites score a victory over the king of Arad at Hormah.

4–9. Departure from Mt. Hor; the brazen serpent.

10–20. Journey to Moab; quotations of poetic fragments relating to the journey; the Song of the Well.

21–32. Sihon, king of the Amorites, defeated in battle.

33–35. Og, king of Bashan, defeated in battle.

22.1. Arrival at the Plains of Moab.

Third Section. 22.2–36.13.

50–56. Laws about exterminating the idols of the Canaanites; the land to be divided among the tribes by lot.

34.1–15. The boundaries of Canaan.

16–29. Names of the princes of the tribes designated to assist Joshua and Eleazar in the apportionment of the land.

35.1–8. The Levitical cities.

9–34. The cities of refuge; the laws of homicide.

36. Zelophehad's daughters, as well as all women entitled to a portion in the land of Canaan, should not marry outside of their tribes.

4. Authorship

Jewish tradition (see B.B. 14b) ascribes the authorship of the entire Pentateuch, with the exception of the last eight verses of Deuteronomy, to Moses, writing under divine inspiration. The belief in the Mosaic authorship of the Pentateuch was never questioned and was so jealously guarded that it was considered heresy to doubt the divine origin of a single sentence or of a single word, even though acknowledging that it came from Moses (Maimonides, *Yad, Teshubah*, 3.8). This belief in the divine origin of the Pentateuch and in its transmission through Moses became in the course of time one of the dogmas of Judaism and is included among the thirteen articles of Maimonides' creed (see his commentary to Mishna Sanh. 11.1).

Guarded and obscure references indicating a doubt as to the divine authorship of some phrases or passages of the Pentateuch may already be found in some medieval Jewish commentaries. However, the tradition continued to be held sacred by Jews as well as by Christians until after the period of the Reformation. It was only during the past two centuries that students arose who began to cast doubt on this tradition and to apply to the Pentateuch the same standards of literary criticism as were applied to all other works of history and literature of antiquity.

The general opinion of modern Bible critics is that the greater part of the Book of Numbers is derived from documents that originated with the priestly guilds of the period of the Babylonian exile and the age which immediately followed it. It is, however, admitted that it also contains some documents of much earlier periods, which a late editor combined with the priestly documents into the present volume. The details of the documentary theory (also known as the Graf-Wellhausen hypothesis, after the early authors of this theory), which is made to apply not only to the Pentateuch but also to the Book of Joshua and to other portions of the Bible, are discussed in most standard works on the Bible and cannot be considered here in detail (see Margolis, *The Hebrew Scriptures in the Making*, Philadelphia, 1922). In the case of the Book of Numbers, it is contended that the narratives and the laws included therein could not have been written by Moses, nor by a writer contemporary with the events described.

It is generally assumed by the proponents of the documentary theory that the text of the Book of Numbers represents a compilation made from the following sources: a) A collection of Judean stories, conveniently designated J, dating from the ninth century before the common era; b) A similar collection made in the eighth century in the Northern Kingdom, designated E; c) A work labeled P and added to JE in the fifth century from a priestly source, describing the origin and institutions of the priestly cult; d) Additions made to JEP by the priestly guilds which produced the book as it is at present before us. More specifically, the sources of the Book of Numbers according to the documentary hypothesis adopted by many modern Bible critics may be summarized as follows:

P is responsible for the following chapters: 1.1–10.28; 13.1–17a, 21b, 25, 26a, 32; 14.1, 2, 5–7, 10, 26–30, 32–39; 15.1–16.11, 16–24, 35–50; 17.1–20.13, 22–29; 21.10, 11; 22.1; 25.6–36.13.

To JE are ascribed the following sections: 10.29–12.16; 13.17b–21a, 22–24, 26b–31, 33; 14.3, 4, 8–9, 11–24, 31, 39b–45; 16.12–15, 25–34; 20.14–21; 21.1–9, 12–32; 22.2–25.5.

Inserted here and there are phrases and words by the final redactors, and some passages are even referred to the Deuteronomist (D) or to later priestly writers. Some also attempted to separate the JE collections into their component parts, applying great ingenuity to their task. It is freely conceded that even those portions definitely assigned to P contain material of a much earlier date, as for example the priestly benediction (6.21–27), or the law about wearing fringes (*Zizit*) on the corners of a garment (15.37–41).

The documentary theory has been strongly assailed in recent years, not only by the strict traditionalists, but also by members of the critical school. The numerous archaeological discoveries made in the last few decades have again opened up the entire question of the institutions and mode of living as reflected in the pages of the books of the Bible and have at the same time caused a revision of the views formerly held regarding the age of the sources of the text. We know now that writing was common in the age of Moses and long before his time and that the state of civilization of Israel and of the other nations with whom Israel's fate was so closely associated was of a much higher degree than was suspected by students of a generation ago. While the strictly orthodox view that every word in the Pentateuch was written by Moses, "by the commandment of God", cannot be maintained now, it is quite possible to follow tradition to the extent that in the main the authorship of the Torah is to be traced to the dominant personality of Moses, admitting at the same time that accretions and alterations crept into it in later times. In their interpretation of the biblical text, the Rabbis already resorted to a principle (עירוב פרשיות) which implies a misplacement of certain words and phrases. Even an orthodox student of the Bible like the late Harold M. Wiener admits that several documents in the Book of Numbers have been misplaced and offers a rearrangement of the material which would obviate many difficulties and compose apparent contradictions (Wiener, *Posthumous Essays*, Oxford, 1932, pp. 37–47). In the present commentary, attention will be directed to the various theories advanced by the critical school regarding certain passages, and their validity appraised. This commentary assumes the position of those who maintain that the book is made up of material emanating from Moses and from the period in which he lived. Whatever changes or emendations have been made in later ages were in the spirit of and in harmony with the original documents. The sacredness with which these writings were regarded and the reverence in which they were held throughout the ages should put us on guard and lead us to assume a most conservative attitude toward the entire subject of modern biblical criticism.

5. The Historic Background

If we were to accept the documentary theory regarding the composition of the Book of Numbers, we should be forced to conclude that the book has but little historical value, since it would present a compilation made many centuries after the events narrated had taken place. At most, these events could then be judged only as legends that survived in the memory of the people, which may have undergone numerous changes in the course of transmission so that they could hardly be utilized as historical material. On the other hand, if we follow the view that most, if not all, of the contents of the book are contemporaneous records, the events as well as the laws contained in this book assume tremendous historical importance, recording as they do the earliest traditions concerning the formative period in Israel's history. The period of the wandering, of which glimpses are afforded us in this book, was the period of the formation of the national character of the people, under the guidance and direction of their great leader, Moses, whose personality looms high in the chapters of this book. We obtain the impression of a people just released from the bonds of slavery, wandering about in the wilderness under the impetus of a hope that soon they will settle in a rich land, a land formerly inhabited by their ancestors and promised to them by their God. This tradition and this hope are constantly kept before them by their leader and are made so vivid and so real as to make all hardships and all sufferings of little consequence. In the course of their travels they come in contact with other tribes and settled nations, some of which are friendly and others hostile. There must have been many wars and treaties regarding which our record is entirely silent. They must have achieved victories and suffered defeats which the chronicler did not find necessary to preserve in his record. Only the narratives of such encounters are presented here as indicate the power of the God of Israel and His protection over His people, and of such contacts as reveal the moral and religious dangers from which the people were saved through the foresight and rigorous discipline of Moses.

It was natural that there should be among them some malcontents who rebelled against the hardships of the apparently aimless wanderings in the wilderness and demanded of Moses a more speedy fulfillment of the promise made by him in the name of God. The chronicler manifests but little sympathy with such complaints. He records those incidents of rebellion against Moses which were followed by the dire punishment of the rebels, and in each instance the figure of Moses emerges with added glory and power. Some of these incidents are introduced to explain the origin of certain institutions, as was evidently the intention in the case of the story of Korah and his followers. In all of these narratives, however, the people are pictured as a normal people, subject to dissension and strife, struggling against most difficult odds to realize a national ambition and to reach the goal that was destined to lead them to a normal life on the land formerly occupied by their ancestors, whose memories were deeply engraved upon their hearts.

Moses, too, is presented here as a normal man, who, subject to the weaknesses and failings to which all men are heir, still becomes the model leader, worthy of the affection and reverence of his people throughout all generations. Not a superman free from all blemish, but a man of flesh and blood easily aroused to anger and to passion, sometimes giving way to discouragement and despondency, but withal possessed of a great love for his people and imbued with an all-pervading ideal to see them established on the basis of a sound morality and of a high religious conception. The book does not gloss over the sins of Moses. One of his sins is made the reason for his failure to accompany his people into the land to which he led them. Modest, self-effacing, and at the same time stern in judgment and insistent upon the full realization of the ideals which he set for his people, Moses, as here presented, undoubtedly preserves the conception which the people formed of the personality who gave tone and character to their national organization and subsequent history.

Imbedded in this book are also references to the internal life of the Israelites in the days of Moses as well as before his time. In some of the laws, notably those pertaining to homicide, we see a picture of primitive society with its feuds and unbridled passions, which the lawgiver seeks to check and to control. Several poetic fragments which found their way into this book, some avowedly taken from older collections (The Book of the Battles of the Lord), and others, like the Song of the Well, derived from the folklore of the people, present an exalted form of expression and portray a fine poetic feeling. The reference to "them that speak in parables" (21.17) indicates that there was a class of singers or makers of parables who were held in high esteem among the people at a very early period. Some of the prophets and the psalmists drew upon incidents recorded here as illustrations of lessons that they wished to convey or as themes for songs that they composed.

6. THE RELIGIOUS BACKGROUND

The idea of God as depicted in this as well as in other books of the Pentateuch is that of a benevolent Father, watching over the destinies of His children, chastising them for their good and demanding unconditional obedience. He is a loving God, but is also the righteous God who demands absolute loyalty of the people to the laws of conduct which He placed before them. He would brook no deviation from the stern rules of morality which He enacted for the benefit of His people; He would permit no weak-kneed adherence but demands complete and perfect faith and confidence. For the sake of the improvement of the people, He would come in close relations with certain individuals to whom He would make His will known and whose mission it was to convey to the people the messages of warning and of comfort, of rebuke and of cheer, which He would entrust to them. Stern in justice, He would still permit these chosen spirits to move Him toward mercy through their pleadings in behalf of His people.

Because of the warmth of the relationship between God and Israel made so prominent in this book, some have gathered that to the mind of the writer God was a local divinity, the God of Israel only, in the same sense as Chemosh was the god of Moab, or Baal the god of the Canaanites. Such an inference is certainly not in harmony with the exalted conception of God which finds expression in every chapter of this book. The God of Israel is the God who guides the fortunes of all peoples; and although He stands in closest relationship to Israel, His chosen people, He has dominion over all peoples. Cf. 16.21; 27.16.

God, indeed, dwells in the midst of Israel, in the sanctuary which they erected, and through His presence the whole camp becomes holy. The ideal of the holiness of God is transferred to the people of God and among them different degrees of holiness are recognized. The immediate vicinity of the sanctuary, where the priests and the Levites were encamped, was most holy, and there the ordinary Israelite might not enter. The whole camp, however, is also holy, for the people are the people of God and partake of His nature. They were to separate themselves from other nations and to dedicate themselves to the higher ideals of life which their religion enjoined. While perhaps not as emphatic regarding the ideal of the universality of God as are the sublime prophecies of Amos, Isaiah or Jeremiah, the conception of God as mirrored in the present book is certainly exalted enough to preclude the idea of a tribal deity, such as was worshiped by the other nations of antiquity.

The elaborate system of sacrifices prescribed in this book is intended for a people settled on a land and not roving about from place to place in the wilderness. Practically all the laws pertaining to sacrifices contained in the Book of Numbers are intended for communal offerings.

Individual sacrifices are dealt with in the Book of Leviticus. The offerings of the princes enumerated in such great detail in chapter 7 were hardly in the nature of sacrifices, although their gifts to the sanctuary were accompanied by a number of animals that were to be used as sacrifices. The prescriptions for the sacrifices to be brought by the woman suspected of adultery, or by the Nazirite, or by the person who wanted to make restitution for a wrong committed against his neighbor are only incidental to the main laws which the respective sections contain. A number of other ceremonial laws will likewise be found in this book, like the laws of defilement from contact with the dead or the law of *Zizit* (fringes), which aim to promote the holiness of the Israelitish camp and to emphasize the distinctiveness of God's people.

The prophetic office and functions are recognized and established, while the power of prophecy vouchsafed to Moses is put in a class by itself, much more exalted than that of any other prophet. God is ready to endow with the gift of prophecy all who are spiritually attuned to the prophetic rôle. Eldad and Medad should not be punished for presuming to utter prophecies, and even a heathen (Balaam) may be granted the power when God chooses to reveal Himself to him. As far as the people of Israel are concerned, Moses would wish that they might all rise to the high estate of spiritual attainment that would make them fit for the prophetic office.

7. References and Abbreviations

ABARBANEL — Isaac Abarbanel or Abravanel (1437–1508), Spanish Jewish statesman and Bible exegete. His commentary on the Pentateuch was first published in Venice, 1589, and often reprinted.

ADLER — Nathan Marcus Adler (1803–1890), Chief Rabbi of England, author of a commentary on the Targum (נתינה לגר), published in the Vilna 1875 edition of the Pentateuch and reprinted in later editions.

Ant. — *Antiquities of the Jews*, see Josephus.

ASHKENAZI — Moses Isaac Tedeschi (Ashkenazi), Italian exegete (1821–1898), author of a series of volumes on the Bible, under the name of הואיל משה, the one on the Pentateuch published in Leghorn, 1881.

B.D.B. — *A Hebrew and English Lexicon of the Old Testament*, based on the *Lexicon* and *Thesaurus* of Gesenius, by F. Brown, C. A. Briggs and S. R. Driver, Cambridge, Mass., 1891.

B.J. — *Bellum Judaicum*, see Josephus.

Biur — A Hebrew commentary on the Bible, emanating from the school of Moses Mendelssohn and based on the latter's German translation. The commentary on the Book of Numbers is by Aaron Jaroslav, working under the direction of Mendelssohn and Wessely. This was frequently reprinted.

DELITZSCH — Friedrich Delitzsch, *Die Lese- und Schreibfehler im alten Testament*, Berlin, 1920.

DILLMANN — August Dillmann, author of *Numeri, Deute-ronomium und Josua*, published in 1886.

EHRLICH — Arnold B. Ehrlich, author of מקרא כפשוטו *Scholien und kritische Bemerkungen zu den heiligen Schriften der Hebräer*. Erster Teil: *Der Pentateuch*, Berlin, 1899.

EHRLICH, *Randglossen* — *Randglossen zur Hebräischen Bibel, Textkritisches, Sprachliches und Sachliches*, 7 vols., Leipzig, 1914.

EPSTEIN — Baruch ha-Levi, author of *Torah Temimah*, Rabbinic references and interpretations to the Torah, printed with the text in five volumes, Vilna, 1904.

EX. R. — Exodus Rabba, Midrashic collection on Exodus, made about the eleventh century (Shemot Rabba).

GES.-K. — *Hebrew Grammar*, by Wilhelm Gesenius, as edited by E. Kautzsch, and translated into English by Collins and Cowley, Oxford, 1910.

GORDON — S. L. Gordon, author of a brief Hebrew commentary on the Pentateuch, which is published with the text and extracts from Rashi, and designed for students, Warsaw, 1920.

GRAY — George Buchanan Gray, author of *A Critical and Exegetical Commentary on Numbers*, New York, 1906 (*The International Critical Commentary*).

HERTZ — *Pentateuch and Haftorahs with Commentary*, edited by the Chief Rabbi, Dr. J. H. Hertz, London, 1936, including the Hebrew text and English notes to the text.

HERXHEIMER — Solomon Herxheimer (1801–1884), German Rabbi, author of *Der Pentateuch im Hebräischen Texte mit worttreuer Übersetzung und mit fortlaufender Erklärung*, Berlin, 1841.

HIRSCH — Samson Raphael Hirsch (1808–1888), Rabbi in Frankfort on-the-Maine, author of a German translation and commentary to the Pentateuch (*Übersetzung und Erklärung des Pentateuchs*), published with the Hebrew text, Frankfort, 1867–78.

HOLZINGER — H. Holzinger, *Numeri erklärt*, Tübingen, 1903 (Marti's *Kurzer Hand-Commentar zum alten Testament*).

IBN EZRA — Abraham ben Meir ibn Ezra (1092–1167), Spanish-Jewish exegete and grammarian, author of a commentary on the Pentateuch, frequently reprinted.

J.E. — *Jewish Encyclopedia*, 12 vols., New York, 1901–1906.

JOSEPHUS — Flavius Josephus, historian of the first century, author of *Antiquities of the Jews* and *Concerning the Jewish Wars with Rome*.

KAHANA — Abraham Kahana, editor of the Hebrew Bible with Hebrew scientific commentary (פירוש מדעי), and author of the commentary to Numbers, Kiev, 1914.

KASPI — Joseph ibn Kaspi (1297–1340), Provençal exegete, author of *Mishneh Kesef*, commentary on the Pentateuch, edited by Isaac Last, Cracow, 1906.

KEIL — *Biblical Commentary on the Old Testament*, by C. F. Keil and F. Delitzsch. Vol. III, *The Pentateuch*, translated by James Martin, Edinburgh, n.d.

KIMHI — David Kimhi (1160–1235), French grammarian and exegete, author of *Sefer ha-Shorashim*, a Hebrew Lexicon.

KÖNIG — F. E. König, author of *Kritische Lehrgebäude der hebräischen Sprache*, 3 vols., 1881–1897.

LAM. R. — Lamentations Rabba, an early midrashic collection on the Book of Lamentations (Ekah Rabba or Rabbati).

LEESER — Isaac Leeser (1806–1868), American Rabbi, translator of the Bible into English, whose translation became the standard version for the Jews of America until the present translation was issued by the Jewish Publication Society (1917). He first issued the Pentateuch, the Hebrew text with English translation and brief notes in English, in 1845, and later the whole Bible appeared in English in 1853.

LUZZATTO — Samuel David Luzzatto (1800–1865), Italian Bible exegete, author of a translation of the Pentateuch in Italian with Hebrew commentary, published in Padua, 1875.

MAIM. — Moses ben Maimon (Rambam), or Maimonides (1135–1204). Reference is made to his *Mishneh Torah*, Code of Laws, in 14 parts, frequently published.

MALBIM — Meir Loeb ben Yehiel Michael (1809–1879), Russian Rabbi and exegete, author of commentary on the Pentateuch (התורה והמצוה), Warsaw, 1874–1880.

McNeile — *The Book of Numbers, in the Revised Version, with Introduction and Notes*, by A. H. McNeile, Cambridge, 1911 (*The Cambridge Bible for Schools and Colleges*).

Meg. Ta'an. — Megillat Ta'anit, an early Tannaitic chronicle of certain eventful days, which were to be celebrated as joyous occasions and on which no mourning was permitted.

Mek. — Mekilta, Tannaitic Midrash to Exodus.

Mendelssohn — Moses Mendelssohn (1729–1786), German Jewish philosopher and translator of the Bible into German; see *Biur*.

Mishna and Talmud, treatises of; referred to in abbreviated form:

'Ab. Zarah	—	'Abodah Zarah
Ab.	—	Pirke Abot
'Arak.	—	'Arakin
B. B.	—	Baba Batra
B. K.	—	Baba Kamma
Ber.	—	Berakot
Bik.	—	Bikkurim
'Eduy.	—	'Eduyyot
'Er.	—	'Erubin
Git.	—	Gittin
Hag.	—	Hagigah
Hal.	—	Hallah

Hor.	—	Horayot
Hul.	—	Hullin
Ket.	—	Ketubot
Kid.	—	Kiddushin
Mak.	—	Makkot
Meg.	—	Megillah
Me'i.	—	Me'ilah
Men.	—	Menahot
Mid.	—	Middot
M. K.	—	Mo'ed Katan
Naz.	—	Nazir
Ned.	—	Nedarim
Nid.	—	Niddah
Par.	—	Parah
Pes.	—	Pesahim
R. H.	—	Rosh ha-Shanah
Sanh.	—	Sanhedrin
Shab.	—	Shabbat
Sheb.	—	Shebu'ot
Sotah	—	Sotah
Suk.	—	Sukkah
Ta'an.	—	Ta'anit
Ter.	—	Terumot
Yeb.	—	Yebamot
Yoma	—	Yoma
Zeb.	—	Zebahim

Num. R. — Numbers Rabba, midrashic collection on Numbers, of about the twelfth century (Bemidbar Rabba).

ORR — James Orr, author of *The Problem of the Old Testament*, considered with reference to recent criticism, New York, 1906.

RAMBAN — Moses ben Nahman (1194–1270?), Spanish Jewish exegete, whose commentary on the Pentateuch has frequently been reprinted.

RASHBAM — Samuel ben Meir (1085?–1174?), French Jewish exegete, grandson of Rashi, whose commentary on the Pentateuch has frequently been reprinted.

RASHI — Solomon ben Isaac (1040–1105), French Jewish exegete whose commentary on the Bible has been the standard commentary for many centuries.

SFORNO — Obadiah ben Jacob Sforno (1475?–1550), Italian Jewish exegete, author of commentary on the Pentateuch, which has frequently been reprinted.

SIFRE — Sifre debe Rab, a Tannaitic Midrash to Numbers and Deuteronomy. (References are to Horowitz's edition, Leipzig, 1916).

SIFRE ZUTA — Tannaitic Midrash to Numbers.

SIFRA — Tannaitic Midrash to Leviticus.

SZANTO — Joseph and Simeon Szanto, who compiled notes on the Pentateuch under the title of בוצר עוללות, published in the back of the Pentateuch edition with the *Biur*, Vienna, 1846.

TAN. — Tanhuma Yelammedenu, a midrashic collection on the Pentateuch, compiled by R. Tanhum ben Abba, in the fourth century. (References here are to Buber's edition, Wilna, 1885.)

YER. — Yerushalmi, the Palestinian Talmud (Talmud Yerushalmi).

ZUNZ — *Der Pentateuch, das ist die fünf Bücher Mosis,* nach dem Masoretischen Texte, unter die Redaction von Dr. Zunz, übersetzt von H. Arnheim und Dr. M. Sachs, Berlin, 1837.

VERSIONS

TARG. — The Aramaic translation of the Pentateuch, usually known as Targum Onkelos, and printed alongside of the Hebrew text, in most editions.

TARGUM JONATHAN — An Aramaic paraphrase, ascribed to Jonathan b. Uzziel, the distinguished pupil of Hillel, but probably of much later origin.

TARG. YER. — Palestinian Targum, fragmentary Aramaic version, homiletic in character, often erroneously referred to as Pseudo-Jonathan.

LXX — Septuagint. The Greek translation of the Bible, ed. H. B. Swete, Cambridge, 1895.

SAM. — Samaritan version of the Hebrew text of the Pentateuch.

SYR. — The Syriac version of the Pentateuch, known as the Peshitta.

VULG. — The Vulgate Latin Translation of the Bible.

R. V. — Revised Version of the English translation of the Bible (1885).

NUMBERS

THE FOURTH BOOK OF MOSES
CALLED
NUMBERS

CHAPTER 1.

1.1–10.10. IN THE WILDERNESS OF SINAI

This section contains a description of the preparations made by Moses for the departure from the wilderness of Sinai on the march further north to the promised land. The tabernacle was erected and consecrated on the first day of the first month of the second year of the exodus, while the Israelites were encamped in the wilderness of Sinai (Ex. 40.17). This was followed by the consecration of Aaron and his sons as priests in the service of the tabernacle (Lev. 8 ff.). During the same time, from the first to the twelfth day of the first month, the princes of the tribes brought their offerings to the tabernacle on successive days (Num. 7). The paschal lamb was offered on the fourteenth day at dusk (9.5), and the law regarding the postponed Passover was promulgated at the same time (9.6–14).

The present section begins with the order given to Moses on the first day of the second month to make preparations for the departure. These preparations include the numbering of the people, the arrangement of the tribes in the camp, the duties of the Levites in connection with the tabernacle and the manner of informing the people when they were to encamp and when they were to break up camp, guided by the position of the cloud and by the blowing of trumpets. While this forms the main subject of this section, it includes also a number of other matters, more or less related to the chief theme. Among these are the detailed account of the offerings of the princes, which really occurred before this date; the laws about the Nazirite and the woman suspected of infidelity, the preparation of the Levites for the service of the tabernacle and a number of miscellaneous laws and ordinances.

1.1–4.49. NUMBERING OF THE ISRAELITES, THEIR ARRANGEMENT IN THE CAMP AND THE DUTIES OF THE LEVITES.

In this section is related the taking of the census, the arrangement of the tribes in the camp and the special census taken of the tribe of Levi, as well as the duties of the members of that tribe when the Israelites were on the march or in camp.

1   AND the LORD spoke unto Moses in the wilderness of
Sinai, in the tent of meeting, on the first day of the second

1.1–20.   THE NUMBERING OF THE ISRAELITES.

Moses is ordered to appoint twelve men, one of each tribe, who
should assist him and Aaron in taking a census of the people. Those
included in this census are all male Israelites, above the age of 20, who
are fit to be mustered into the army. The order is carried out and the
census is taken.

1. *in the wilderness of Sinai*] The part of the Arabian peninsula
which is at the head of the Red Sea, bounded by the Gulf of Suez on
the left and the Gulf of Akabah on the right. "Although formerly
restricted to the triangular region lying between the gulfs of Suez and
Aqaba, it is now customary and convenient to apply the name Sinai
to the entire country, 23,000 square miles in area, bounded on the
north by the Mediterranean; on the south by the Red Sea; on the
west by the Canal and the Gulf of Suez; and on the east by the Gulf
of Aqaba and the old Egyptian-Turkish boundary, which is now the
frontier between Egyptian territory and the mandated portion of
Palestine under British administration. With the exception of the
southern part of the last mentioned frontier — which cuts through a
small area draining into the Wadi el-Araba and the Dead Sea — the
boundaries are natural limits of a self-contained and unique topo-
graphical and geologic unit" (H. Llewellyn Beadnell, *The Wilderness
of Sinai*, London, 1927, pp. 3–4).

It is in this area that tradition found the celebrated Mount Sinai,
from which the revelation is recorded to have been made. The present
name of the particular hill is Jebel Musa, the northernmost peak
of which is Ras-es-Sufsafeh, 6937 feet high, which is regarded as
the place from which the Law was promulgated. However, other
mountains in the vicinity and, according to some critics, at a considerable distance from the Sinai peninsula, as far as Midian and Seir,
have severally been considered as the site of the mountain of revelation (see Oesterly and Robinson, *Hebrew Religion*, N. Y., 1930, pp.
106 ff.). However, many Bible students still adhere to the old identification of Mt. Sinai with the modern Jebel Musa.

in the tent of meeting] The name usually given to the tabernacle,
"where I will meet with you, to speak there unto thee" (Ex. 29.42),
and more specifically in Ex. 25.22. Whether Moses was at the time

month, in the second year after they were come out of the
land of Egypt, saying: 'Take ye the sum of all the congrega- 2
tion of the children of Israel, by their families, by their
fathers' houses, according to the number of names, every
male, by their polls; from twenty years old and upward, 3

inside or outside of the tabernacle is not definitely stated here (comp.
Lev. 1.1).

on the first day of the second month] I. e. one month after the completion of the tabernacle (Ex. 40.17). According to tradition, the
laws contained in the book of Leviticus were transmitted by Moses
during this intervening month. The first of the month, being observed
as a holiday, was regarded as a proper time for making announcements
and for imparting instruction (Deut. 1.3; Ezek. 26.1; 29.17; 31.1; 32.1;
45.18; Ezra 7.9; II Chron. 29.17).

2. *Take ye*] I. e. Moses, Aaron and the chiefs of the tribes (vv.
3, 4), hence the plural.

by their families] Not only the sum of the whole nation, but also
the number of people in each clan and in each family. It appears that
the people were divided into tribes (שבט), each tribe into clans (משפחה)
and each clan again into families (בית אב). This method of division is
followed also in Josh. 7.16–18, in connection with the story of Achan.
However, these terms are used rather loosely in the Bible to denote
one or the other of these divisions. Rashi and ibn Ezra take the phrase
"by their fathers' houses" as descriptive of the manner of counting,
that it shall be in accordance with the paternal and not the maternal
relationship.

the number of names] Possibly kept in a register (Ehrlich).

every male] Since this was chiefly a military census, women and
minors as well as the Levitical tribe were excluded.

by their polls] Head by head. In Ex. 30.12 ff., it is stated that when
the people were counted it was done by means of collecting half a shekel
from each and then counting the number of half shekels (see Rashi).

3. *from twenty years old*] The age of military service (Ex. 30.14),
terminating apparently at death or complete disability (comp. Sforno
to v. 45, quoting a rabbinic tradition, that those counted were only
from twenty to sixty years of age, since those over 60 were retired
from office). In the case of the Levites, the age of service was from
thirty to fifty (4.23).

all that are able to go forth to war in Israel: ye shall number
4 them by their hosts, even thou and Aaron. And with you there
shall be a man of every tribe, every one head of his fathers'
5 house. And these are the names of the men that shall stand
6 with you: of Reuben, Elizur the son of Shedeur. Of Simeon,
7 Shelumiel the son of Zurishaddai. Of Judah, Nahshon the

ye shall number] The Heb. term פקד also implies the notion of mustering and enrolling for service.

4. *And with you*] The tribal representatives assist not only in the
numbering, but also in the establishment of relationships and in guarding against any inaccuracy, which may be discreditable to the tribe
or clan (Luzzatto).

every one head] The various subdivisions of the tribe each had its
own chief, out of which the tribal chief was selected (see Friedman,
Bet Talmud, II, 77). Leeser has: "a man who is the head of his family
division." (Graetz's emendation of אשר for איש is unnecessary and
even awkward).

5. *stand with you*] Attend, serve with you. The order of the tribes
here is not according to the seniority of the sons of Jacob (Gen. chs.
29–30), the five sons of Leah (omitting Levi) being mentioned first,
then the two sons of Rachel, then Dan, the oldest son of the concubines
(Bilhah), then Asher, the son of Zilpah, encamped next to Dan (2.27),
then Gad, second son of Zilpah, and last Naphtali, second son of Bilhah.
Ephraim is mentioned before Manasseh, in accordance with the promise
of Jacob (Gen. 48.19, 20; see ibn Ezra). The names are differently
arranged in Gen. 49 (Blessing of Jacob); 46.8–25; 35.23–26 and in
Ex. 1.2–4.

Elizur] God is a rock, or my God is a rock, found also in the form
Zuriel, my rock is God (3.35).

Shedeur] Shaddai (the Almighty) is a flame.

6. *Shelumiel*] My peace is God, or at peace with God, or God is
my friend (cf. 34, 27). Judith (8.1) traces her genealogy to this Shelumiel.

Zurishaddai] My rock is the Almighty.

7. *Nahshon*] A formation from נחש (a serpent, also used as a proper
name, I Sam. 11.1; II Sam. 17.23). His sister Elisheba was the wife
of Aaron (Ex. 6.23; comp. Ruth 4.20).

son of Amminadab. Of Issachar, Nethanel the son of Zuar. Of 8-9
Zebulun, Eliab the son of Helon. Of the children of Joseph: 10
of Ephraim, Elishama the son of Ammihud; of Manasseh,
Gamaliel the son of Pedahzur. Of Benjamin, Abidan the 11
son of Gideoni. Of Dan, Ahiezer the son of Ammishaddai. 12
Of Asher, Pagiel the son of Ochran. Of Gad, Eliasaph the 13-4
son of Deuel. Of Naphtali, Ahira the son of Enan.' These 15-6
were the elect of the congregation, the princes of the tribes

Amminadab] My kinsman is noble, kinsman in this case may refer
to God.

8. *Nethanel*] God hath given.

Zuar] Little one, or insignificant one; Zoar is found as the name
of a town (Gen. 13.10).

9. *Eliab*] God, or my God, is father; comp. Abiel (I Sam. 9.1),
my father is God.

Helon] Also found as the name of a town in Moab (Holan, Jer.
48.21), in Judah (Josh. 15.51) and of a priestly city (ib. 21.15); comp.
I Chron. 6.43 (Hilen); possibly denoting sandy soil.

10. *Elishama*] God has heard.

Ammihud] My kinsman (God) is majesty, or glorious.

Gamaliel] Reward of God, or God is (my) reward.

Pedahzur] The rock has redeemed.

11. *Abidan*] My father is judge, or the father has judged.

12. *Ahiezer*] My brother is help, or the brother is a help.

Ammishaddai] My kinsman (God) is Shaddai (the Almighty).

13. *Pagiel*] Perhaps encountered by God, or entreated by God
(Isa. 53.12).

Ochran] Possibly disturber or troubler.

14. *Eliasaph*] God has added.

Deuel] Possibly God knows, related to Eliadah (II Sam. 5.16) and
Eldaah (Gen. 25.4). Another reading here (LXX, Pesh.) is Reuel,
God is a friend (as in 2.14).

15. *Ahira*] My brother is evil, or my brother and friend.

Enan] A small well, comp. Hazar-enan, 34.9, 10; Hazar-enon,
Ezek. 47.17.

16. *the elect of the congregation*] Lit. the summoned ones, those
who are usually called to congregational assemblies (Rashi, ibn Ezra).

of their fathers; they were the heads of the thousands of
17 Israel. And Moses and Aaron took these men that are
18 pointed out by name. And they assembled all the congregation together on the first day of the second month, and they
declared their pedigrees after their families, by their
fathers' houses, according to the number of names, from
19 twenty years old and upward, by their polls. As the Lord
commanded Moses, so did he number them in the wilderness of Sinai.

20   And the children of Reuben, Israel's first-born, their
generations, by their families, by their fathers' houses,

LXX has "councillors" and Saadia takes it in an active sense, the
summoners or muezzins, comp. 26.9.

tribes of their fathers] Father's houses, the component parts of the
tribe.

heads of the.thousands of Israel] The division into thousands was
made for civil (Ex. 18.21) or for military purposes (II Sam. 18.1). The
term may refer to a definite division of a tribe and may correspond
to "family" in v. 2 (cf. II Sam. 10.19), or it may mean an indefinite
aggregate of people belonging to the same clan.

17. *pointed out by name*] Whose names were mentioned above.

18. *they declared their pedigrees*] They registered themselves
according to their families and tribes (Rashi; comp. ibn Ezra, who
adds that the age of each was also registered).

19. *so did he number them*] Moses, upon whom the responsibility
rested.

20–47. The Total Number of All the Tribes.

The results of the census are given here in detail for each tribe and
then the total for all Israel, exclusive of the Levites, who were of the
age of twenty or over. See note at the end of the chapter.

20. *their generations*] Used in the sense of a genealogical division
according to families and fathers' houses. The tribes are enumerated
here in the order in which they were encamped as described in ch. 2.

according to the number of names, by their polls, every
male from twenty years old and upward, all that were
able to go forth to war; those that were numbered of them, 21
of the tribe of Reuben, were forty and six thousand and
five hundred.

Of the children of Simeon, their generations, by their 22
families, by their fathers' houses, those that were numbered
thereof, according to the number of names, by their polls,
every male from twenty years old and upward, all that
were able to go forth to war; those that were numbered of 23
them, of the tribe of Simeon, were fifty and nine thousand
and three hundred.

Of the children of Gad, their generations, by their 24
families, by their fathers' houses, according to the number
of names, from twenty years old and upward, all that were
able to go forth to war; those that were numbered of them, 25
of the tribe of Gad, were forty and five thousand six hundred and fifty.

Of the children of Judah, their generations, by their 26
families, by their fathers' houses, according to the number
of names, from twenty years old and upward, all that were
able to go forth to war; those that were numbered of them, 27
of the tribe of Judah, were threescore and fourteen thousand
and six hundred.

Of the children of Issachar, their generations, by their 28
families, by their fathers' houses, according to the number
of names, from twenty years old and upward, all that were

29 able to go forth to war; those that were numbered of them, of the tribe of Issachar, were fifty and four thousand and four hundred.

30 Of the children of Zebulun, their generations, by their families, by their fathers' houses, according to the number of names, from twenty years old and upward, all that were

31 able to go forth to war; those that were numbered of them, of the tribe of Zebulun, were fifty and seven thousand and four hundred.

32 Of the children of Joseph, namely, of the children of Ephraim, their generations, by their families, by their fathers' houses, according to the number of names, from twenty years old and upward, all that were able to go forth

33 to war; those that were numbered of them, of the tribe of Ephraim, were forty thousand and five hundred.

34 Of the children of Manasseh, their generations, by their families, by their fathers' houses, according to the number of names, from twenty years old and upward, all that were

35 able to go forth to war; those that were numbered of them, of the tribe of Manasseh, were thirty and two thousand and two hundred.

36 Of the children of Benjamin, their generations, by their families, by their fathers' houses, according to the number of names, from twenty years old and upward, all that were

37 able to go forth to war; those that were numbered of them, of the tribe of Benjamin, were thirty and five thousand and four hundred.

Of the children of Dan, their generations, by their 38
families, by their fathers' houses, according to the number
of names, from twenty years old and upward, all that were
able to go forth to war; those that were numbered of them, 39
of the tribe of Dan, were threescore and two thousand and
seven hundred.

Of the children of Asher, their generations, by their 40
families, by their fathers' houses, according to the number
of names, from twenty years old and upward, all that were
able to go forth to war; those that were numbered of them, 41
of the tribe of Asher, were forty and one thousand and five
hundred.

Of the children of Naphtali, their generations, by their 42
families, by their fathers' houses, according to the number
of names, from twenty years old and upward, all that were
able to go forth to war; those that were numbered of them, 43
of the tribe of Naphtali, were fifty and three thousand and
four hundred.

These are those that were numbered, which Moses and 44
Aaron numbered, and the princes of Israel, being twelve
men; they were each one for his fathers' house. And all 45
those that were numbered of the children of Israel by their
fathers' houses, from twenty years old and upward, all
that were able to go forth to war in Israel; even all those 46
that were numbered were six hundred thousand and three
thousand and five hundred and fifty. But the Levites 47
after the tribe of their fathers were not numbered among
them.

48-49   And the LORD spoke unto Moses, saying: 'Howbeit the tribe of Levi thou shalt not number, neither shalt thou
50 take the sum of them among the children of Israel; but appoint thou the Levites over the tabernacle of the testimony, and over all the furniture thereof, and over all that belongeth to it; they shall bear the tabernacle, and all the

48-54. LEVITES NOT INCLUDED IN TOTAL.
THE FUNCTIONS OF THE LEVITES.

The Levites were not included in the census (v. 47), in accordance with the direct divine command given to Moses. The work of the Levites was mainly connected with the sanctuary and they were apparently not required to do any military service. The fact that no chief was appointed from among them, although Aaron might have served as such, was an intimation from the start that they would not be included in the numbering (Ramban). Some explain the peculiar form הָתְפָּקְדוּ in v. 47 to be a compound of Hophal and Hithpael and to mean that they neither took their own census nor were they numbered by the officials appointed for the purpose (Sforno), or that they were not ordered to be numbered (*Biur*, comp. Luzzatto). R. V., also Leeser, begin v. 48 with the preposition *For*, indicating that the following section is in explanation of v. 47. This, however, is inadmissible on grammatical grounds (see Driver, *Hebrew Tenses*, 76).

49. *thou shalt not number*] This term also denotes "mustering in" (see note on v. 3), so that the duplication here (number and take the sum of) may be accounted for by taking the first expression to refer to the rule that the Levites were not to be enrolled in the army and the second that they shall not be numbered together with the Israelites (cf. Rashbam, Sforno).

50. *but appoint thou*] The reason why they should not be numbered is because they are appointed to do the work of the sanctuary (ibn Ezra).

tabernacle of the testimony] The tabernacle containing the testimony, the tables on which the Ten Words (comp. Ex. 31.18) were engraved, the most important article contained therein.

they shall bear . . . . they shall minister] They shall carry its parts while the Israelites are on the march, and they shall minister in it when they are encamped (ibn Ezra).

furniture thereof; and they shall minister unto it, and shall encamp round about the tabernacle. And when the taber- 51 nacle setteth forward, the Levites shall take it down; and when the tabernacle is to be pitched, the Levites shall set it up; and the common man that draweth nigh shall be put to death. And the children of Israel shall pitch their 52 tents, every man with his own camp, and every man with his own standard, according to their hosts. But the Levites 53 shall pitch round about the tabernacle of the testimony, that there be no wrath upon the congregation of the children of Israel; and the Levites shall keep the charge of the tabernacle of the testimony.' Thus did the children 54 of Israel; according to all that the LORD commanded Moses, so did they.

51. *and the common man*] I. e. the non-Levite, the layman (Targum), not the stranger (R. V., Leeser) in the sense of foreigner, but one not belonging to the tribe (comp. Shab. 31a).

that draweth nigh] To perform any of the duties assigned to the Levites (18.4), in the same manner as the Levite is excluded from doing any of the works which were assigned to the priests (3.10; 18.7).

shall be put to death] The general opinion among the Rabbis is that the offence is not subject to capital punishment, but to death by divine action (מיתה בידי שמים), although the opinion of R. Akiba is that the punishment intended here was strangulation (Sanh. 81b; Maim., *Biat ha-Mikdash*, IX, 31; comp. ibn Ezra, and Adler to Targum).

53. *that there be no wrath*] The Levites shall encamp round about the sanctuary, so as to keep all laymen away from coming near it, and thus prevent God's anger from being aroused against them (cf. 8.19; 17.11; II Sam. 6.7).

the charge] The office and function of the priests and the Levites (3.38; 31.30, 47).

54. *Thus did the children of Israel*] A general summary of all that is contained in this chapter. Ibn Ezra says that this refers to the last mentioned law that the Israelites kept at a distance from the tabernacle, as they were commanded.

The Census.

The total number of male Israelites over the age of 20 is found to be 603,550, corresponding exactly to the totals of all the tribes, and in agreement with the number given in Ex. 38.26, as derived from the poll-tax of half a shekel imposed upon all those of 20 years of age and over. In Ex. 12.37 and in Num. 11.21 only the approximate number of 600,000 is given. In the second census taken in the fortieth year (ch. 26), the total number was 601,730, a decrease of 1,820. This number was of those who were less than twenty years of age at the time of the exodus, or who were born in the wilderness (with the exception of Joshua and Caleb).

The census of the Levites (ch. 3) yielded a total of 22,000 (or, more exactly, 22,300) in the first census, and in the second census (26.62) of 23,000. This included all Levites above one month old, while the number of Levites between the ages of 30 and 50 was 8580. The total number of the first-born of the Israelites, above a month old, is given (3.43) as 22,273.

These figures present many difficulties so that many modern Bible critics regard them as pure inventions on the part of an editor (Wellhausen, *Prolegomena*, p. 347). The main difficulties are as follows: 1. A population of 600,000 fighting men over the age of 20 would represent a total population of over 2,000,000. The impression one gets from the reading of the text is that of a much smaller group of people. Besides, a population as large as that could not possibly have subsisted in the Sinaitic peninsula, which now has no more than from four to six thousand inhabitants. 2. The number of the first-born males is given as 22,273. If the female first-born were of approximately the same number, it would follow that there were from 40 to 50 children to a family. If the first-born here is intended to be the first-born of the mother only, it would follow that there were approximately about 45,000 mothers in all of Israel. Since the number of women over the age of 20 was probably about the same as the number of men, it would follow that only one in 14 or 15 women was a mother. 3. In references in other portions of the Bible, the fighting forces of the different tribes are by far less than assumed in this census. According to Judges 5.8, six tribes could muster a fighting force of only 40,000 persons, while the same six tribes are represented here as having a fighting force of 273,300, and in the second census of 301,000.

More conservative commentators have endeavored to remove these difficulties in one way or another. In regard to the first difficulty, it is suggested that the area might have included the whole of the Arabian desert, capable of holding a much larger population, especially if we believe that food was obtained in a miraculous way. It is furthermore pointed out that when David had a census taken of Israel, it was found that there were 800,000 fighting men in Israel and 500,000 in Judah, which would give a population of nearly five million for the whole of Palestine, making about 12,500 inhabitants to every square mile. If Palestine could sustain a population of five million at the time of David, it is likely that the Arabian peninsula could sustain a population of two million.

A more serious difficulty is the great discrepancy between the number of first-born and the total number. Wellhausen suggests that the first-born were actually sacrificed in ancient Israel, hence most of the first-born males disappeared in this way. But this theory is not seriously considered even by modern critics. Jakob Neubauer (*Bibelwissenschaftliche Irrungen*, Berlin, 1917, pp. 200–207) offers the following explanation.

1. More of the first-born found their death through the edict of Pharaoh to destroy all male children (Ex. 1.19, 22), because it was more difficult to hide them than other children. The woman, in her first experience of childbirth, needs the help of a midwife more than the woman who has had children before, hence could not hide the birth of a child from the eyes of Pharaoh's officials.

2. The Bible often speaks of the fruitfulness of the Jewish women in Egypt (Ex. 1.7, 12), and the Rabbis have preserved a tradition that in Egypt Jewish women gave birth to six children at one time (Tanhuma, Shemot, 6; Pesikta, Beshallah). The birth of more children than one at a time is also referred to in other places in the Bible (comp. Ex. 21.22). Since the first-born was the only one who "openeth the womb", the proportion between the first-born and other children was much smaller than would be in modern society.

3. The first-born, as indicated before, was only he who was actually the first child born of a mother. If the birth was preceded by a miscarriage or by an abortion, this child would not be considered first-born. There may have been thousands who were the oldest in their families and who for one reason or another were not regarded as first-born.

4. According to the biblical account, especially as interpreted by the Rabbis, the first-born acted as the priests in their respective families, and it is therefore possible that the same rules applied to them as later applied to the priests, viz. that no one having a deformity or physical blemish could perform the duties of the priesthood. This would further reduce their number.

It has also been contended that the first-born included here were only those who were born since the exodus (Keil), for the sanctification of the first-born is based upon the miraculous survival of the first-born of the Israelites when those of the Egyptians died (Ex. 13.11). In order to explain how such a large number of first-born should be born in one year, it is suggested that the hope of the redemption gave rise to many marriages, which were delayed during the period of greatest persecution.

A novel suggestion is made by Petrie (*Researches in Sinai*, 207–217) to the effect that the term אלף does not mean a thousand, but inmates of a household or of a tent, so that the word here translated "thousands" should be rendered "family groups" in each tribe, and the hundreds are the actual number of individuals above the age of twenty in the tribe. This theory, although very attractive, does not remove all the difficulties and indeed creates new ones which are almost insuperable.

While we are constrained to admit that the efforts of the commentators who seek to maintain the traditional point of view are not convincing, the critics are in no less a quandary to explain the reason for the manipulation of these figures on the part of an editor (Gray, 14). The attempt made by Kautzsch to show that this is a Midrash, which relied on the *Gematria* (the numerical value of the Hebrew letters) of *Bene Yisrael*, which equals 603, the thousands of the total here given, or the view of Holzinger who shows that the words *Kol Zakar*, equaling 277, should be subtracted from 550, giving us the number 273, the surplus of the first-born over the Levites, is more fanciful than any advanced by the conservative exegetes. That the number 600,000 was believed to be the total number of Israelites who went out of Egypt is evidenced from the persistency with which it is repeated in various parts of the Bible. One can hardly compare conditions of living in those primitive ages with statistics of modern days, and conclude that since they do not tally the traditional number must be fictitious. Still less is it legitimate to compare data of births and deaths of ancient times with similar data of the present, since social conditions were so vastly different then from what they are now. Without insisting on the accuracy of all the details, it is safe to assume that the text here deals with a genuine tradition which prevailed throughout Israel. If there are any discrepancies, these must be attributed to our lack of understanding of conditions or of the terminology used, although it is not impossible that in some details carelessness of scribes or editors or a desire to be exact and consistent is responsible for some of the inaccuracies.

CHAPTER **2.**

2.1–34. THE ARRANGEMENT OF THE CAMP.

Moses is ordered to arrange the tribes in the camp in an orderly fashion, each one encamped under its proper standard, and the same order is to prevail also when they are on the march. The camp is here conceived of as being quadrilateral in shape, as in the accompanying diagram. The tabernacle is situated in the center, the Levitical families being grouped round about it on the four sides and the tribes arranged in threes on the outside. Each group of three tribes is called a "camp" and the name of the most important of the three is the name given to the camp. The tabernacle, the symbol of God's presence in the midst of Israel, in the center of the entire camp, is surrounded by the priests and the Levites, who are to guard against any defilement of the sanctuary and against an outsider coming near the holy objects. There is a difference of opinion among ancient as well as among modern commentators as to the manner in which the camp moved when on march according to this description. This will be referred to in the notes.

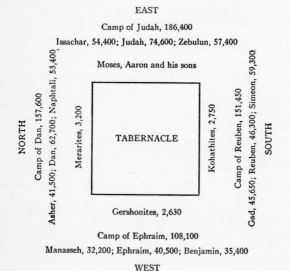

EAST

Camp of Judah, 186,400

Issachar, 54,400; Judah, 74,600; Zebulun, 57,400

Moses, Aaron and his sons

NORTH

Camp of Dan, 157,600

Asher, 41,500; Dan, 62,700; Naphtali, 53,400

Merarites, 3,200

TABERNACLE

Kohathites, 2,750

Camp of Reuben, 151,450

Gad, 45,650; Reuben, 46,300; Simeon, 59,300

SOUTH

Gershonites, 2,630

Camp of Ephraim, 108,100

Manasseh, 32,200; Ephraim, 40,500; Benjamin, 35,400

WEST

2 And the LORD spoke unto Moses and unto Aaron saying:
2 'The children of Israel shall pitch by their fathers' houses;
every man with his own standard, according to the ensigns;
a good way off shall they pitch round about the tent of
3 meeting. Now those that pitch on the east side toward

2. *every man with his own standard*] The word דגל here translated
"standard" probably comes from a root denoting "to look", "to behold"
(Cant. 5.10), hence a standard or banner. Here, however, a secondary
sense may be implied, a legion or battalion grouped around a single
standard (Targum, LXX, comp. Luzzatto). Rabbinic tradition has
it that each unit of three tribes had its own standard, bearing a certain
figure: Reuben, the likeness of a man (cf. Gen. 30.14); Judah, the
figure of a lion (Gen. 49.9); Ephraim, the figure of an ox (Deut. 33.17);
and Dan, the figure of an eagle (although Dan is compared to a serpent
in Jacob's blessing, Gen. 49.17, the eagle was chosen, because it is the
enemy of the serpent; Jerome Prado, quoted by Keil, 17 n.), thus
completing the four cherubic forms described by Ezekiel (1.10; ibn
Ezra; comp. Num. R. 2.6, where each individual tribe is also assumed
to have a standard with a special figure).

ensigns] Besides the standards of each unit of three tribes, each
tribe also had its ensign, possibly consisting of a pole, with a flag of a
different color for each (Rashi). The words מטה and שבט denoting tribe
also mean stick or staff. The modern bedouins also use the lance or
the staff, which is placed in the ground by the chief as a sign where
the clan should encamp. Rabbinic tradition has it that each tribe had
its own flag and each flag was of the same color as the stone in the
high priest's breast-plate corresponding to that tribe (Ex. 39.14),
with the name of the tribe embroidered on it (Num. R. 2.7).

a good way off] Following Rashi and ibn Ezra, R. V. has "over
against". The Rabbis say that the distance from the tabernacle to
the camps of the Israelites was 2000 cubits (cf. Josh. 3.4; Num. R. 2.8;
Tanhuma, Bemidbar, 9).

3. *the east side*] Of the tent of meeting.

toward the sunrising] A redundancy for the sake of greater clearness
(Kimhi, *Shorashim*), found in this combination in a number of other
places (3.38; 34.15; Ex. 27.13; 38.13; Josh. 19.13). Ibn Ezra's explanation that קדמה here refers to the front, i. e. that Judah was in front of
the three tribes encamped on the east side, is strained.

the sunrising shall be they of the standard of the camp of
Judah, according to their hosts; the prince of the children
of Judah being Nahshon the son of Amminadab, and his 4
host, and those that were numbered of them, threescore
and fourteen thousand and six hundred; and those that 5
pitch next unto him shall be the tribe of Issachar; the
prince of the children of Issachar being Nethanel the son
of Zuar, and his host, even those that were numbered 6
thereof, fifty and four thousand and four hundred; and 7
the tribe of Zebulun; the prince of the children of Zebulun
being Eliab the son of Helon, and his host, and those that 8
were numbered thereof, fifty and seven thousand and four
hundred; all that were numbered of the camp of Judah 9
being a hundred thousand and fourscore thousand and
six thousand and four hundred, according to their hosts;
they shall set forth first.

   camp of Judah] Each unit of three camps is named after the most
important tribe, mentioned first, included in it, and the total of the
unit is credited to it.
   4. *and his host*] "His" may refer to the prince mentioned last
(*Biur*).
   numbered of them] So nine times in this section, while three times
(vv. 6, 8, 11) the sing. suffix is used, translated here "thereof". The
word "host" to which it refers is a collective noun and may be used
as a sing. or a pl. (ibn Ezra).
   5. *next unto him*] Judah in the middle and Issachar and Zebulun
on either side of Judah. Similarly in the other three units, the most
important tribe was placed in the middle and the other two on each
side of it. According to ibn Ezra, the tribes were not in a straight line,
but one behind the other, so here Judah was in front, Issachar behind
it and Zebulun behind Issachar (see note on v. 3).
   9. *they shall set forth first*] "When they saw the cloud of glory
depart, the priests blew their trumpets, and the camp of Judah pro-

10   On the south side shall be the standard of the camp of Reuben according to their hosts; the prince of the children 11 of Reuben being Elizur the son of Shedeur, and his host, and those that were numbered thereof, forty and six 12 thousand and five hundred; and those that pitch next unto him shall be the tribe of Simeon; the prince of the children 13 of Simeon being Shelumiel the son of Zurishaddai, and his host, and those that were numbered of them, fifty and 14 nine thousand and three hundred; and the tribe of Gad; the prince of the children of Gad being Eliasaph the son 15 of Reuel, and his host, even those that were numbered of them, forty and five thousand and six hundred and fifty; 16 all that were numbered of the camp of Reuben being a hundred thousand and fifty and one thousand and four hundred and fifty, according to their hosts; and they shall set forth second.

17   Then the tent of meeting, with the camp of the Levites, shall set forward in the midst of the camps; as they encamp, so shall they set forward, every man in his place, by their standards.

---

ceeded on the journey. They proceeded in the same manner in which they were encamped, the Levites and the wagons (containing the tabernacle) in the middle, Judah in the east, Reuben in the south, Ephraim in the west and Dan in the north" (Rashi).

17. *with the camp*] "With" is not in the Heb. text and the better rendering would be "which is" the camp, making the tent of the Levites an appositional phrase of "the tent of meeting" (Mendelssohn, Leeser, see also Luzzatto).

in the midst of the camps] Apparently meaning in the midst of all the four camps, first Judah from the east, then Reuben from the south, and then the Levites proceed from the middle, followed by the other

On the west side shall be the standard of the camp of 18
Ephraim according to their hosts; the prince of the children
of Ephraim being Elishama the son of Ammihud, and his 19
host, and those that were numbered of them, forty thousand
and five hundred; and next unto him shall be the tribe of 20
Manasseh; the prince of the children of Manasseh being
Gamaliel the son of Pedahzur, and his host, and those 21
that were numbered of them, thirty and two thousand and
two hundred; and the tribe of Benjamin; the prince of the 22
children of Benjamin being Abidan the son of Gideoni,
and his host, and those that were numbered of them, 23
thirty and five thousand and four hundred; all that were 24
numbered of the camp of Ephraim being a hundred thousand and eight thousand and a hundred, according to
their hosts; and they shall set forth third.

two camps, Ephraim on the west and Dan on the north, so that the
Levites proceeded as they were encamped, in the midst of the entire
camp. This, however, does not agree with the description in 10.14–28,
where the order of procedure is given as follows: Judah, Gershon,
Merari, Reuben, Kohath and the tabernacle, Ephraim and Dan. Ibn
Ezra suggest that "in the midst of the camps" here means that Gershon
and Merari marched between Judah and Reuben, Kohath between
Judah and Ephraim, but following upon Reuben. According to this,
the tabernacle with the Kohathites and the priests really were in the
middle of the camp, although the Gershonites and Merarites proceeded
ahead of Reuben. The expression "as they encamp, so shall they set
forward" applies to the Israelitish camps and not the camp of the
Levites (comp. Sforno). This assumption is perhaps supported by
the phrase "by their standards", which can only refer to the Israelites
and not to the Levites. If, however, the clause includes also the Levites,
we shall have to assume that they also were divided into four com-
panies, each having a set place and standard.

25 On the north side shall be the standard of the camp of Dan according to their hosts; the prince of the children 26 of Dan being Ahiezer the son of Ammishaddai, and his host, and those that were numbered of them, threescore 27 and two thousand and seven hundred; and those that pitch next unto him shall be the tribe of Asher; the prince 28 of the children of Asher being Pagiel the son of Ochran, and his host, and those that were numbered of them, forty 29 and one thousand and five hundred; and the tribe of Naphtali; the prince of the children of Naphtali being 30 Ahira the son of Enan, and his host, and those that were numbered of them, fifty and three thousand and four 31 hundred; all that were numbered of the camp of Dan being a hundred thousand and fifty and seven thousand and six hundred; they shall set forth hindmost by their standards.'

32 These are they that were numbered of the children of Israel by their fathers' houses; all that were numbered of the camps according to their hosts were six hundred thousand and three thousand and five hundred and fifty. 33 But the Levites were not numbered among the children 34 of Israel; as the LORD commanded Moses. Thus did the children of Israel: according to all that the LORD commanded Moses, so they pitched by their standards, and so they set forward, each one according to its families, and according to its fathers' houses.

31. *by their standards*] The pl. here is rather strange unless it refers to all the four standards, or it is used here as a synonym of לצבאתם, the word used in connection with the first three camps (note on v. 2).

32–33. A repetition of 1.46, 47.

Now these are the generations of Aaron and Moses in **3**
the day that the LORD spoke with Moses in mount Sinai.
And these are the names of the sons of Aaron: Nadab the 2
first-born, and Abihu, Eleazar, and Ithamar. These are 3
the names of the sons of Aaron, the priests that were
anointed, whom he consecrated to minister in the priest's

CHAPTER 3.

3.1–4. THE SONS OF AARON.

The family of Aaron, although part of the Levitical tribe, is singled
out and described first, in the list of the Levites, since this family furnished the priests, the consecrated Levites who stood in more intimate
relation with the service of the sanctuary.

1. *generations of Aaron and Moses*]   The family of Moses is given
later with the family of Amram (v. 27), while here the family of
Aaron alone is given (cf. I. Chron. 23.13–14). See Sanh. 19b for the
homiletic explanation that the descendants of Aaron are regarded as
the children of Moses because Moses taught them the Law.

in mount Sinai]   Before the tabernacle was erected, when all the
four sons of Aaron were alive, while after the erection of the tabernacle the expression used is "the wilderness of Sinai" (Rashbam, ibn
Ezra, *Biur*). It is also possible to assume that the superscription
"These are the generations of Aaron and Moses" is intended for the
whole chapter, describing the Levites, who are thus associated with
the two most distinguished representatives of their tribe (Keil).

3. *that were anointed*]   Although the high priest alone is described
as having been anointed (Ex. 29.7; Lev. 8.12), the four sons of Aaron
were also anointed with their father, since their priesthood was by
divine appointment and not through inheritance. "And their anointing shall be unto them for an everlasting priesthood throughout their
generations" (Ex. 40.15).

whom he consecrated to minister]   Lit. "whose hands he filled", an
expression frequently used in the sense of appointment to office (Ex.
28.41; Judg. 17.5, 12).

4 office. And Nadab and Abihu died before the LORD, when they offered strange fire before the LORD, in the wilderness of Sinai, and they had no children; and Eleazar and Ithamar ministered in the priest's office in the presence of Aaron their father.

5-6   And the LORD spoke unto Moses, saying: 'Bring the tribe of Levi near, and set them before Aaron the priest,
7 that they may minister unto him. And they shall keep

4. *before the Lord*]   Suggesting an unnatural death as a punishment for a sin committed against God (see 14.37; II Sam. 21.9). The incident is related in Lev. 10.1–7.

strange fire]   Not in accordance with the divine command (Lev. 10.1), "strange" indicating perhaps that the fire was obtained from another place than the altar of burnt-offerings.

had no children]   For if they had children, their children would have assumed the priestly office after them (Sifre to Lev. 10.12; 16.32). This fact is not recorded in Lev., but is mentioned in I Chron. 24.2 (see Ehrlich, who advances the theory that where a person was punished with death, his children were placed outside of the community).

in the presence of]   Under his jurisdiction, or during his lifetime (Rashi). Ramban transposed this phrase, placing it after "before the LORD", and renders: "And Nadab and Abihu died before the Lord, in the presence of Aaron their father (cf. Gen. 11.28) .... and Eleazar and Ithamar ministered in the priest's office" (followed by Luzzatto and *Biur*).

5–10.   DUTIES OF LEVITES.

The tribe of Levi, exclusive of the priestly family, is designated to act in the capacity of ministers in the tabernacle, to assist the priests in their duties. The Levites are conceived as a gift given by Israel to Aaron and his family, the priests, to do the more menial labors in the sanctuary.

6. *set them before*]   Cause them to attend upon, to serve (I Kings 17.1; 18.15).

unto him]   Aaron, the representative of the priests, to whom the Levites were to minister.

his charge, and the charge of the whole congregation
before the tent of meeting, to do the service of the tabernacle. And they shall keep all the furniture of the tent of 8
meeting, and the charge of the children of Israel, to do the
service of the tabernacle. And thou shalt give the Levites 9
unto Aaron and to his sons; they are wholly given unto
him from the children of Israel. And thou shalt appoint 10
Aaron and his sons, that they may keep their priesthood;

7. *his charge*] They shall perform the duties imposed upon them
by the priests in connection with the public worship, and also attend
to the preparation of the sacrifices brought by individual members
of the community (ibn Ezra).

8. *the charge of the children of Israel*] The duties that should be
performed by the children of Israel as a whole (Rashi; comp. 18.21, 31).
Ibn Ezra suggests that this refers to the duty of the Levites to guard
against the Israelites coming close to the tabernacle, which was pro-
hibited to them (1.51), but the construction of the verse does not
permit it.

9. *they are wholly given unto him*] LXX and Sam. have "unto
Me", as in 8.16–19, where it is said that the Levites were given to
God by Israel, and then by Him to Aaron and his sons (comp. 18.6).
"Wholly given" translates the duplication נתונם נתונם, used here for
emphasis. Luzzatto makes the first נתונם a noun (like נתינים, I Chron.
9.12) and the second a participle, i. e. they are given to him as Nethinim, servants. The Nethinim are mentioned as a class of menial Temple
servants in Ezra (2.43) and in Neh. (7.46), although their origin is
obscure. The Rabbis regarded them as aliens, members of conquered
tribes, with whom the Israelites were forbidden to intermarry (Mishna
Yeb. 2.4). The use of this word here in the meaning given is not warranted and the confusion of the Levites with the late Nethinim is
not admissible.

from the children of Israel] From among the children of Israel one
tribe is set aside to render service to the priests (Rashi), as if it were
written מתוך (Sam. and Syr. v. 12; 8.16).

10. *may keep their priesthood*] From pollution of any kind (ibn
Ezra). They should be careful with the work assigned to them, such

and the common man that draweth nigh shall be put to death.'

11-12   And the LORD spoke unto Moses, saying: 'And I, behold, I have taken the Levites from among the children of Israel instead of every first-born that openeth the womb among the children of Israel; and the Levites shall be Mine;

as the offering of the sacrifices and of the incense, and not allow any stranger, i. e. a non-priest, be he a Levite or an Israelite, to perform any of the priestly duties (Rashi, see Luzzatto, *Biur*). LXX adds "and anything that pertaineth to the altar, and to that within the veil", as in 18.7.

11-14. LEVITES TAKE PLACE OF FIRST-BORN.

The Levites are substituted for the first-born, who became devoted to God in consequence of the miracle, when they were spared at the time of the plague of the first-born in Egypt. This idea is further elaborated in vv. 40-51.

12. *And I, behold, I*] I have the right to assign the Levites as assistants to Aaron and his sons, because they take the place of the first-born, who belong to Me (Rashi). The first-born, both of men and of beasts, were sacred to God (Ex. 22.28, 29; 13.1); the first-born of clean animals were to be offered, and of unclean animals to be exchanged for clean animals, and the first-born of man to be redeemed by the payment of a sum of money (Ex. 13.11-13; 34.19-20; Num. 18.14-18). It is possible to assume that at a very early age the first-born of man also were sacrificed, and that the ransom of money was instituted as a substitute, although the rabbinic tradition, based on this and on vv. 40-51, is that the first-born at one time acted as the priests in each household, whose functions were later transferred to the Levites, because the first-born participated in the worship of the Golden Calf, while the Levites acted as the champions of the true faith. Ex. 32.26-28 (Rashi).

and the Levites shall be Mine] Dedicated to My service (Targum, ibn Ezra, cf. Ex. 13.2).

for all the first-born are Mine: on the day that I 13
smote all the first-born in the land of Egypt I hallowed
unto Me all the first-born in Israel, both man and beast,
Mine they shall be: I am the LORD.'

And the LORD spoke unto Moses in the wilderness of 14
Sinai, saying: 'Number the children of Levi by their 15
fathers' houses, by their families; every male from a month
old and upward shalt thou number them.' And Moses 16
numbered them according to the word of the LORD, as he
was commanded. And these were the sons of Levi by their 17
names: Gershon, and Kohath, and Merari. And these are 18
the names of the sons of Gershon by their families: Libni
and Shimei. And the sons of Kohath by their families: 19

13. The idea is more fully given in Ex. 13.14–15.
I am the Lord] A formula used to emphasize the importance of a
command.

14–39. THE NUMBERING OF THE LEVITES.

The Levitical families and their numbers are here given and the
functions of each family in connection with the tabernacle are described.
The census of the Levites includes all those over one month old.
15. *from a month old*] Since they were to be substituted for the
first-born, who were to be redeemed only after reaching the age of
one month (18.16), the Levites were also numbered from the age of
one month and upwards, although for the purpose of assuming office
they were numbered later from the ages of 30 to 50 (4.47). The redemption of the first-born is observed also in modern times, but only
after the child has reached the age of one month, when it is assumed
to be healthy and likely to continue a normal life (בן קיימא; Tanhuma,
Bemidbar, 21; comp. ibn Ezra, who associates it with the belief in
the effect of the revolution of the moon on the life of the new-born
infant). In Jewish law, the infant less than a month old is not treated
as a living person and, if it dies, no mourning need be observed by its
parents, since it is looked upon as a still-born child (M. K. 24b).

20 Amram and Izhar, Hebron and Uzziel. And the sons of
Merari by their families: Mahli and Mushi. These are the
families of the Levites according to their fathers' houses.
21 Of Gershon was the family of the Libnites, and the
family of the Shimeites; these are the families of the
22 Gershonites. Those that were numbered of them, according to the number of all the males, from a month old and
upward, even those that were numbered of them were
23 seven thousand and five hundred. The families of the
Gershonites were to pitch behind the tabernacle westward;
24 the prince of the fathers' house of the Gershonites being
25 Eliasaph the son of Lael, and the charge of the sons of
Gershon in the tent of meeting the tabernacle, and the
Tent, the covering thereof, and the screen for the door of

21. *Of Gershon*] Those that were numbered (v. 22) of Gershon
were the families of Libni and of Shimei (Rashi, ibn Ezra). This accounts for the repetition of פקדיהם in v. 22. Syr. omits the second
פקדיהם. It is suggested that it was transposed here from the beginning
of v. 28, where it is missing (Gray).
23. *behind*] When facing the east.
westward] Lit. towards the sea, the Mediterranean, west of Palestine.
25. *and the charge*] Although here the census of the Levites of
one month old and over is given, and not the number of those to be
enrolled for service from 30 to 50 years of age, still the position of each
of the three families and the objects given in charge of each are mentioned in a general way. In ch. 4 this is given in greater detail.
the tabernacle] Refers to the ten linen curtains hung on the inside
(Ex. 26.1-6), since the framework was assigned to the Merarites (v. 36).
the Tent] The eleven curtains of goats' hair used as the covering
(ib. 7-13).
the covering thereof] The second covering on top made "of rams'
skins dyed red" and of sealskins (ib. v. 14).
the screen] On the east side, where there were no boards (ib. v. 36).

the tent of meeting, and the hangings of the court, and 26
the screen for the door of the court—which is by the tabernacle, and by the altar, round about—and the cords of it,
even whatsoever pertaineth to the service thereof.

And of Kohath was the family of the Amramites, and 27
the family of the Izharites, and the family of the Hebronites, and the family of the Uzzielites; these are the families
of the Kohathites: according to the number of all the males, 28
from a month old and upward, eight thousand and six
hundred, keepers of the charge of the sanctuary. The 29
families of the sons of Kohath were to pitch on the side
of the tabernacle southward; the prince of the fathers' 30
house of the families of the Kohathites being Elizaphan
the son of Uzziel, and their charge the ark, and the table, 31

26. *the hangings of the court*] Ex. 27.9–15.

the screen] Ib. v. 16.

which is by the tabernacle] The court which encloses both the tabernacle and the altar of burnt-offerings which stood within it (comp.
Rashi to 4.26, who makes it refer to the hangings together with the
screen surrounding and protecting both the tabernacle and the altar;
see *Biur*).

and the cords of it] Of the tent, by which the outer coverings were
fastened down, while the cords of the hangings of the court were carried
by the Merarites (v. 37, Rashi).

the service thereof] According to the more definite instructions given
further (4.25–27).

27. *Amramites*] Referring to the descendants of Moses only, since
Aaron and his sons were not included among them; or, perhaps, Amram
had other sons not mentioned elsewhere.

28. *keepers of the charge of the sanctuary*] This phrase occurs only
here and in v. 32, because the Kohathites had charge of the most
sacred objects, such as the ark, the table, the candlestick and the altars.

and the candlestick, and the altars, and the vessels of the
sanctuary wherewith the priests minister, and the screen,
32 and all that pertaineth to the service thereof; Eleazar the
son of Aaron the priest being prince of the princes of the
Levites, and having the oversight of them that keep the
charge of the sanctuary.

33 Of Merari was the family of the Mahlites, and the
family of the Mushites; these are the families of Merari.
34 And those that were numbered of them, according to the
number of all the males, from a month old and upward,
35 were six thousand and two hundred; the prince of the
fathers' house of the families of Merari being Zuriel the son
of Abihail; they were to pitch on the side of the tabernacle
36 northward; the appointed charge of the sons of Merari
being the boards of the tabernacle, and the bars thereof,

31. *and the altars*] The altar of burnt-offerings (Ex. 27.1–8) and
the altar of incense (ib. 30.1–10).

vessels of the sanctuary] The vessels pertaining to the objects enumerated as described in ch. 4.

screen] The veil that separated the "holy" place from the "most
holy" (Ex. 26.31–33).

32. Eleazar, the son of Aaron, himself a Kohathite, was made chief
of the tribe of Levi and overseer of the work assigned to the three
families of the tribe (comp. 17.16–28, where Aaron appears to be
regarded as the prince of the tribe of Levi).

prince of the princes] Of the three princes (vv. 24, 30, 35). Targum
renders אמרכלא, probably a Persian word meaning supervisor (Kohut,
Aruch, s. v., comp. Yer. Shab. 10.3).

oversight] An abstract noun used in a concrete sense (BDB פְּקֻדָּה).
Targum renders rather freely: "under whose direction all officials who
keep the charge of the sanctuary were appointed."

36. See Ex. 26.15–30.

and the pillars thereof, and the sockets thereof, and all
the instruments thereof, and all that pertaineth to the
service thereof; and the pillars of the court round about, 37
and their sockets, and their pins, and their cords. And 38
those that were to pitch before the tabernacle eastward,
before the tent of meeting toward the sunrising, were
Moses, and Aaron and his sons, keeping the charge of the
sanctuary, even the charge for the children of Israel; and
the common man that drew nigh was to be put to death.
All that were numbered of the Levites, whom Moses and 39
Aaron numbered at the commandment of the LORD, by
their families, all the males from a month old and upward,
were twenty and two thousand.

37. See Ex. 27.10–19.

38. *before the tabernacle eastward*] Omitted in LXX; cf. 2.3.

Moses] But not his children, who were included with the Kohathites
in the family of Amram.

even the charge for the children of Israel] That which had to be
attended to in behalf of the Israelites, who could not themselves come
near to the sanctuary (comp. on v. 8). The priests were to do the work
incumbent upon the Israelites, as the offering of sacrifices, since
the Israelites could not perform these functions themselves (*Biur*,
Luzzatto).

39. *and Aaron*] In the Hebrew text, the word ואהרן has masoretic
dots over it, which gave rise to the suspicion that the word should be
omitted, possibly because the order was given to Moses alone (vv. 5, 14).
This word is actually omitted in the Syr. and Sam. versions. This,
however, is not conclusive, since in 4.1, 34, 37, 41, 45, 46, Aaron is
mentioned together with Moses in the census taken of the Levites who
were mustered into service and there is no reason why Aaron should
have been excluded here (see Szanto, Keil). According to rabbinic
tradition, the Masoretic dots indicate that Aaron was not included
in the sum total of the Levites (Bek. 4a).

twenty and two thousand] But actually there were 22,300 (Gershonites 7,500; Kohathites 8,600; and Merarites 6,200). That the number

40   And the LORD said unto Moses: 'Number all the first-born males of the children of Israel from a month old and
41   upward, and take the number of their names. And thou shalt take the Levites for Me, even the LORD, instead of all the first-born among the children of Israel; and the cattle of the Levites instead of all the firstlings among

22,000 is intended to be exact is clearly seen below, where the additional 273 first-born over the 22,000 had to be redeemed. The suggestion is made by some modern commentators that an error crept in in the number of the Kohathites and that instead of 8,600 there should be 8,300 (שלש instead of שש). The Rabbis explain this difficulty by assuming that there were 300 first-born among the Levites, who could not be exchanged for the first-born (Bek. 5a), hence "all that were numbered of the Levites" refers only to such Levites as could be substituted for the first-born. While this explanation seems plausible, it is strange that no reference to it should have been made in the text.

40–51. THE NUMBER OF THE FIRST-BORN AMONG THE ISRAELITES.

The substitution of the Levites for the first-born was to be person for person, hence the first-born of one month old and over had to be counted. Their number exceeded that of the Levites by 273, who were ordered to be redeemed at the rate of five shekels per person and the redemption money given to the priests. The first-born of the cattle of the Israelites had also to be redeemed by the cattle of the Levites.

40. *a month old*] See on v. 15.

41. *for Me, even the Lord*] The usual rendering is "for Me; I am the Lord" (R. V., Leeser), but our translation is corroborated by I Kings 1.26; I Sam. 25.24 (Luzzatto).

and the cattle of the Levites] This is apparently in contradiction to 18.15, 17, where it is distinctly said that the first-born of clean animals may not be redeemed, but had to be sacrificed. The Rabbis, therefore, are of the opinion that this refers to the first-born of unclean beasts, which are redeemed by the cattle of the Levites (Bek. 4b). In this case, the redemption could not be head for head in exact number, but all the first-born cattle were for the time redeemed by the cattle of the Levites. Gray's emendation כל בהמת בכור, as in v. 45, rendering:

the cattle of the children of Israel.' And Moses numbered, 42
as the LORD commanded him, all the first-born among the
children of Israel. And all the first-born males according 43
to the number of names, from a month old and upward,
of those that were numbered of them, were twenty and
two thousand two hundred and threescore and thirteen.

And the LORD spoke unto Moses, saying: 'Take the 44-45
Levites instead of all the first-born among the children
of Israel, and the cattle of the Levites instead of their
cattle; and the Levites shall be Mine, even the LORD's.
And as for the redemption of the two hundred and three- 46
score and thirteen of the first-born of the children of Israel,
that are over and above the number of the Levites, thou 47
shalt take five shekels apiece by the poll; after the shekel
of the sanctuary shalt thou take them—the shekel is

"the cattle of the Levites instead of the cattle of the first-born among
the children of Israel", assumes that when the first-born were made
sacred to God, all their belongings were likewise made sacred, and now
when they were exchanged by the Levites, their cattle also had to be
redeemed by the cattle of the Levites, which has henceforth become
sacred.

45. *instead of their cattle*] If Gray's emendation is accepted (see
previous note), "their" will refer to the first-born; if the traditional
rendering is followed, "their" will refer to "the children of Israel",
and include only the first-born cattle.

46. *And as for the redemption*] Taking the word פדויי as the
construct of a noun פדוי, meaning the ransom-money (Targum, Kimhi)
and not as pass. part. (ibn Ezra; see *Biur*, BDB).

47. *after the shekel of the sanctuary*] Comp. Ex. 30.13. The shekel
of the sanctuary is the silver shekel, equal to 224½ gr. (about ½ oz.),
the modern equivalent being estimated at 2s. 9d. or about 67 cents,
so that five shekels will amount to ca. 13s. 9d. or $3.35 (BDB).
Kennedy's estimate (Hastings, *Dict. of the Bible*, s. v. Money) is a little
lower, about 12 s., the shekel being equal to 2s. 5d.

48 twenty gerahs. And thou shalt give the money wherewith they that remain over of them are redeemed unto Aaron **49** and to his sons.' And Moses took the redemption-money from them that were over and above them that were **50** redeemed by the Levites; from the first-born of the children of Israel took he the money: a thousand three hundred and threescore and five shekels, after the shekel of the **51** sanctuary. And Moses gave the redemption-money unto Aaron and to his sons, according to the word of the LORD, as the LORD commanded Moses.

49. *from them that were over and above them*] The Rabbis explain that this was determined by lot. Moses took 22,000 cards on which was written the word "Levite", and 273 cards with the words "five shekels", and put them all in a box. All the first-born then drew lots. Those who drew the lot with the word "Levite" were immediately redeemed, and the others were redeemed only on the payment of the five shekels (Num. R. 4.10; Tanhuma, Bemidbar, 25; Sanh. 17a). Luzzatto suggests that the redemption-money, 1365 shekels, was distributed among *all* the first-born and not only among the 273 who exceeded the number of the Levites, so that each one had to pay about .06 of a shekel. His view is supported by the expression "from the first-born of the children of Israel" in the following verse, which apparently includes all the first-born. This, however, is not the traditional rendering.

CHAPTER **4.**

1–49.   CENSUS OF LEVITES FIT FOR SERVICE.

A census was taken of the Levites, of one month old and upwards, in order to effect the exchange for the first-born. This is described in ch. 3. Another census had to be taken of the Levites of the ages of 30 to 50 in order to establish the number that could be relied upon for the service of the tabernacle. This census is now taken, and in the same chapter are also described in detail the functions in connection with the sanctuary of each of the three families of the Levites.

And the LORD spoke unto Moses and unto Aaron, **4**
saying: 'Take the sum of the sons of Kohath from among 2
the sons of Levi, by their families, by their fathers' houses,
from thirty years old and upward even until fifty years 3
old, all that enter upon the service, to do work in the tent

2. *sons of Kohath*] In numbering the Levites fit for active service
in the tabernacle, the Kohathites and not the Gershonites (3.17, 20)
are mentioned first, because of the more important part assigned to
the former. In ch. 3 the Levites are mentioned in order of seniority,
and here in the order of the importance of the respective duties assigned
to each (Num. R. 4.11).
3. The term of service of the Levites given here is from 30 to 50
years of age, while in 8.23–26 the period of service for the Levites is
from 25 to 50. The opinion of the Rabbis is that at 25 the Levites
were to report for service and for five years they had to serve an
apprenticeship, under supervision, until they reached the age of 30,
when they became full-fledged workers in the sanctuary (Hul. 24a).
Another explanation, offered by Rashbam, is that the Levites from
the age of 25 to the age of 30 and from the age of 50 upwards were
assigned to the duty of guarding the tabernacle, but were not expected
to do the heavy work of carrying the parts of the tent, which was left
to those between the ages of 30 and 50. The LXX has 25 in this chapter
as well as in ch. 8. In I Chron. 23.24–27 (cf. Ezra 3.8; II Chron. 31.17;
but comp. I Chron. 23.3), it appears that David ordered the Levites
to be mustered into service at the age of 20, and no upward limit is
given. This may be accounted for by the fact that in connection with
the Temple service a larger force was required (Sifre 63; comp. Epstein
to 8.26 and Ehrlich to 8.23). Another suggestion has been made that
the present law was only temporary, when strong men were required
to carry the heavy parts of the tabernacle from place to place, while
the age given in ch. 8 represents the regular custom prevalent at all
future times for the Levites who should do service in the sanctuary
(Keil). Modern critics assign the three texts in which different ages
of admission for Levites into service are given to three different
periods (Gray, McNeile).
the service] The word צבא, primarily used for military service, is
used here in connection with the service of the sanctuary. It is interesting to note that in the case of military service the verb used is יצא,

4 of meeting. This is the service of the sons of Kohath in
5 the tent of meeting, about the most holy things: when the
camp setteth forward, Aaron shall go in, and his sons,
and they shall take down the veil of the screen, and cover
6 the ark of the testimony with it; and shall put thereon a
covering of sealskin, and shall spread over it a cloth all
7 of blue, and shall set the staves thereof. And upon the

to go out (1.3, 20), or עלה, to go up (Josh. 22.12, 33), while here בא,
to come in or enter, is used. It is possible that the Levites were also
organized in the same manner as the army, with officers and rules
(McNeile).

4. *the most holy things*] Such as the ark, the candlestick and the
altars (Ex. 30.29). The articles were arranged and covered up by the
priests before the Kohathites were permitted to carry them (v. 15),
since the Levites were forbidden to touch these objects or even to
look at them.

5. *when the camp setteth forward*] When the camp is about to set
forth (Mendelssohn), or when the first two divisions, Judah and
Reuben, begin to move (Rashbam), or when the cloud of glory is lifted
from the tabernacle, as a sign for departure (Rashi).

the veil of the screen] The curtain that separated the sanctuary
from the holy of holies was used as a covering for the ark, and this in
turn was covered with sealskins and a blue cloth (v. 6).

6. *thereon*] Over the covering of the veil placed upon the ark.
The sealskins served as a protection, both for the ark and for the veil,
against rain or dust, and over the sealskins the cloth of blue was placed
as an ornament, perhaps in order to hide the skins from view or so
as to make the ark conspicuous, while in the case of the other objects
the skins were on the outside (Ramban, but comp. ibn Ezra).

and shall set the staves thereof] Ready to be carried. The staves were
never removed from the ark (Ex. 25.15), and the priests were ordered
to adjust them so that they should balance properly and be more
convenient for carrying. The rendering of the R. V., "put in", is
therefore incorrect; "set" or "adjust" is better (comp. Yoma 72a and
Tosafot, s. v. כתיב, see Ehrlich to Ex. 25.15).

table of showbread they shall spread a cloth of blue, and
put thereon the dishes, and the pans, and the bowls, and the
jars wherewith to pour out; and the continual bread shall
remain thereon. And they shall spread upon them a cloth 8
of scarlet, and cover the same with a covering of sealskin,
and shall set the staves thereof. And they shall take a 9
cloth of blue, and cover the candlestick of the light, and
its lamps, and its tongs, and its snuffdishes, and all the
oil vessels thereof, wherewith they minister unto it. And 10
they shall put it and all the vessels thereof within a covering of sealskin, and shall put it upon a bar. And upon the 11

7. *table of showbread*] The word לחם, bread, is understood here
(see Targum). The showbread (לחם הפנים) is so called because it was
placed in the sanctuary, in the presence of God. The twelve loaves
were arranged on the table, in two rows, every Sabbath (Lev. 24.5–9).

thereon] On the cloth of blue all the appurtenances of the table
were arranged.

shall remain] I. e. the cloth of blue shall be spread over the table
while the bread is on it (the table) (Ramban). The bread is called here
"continual", because it was never to be absent from the table (Ex. 25.30;
Lev. 24.8).

8. The cloth of scarlet was spread over the utensils and over the
table, and over that cloth the sealskins were placed, so that the table,
like the ark, had three covers, while the other objects had only two
covers.

the staves] Ex. 25.28.

9. *oil vessels*] Vessels in which the oil for the candlestick was
kept. For a detailed description of the utensils of the candlestick
see Ex. 25.40. The expression "the candlestick of light" is found only
here and in Ex. 35.14, otherwise it is referred to simply as the candlestick. In some editions of the Targum (see ed. Berliner) the rendering
is כלי שרת=מני שמושא מני שמושא, "vessels of ministry", as in v. 12 (see Adler).

10. *upon a bar*] The sealskin was fixed in the form of a bag
(Rashi מרצף) and then attached to a bar by means of ropes or hooks
(Luzzatto). Gray is of the opinion that the word מוט here, in v. 12

golden altar they shall spread a cloth of blue, and cover it
with a covering of sealskin, and shall set the staves thereof.
12 And they shall take all the vessels of ministry, wherewith
they minister in the sanctuary, and put them in a cloth
of blue, and cover them with a covering of sealskin, and
13 shall put them on a bar. And they shall take away the
ashes from the altar, and spread a purple cloth thereon.
14 And they shall put upon it all the vessels thereof, wherewith they minister about it, the fire-pans, the flesh-hooks,
and the shovels, and the basins, all the vessels of the altar;
and they shall spread upon it a covering of sealskin, and
15 set the staves thereof. And when Aaron and his sons have

and in 13.23, means "something with a considerable flat surface on
which a variety of objects could be placed and carried".

11.   *golden altar*]   The altar of incense, described in Ex. 30.1–6,
also 40.5, 26, 27.

12.   *vessels of ministry*]   The vessels used in connection with the
offering of incense (Rashi).

13.   *from the altar*]   Of brass or of burnt-offerings (Ex. 27.1–8, see
Rashi to v. 3).   The perpetual fire (Lev. 6.6), according to the Rabbis,
remained on the altar, covered with a brass pan (פסכתר), over which
the purple cloth was spread.   Another opinion has it that the fire was
extinguished during the journey (Yer. Yoma 4.6; comp. Epstein ad loc.
and to Lev. 6.6; see Rashi, Malbim).

14.   *upon it*]   The purple cloth.

fire-pans]   Used to snatch up live coals.

flesh-hooks]   Used to turn the sacrificial animal so that it be well-
done.

shovels]   Used to remove the ashes.

basins]   In which the meat of the sacrifice was placed (cf. Ex. **27.3**).

the staves]   In the brazen rings fixed on the four corners of the net-
work of brass, placed as a grating upon the altar (Ex. 27.4), ready to
be carried (Luzzatto).   The LXX and Sam. add at the end of this

made an end of covering the holy furniture, and all the
holy vessels, as the camp is to set forward—after that, the
sons of Kohath shall come to bear them; but they shall
not touch the holy things, lest they die. These things are
the burden of the sons of Kohath in the tent of meeting.
And the charge of Eleazar the son of Aaron the priest shall 16
be the oil for the light, and the sweet incense, and the
continual meal-offering, and the anointing oil: he shall

verse: "and they shall take a purple cloth and cover the laver and its
base and they shall put them within a covering of sealskins and they
shall put them on a bar". This was probably suggested by other
passages in which the laver is included (Ex. 30.29; 31.9; 35.16), and
is not a translation of a text that contained this passage. The laver
was probably carried without any covering at all (Keil).

15. *holy furniture*] The word "furniture" is not in the Heb.
text, but understood in the collective noun קדש. R. V. and Leeser
render "sanctuary", which is meaningless, since the sanctuary itself
was not covered.

but they shall not touch] Or better "so that they shall not touch",
i. e. they shall carry them without touching them, defining the manner
of carrying them by means of staves and poles, without touching the
objects themselves (Gray).

lest they die] Comp. II Sam. 6.6, 7.

These things] After the priests prepared the objects, as described
in vv. 5–14, the Kohathites were to carry them.

16. *And the charge of Eleazar*] Eleazar was not to carry these
things personally (Rashi, see Yer. Shab. 10.3), but to have general
supervision over them and see that they were handled by scrupulous
and reliable members of the Kohathite family (ibn Ezra, Ramban,
Luzzatto).

continual meal-offering] Probably the meal-offering brought daily
by the "anointed priest" on behalf of himself and the other priests
(Lev. 6.13–15), or the meal-offering that accompanied the burnt-
offering (עלת תמיד) which was brought twice daily (Ex. 29.38–40).

have the charge of all the tabernacle, and of all-that therein
is, whether it be the sanctuary, or the furniture thereof.'
17 And the LORD spoke unto Moses and unto Aaron,
18 saying: 'Cut ye not off the tribe of the families of the
19 Kohathites from among the Levites; but thus do unto
them, that they may live, and not die, when they approach
unto the most holy things: Aaron and his sons shall go in, and
appoint them every one to his service and to his burden;
20 but they shall not go in to see the holy things as they are
being covered, lest they die.'

charge of all the tabernacle] That is the part assigned to the Kohathites, while the portions carried by the Gershonites and Merarites were
under the supervision of Ithamar (vv. 28, 33; Rashi, comp. ibn Ezra
and Ramban).

the sanctuary] Referring to the holy objects in the sanctuary, as
in v. 15. A more satisfactory explanation would be that Eleazar,
besides having charge of the specific things enumerated, had also
general charge of the whole of the tabernacle and its furniture, as being
the head of the whole tribe in its relation to the sanctuary (3.32).

18. *Cut ye not off*] A more definite statement of what is implied
in v. 15. Moses and Aaron are told that they should see to it that the
arrangements are carried out in every detail so that there be no irregu-
larity which might cause the Kohathites to come in direct contact with
the holy objects, which would lead to their destruction (Sforno).

the tribe] It is rather unusual to employ the word שבט (tribe) for
the subdivision of a tribe, as is the case here (see Gray).

19. *appoint them*] Aaron and his sons should appoint each one to
his task and have him perform his work under their immediate supervision. The Kohathites should not come in until after everything is
covered, so that they should not see (v. 20) the holy objects or touch
them (Yoma 54a; Sanh. 86b). Looking at sacred objects was also
regarded as a capital offence (I Sam. 6.19; cf. Ramban, ibn Ezra).

20. *as they are being covered*] Following Targum, Rashi (comp.
Rashi to Yoma 54a), ibn Ezra II; others render "uncovered" (ibn
Ezra I, Rashbam). The word כבלע comes from a root meaning "to

And the LORD spoke unto Moses, saying: 'Take the 21-22
sum of the sons of Gershon also, by their fathers' houses,
by their families; from thirty years old and upward until 23
fifty years old shalt thou number them: all that enter in
to wait upon the service, to do service in the tent of meeting.
This is the service of the families of the Gershonites, in 24
serving and in bearing burdens: they shall bear the curtains 25
of the tabernacle, and the tent of meeting, its covering,
and the covering of sealskin that is above upon it, and the
screen for the door of the tent of meeting; and the hangings 26
of the court, and the screen for the door of the gate of the
court, which is by the tabernacle and by the altar round
about, and their cords, and all the instruments of their
service, and whatsoever there may be to do with them,

swallow", hence engulf, cover up. Some, however, take it in a figurative sense, "as a swallowing of spittle", i. e. for a moment (R. V.,
Luzzatto, BDB).

22. *also*] Referring to v. 2; cf. 3.21–26.

23. *to wait upon the service*] Lit. to be mustered into the service.
Leeser, following Mendelssohn, has "all that are fitted for the service".

24. *in serving and in bearing burdens*] "In serving", i. e. dismantling and putting together the various parts entrusted to them,
and "bearing" the same when on the journey. The Kohathites were
not present at the dismantling (v. 20), hence their work consisted only
in carrying the objects (v. 15).

25. *the tent of meeting*] The curtains made of goats' hair and used
as a roof for the tabernacle (Ex. 36.14–19).

its covering] The rams' skins, dyed red (ib. v. 19).

26. *by the tabernacle*] Surrounding the tabernacle and the altar
(cf. 3.26 note).

instruments] Such as tools, nails, etc.

to do with them] With the instruments; or "all that may have to be
done with regard to them, e. g. the undoing of the hooks and loops,

27 therein shall they serve. At the commandment of Aaron
and his sons shall be all the service of the sons of the
Gershonites, in all their burden, and in all their service;
and ye shall appoint unto them in charge all their burden.
28 This is the service of the families of the sons of the Gershonites in the tent of meeting; and their charge shall be under
the hand of Ithamar the son of Aaron the priest.

29   As for the sons of Merari, thou shalt number them by
30 their families, by their fathers' houses; from thirty years
old and upward even unto fifty years old shalt thou number
them, every one that entereth upon the service, to do the
31 work of the tent of meeting. And this is the charge of
their burden, according to all their service in the tent of
meeting: the boards of the tabernacle, and the bars thereof,
32 and the pillars thereof, and the sockets thereof; and the
pillars of the court round about, and their sockets, and
their pins, and their cords, even all their appurtenance,
and all that pertaineth to their service; and by name ye

the rolling up of the strips of curtain, and so on" (McNeile). Targum
has: "all that would be delivered unto them", the Gershonites (Rashi).

   27. *at the commandment*] The priests should appoint the individuals to do the work, while Ithamar is to see to it that the orders
are carried out (Ramban).

   and ye shall appoint] Moses and Aaron.

   in charge] According to LXX the reading here is similar to that
of v. 32, "and ye shall appoint to them *by name* the things committed
to their charge to carry".

   32. *their cords*] The cords of the pillars, since the cords and the
pins of the hangings were in charge of the Gershonites (v. 26; Rashi,
cf. Ramban).

   and by name] Each one by name mentioned to do specific work
(Ramban). It is perhaps better to refer this to the objects which were

shall appoint the instruments of the charge of their burden. This is the service of the families of the sons of Merari, 33 according to all their service, in the tent of meeting, under the hand of Ithamar the son of Aaron the priest.'

And Moses and Aaron and the princes of the congrega- 34 tion numbered the sons of the Kohathites by their families, and by their fathers' houses, from thirty years old and 35 upward even unto fifty years old, every one that entered upon the service, for service in the tent of meeting. And 36 those that were numbered of them by their families were two thousand seven hundred and fifty. These are they 37 that were numbered of the families of the Kohathites, of all that did serve in the tent of meeting, whom Moses and Aaron numbered according to the commandment of the LORD by the hand of Moses.

And those that were numbered of the sons of Gershon, 38 by their families, and by their fathers' houses, from thirty 39 years old and upward even unto fifty years old, every one that entered upon the service, for service in the tent of meeting, even those that were numbered of them, by their 40 families, by their fathers' houses, were two thousand and six hundred and thirty. These are they that were numbered 41 of the families of the sons of Gershon, of all that did serve in the tent of meeting, whom Moses and Aaron numbered according to the commandment of the LORD.

known by definite names for the purpose of identification. These names were not necessarily proper names, although we find proper names for two pillars, Jachin and Boaz (I Kings 7.21; see BDB, 127a), in the Temple (Herxheimer, Malbim).

42   And those that were numbered of the families of the
sons of Merari, by their families, by their fathers' houses,
43 from thirty years old and upward even unto fifty years
old, every one that entered upon the service, for service
44 in the tent of meeting, even those that were numbered of
them by their families, were three thousand and two
45 hundred. These are they that were numbered of the
families of the sons of Merari, whom Moses and Aaron
numbered according to the commandment of the LORD
by the hand of Moses.

46   All those that were numbered of the Levites, whom
Moses and Aaron and the princes of Israel numbered, by
47 their families, and by their fathers' houses, from thirty
years old and upward even unto fifty years old, every one
that entered in to do the work of service, and the work of
48 bearing burdens in the tent of meeting, even those that
were numbered of them, were eight thousand and five
49 hundred and fourscore. According to the commandment
of the LORD they were appointed by the hand of Moses,
every one to his service, and to his burden; they were also
numbered, as the LORD commanded Moses.

47. *the work of service*] Rashi interprets this to refer to the music
furnished by the Levites while the sacrifices were being offered ('Arak.
11a), but the phrase may include the priests, who were to do the service
in the tabernacle but not to carry burdens (*Biur*).

49. *they were also numbered*] Referring to the Levites and meaning
that not only was the appointment, "every one to his service", by the
order of God, but the numbering also was by divine command (Rashi,
Biur). It is also possible to translate ופקדיו as things mustered in, the
assignments made to each one. While the construction is difficult, the
meaning is plain and there is no need for emendation of the text (see
ibn Ezra, Ramban, comp. Szanto).

And the LORD spoke unto Moses, saying: 'Com- 2 **5**
mand the children of Israel, that they put out of
the camp every leper, and every one that hath an
issue, and whosoever is unclean by the dead; both 3

CHAPTER **5.**

1–4. UNCLEAN PERSONS TO BE EXCLUDED FROM THE CAMPS.

After the description of the arrangement of the camp in chs.
1–4, comes the regulation concerning the preservation of the sacredness and purity of the camp. Any person who was in a state of ritual
uncleanness should be placed beyond the precincts of the camp, so that
he might not, by his presence, render the camp unclean. The Rabbis
speak of three distinct divisions or spheres in the Israelitish camp in
the wilderness: The tabernacle, known as the camp of the Shekinah
(the presence of God); the camp of the Levites round about the tabernacle; the camp of the Israelites, arranged around the Levitical camp.
The leper was put out of all the three camps; "the one that hath an
issue" was put out of the camp of the tabernacle and of the Levites,
but could remain in the Israelitish camp; the one who came in contact
with a dead body might not enter the tabernacle, but was allowed to
remain in the other two camps (Pes. 67a).

2. *every leper*] The details of the laws pertaining to the leper are
found in Lev. chs. 13, 14.

that hath an issue] A diseased flux or menstruation, described in
Lev. 15.

unclean by the dead] By contact with a dead body, described in
ch. 19. These three classes of uncleanness are all such as require segregation for at least seven days and render others with whom they come
in contact also unclean. The removal from the camp is nowhere else
mentioned, except in the case of the leper (Lev. 13.46). It is not likely
that this refers only to the military camp, regarding which the regulations were more stringent (comp. 31.19; Deut. 23.10, 11), since here
women are also included (v. 3), although it is possible that some women
also accompanied military camps. Here, however, the contents point
to the arrangement of the ordinary camp and not to that of a military
camp (Holzinger, Gray). The Rabbis extended this law to apply also to
Temple times, when the leper was not permitted to enter Jerusalem,

male and female shall ye put out, without the camp shall
ye put them; that they defile not their camp, in the midst
4 whereof I dwell.' And the children of Israel did so, and
put them out without the camp; as the LORD spoke unto
Moses, so did the children of Israel.

5-6　　And the LORD spoke unto Moses, saying: Speak unto
the children of Israel:

When a man or woman shall-commit any sin that men
commit, to commit a trespass against the LORD, and that

the person who "hath an issue" was excluded from the Temple mount
and the person who became unclean through contact with a dead body
was not permitted to enter the Temple proper (Sifre 1; Zeb. 116a,
Maim., *Biat ha-Mikdash*, III).

3. *male and female*]　Including also minors (Sifre 1).

that they defile not their camp]　The three classes of unclean persons
should also not come in contact with one another so that they do not
cause defilement to each other (Pes. 67a).

4. *and put them out*]　Ibn Ezra suggests that these unclean
persons followed the camp somewhere between the camps of Dan and
Ephraim, but admits that this is only a conjecture.

5–10.　OFFERING OF CONFESSED ROBBER.

This section is supplementary to the law of Lev. 5.20–26, where it is
provided that if any one wrong his neighbor by robbery or in some
other way and confess his guilt, he should restore the property plus
one fifth of it to the person wronged, and besides that should bring a
guilt-offering to God in atonement for his sin. Here an additional
provision is made that in case the rightful owner is dead and left no
heirs (*Goël*), the property should be given to the priest. The reason
for the repetition of the law here is probably because of this addition
by which it becomes related to the laws pertaining to the priests and
the Levites.

6. *any sin that men commit*]　Specified in Lev. 5.21, 22. It may
also be translated objectively, "any sin committed against men"
(Mendelssohn).

a trespass against the Lord]　A sin against man also involves a sin

soul be guilty; then they shall confess their sin which they 7
have done; and he shall make restitution for his guilt in
full, and add unto it the fifth part thereof, and give it unto
him in respect of whom he hath been guilty. But if the 8
man have no kinsman to whom restitution may be made
for the guilt, the restitution for guilt which is made shall
be the LORD's, even the priest's; besides the ram of the

against God (Lev. 5.21). A sin against man cannot be atoned for by
an offering unless full restitution was made to the offended party. But
restitution does not wipe out the sin unless it be accompanied by a
guilt-offering. Some understand by this clause that the offender had
previously perjured himself (ib. v. 22), for which he has to atone by
bringing a sacrifice to God, since the oath usually included the name
of God (Rashi, Ramban).

and that soul be guilty] Of any of the sins enumerated in Lev. 5.21, 22.
It is also possible to render this verb "recognize his guilt" (Mendelssohn).

7. *they shall confess*] Implying that a public confession is required,
although it is possible to make this clause part of the condition (cf.
Lev. 5.5).

in full] I. e. the principal; lit. in its sum (1.2), in its entirety.

the fifth part thereof] The same ratio of restitution is prescribed also
in the case of one who eats sacred food unwittingly (Lev. 22.14); of
an unclean animal vowed to the sanctuary (ib. 27.11–13); of a firstling
of an unclean animal (ib. v. 27); or of the redemption of the tithe of
grain (ib. v. 31).

8. *kinsman*] The word used here, *Goël*, is a technical term denoting the nearest relative, upon whom rested the obligation to redeem
the family estate (Lev. 25.25; Ruth 4.1–6) or to ransom a relative who
sold himself into slavery on account of poverty (Lev. 25.48). The
Rabbis, finding it difficult to conceive of a person who had no relatives
at all, make this apply to the case when the person wronged was a
proselyte who died without leaving heirs in the Jewish fold (Sifre 4;
B. K. 109b).

the Lord's, even the priest's] The restitution, the principal with the
additional one fifth (B. K. 109a), should be made to the Lord and

atonement, whereby atonement shall be made for him.
9 And every heave-offering of all the holy things of the
children of Israel, which they present unto the priest,
10 shall be his. And every man's hallowed things shall be
his: whatsoever any man giveth the priest, it shall be his.

given to the priest as the representative of the Lord (Rashi, comp.
ibn Ezra).

ram of the atonement] The guilt-offering described in Lev. 5.25, which
belongs to the priest anyhow (ib. 7.7).

9. *heave-offering of all the holy things*] All kinds of contributions
that belong to the priests should go to the individual priest to whom the
offering was made and not to the community of priests for subsequent
apportionment (Lev. 7.7–9, 14). The term "heave-offering" is often
applied to the grain-tax given to the priests (15.19–21; 18.24). Some
of the Rabbis make the phrase here refer to the first-fruits that were
brought to the Temple and given to the officiating priest (Ex. 23.19;
Sifre 5). The verse here, however, obviously intends to include all
kinds of offerings that go to the priests (comp. 18.8).

10. *shall be his*] I. e. the man who makes the offering, who has
the privilege of giving it to any priest that he may desire (Sifre 6;
Rashi; not like Gray, who makes "his" refer to the priest). However,
after the man delivered it to a certain priest, he cannot take it away
from him and give it to another priest (Sforno).

11–31. LAW PERTAINING TO A WOMAN SUSPECTED OF ADULTERY.

This section contains the law about a married woman who is suspected of infidelity by her husband, who, however, is unable to sub-
stantiate his suspicion legally. It is placed here because it contains
provisions which come within the province of the duties and functions
of the priesthood.

Adultery in the case of a married woman, legally proved, is a capital
offence and punishment is visited on both the woman and her paramour
(Lev. 20.10; Deut. 22.22). In accordance with rabbinic tradition
(Sanh. 52a), the punishment was death by strangulation. In the case
where the fact cannot be established by the testimony of witnesses,
as the criminal law requires, and there is merely a suspicion arousing

And the LORD spoke unto Moses, saying: Speak unto 11-12
the children of Israel, and say unto them:

the jealousy of her husband, whether the suspicion rests on facts or
not, the law here prescribes a test by which the truth may be discovered
or a confession obtained. A matter of such great importance as the
preservation of the marital ties and the maintenance of the moral
standards of the community could not be left in doubt, and if human
judges are unable to determine the truth, divine aid is invoked.

The rabbinic law provides that when the husband determines to
place the case before the authorities on the ground of his suspicions,
the woman must become a stranger to him and all conjugal relations
must be interrupted, until her innocence is established through the
test. If the woman refuses to undergo the test, she should be divorced,
since her refusal is interpreted as an admission of guilt, although no
punishment can be meted out to her under these conditions since there
is no legal evidence.

The test itself, as given here, consists in the presentation of the
woman by her husband to the priest. The husband must bring at the
same time a meal-offering of coarse barley-flour. The woman is placed
in a conspicuous corner in front of the sanctuary, her hair loosened,
her garments disarranged, with the meal-offering in her hands. The
priest stands in front of her, with an earthen vessel containing holy
water taken from the laver, mingled with dust taken from the floor of
the sanctuary. He then pronounces the formula, declaring that if she
be innocent nothing will happen to her, but if she be guilty, the water
will cause her "thigh to fall away and her belly to swell", a disease
which is described as dropsy of the womb. The woman confirms the
oath by responding "Amen, Amen." The same formula is then written
on a scroll and washed off into the water, which she is made to drink,
after the meal-offering is sacrificed on the altar. If she is guilty, the
threatened disease attacks her and she becomes accursed among her
people; if she is innocent, the promise is made to her that she will again
become a mother and all reproach is removed from her.

The test is probably a modification of the practice of an ordeal found
among many ancient peoples and among some African tribes even at
the present time. The Code of Hammurabi (Johns, *The Oldest Code of
Laws in the World*, Edinburgh, 1903) has the following rules: "131. If
the wife of a man her husband has accused her, and she has not been

If any man's wife go aside, and act unfaithfully against

caught in lying with another male, she shall swear by God and return
to her house. 132. If a wife of a man on account of another male has
had the finger pointed at her, and has not been caught in lying with
another male, for her husband she shall plunge in the holy river." Thus
when the suspicion is raised by the husband only and has not been
confirmed by outside rumor, she needs take only an oath to clear herself. When, however, the suspicion is entertained also by others outside of her husband, she has to go through the more severe test of the
ordeal by water (see Barton, *Archaeology and the Bible*, Philadelphia,
1916, p. 328).

It is to be noted that in the form in which the ordeal is found here,
there is no prejudice against the woman; the drink administered to her
contained no dangerous or poisonous ingredients (comp. Luzzatto to
v. 18) and the process was not intended primarily as a punishment
but rather as a test, which might lead to a confession and to the establishment of the truth, through the intervention of God. The Rabbis
also stress the fact that the accusing husband must be free from all
guilt himself, otherwise the test will not be efficacious. They further
say that in a period of great immorality, R. Johanan b. Zakkai entirely
abolished the rite. The text does not mention how soon the result that
is foretold would become evident. It appears, however, that an immediate result was expected, and so it was also understood by the Rabbis
(Sotah 20a, b), although it is also said that because of certain merits
that she may have or certain good deeds that she may have performed,
the punishment might be delayed for as long as three years.

The Mishna devotes a whole treatise to the discussion of the details
of this law, and there is an extensive Gemara to it both in the Palestinian and Babylonian editions of the Talmud. References to this
treatise (Sotah) will be made in the notes to the text. For further
discussion of the subject, the reader is referred to Frazer, *Folk-Lore in
the Old Testament*, London, 1919, vol. III, pp. 304–414; Hastings,
Dictionary of the Bible, III, 273–4; Gray, *Numbers*, 43–56; Kennedy,
Leviticus and Numbers, Century Bible, 214; Morgenstern, in *Hebrew
Union College Jubilee Volume*, 1925, pp. 113–143.

12. *go aside*] Stray from the right path. It is from this verb that
the technical name, Sotah, as applied to a woman under suspicion, is
derived.

act unfaithfully] The root used here, מעל, is the same as in v. 6,

him, and a man lie with her carnally, and it be hid from 13
the eyes of her husband, she being defiled secretly, and
there be no witness against her, neither she be taken in
the act; and the spirit of jealousy come upon him, and he 14
be jealous of his wife, and she be defiled; or if the spirit of
jealousy come upon him, and he be jealous of his wife,

"trespass against the Lord", indicating deceit, falsification (Sifre 7;
Me'i. 18a).

13. *hid from the eyes of her husband*] But if the husband knew of
it and made no protests, the test cannot be made (Sifre 7).

she being defiled secretly] Both A. V. and R. V. have "and be kept
close, and she be defiled", which is grammatically inadmissible. Gray
has "and she be undetected, though she as a matter of fact defiled herself". The Rabbis assume that the "defilement" consisted in the fact
that she had a secret rendezvous with a man (Sotah 4a, Yer. Sotah,
1.2). This is approved by Luzzatto and others. Our rendering may
have the same connotation, namely that the husband knew that she
had secret meetings with the man, but was unable to establish her
guilt (see Zunz).

no witness] But if there was even one witness, although she could
not be legally convicted through his testimony since the evidence of
at least two witnesses was required for conviction (Deut. 17.6; 19.15),
the test cannot be made (Sotah 31a; comp. Yer. Sotah 6.2).

neither she be taken in the act] The traditional rendering of the word
נתפשה is "seized against her will", i. e. that it was not a case of rape
(Rashi, Rashbam, after Sifre, Ket. 51b; ibn Ezra, Luzzatto and others
take the word in the sense given to it in our translation).

14. *spirit of jealousy*] Suspicion leading to jealousy (cf. Hos. 10.11).

and he be jealous] According to the Rabbis, the test is given only
when the husband gave expression to his suspicions by warning
her in the presence of two witnesses and forbidding her to have any
communication with the man under suspicion, and she defied his orders
and continued her friendship with the man, but no evidence of actual
defilement was present (Sotah 1.1).

15 and she be not defiled; then shall the man bring his wife
unto the priest, and shall bring her offering for her, the
tenth part of an ephah of barley meal; he shall pour no
oil upon it, nor put frankincense thereon; for it is a meal-
offering of jealousy, a meal-offering of memorial, bringing
16 iniquity to remembrance. And the priest shall bring her
17 near, and set her before the LORD. And the priest shall

15. *shall the man bring his wife*] Even against her will (ibn Ezra).
This rendering is opposed to the rabbinic law that if she refuses to go
through the test before the potion was prepared, she must leave her
husband, but is entitled to her marriage portion (*ketubah*). (See Sotah
4.1, comp. ib. 20a).

her offering for her] Not necessarily in the sense of an atonement
for her but rather on her account. The husband brings the offering
because he is seeking the help of God in his predicament.

the tenth part of an ephah] A little less than seven pints.

of barley meal] The commonest kind of flour, about one half the
value of wheat flour (II Kings 7.1), a mark of poverty and mourning,
as opposed to the regular meal-offering which was made of fine flour
(Lev. 2.1 ff.). Cf. the rabbinic interpretation: "She acted in a bestial
manner, therefore her sacrifice is to be of the food of beasts", Sotah
2.1. For the same reason, no oil or frankincense is to be used with it,
as in the case of the poor man's offering (Lev. 5.11).

meal-offering of memorial] This expression is usually employed in
a favorable sense, hence the phrase "bringing iniquity to remembrance"
is added to indicate that here it is used in an unfavorable sense (comp.
Ezek. 29.16; Sifre 8).

16. *set her before the Lord*] Before the altar or before the tabernacle. Ibn Ezra makes "her" refer to the meal-offering and not the
woman, thus removing the difficulty of the repetition in v. 18, but the
verb used here will not permit of such an interpretation. In later times,
according to rabbinic tradition, the woman was placed before the
eastern (Nicanor) gate of the Temple (Sotah 1.5; Sifre 9), the gate used
by most people on entering or leaving the sanctuary, so as to give
publicity to the affair (Sotah 8a).

take holy water in an earthen vessel; and of the dust that
is on the floor of the tabernacle the priest shall take, and
put it into the water. And the priest shall set the woman 18
before the LORD, and let the hair of the woman's head go
loose, and put the meal-offering of memorial in her hands,

17. *holy water*] Water taken from the holy laver which stood in
the court of the tabernacle (Targum, Sotah 2.2 and most of old Jewish
commentators). LXX has "pure living water", after the analogy of
19.17, Lev. 14.5; comp. Ezek. 36.25; it may have read מים חיים (comp.
W. R. Smith, *Religion of the Semites*, p. 181, and Oesterly and Robinson,
Hebrew Religion, 1930, p. 32 ff.).

earthen vessel] Also in Lev. 14.5, 50. The vessel was perhaps
destroyed after this use was made of it (comp. Lev. 6.21).

the dust] To enhance the holiness of the drink to be administered
to her. There was in the Temple, according to the Rabbis, a space one
cubit square, which was covered with a marble slab, to which a ring
was affixed. The priest would raise the slab by means of the ring, take
out the dust and place it on the surface of the water so that the dust
should be visible to the eye (Sotah 2.2).

18. *And the priest*] A repetition of v. 16, unless we accept as the
object of the verb there the meal-offering and not the woman. Rashi,
following the agadic interpretation, says that she was taken from place
to place in order to confuse her so that she may be led to confess (Num.
R. 9.13 and יוסף עץ ad loc.).

let the hair . . . . go loose] As a mark of humiliation (Lev. 10.6; 13.45;
21.10). According to the Rabbis, the priest also tore her upper garment, laying bare her bosom, in order to further disgrace her. She was
dressed in black and coarse garments, and was not to have any ornaments on her. The public, excepting the woman's servants, were
permitted to see her in this condition (Sifre 11; Sotah 1.5, 6).

in her hands] The sacrifice was often placed on the hands of the
one who brought it before it was offered, as in the case of the Nazirite
(6.19) and of the initiation of Aaron and his sons (Ex. 29. 24; Lev. 8.27),
although the Rabbis suggest that this also was done in order to weary
her and lead her to confess (Sifre 11; Sotah 14a).

which is the meal-offering of jealousy; and the priest shall
have in his hand the water of bitterness that causeth the
19 curse.   And the priest shall cause her to swear, and shall
say unto the woman: 'If no man have lain with thee, and
if thou hast not gone aside to uncleanness, being under
thy husband, be thou free from this water of bitterness

water of bitterness]   Called so because of the effect that it may have
upon her (Sifre 11). Some of the Rabbis believed that a bitter ingredient was placed into the water (Sotah 20a; comp. ibn Ezra and Luzzatto). LXX has "the waters of purgation" or ordeal.

that causeth the curse]   Not the "cursed water", for the same water is
designated also (v. 17) as "holy water". The suggestion that the word
מאררים comes from a root אור meaning light and should be rendered as
waters of examination, that bring the truth to light (Szanto), or that
it should be האורים with reference to Urim and Thummim, *Orakelwasser*
(Ehrlich, *Randglossen*), is far fetched (comp. Luzzatto to v. 22, quoting
Sam. and rendering המבארים "that make clear").

19. *cause her to swear*]   The priest pronounced the oath and the
woman replied: "Amen, Amen" (v. 22).

and shall say]   In any language that the woman understands (Sifre
12; Sotah 32b).

gone aside to uncleanness]   In explanation of "no man have lain with
thee" as referring to another man, outside of her husband (Ramban).

under thy husband]   While married to him and under his authority
(cf. Ezek. 23.5; Sotah 4.1). Targum renders "besides" instead of
"under" (cf. Adler).

be thou free]   Unpunished, the water shall have no deleterious effect
and she shall be declared innocent (comp. Ex. 21.19; I Sam. 26.9;
Prov. 6.29). The Rabbis relate that before administering the oath the
priest would direct to her persuasive words in order to lead her to confess. He would say: Perhaps you yielded to the temptation when you
were in a state of drunkenness or of youthful excitement. Many
another one has likewise fallen in consequence of such allurements.
Do not allow the holy name of God to be burned for nought. He would

that causeth the curse; but if thou hast gone aside, being 20
under thy husband, and if thou be defiled, and some man
have lain with thee besides thy husband—then the priest 21
shall cause the woman to swear with the oath of cursing,
and the priest shall say unto the woman—the LORD make
thee a curse and an oath among thy people, when the
LORD doth make thy thigh to fall away, and thy belly to

also relate to her incidents of a similar nature and thus lead her on to
make a confession if she was really guilty (Sifre 12; Sotah 7a; Num. R.
9.14).

   20. *but if thou hast gone aside*] כי is used here in the sense of אם, if
(Rashi, cf. 10.32; II Sam. 19.8).

   21. *then the priest*] Repeated here from v. 19, possibly because of
the lengthy interruption (Luzzatto), or the whole clause is to be understood in the sense "the priest shall proceed to say" (Keil). Some consider this a later gloss, inserted to emphasize God's part in the pro-
ceedings. Not the water, but God brings the punishment. The rabbinic explanation of the repetition is that the priest pronounces the
oath by himself, that her assertion of innocence is true, and then pronounces the "oath of cursing" in case her statement was false (Sotah
19a; see Malbim).

   make thee a curse and an oath] That this woman be used as an
example by people who wish to pronounce a curse on some one or to
take an oath. "May my fate be like the fate of that woman if I do not
speak the truth" (Jer. 29.22; Isa. 65.15; Rashi).

   thy thigh] Meaning loins, seat of procreative power, euphemism
for רחם (comp. Gen. 42.26; Ex. 1.5).

   to fall away] To waste away. The exact nature of the disease
intended here is not known. Some understand by it dropsy of the
ovary (*hydrops ovarii*), "in which a tumor is formed in the place of the
ovarium, which may swell so as to contain 100 lbs. of fluid and which
makes the patient dreadfully emaciated" (Michaelis, quoted by Keil,
comp. Ehrlich, *Randglossen*). The Rabbis saw in this punishment a
corroboration of the principle of making the punishment fit the crime
(Sotah 1.7; comp. Sotah 9b, the explanation given for the reverse order
followed in vv. 22, 27).

22 swell; and this water that causeth the curse shall go into
thy bowels, and make thy belly to swell, and thy thigh to
fall away'; and the woman shall say: 'Amen, Amen.'
23 And the priest shall write these curses in a scroll, and he
24 shall blot them out into the water of bitterness. And he
shall make the woman drink the water of bitterness that

22. *And this water*] After pronouncing the curse, the priest declares
what will actually happen to her if she is guilty. Those who regard
v. 21 as a gloss, make this follow directly upon v. 20.

Amen, Amen] An expression of confirmation; verily, truly (Deut.
27.15–26). The repetition of the word is also found at the end of dox-
ologies (Ps. 41.14; 72.19; 89.53) and in solemn confirmation (Neh. 8.6).
The Rabbis interpret this repetition homiletically in a number of ways
(Sotah 18a, b).

23. *shall write*] The words of the curses in v. 19, beginning with
"if no man", then v. 20, v. 21, beginning with "the Lord make thee"
to v. 22, "to fall away" (Sotah 2.3; Maim. *Sotah*, III.7, 8). The Rabbis
specify the material on which and with which the writing should be
made. The scroll must be made of the skin of a clean animal like the
parchment used for the scrolls of the law, and the ink should have no
vitriol (or *atramentum sutorum*, an ingredient used in shoe-blacking
and in ink) in it, so that no trace of it be left on the scroll after the
writing is erased (Sotah 2.4).

these curses] Comp. Sulzberger, *Ancient Hebrew Law of Homicide*,
p. 148, for the development of the meaning of the word *alah*.

into the water] So that the water contained two ingredients: the
dust from the soil of the sanctuary and the erasure of the words of the
curse. See Gray, p. 54, and quotations there for the belief in the efficacy
of eating or drinking charms containing written words.

24. *And he shall make*] The order of the process was as follows:
The pronouncement of the oath by the priest, after which the woman
responds: Amen, Amen; writing it on a scroll; blotting out the writing
into the water; offering the meal-offering; causing the woman to drink
of the water. This verse is, therefore, only explanatory, telling of the
purpose of erasing the writing into the water, while the description of
the process continues in v. 25 (Rashi, *Biur*; cf. Gray, who regards this
verse also as a gloss; comp. Sotah 3.2).

causeth the curse; and the water that causeth the curse shall enter into her and become bitter. And the priest 25 shall take the meal-offering of jealousy out of the woman's hand, and shall wave the meal-offering before the LORD, and bring it unto the altar. And the priest shall take a 26 handful of the meal-offering, as the memorial-part thereof, and make it smoke upon the altar, and afterward shall make the woman drink the water. And when he hath 27 made her drink the water, then it shall come to pass, if she be defiled, and have acted unfaithfully against her husband, that the water that causeth the curse shall enter into her and become bitter, and her belly shall swell, and her thigh shall fall away; and the woman shall be a curse

and become bitter]   Causing pain and suffering.

25.   *shall wave*]   The priest placed his hand under the hand of the woman, and together they waved the offering (Sotah 19a).

26.   *a handful*]   Lit. enclose with the fist (Lev. 2.2).

memorial-part thereof]   The part of the meal-offering which is burnt on the altar (Lev. 2.2, 9, 16; 5.12; 6.8; 24.7), thus bringing the offering to the attention of God (Rashi); or to be a remembrance to the woman in the future for good or for evil (ibn Ezra); or as a remembrance for other women to follow the path of chastity (Sotah 7b).

make it smoke]   The word קטר is used in connection with sacrifices or with incense used in sacrificial worship.

27.   *And when*]   LXX and Syr. omit the first two words of this verse, which seem to be a repetition of the last phrase of v. 26. The translation "and when he hath made her drink, etc.", although not in the Heb. text, is possible. The sense would be: after he finished giving her to drink, the following will result. The Rabbis base upon this repetition the law that before the writing on the scroll was erased, she might refuse to drink of the water if she chose, but after the scroll had been erased she was forced to drink, unless she confessed herself guilty (Sotah 3.2).

28 among her people. And if the woman be not defiled, but
be clean; then she shall be cleared, and shall conceive seed.
29 This is the law of jealousy, when a wife, being under her
30 husband, goeth aside, and is defiled; or when the spirit of
jealousy cometh upon a man, and he be jealous over his
wife; then shall he set the woman before the LORD, and
31 the priest shall execute upon her all this law. And the
man shall be clear from iniquity, and that woman shall
bear her iniquity.

28. *but be clean*] The positive assertion after the negative for
emphasis. The Rabbis have the principle that every woman should
be considered chaste until proved guilty, and they deride the Rabbi
who locked his wife in the house when he went out for fear that she
might be led to misconduct in his absence (Yer. Kid. 4.4; Git. 90a).

shall be cleared] Proved innocent, cleared of all guilt and the suspicion of guilt.

shall conceive seed] Permission to return to her husband and live
with him again, although she caused the suspicion by her improper
conduct (Num. R. 9.31). It may also be regarded as a blessing or
reward for the humiliation suffered by her (comp. Sotah 26a).

29. *This is the law*] A summary of this section, in a formal way
(cf. Lev. 11.46 et al.).

30. *spirit of jealousy*] Even though he is not able to give a satisfactory explanation of his suspicions. The husband, however, should
not cause his wife to go through this humiliating ceremony because of
a quarrel or in the spirit of fun, when he himself has no suspicion of
her unfaithfulness (Yer. Sotah 1.1).

then shall he set] The husband, comp. v. 11.

31. *clear from iniquity*] In either case no blame is to be attached
to the husband, while the woman, if guilty, will suffer the punishment,
and even if not guilty of actual defilement, will suffer disgrace because
of her unseemly conduct which provoked the suspicion (Sforno). The
Rabbis deduce from this phrase the law that only when the husband
is entirely guiltless of any misconduct will the test be effective (Sotah
47b), so that when immorality increased in Israel, the whole process
of the "bitter waters" was abolished by R. Johanan b. Zakkai (see
Ramban, Sotah 9.9).

And the Lord spoke unto Moses, saying: Speak unto 2 **6**
the children of Israel, and say unto them:

CHAPTER 6.

1–21. The Laws of the Nazirite

This section deals with the law of the Nazirite. If a man takes upon himself the Nazirite vow, he must abstain from drinking wine or any product of the grape; he must not cut his hair; and he must avoid contact with a dead body. If by accident he becomes defiled by contact with a dead body, his Naziriteship is interrupted and he has to begin the fulfillment of his vow anew, after having brought the prescribed offerings in atonement of his sin. After the fulfillment of his vow, he must have his hair cut and offer a prescribed order of sacrifices.

The reason for the introduction of this law here is variously given. The Rabbis found in the juxtaposition of this law with the law of the married woman suspected of adultery an opportunity for a number of homiletic speculations (Num. R. 10.4 ff.; Sotah 2a). The most obvious connection with the preceding text is the part played by the priest in the ceremonies connected with the Nazirite (comp. ibn Ezra to 5.31).

The institution of the Nazirite, which is nowhere else found in the Pentateuch, was probably one of the oldest in Israel. Still, the references to it, even in the narrative portions of the Bible, are very scant and incomplete. Samson is called a Nazirite (Judg. 13.5), although the only condition made in his case is that no razor shall come upon his head, but his mother was told not to drink wine or eat any unclean thing during the period of her pregnancy (ib. vv. 4, 7, 14). With regard to Samuel, who also is mentioned as a Nazirite, it is said that "no razor shall come upon his head" (I Sam. 1.11), but no mention is made of any other restriction. The tradition about the Rechabites, a semi-Jewish sect, mentions only their abstinence from wine and the fact that they led a nomad life (Jer. 35.2–19). Amos, referring to the Nazirites (2.12, 13), seems to imply that their abstinence from wine was their main characteristic. Nazirites were numerous during the period of the second Temple and references to them are made in the Apocrypha (I Macc. 3.49), by Josephus (*Ant.* xix.6.1), and in the Mishna (Naz. 3.6; 5.4; comp. Yer. Ber. 11b, where it is mentioned that 300 Nazirites

came to Jerusalem at one time before Simeon ben Shatah, who lived
in the first century B.C.E.). It has been suggested that John the
Baptist was a Nazirite (Luke 1.15) and that the institution flourished
among the early Jewish Christians (Acts 21.17 ff.; comp. Hastings,
Dictionary of the Bible, III, 500).

The outstanding difference between the few instances of Nazirites
mentioned in the Bible and the law here is that here the law obviously
speaks of one who took the vow for a limited period (according to the
Rabbis, a minimum of 30 days, Naz. 1.3). Samson was a Nazirite for
life, as were also Samuel and Absalom, if the tradition about them is
historical (Naz. 4b). The Rechabites were certainly life Nazirites, if
they may be considered as Nazirites at all (see Oesterly and Robinson,
Hebrew Religion, 184–6). The Rabbis distinguish between a life-long
Nazirite, who may cut his hair once a year if it becomes too heavy,
and a Samson-Nazirite who may never cut his hair, but may defile
himself through contact with a dead body (ib. based on II Sam. 14.26).
According to rabbinic tradition both the temporary and the life-long
Nazirite existed simultaneously in Israel. That the life-long Nazirite,
with his long flowing hair, was a common phenomenon in ancient Israel
is evidenced by the metaphorical use made of the word Nazir in the
Bible (cf. Lev. 25.5, 11).

It has been suggested that in its origin this institution was "a reac-
tion in favor of the primitive simplicity of Israel in the days before it
came in contact with Canaanite civilization and Canaanite religion"
(W. R. Smith, *Prophets of Israel*, 84 ff.; comp. Bar Tubyah, *Sefer ha-
Nezirim*, I, 12 ff.). It was not originally connected with asceticism of
any kind, but with the desire to maintain the simplicity of the old
nomad life as against the agricultural life, in which the cultivation of
the vine was one of the most conspicuous elements in Canaan. Later,
these Nazirites formed a distinct class in the community, a living
protest against the sensuous and self-indulgent habits of the Canaanites, which were gradually being adopted by the Israelitish settlers of
the land. While these were probably life-long Nazirites, and the case
of the Rechabites may be only an example of many such groups that
existed both in the northern and in the southern parts of the country,
who were regarded by the people as men of God and classed together
with the prophets (Amos 2.12), there were later individuals who
assumed the vow for a longer or a shorter period, because of some
misfortune or because of the hope of attaining a certain wish. The
Mishna mentions different reasons that might have prompted one to

When either man or woman shall clearly utter a vow,
the vow of a Nazirite, to consecrate himself unto the

become a Nazirite. "The pious in ancient times took such a vow that
they might have the opportunity of bringing a sin-offering" (Ned.10b).
It is related of Simeon the Just that he praised a shepherd-boy who had
become a Nazirite because he was tempted to sin when he realized the
beauty of his hair (Naz. 4b). It was thus in later times that an element
of asceticism was introduced into this institution, and it was because
of this that the Rabbis regarded it with disfavor (Ned. 9a; Ta'an. 11a).

It seems that the most prominent feature of the institution in ancient
times was the abstention from cutting the hair, perhaps because it was
the visible sign by which the Nazirite was recognized. The long hair
was the symbol of his consecration to God, and when the period of the
Naziriteship was completed, the hair was to be burnt together with
the sacrifice, as an offering to God. Many ancient peoples regarded
the hair as the seat of life and strength and it was therefore considered
sacred (W. R. Smith, *Religion of the Semites*, 2nd ed., 483; cf. Keil).
It is for this reason that the Nazirite, who was supposed to be on a
higher level of holiness even than the priest, must avoid all contact
with a dead body, even that of his closest relative, since such contact
brought defilement. For further reference see Gray, *Numbers*, 56–74.
Jew. Ency., s. v. Nazirite; Hastings, *Dictionary of the Bible*, s. v.
Nazirite.

2. *or woman*] The Nazirite vow of a woman is subject to the laws
governing all vows made by women as explained in 30.3 ff. The Rabbis
refer to a famous case when Queen Helene observed Naziriteship for
14 or 21 years, as a token of her gratitude for the safe return of her son
from a battle (Naz. 3.6; comp. ibid. 4.1).

clearly utter] The original meaning of the word used here יפלא
is not certain. R. V. and Leeser have "make a special vow"; ibn Ezra
renders: "make a remarkable vow", something that attracts attention,
and he is followed by Mendelssohn and Herxheimer; BDB has "make
a hard, difficult vow". The verb is especially used with vows (15.3, 8;
Lev. 22.21; 27.2).

the vow of a Nazirite] The Heb. root נזר means to set aside, dedicate,
separate, in a religious and ceremonial sense (cf. Lev. 15.31; see Introductory note to this chapter).

to consecrate himself] Lit. to become a Nazir. "A Nazir of God"

3 LORD, he shall abstain from wine and strong drink: he shall drink no vinegar of wine, or vinegar of strong drink, neither shall he drink any liquor of grapes, nor eat fresh 4 grapes or dried. All the days of his Naziriteship shall he eat nothing that is made of the grape-vine, from the 5 pressed grapes even to the grape-stone. All the days of his vow of Naziriteship there shall no razor come upon

was probably the original full form of the term (Judg. 13.5, 7), which was shortened to Nazir.

3. *strong drink*] Even though not produced from the grapes, including all kinds of intoxicating liquors. Targum renders "old and new wine" (cf. Adler), and is followed by Rashi and ibn Ezra. One of the Rabbis suggests that יין refers to diluted wine, while שכר (LXX transliterates but does not translate) is undiluted wine. The rabbinic view is that the prohibition includes the produce of the grape, but not other liquors (Sifre 24; Naz. 4a; 34b).

vinegar] Prepared from liquor which turned sour, and used as a condiment (Ruth 2.14).

liquor of grapes] Grape-juice, unfermented, even though not intoxicating (Naz. 37a).

dried] dried grapes were made into cakes and used as food (II Sam. 6.19; Cant. 2.5; Hos. 3.1).

4. *made of the grape-vine*] Comp. Judg. 13.14.

from the pressed grapes even to the grape-stone] The two Heb. words used here are hapaxlegomena and their meaning can be determined from the context only. R. V. has "from the kernels even to the husk" (Targum, Rashi, cf. Naz. 39a). Our rendering reverses the meaning of the two words (comp. LXX, Syr. and Vulg., ibn Ezra and Luzzatto). The pressed grapes are the husks after the juice has been extracted (R. Judah in Naz. 34b; comp. Luzzatto). The Nazir is warned against eating or drinking anything that has any relation to the grape. There was an ancient popular saying, quoted in the Talmud: "Go hence, go hence, Nazirite; make a detour, make a detour, and come not near the vineyard" (Shab. 13a; Yeb. 46a).

5. *no razor*] Not limited to shaving, but the cutting of the hair with any other instrument is also included, as is explained in the second half of the verse (Naz. 39b; Sotah 16a).

his head; until the days be fulfilled, in which he consecrateth himself unto the Lord, he shall be holy, he shall let
the locks of the hair of his head grow long. All the days 6
that he consecrateth himself unto the Lord he shall not
come near to a dead body. He shall not make himself 7
unclean for his father, or for his mother, for his brother,
or for his sister, when they die; because his consecration
unto God is upon his head. All the days of his Nazirite- 8
ship he is holy unto the Lord. And if any man die very 9
suddenly beside him, and he defile his consecrated head,

he shall be holy]   To leave the hair grow long was the visible sign of
consecration. The law is more stringent with the Nazirite than with
the priests (Lev. 10.6; 21.5; Ezek. 44.20). Rashi renders here "it shall
be holy", referring to the hair (Sifre 25).

6.   The Nazirite must not come in contact with a dead body, even
that of his nearest relative, the same as the high priest (Lev. 21.11),
while the common priests might defile themselves by contact with the
dead bodies of certain of their relatives (ib. vv. 1–4). Samson certainly
did not observe this provision, as he often came in contact with dead
bodies (Judg. 14.19; 15.8). The Rabbis solve the difficulty by drawing
a distinction between the Samson type of Nazirite who did not have to
bring a sin-offering in case he became defiled through contact with a
dead body and the ordinary life-long Nazirite (נזיר עולם), who had to
offer the prescribed sacrifices (vv. 9–12) every time he was defiled by
contact with the dead (Naz. 4a, b).

7.   *consecration unto God*]   The Naziriteship, which he wears as a
crown on his head (cf. ibn Ezra). In Lev. 25.5, 11, the word Nazir is
used for untrimmed vine, like the Nazirite with the unshorn hair.

9.   *very suddenly*]   So that he had no time to leave the place before
he became defiled by being in the same house with the dead (cf. 19.14).

his consecrated head]   R. V. has "the head of his separation", meaning the head with the long hair, the symbol of his Naziriteship.

then he shall shave his head in the day of his cleansing,
10 on the seventh day shall he shave it. And on the eighth
day he shall bring two turtle-doves, or two young pigeons,
11 to the priest, to the door of the tent of meeting. And the
priest shall prepare one for a sin-offering, and the other
for a burnt-offering, and make atonement for him, for
that he sinned by reason of the dead; and he shall hallow
12 his head that same day. And he shall consecrate unto the
LORD the days of his Naziriteship, and shall bring a
he-lamb of the first year for a guilt-offering; but the

shave his head] The hair which has become defiled shall be shaved
off and buried, according to rabbinic tradition (Tem. 7.4).

of his cleansing] When he becomes clean, after the water of purification has been sprinkled upon him, as required by the law (19.11, 12).

10. *two turtle-doves*] The most inexpensive of animal sacrifices
(Lev. 5.7; 12.8).

11. *he sinned by reason of the dead*] Although it was unavoidable,
it is nevertheless regarded as a sin which requires atonement. The
sin-offering is prescribed also in other cases of inadvertent transgressions (15.24, 27; Lev. 4.2, 13 ff.).

hallow his head] I. e. he resumes his Naziriteship, after it had been
defiled (v. 9; Rashi).

12. *and he shall consecrate*] He shall begin again the fulfillment of
his vow, counting from that day as many days as he originally vowed.

of the first year] Of its life.

for a guilt-offering] This was usually brought in cases involving an
act of reparation for some wrong done (5.8–9). Why the Nazirite was
to bring a guilt-offering in this case is not made clear. Some consider
this as a reparation for some unknown sin which he must have committed to bring him into such a predicament (comp. Lev. 14.12, 21;
ibn Ezra to v. 11). Others regard this as a form of recompense to God
for the delay caused in the discharge of his vow (Gray). The Rabbis
find a reason for it in his carelessness in permitting himself to become
defiled (Num. R. 10.34).

former days shall be void, because his consecration was defiled.

And this is the law of the Nazirite, when the days of his 13 consecration are fulfilled: he shall bring it unto the door of the tent of meeting; and he shall present his offering 14

shall be void] Lit. shall fall, shall not be considered. In the case of Queen Helene, it is related in the Mishna (Naz. 3.6), that she had taken a vow to be a Nazirite for seven years and at the end of the period she became accidentally defiled, so that she had to observe her vow for another period of seven years.

his consecration] "His Naziriteship" would be a better rendering.

13–21. The Conclusion of the Nazirite Period

The Nazirite, on the completion of the fulfillment of his vow, must bring a burnt-offering, a sin-offering and a peace-offering, together with the accompanying meal-offering and libations. He should have his head shaved and the hair burnt. After the priest makes a wave-offering, the Nazirite is regarded as having absolved his vow and he may drink wine.

13. *he shall bring it*] His head with the unshorn hair, to show that he completed the period of his vow (Luzzatto; König, III, 324; but comp. Ashkenazi). Rashi, following Sifre 32 and Jonathan b. Uziel, renders "he shall bring himself" (see Leeser, "shall he present himself"). Ibn Ezra, adopting Rashi's rendering, suggests also the possibility of making the priest the subject of the verb here, although there is no reason why it should be necessary for some one else to bring him, when he would probably be happy to come himself (comp. Luzzatto and R. V., "he shall be brought"). Rashbam makes "it" refer to the sacrifice described in v. 15, a view also adopted by Dillmann (see Gray).

14. The three offerings which the Nazirite was to offer were: 1. A burnt-offering, which is always a male (Lev. 1.3, 10; 22.18, 19); 2. A sin-offering which is always a female (Lev. 4.28, 32; 5.6); 3. A peace-offering, which may be either a male or a female (Lev. 3.1, 16).

unto the Lord, one he-lamb of the first year without
blemish for a burnt-offering, and one ewe-lamb of the
first year without blemish for a sin-offering, and one ram
15 without blemish for peace-offerings, and a basket of
unleavened bread, cakes of fine flour mingled with oil,
and unleavened wafers spread with oil, and their meal-
16 offering, and their drink-offerings. And the priest shall
bring them before the Lord, and shall offer his sin-offering,
17 and his burnt-offering. And he shall offer the ram for a
sacrifice of peace-offerings unto the Lord, with the basket

The peace-offering and the burnt-offering had to be accompanied by
the prescribed meal-offering and libations.

The burnt-offering was given to God, in gratitude for the privilege
of having been able to fulfill his vow. The sin-offering was brought
probably for the reason that he may have unconsciously defiled his
Naziriteship. Some suggest that the sin-offering had as its reason the
fact that he had committed a sin by denying himself the legitimate
pleasures of life, which is disapproved of by Jewish law and teaching
(Ned. 10b; Maim., *De'ot*, III.1); while others again say that the
Nazirite by leaving his consecrated state and returning to the sinful
world is in need of an atonement (Ramban). The peace-offering was
here, as usual, partaken of at a consecrated family feast, in celebration
of the completion of the fulfillment of his vow (ibn Ezra).

15. *a basket of unleavened bread*] Which was eaten at the festive
meal, at which the meat of the peace-offering was served. Two kinds
of cakes are mentioned here; one made of dough which had oil in it,
and the other of ordinary dough, but the cakes had oil spread on
their surface after baking (Lev. 7.12). There were ten cakes of each
kind (Men. 77b).

and their meal-offering] Usual with peace-offerings and burnt-
offerings (15.4–6), but not with sin-offerings (Sifre 34; Men. 91b).
The exact amount of the meal-offering and the libation is given in 15.4, 7.

17. *with the basket*] Which went together with the peace-offering
(see on v. 15).

of unleavened bread; the priest shall offer also the meal-offering thereof, and the drink-offering thereof. And the 18 Nazirite shall shave his consecrated head at the door of the tent of meeting, and shall take the hair of his conse-crated head, and put it on the fire which is under the sacrifice of peace-offerings. And the priest shall take the 19 shoulder of the ram when it is sodden, and one unleavened cake out of the basket, and one unleavened wafer, and shall put them upon the hands of the Nazirite, after he hath shaven his consecrated head. And the priest shall 20 wave them for a wave-offering before the LORD; this is holy for the priest, together with the breast of waving

the meal-offering] Of the peace-offering. The burnt-offering was also accompanied by a meal-offering and libations, although not specified here.

18. *at the door of the tent of meeting*] Where the altar was situated (Ex. 40.6). Some of the Rabbis were of the opinion that the shaving was not done in the sanctuary proper, as this would be unseemly. Others think that the male Nazirite was shaved at the door of the sanctuary, but not the female Nazirite (Naz. 45a). In the description of the Temple, the Mishna (Mid. 2.5) provides for a special room (לשכת הנזירים), where the Nazirites had their heads shaved and where the meat of the peace-offering was cooked.

on the fire] Which is under the pot in which the meat of the peace-offering was boiled (Targum, Rashi following Naz. 45a), and not on the fire which is on the altar.

19. *when it is sodden*] After it was boiled (cf. I Sam. 2.15; see Hul. 98a, b).

20. *wave them*] The priest lifted his share of the offering and moved it towards the altar and back again, to indicate its presentation to God and then its return by God to the priest (BDB 632a).

this is holy for the priest] The shoulder and the cakes as well as the "breast of waving and the thigh of heaving", which belonged to the priest in the case of any peace-offering (Lev. 7.34). In this case, the

and the thigh of heaving; and after that the Nazirite may
21 drink wine. This is the law of the Nazirite who voweth,
and of his offering unto the LORD for his Naziriteship,
beside that for which his means suffice; according to his
vow which he voweth, so he must do after the law of his
Naziriteship.

22-23   And the LORD spoke unto Moses, saying: 'Speak unto

priest obtains a larger portion, including also the shoulder (comp.
Deut. 18.3).

thigh of heaving] The right thigh which was given to the priest
(Lev. 7.32; Num. 18.18).

drink wine] Probably served at the sacrificial meal, at which the
meat of the peace-offering was served and of which the Nazirite and
his friends partook (see Keil).

21. This is a summary of the law of the Nazirite, in which the
stress is laid on the sacrifices to be offered and the intimation is given
that this is the minimum required, although one may add many other
freewill-offerings if one can afford it.

his means suffice] R. V. has "he is able to get"; meaning that
he may add more offerings according to his means (Sifre 38).

according to his vow] In addition to the Nazirite vow, which implied
the three prescribed sacrifices mentioned, one could assume other
vows to present sacrificial gifts in connection with his Naziriteship,
all of which should be discharged at the same time. If he is too poor
to bring even the prescribed offerings, his friends or members of the
community would contribute toward defraying the necessary expenses
(Tem. 10a).

22–27.   THE PRIESTLY BLESSING

The beautiful priestly blessing appropriately concludes this section
relating to the functions of the priesthood. In Lev. 9.22, it is mentioned
that Aaron raised his hands and blessed the people, after he offered
the sacrifices, but the text of the blessing is not given there. The
suggestion is made that this was the usual blessing which the priest
gave to every individual who offered a sacrifice, and it is therefore
mentioned here immediately after the conclusion of the description of

Aaron and unto his sons, saying: On this wise ye shall bless the children of Israel; ye shall say unto them:

The LORD bless thee, and keep thee;   **24**

the sacrifices offered by the Nazirite (ibn Ezra). The text here, however, points to a communal rather than an individual blessing.

In Temple times, the blessing was offered by the priests every day, in connection with the morning sacrifice. The priests stationed themselves on the steps of the hall of the sanctuary, with their hands raised over their heads, and delivered the threefold blessing, pronouncing the name of God as it is written (the tetragrammaton). In the synagogues also, the blessing was pronounced by the priests daily, but there the name *Adonai* was substituted for the tetragrammaton and some other changes were made (Tam. 7.2; Sotah 37b). In most synagogues the custom is still observed during the services on the festivals.

The three verses making up the priestly blessing are of unequal size, the first consisting only of three words, the second of five and the third of seven. The name of God is mentioned in each verse. The expression used here makes it apparently obligatory upon the priests to pronounce this blessing upon the people. It does not, however, limit this function to the priests alone. The whole tribe of Levi was set aside to bless Israel in the name of God (Deut. 10.8; 21.5), and we also find King David blessing the people in the name of God (II Sam. 6.18; comp. I Kings 8.55).

23. *on this wise*] In the following manner. The rabbis took the phrase literally and declared that the blessing must be pronounced as it is found here, i. e. in the Hebrew language (Sotah 38a; Yer. Meg. 4.11). Rashbam suggests that this phrase is intended to emphasize that the blessing should be regarded as a prayer to God and not as a blessing by the priests, indicating that the priest is powerless to bless and that all he can do is to invoke God's blessing, as is intimated in v. 27 (Sifre 43; Num. R. 11.22).

24. *bless thee*] Referring to material blessings, such as are enumerated in Deut. 28.3 ff. (Sifre 40).

keep thee] From evil (Ps. 121.7), also in a material sense, so that the blessing may remain with thee (Rashi; ibn Ezra).

25 The LORD make His face to shine upon thee, and be gracious unto thee;

26 The LORD lift up His countenance upon thee, and give thee peace.

27 So shall they put My name upon the children of Israel, and I will bless them.'

25. *make His face to shine upon thee*] Be well-disposed towards thee (Ps. 16.15). The Rabbis refer this to the blessing of the knowledge of the Torah, which is called light (Prov. 6.23; Sifre 41).

be gracious unto thee] To grant your requests and prayers (ibn Ezra); or to give you grace in His eyes or in the eyes of men (Rashi, Ramban; cf. Sifre ib.).

26. *lift up His countenance upon thee*] Indicative of His favor, while when He hides His face, it is a sign of His anger (Ps. 30.8; 104.28). Rashi renders this in the sense that He may suppress His anger against you even when you sin and provoke Him (cf. Sifre 42).

peace] Tranquillity, absence of strife (Lev. 26.6), as well as happiness and general welfare (comp. II Kings 4.26; *Biur*).

27. *so shall they put My name*] They shall bless them in My name (see on v. 23) and I shall execute the blessing. "Man does not always know what is best for him, but I shall bless him in accordance with My knowledge" (*Biur*). The Rabbis deduce from this phrase that in the benediction the priests should pronounce God's name as it is written (tetragrammaton) (Sifre 39.42). Other elements which were regarded essential in the proper discharge of this function were that the priests should recite the blessing while standing, that their hands should be raised above their heads and that the words should be given in Hebrew (ib.).

bless them] The children of Israel. Another possible interpretation is that the word "them" refers to the priests. God will bless the priests if they obey His commandment and pronounce the blessing over Israel (Rashi, ibn Ezra; following the opinion of R. Ishmael in Hul. 49a; comp. Malbim).

And it came to pass on the day that Moses had made **7**
an end of setting up the tabernacle, and had anointed it
and sanctified it, and all the furniture thereof, and the
altar and all the vessels thereof, and had anointed them

CHAPTER 7.

1-88. THE OFFERINGS OF THE PRINCES.

The tabernacle was completed on the first day of the first month of
the second year of the Exodus. On that day, the tabernacle was set
up, and then, together with all its furniture and sacred vessels,
anointed by Moses (Ex. 40.2). The princes of the tribes, in the order
in which they were encamped (ch. 2), each brought an offering to the
tabernacle on successive days, beginning with the first and concluding
with the twelfth day of the month. The offerings consisted first of six
wagons and of twelve oxen, one wagon donated by two princes and
one ox by each one of them, to be used for transporting the tabernacle
from place to place. These were handed over to the Gershonites and
Merarites (vv. 2–9). Then each prince made an offering consisting of
gold and silver vessels, a number of sacrificial animals and meal-
offerings, each one giving exactly the same amount and quantity, on
successive days (vv. 12–83). This is followed by a summary of all the
articles and offerings brought by them (84–88).

1. *on the day*]   The first day of Nisan, one month before the counting of the people, mentioned in 1.1 ff.. The priests were consecrated
during the seven days preceding this, i. e. beginning with the 23rd day
of Adar (Lev. 8.33–35), during which time, according to rabbinic
tradition, Moses practiced the putting together and the dismembering
of the tabernacle, and on the eighth day (Lev. 9.1), i. e. the first day
of Nisan, the tabernacle was put together and anointed (Ex. 40.17;
30.26–29; Lev. 8.10 ff.; Sifre 44; Num. R. 12.18; 13.2; Yer. Yoma 1.1).
The expression in v. 2, "over them that were numbered", however,
would imply that the presentation of the gifts of the princes occurred
after the census of ch. 1 and the appointment of the princes, and in
order to remove this difficulty some commentators are of the opinion
that this does not refer to the first day of Nisan, but to a date after
the census was taken, understanding the term "made an end" to include
the counting of the people, the setting up of the Levites and allotting

2 and sanctified them; that the princes of Israel, the heads
of their fathers' houses, offered—these were the princes
of the tribes, these are they that were over them that were
3 numbered. And they brought their offering before the
LORD, six covered wagons, and twelve oxen: a wagon for
every two of the princes, and for each one an ox; and they
4 presented them before the tabernacle. And the LORD

their respective functions to them, all of which would be included in
the work of "setting up" (Szanto; comp. Gray and McNeile).

and sanctified them] Dedicated them to the service for which they
were intended. Ibn Ezra's suggestion that the consecration consisted
in pouring the blood of a sacrifice upon the altar (Lev. 8.15) is rightly
opposed by Ramban, since this cannot apply to the tabernacle as a
whole or to the other vessels, in connection with all of which this term
is used (Ex. 40.9–13).

2. *the princes of Israel*] The twelve persons enumerated in 1.5–15.

offered] Explained in v. 3, where the verb had to be repeated because of the parenthetic clause here.

that were over them] Who were appointed to assist Moses and Aaron
in the work of taking the census of the people (1.4, 16).

3. *covered wagons*] Various other renderings have been offered
for this rather rare word (cf. Isa. 66.20). Some render the expression
"wagons used in military service" (perhaps reading צבא; see Rashbam);
others translate "made ready" (Syr.; Targum Yer. מזווגן which, however, may mean "with a pair, for two oxen", so *Biur, "zwei-
spännig"*, or "two-wheeled wagons", see Keil, and Kohut, 145, 352);
others again take it from the root צבה, to swell, "filled" with the gifts
which they brought, as enumerated later (Ramban; comp. Sifre 45,
Num. R. 12.22).

before the tabernacle] According to the interpretation of the Rabbis,
Moses was not certain whether he should accept these, since the command was that the Levites should *carry* the objects and therefore the
wagons and the oxen were placed before the tabernacle until Moses
received a divine message (v. 5) approving of the gift and of the use
to be made of it (Num. R. 12.23; see Rashi and Sforno).

spoke unto Moses, saying: 'Take it of them, that they 5
may be to do the service of the tent of meeting; and thou
shalt give them unto the Levites, to every man according
to his service.' And Moses took the wagons and the oxen, 6
and gave them unto the Levites. Two wagons and four 7
oxen he gave unto the sons of Gershon, according to their
service. And four wagons and eight oxen he gave unto 8
the sons of Merari, according unto their service, under
the hand of Ithamar the son of Aaron the priest. But 9
unto the sons of Kohath he gave none, because the service
of the holy things belonged unto them: they bore them
upon their shoulders. And the princes brought the dedi- 10
cation-offering of the altar in the day that it was anointed,

5. *to do the service*] To carry the parts of the tabernacle from place
to place.

according to his service] Those of the Levites who had the heavier
objects to carry should be given more wagons and oxen than the others,
as explained further.

8. *under the hand of*] Under the supervision of Ithamar, who had
charge over both the Gershonites and the Merarites (4.28, 33).

9. *of the holy things*] Such as the ark, the table, the candlestick,
which were to be carried by them personally and not placed on wagons.

upon their shoulders] When King David brought the ark from
Baale-judah it is said that the ark was taken in a new wagon (II Sam.
6.3). The Rabbis regarded this as a grave offense, which was not cor-
rected by David until after the death of Uzza (I Chron. 15.11–15;
Sifre 46; Sotah 35a).

10. *dedication-offering*] Or *at* the dedication of the altar (as in
v. 11), or *for* (R. V.), when the altar was ready to have offerings made
on it (Rashi). From this verse it appears that all the princes first
brought their offerings on the same day (comp. note to v. 3, where the
opinion of Ramban is quoted, which implies that the wagons contained
the offerings of the princes, see *Biur*), but were told to offer in a formal
way, each one on a separate day (Sifre 47, Num. R. 12.26).

even the princes brought their offering before the altar.
11 And the LORD said unto Moses: 'They shall present their offering, each prince on his day, for the dedication of the altar.'

12 And he that presented his offering the first day was Nahshon the son of Amminadab, of the tribe of Judah; 13 and his offering was one silver dish, the weight thereof was a hundred and thirty shekels, one silver basin of seventy shekels, after the shekel of the sanctuary; both of them full of fine flour mingled with oil for a meal-offering; 14-15 one golden pan of ten shekels, full of incense; one young bullock, one ram, one he-lamb of the first year, for a burnt-

12. The order followed here is the same as that which was followed when they were encamped or when on the journey (ch. 2). The offerings of each prince consisted of the representative types of sacrifices — the meal-offering, the incense, the burnt-offering, the sin-offering and the peace-offering. At the dedication of the Temple of Solomon, only peace-offerings were brought (I Kings 8.62; II Chron. 7.5; comp. Neh. 12.43; I Macc. 4.53–54). Although the offerings of all the princes were identical, they are repeated in each case. The Rabbis offered a number of homiletic interpretations for this redundancy (see Ramban).

13. *silver dish*] The Rabbis understood by it a dish in which the showbread was baked (Ex. 25.29; 37.16; Men. 97a).

silver basin] A vessel used to receive the blood of sacrifices, from which it was later taken and sprinkled on the altar (Ex. 27.3; 38.3).

14. *one golden pan*] The weight of ten *silver* shekels (Sifre 49), used to hold the frankincense kept on the table with the showbread (Ex. 25.29; Lev. 24.7).

full of incense] This was regarded as an exceptional case when incense was offered on the *brazen* altar and in connection with an *individual* offering (Men. 50a).

15. *of the first year*] Within the first year of its life (cf. Num. R. 13.12).

offering; one male of the goats for a sin-offering; and for 16-17
the sacrifice of peace-offerings, two oxen, five rams, five
he-goats, five he-lambs of the first year. This was the
offering of Nahshon the son of Amminadab.

On the second day Nethanel the son of Zuar, prince of 18
Issachar, did offer: he presented for his offering one silver 19
dish, the weight thereof was a hundred and thirty shekels,
one silver basin of seventy shekels, after the shekel of the
sanctuary; both of them full of fine flour mingled with
oil for a meal-offering; one golden pan of ten shekels, full 20
of incense; one young bullock, one ram, one he-lamb of 21
the first year, for a burnt-offering; one male of the goats 22
for a sin-offering; and for the sacrifice of peace-offerings, 23
two oxen, five rams, five he-goats, five he-lambs of the
first year. This was the offering of Nethanel the son of
Zuar.

On the third day Eliab the son of Helon, prince of the 24
children of Zebulun: his offering was one silver dish, the 25
weight thereof was a hundred and thirty shekels, one
silver basin of seventy shekels, after the shekel of the
sanctuary; both of them full of fine flour mingled with
oil for a meal-offering; one golden pan of ten shekels, full 26
of incense; one young bullock, one ram, one he-lamb of 27
the first year, for a burnt-offering; one male of the goats 28
for a sin-offering; and for the sacrifice of peace-offerings, 29
two oxen, five rams, five he-goats, five he-lambs of the
first year. This was the offering of Eliab the son of Helon.

On the fourth day Elizur the son of Shedeur, prince of 30
the children of Reuben: his offering was one silver dish, 31

the weight thereof was a hundred and thirty shekels, one silver basin of seventy shekels, after the shekel of the sanctuary; both of them full of fine flour mingled with oil 32 for a meal-offering; one golden pan of ten shekels, full of 33 incense; one young bullock, one ram, one he-lamb of the 34 first year, for a burnt-offering; one male of the goats for 35 a sin-offering; and for the sacrifice of peace-offerings, two oxen, five rams, five he-goats, five he-lambs of the first year. This was the offering of Elizur the son of Shedeur.

36   On the fifth day Shelumiel the son of Zurishaddai, 37 prince of the children of Simeon: his offering was one silver dish, the weight thereof was a hundred and thirty shekels, one silver basin of seventy shekels, after the shekel of the sanctuary; both of them full of fine flour 38 mingled with oil for a meal-offering; one golden pan of 39 ten shekels, full of incense; one young bullock, one ram, 40 one he-lamb of the first year, for a burnt-offering; one 41 male of the goats for a sin-offering; and for the sacrifice of peace-offerings, two oxen, five rams, five he-goats, five he-lambs of the first year. This was the offering of Shelumiel the son of Zurishaddai.

42   On the sixth day Eliasaph the son of Deuel, prince of 43 the children of Gad: his offering was one silver dish, the weight thereof was a hundred and thirty shekels, one silver basin of seventy shekels, after the shekel of the sanctuary; both of them full of fine flour mingled with oil 44 for a meal-offering; one golden pan of ten shekels, full of 45 incense; one young bullock, one ram, one he-lamb of the 46 first year, for a burnt-offering; one male of the goats for

a sin-offering; and for the sacrifice of peace-offerings, two 47
oxen, five rams, five he-goats, five he-lambs of the first
year. This was the offering of Eliasaph the son of Deuel.

On the seventh day Elishama the son of Ammihud, 48
prince of the children of Ephraim: his offering was one 49
silver dish, the weight thereof was a hundred and thirty
shekels, one silver basin of seventy shekels, after the
shekel of the sanctuary; both of them full of fine flour
mingled with oil for a meal-offering; one golden pan of 50
ten shekels, full of incense; one young bullock, one ram, 51
one he-lamb of the first year, for a burnt-offering; one 52
male of the goats for a sin-offering; and for the sacrifice 53
of peace-offerings, two oxen, five rams, five he-goats, five
he-lambs of the first year. This was the offering of Elishama the son of Ammihud.

On the eighth day Gamaliel the son of Pedahzur, prince 54
of the children of Manasseh: his offering was one silver 55
dish, the weight thereof was a hundred and thirty shekels,
one silver basin of seventy shekels, after the shekel of the
sanctuary; both of them full of fine flour mingled with oil
for a meal-offering; one golden pan of ten shekels, full of 56
incense; one young bullock, one ram, one he-lamb of the 57
first year, for a burnt-offering; one male of the goats for 58

48. *seventh day*] If the tradition is correct, the first of Nisan was
on a Sunday and the offering of Elishama was brought on the Sabbath.
In any event, if the offerings were brought on successive days without
interruption, there must have been a Sabbath in the course of twelve
days. This would be contrary to the law which does not permit the
offering of individual sacrifices on the Sabbath. This, however, was
regarded as an exception by the express command of God (Num. R.
14.5; Tanhuma, Naso, 31, 32; comp. ibn Ezra).

59 a sin-offering; and for the sacrifice of peace-offerings, two oxen, five rams, five he-goats, five he-lambs of the first year. This was the offering of Gamaliel the son of Pedahzur.

60   On the ninth day Abidan the son of Gideoni, prince of 61 the children of Benjamin: his offering was one silver dish, the weight thereof was a hundred and thirty shekels, one silver basin of seventy shekels, after the shekel of the sanctuary; both of them full of fine flour mingled with oil 62 for a meal-offering; one golden pan of ten shekels, full of 63 incense; one young bullock, one ram, one he-lamb of the 64 first year, for a burnt-offering; one male of the goats for 65 a sin-offering; and for the sacrifice of peace-offerings, two oxen, five rams, five he-goats, five he-lambs of the first year. This was the offering of Abidan the son of Gideoni.

66   On the tenth day Ahiezer the son of Ammishaddai, 67 prince of the children of Dan: his offering was one silver dish, the weight thereof was a hundred and thirty shekels, one silver basin of seventy shekels, after the shekel of the sanctuary; both of them full of fine flour mingled with oil 68 for a meal-offering; one golden pan of ten shekels, full of 69 incense; one young bullock, one ram, one he-lamb of the 70 first year, for a burnt-offering; one male of the goats for 71 a sin-offering; and for the sacrifice of peace-offerings, two oxen, five rams, five he-goats, five he-lambs of the first year. This was the offering of Ahiezer the son of Ammi-shaddai.

72   On the eleventh day Pagiel the son of Ochran, prince 73 of the children of Asher: his offering was one silver dish, the weight thereof was a hundred and thirty shekels, one

silver basin of seventy shekels, after the shekel of the
sanctuary; both of them full of fine flour mingled with oil
for a meal-offering; one golden pan of ten shekels, full of 74
incense; one young bullock, one ram, one he-lamb of the 75
first year, for a burnt-offering; one male of the goats for 76
a sin-offering; and for the sacrifice of peace-offerings, two 77
oxen, five rams, five he-goats, five he-lambs of the first
year. This was the offering of Pagiel the son of Ochran.

On the twelfth day Ahira the son of Enan, prince of the 78
children of Naphtali: his offering was one silver dish, the 79
weight thereof was a hundred and thirty shekels, one
silver basin of seventy shekels, after the shekel of the
sanctuary; both of them full of fine flour mingled with oil
for a meal-offering; one golden pan of ten shekels, full of 80
incense; one young bullock, one ram, one he-lamb of the 81
first year, for a burnt-offering; one male of the goats for 82
a sin-offering; and for the sacrifice of peace-offerings, two 83
oxen, five rams, five he-goats, five he-lambs of the first
year. This was the offering of Ahira the son of Enan.

This was the dedication-offering of the altar, in the day 84
when it was anointed, at the hands of the princes of Israel:
twelve silver dishes, twelve silver basins, twelve golden
pans; each silver dish weighing a hundred and thirty 85
shekels, and each basin seventy; all the silver of the vessels
two thousand and four hundred shekels, after the shekel

84. *in the day*] Not exactly the day, but the period (comp. v. 88;
Biur), or the *beginning* of the dedication was made on the day of anoint-
ment (Rashbam, Rashi, comp. Sifre 53, Num. R. 14.26).

86 of the sanctuary; twelve golden pans, full of incense, weighing ten shekels apiece, after the shekel of the sanctuary;
all the gold of the pans a hundred and twenty shekels;
87 all the oxen for the burnt-offering twelve bullocks, the
rams twelve, the he-lambs of the first year twelve, and
their meal-offering; and the males of the goats for a sin-
88 offering twelve; and all the oxen for the sacrifice of peace-
offerings twenty and four bullocks, the rams sixty, the
he-goats sixty, the he-lambs of the first year sixty. This
was the dedication-offering of the altar, after that it was
89 anointed. And when Moses went into the tent of meeting
that He might speak with him, then he heard the Voice

89. This verse, apparently unconnected with either the preceding
or the following, has given much trouble to commentators. The view
advocated by modern critics is that this is "an isolated fragment of a
narrative which recorded the fulfillment of the promise made in Ex.
25.22" (Gray), where Moses is promised that God would speak to him
"from above the ark-cover, from between the two cherubim which
are upon the ark of the testimony". What preceded this and what
followed it has been lost. Ibn Ezra's suggestion that the whole chapter
of the princes' offerings belongs at the end of Exodus and that this
verse belongs to Lev. 1.1 is far-fetched. It seems, however, that the
difficulty has been greatly exaggerated. After describing the details
of the dedication of the tabernacle and of the altar, the narrator relates
the manner in which revelation was made to Moses in the sanctuary,
the tent of meeting between God and Moses, for the purpose of making
His will known to the people (no longer from Mt. Sinai, *Biur*). This
verse, therefore, is not intended to relate what happened at one particular time, but the habitual way in which God communicated with
Moses (comp. Keil; see Sifre 58; Num. R. 14.36).

that He might speak with him] Following Luzzatto, as against A. V.,
Mendelssohn and Leeser (comp. Ex. 25.22).

he heard] Even though the voice was exceedingly loud, no one else
heard it besides Moses (Num. R. 14.35).

speaking unto him from above the ark-cover that was
upon the ark of the testimony, from between the two
cherubim; and He spoke unto him.

And the LORD spoke unto Moses, saying: 'Speak unto 2 **8**
Aaron, and say unto him: When thou lightest the lamps,
the seven lamps shall give light in front of the candlestick.'

speaking unto him]   The verb used here is in the reflexive (Hithpael),
hence the interpretation given by Rashi as God speaking to Himself
and Moses overhearing it. A slight emendation (מְדַבֵּר) would make it
an ordinary Piel, the usual form of this verb (Gray; comp. ibn Ezra
and *Biur*).

and He spoke unto him]   Always, indicating habitual action (ibn
Ezra).

CHAPTER 8.

1–4. THE GOLDEN CANDLESTICK.

The golden candlestick, described in Ex. 25.31–40; 37.17–24, was
placed in the holy place and was probably the only source of light in
the tabernacle. Although the manner in which it was to be arranged
and kept is described fully in Ex. 27.20–21 and Lev. 24.2–4, it is repeated
here in the order in which the various parts of the tabernacle began to
function. The Rabbis interpreted this repetition homiletically, that
Aaron was displeased when the princes of all the tribes brought their
offerings, while the tribe of Levi made no contribution. Then God said
to him that his functions of keeping the lights of the candlestick burning were of greater importance than the gifts of the princes (Num. R.
15.2, 5).

2. *when thou lightest*]   The verb עלה in Hiphil, as used here, has
the meaning of causing the flame to go up, hence lighting. R. V. margin
has "when thou settest up", meaning the raising of the lamp, made of
small bowls of oil with wicks, upon the lamp-stand.

in front]   The candles should be lighted in a manner that the light
should fall in front (Ex. 25.37), over the table of the showbread which

3 And Aaron did so: he lighted the lamps thereof so as to
give light in front of the candlestick, as the LORD com-
4 manded Moses. And this was the work of the candlestick,
beaten work of gold; unto the base thereof, and unto the
flowers thereof, it was beaten work; according unto the
pattern which the LORD had shown Moses, so he made
the candlestick.

stood on the north-side, opposite the candlestick. The rabbinic interpretation is that the three branches on either side of the middle lamp,
which was regarded as *the candlestick*, should be turned towards it, so
that the light from the three eastern lamps and from the three western
lamps should strike the middle lamp (Sifre 59; Meg. 21b; comp. Rashi
and Sforno).

3. *Aaron did so*] Himself, although ordinarily this function might
be performed by any one of the priests (Ex. 28.21; see Ramban).

4. *beaten work of gold*] Made of a single solid piece of gold and not
composed of pieces (Ex. 25.36; 37.17). The same requirement was
made in case of the cherubim (Ex. 25.18; 37.7) and of the two silver
trumpets (Num. 10.2).

the base thereof] I. e. both base and flowers, the heaviest portion
and the most delicate part of it, were beaten out of the same solid piece
of gold.

5–22. THE LEVITES PRESENTED TO THE SERVICE OF THE TABERNACLE.

In ch. 3, the families of the Levites are enumerated and their respective positions in the camp described. There it is also indicated that they
were chosen to act as ministers in the tabernacle in the place of the
first-born of the Israelites, by the process of redemption. In ch. 4, the
respective functions of the Levitical families are given in detail. Before
entering upon their duties, however, the Levites had to be purified and
formally presented to God by the Israelites, whose representatives they
were henceforth to be. The priests were "consecrated" by means of
an elaborate ceremony, described in Ex. 29.1 ff. and Lev. 8.1 ff., while
the Levites were merely "purified", that is made ritually clean. The
priests, because of the higher kind of service which they were to render,

And the LORD spoke unto Moses, saying: 'Take the 5-6
Levites from among the children of Israel, and cleanse
them. And thus shalt thou do unto them, to cleanse them: 7
sprinkle the water of purification upon them, and let them
cause a razor to pass over all their flesh, and let them

were consecrated, made holy, that is separated from, and set above
the others, the double significance of the Hebrew term for holy.

The process of the presentation of the Levites to the service of the
tabernacle is described here as follows: After they went through the
prescribed form of ritual purification, they were presented by Moses
in the court of the tabernacle, in the presence of the congregation, or
its representatives. They were then taken into the tabernacle, and the
representatives of the congregation laid their hands on the heads of
the Levites, who were thus treated as a sacrifice brought by the entire
congregation to God. Aaron then offered them up as a wave-offering,
following the same ceremony as was followed in the case of sacrifices,
which was an indication that God received the offering with favor.
The Levites then placed their hands on the heads of the sacrifices,
which were symbolically to take the place of the Levites. Then Moses
placed the Levites in front of Aaron and offered them again as a wave-
offering to indicate that God gave them over to the Aaronites, whom
they were to assist in the service of the tabernacle.

6. *Take*] Separate them from the rest of the people (ibn Ezra),
or simply bring them near (Targum).

cleanse them] Referring to ritual purification, as described further.

7. *And thus shalt thou*] Comp. Ex. 29.1.

water of purification] Lit. "water of sin", that is water causing purification from sin, as in 19.9, "a water of sprinkling; it is a purification
from sin", there referring to the water in which the ashes of the red
heifer were mingled and later sprinkled upon those who became defiled
by having come in contact with a dead body. The traditional interpretation has it that the water used here was the same as that described
in 19.9, and it was sprinkled upon the Levites because of the possibility
that some of them had been defiled (Rashi, Luzzatto). Modern commentators understand by it ordinary pure water taken from the laver,
the same kind that was used by the priests to bathe when they were
consecrated (Ex. 29.4; Lev. 8.6; Keil, cf. Holzinger).

and let them cause a razor] Probably in the same manner as is pre-

8 wash their clothes, and cleanse themselves. Then let them
take a young bullock, and its meal-offering, fine flour mingled with oil, and another young bullock shalt thou take for
9 a sin-offering. And thou shalt present the Levites before
the tent of meeting; and thou shalt assemble the whole
10 congregation of the children of Israel. And thou shalt
present the Levites before the LORD; and the children of

scribed in the case of the leper, after he became well again (Lev. 14.8),
when the hair of the whole body was shaven. It is, however, likely that
the expression used here indicates that the hair of the whole body was
cut off, but not as close as was required in the case of the leper and of
the Nazirite (6.9) (Keil, Gray; comp. Pes. R. quoted by Epstein).
Ibn Ezra assumes that the sprinkling of the water of purification took place after the hair was cut off and the garments washed,
and he therefore translates, "*after* they caused a razor, etc." (comp.
Biur).

wash their clothes] This was also required in the case of the leper
(Lev. 14.8) and of all Israelites in the preparation for the Revelation
(Ex. 19.10). This was not required of the priests when they were consecrated, because they were furnished with official vestments at the
time of their consecration (Ex. 29.8, 9; Lev. 8.13).

and cleanse themselves] Implying another process, possibly bathing
of the entire body in water (as Gen. 35.2; Luzzatto). Mendelssohn
and Leeser have "and so shall they be clean", i. e. after having performed the prescribed duties of shaving, washing their garments and
having the waters of purification sprinkled on them, they shall be
considered ritually clean.

8. *young bullock*] For a burnt-offering (v. 12; Lev. 1.3, 5).

shalt thou take] Referring back to Moses, although the reason for
the change of subject is not clear. Ibn Ezra reads "order them to take"
but this is not in the text.

9. *the whole congregation*] Possibly only the representatives of the
congregation are meant here, or the general assembly of the nation.

10. *before the Lord*] After the people were assembled, the Levites
were taken into the sanctuary. Some regard this repetition as a continuation of the narrative "and when thou hast brought them, etc."

Israel shall lay their hands upon the Levites. And Aaron 11
shall offer the Levites before the LORD for a wave-offering
from the children of Israel, that they may be to do the
service of the LORD. And the Levites shall lay their hands 12
upon the heads of the bullocks; and offer thou the one for
a sin-offering, and the other for a burnt-offering, unto the
LORD, to make atonement for the Levites. And thou 13
shalt set the Levites before Aaron, and before his sons,
and offer them for a wave-offering unto the LORD. Thus 14

lay their hands] The symbol of the appointment to office, or the
ceremony followed in all sacrifices by those who offered them (Lev. 1.4;
Rashi). The "children of Israel" here must refer to the representatives
of the people or to the heads of the tribes (Keil, McNeile).

11. *for a wave-offering*] The ceremony of waving part of a sacrifice
consisted in moving it towards the altar and then back again, indicating
first its presentation to God and then its return by Him to the priests
(Lev. 23.11; Ex. 29.26), although the ceremony is also mentioned in
connection with offerings which were burnt entirely on the altar (Ex.
29.27). Here the ceremony signified that the Levites were set aside
for the service of God, who in turn gave them back to minister to the
priests in the tabernacle. It is hardly likely that this was carried out
literally. The ceremony may have consisted merely in leading the
Levites around the altar (Luzzatto) or to and fro in the direction of
the holy of holies (Hertz), or the word may have here the general
significance of making a sacred gift (comp. Ehrlich to Lev. 8.27).

12. *lay their hands*] Indicating that the sacrifices were made in
their behalf to serve as an atonement for their sins (Lev. 4.1).

and offer thou] Moses should cause the offering to be made, but the
actual offering was performed by the priests (ibn Ezra). Ehrlich emends
עָשָׂה, "and he (Aaron) shall offer".

13. *and offer them*] This is directed to Moses who should set the
Levites aside as assistants to the Aaronites in the service of the tabernacle. Rashi explains the three expressions of תנופה (offering) mentioned here (vv. 11, 13, 15) to refer to the three families of the Levites,
Gershon, Kohath and Merari. There are probably two distinct processes indicated here, the offering by Aaron as the gift of the Israelites to
God and the offering by Moses symbolic of the giving of the Levites to

shalt thou separate the Levites from among the children
15 of Israel; and the Levites shall be Mine. And after that
shall the Levites go in to do the service of the tent of meeting; and thou shalt cleanse them, and offer them for a
16 wave-offering. For they are wholly given unto Me from
among the children of Israel; instead of all that openeth
the womb, even the first-born of all the children of Israel,
17 have I taken them unto Me. For all the first-born among
the children of Israel are Mine, both man and beast; on
the day that I smote all the first-born in the land of Egypt
18 I sanctified them for Myself. And I have taken the Levites
instead of all the first-born among the children of Israel.

the priests by God, while the third expression is merely a summary, as
explained in v. 15. It is not idiomatic Hebrew to render this as "causing
to offer", meaning that Moses caused Aaron to make the offering,
and making this identical with the process described in v. 11 (ibn Ezra).

14. *Thus shalt thou separate*]   In the manner prescribed above, the
Levites shall become separated from the rest of Israel, even as Israel
is to be separated from the nations of the world (Lev. 20.26).

shall be Mine]   Shall minister before Me (Targum, to avoid anthropomorphism, as also in 3.12).

15. *and thou shalt cleanse them*]   This cannot refer to another process of cleansing and waving and should therefore be rendered "after
thou shalt have cleansed them" (Mendelssohn), i. e. after the process
of cleansing and waving described above has been completed, they shall
enter upon their functions.

16.   The first part of this verse follows closely upon 3.9, and the
second part upon 3.12.

wholly given]   Set aside (Targum).

the first-born of all the children of Israel]   Or "of every first-born of
the children of Israel" (Mendelssohn and Leeser), or perhaps, "the
first-born of everything belonging to the children of Israel", including
men and beasts, with reference to the following verse and 3.41.

17.   Comp. 3.13.

18.   Comp. 3.12.

And I have given the Levites—they are given to Aaron   19
and to his sons from among the children of Israel, to do
the service of the children of Israel in the tent of meeting,
and to make atonement for the children of Israel, that
there be no plague among the children of Israel, through
the children of Israel coming nigh unto the sanctuary.'
Thus did Moses, and Aaron, and all the congregation of   20
the children of Israel, unto the Levites; according unto
all that the LORD commanded Moses touching the Levites,
so did the children of Israel unto them. And the Levites   21
purified themselves, and they washed their clothes; and
Aaron offered them for a sacred gift before the LORD; and

19. *and I have given*] Since they belong to Me, I can dispose of
them at will.

they are given] Comp. 3.9 and note. R. V. "as a gift".

the service of the children of Israel] The service which they should
render through their representatives, the first-born.

to make atonement] Not in the usual sense of the term, to atone for
sins committed, but to guard against sins being committed, as is explained further, by keeping the Israelites away from the sanctuary
and thereby saving them from the calamity that might befall them.
Ibn Ezra renders the word לכפר in the sense of ransom (כֹּפֶר), the
Levites serving as a ransom (*Lösegeld*, Mendelssohn) for the children
of Israel (comp. Ex. 30.12, 15, 16).

no plague] The usual consequence of disobeying the word of God
and arousing His anger, in this case by coming too close to the sanctuary (1.53; 3.38). The "children of Israel" is repeated five times in
this verse, so as to emphasize the distinction between them and Aaron
and his sons and the Levites (Luzzatto, see Rashi).

20. *touching the Levites*] With regard to them, including the cleansing, the sacrifices and the waving, as described in v. 21.

21. *purified themselves*] By having the "water of purification" sprinkled upon them (v. 7; comp. 31.19; comp. Gray, "unsinned themselves").

for a sacred gift] In vv. 11, 13, 15, the same word is rendered "for
a wave-offering" (comp. note to v. 11).

22 Aaron made atonement for them to cleanse them. And
after that went the Levites in to do their service in the
tent of meeting before Aaron, and before his sons; as the
LORD had commanded Moses concerning the Levites, so
did they unto them.

23-24   And the LORD spoke unto Moses, saying: 'This is that
which pertaineth unto the Levites: from twenty and five
years old and upward they shall go in to perform the
25 service in the work of the tent of meeting; and from the
age of fifty years they shall return from the service of the
26 work, and shall serve no more; but shall minister with
their brethren in the tent of meeting, to keep the charge,
but they shall do no manner of service. Thus shalt thou
do unto the Levites touching their charges.'

made atonement for them to cleanse them] Comp. Lev. 16.30. By
the atonement made for them through the offering of the sacrifices,
they became cleansed (BDB, s. v. כפר).

23–26. Here the age of the Levitical service is given as from 25 to
50. After the age of 50, they are permitted to retire, although they
may still do certain kinds of work to assist their younger brethren, in
loading the wagons, accompanying them in song and guarding the
gates of the tabernacle (Sifre 63). On the contradiction between the
ages given here (25 to 50) and those given in 4.3, 23, 30 (30 to 50) see
note to 4.3.

24. *This is that which pertaineth*] Referring to the following regulation. A word like "the law" (תורה) or "what thou shalt do" (תעשה, Ex.
29.1 and here v. 26) is to be understood here. Ibn Ezra renders, "This
is the age-limit" (קצבה).

to perform] R. V. "to wait upon," as also in v. 25.

26. *minister with*] Targum; not "minister to" or "wait on"
(Mendelssohn, Leeser).

keep the charge] To be on hand near the sanctuary and to be of
assistance whenever required (Rashi).

And the Lᴏʀᴅ spoke unto Moses in the wilderness of **9**
Sinai, in the first month of the second year after they were
come out of the land of Egypt, saying: 'Let the children ₂

CHAPTER **9.**

Tʜᴇ Sᴇᴄᴏɴᴅ Pᴀssᴏᴠᴇʀ.

The observance of the first, and according to the Rabbis, the only
Passover in the wilderness (Sifre 67, comp. Ramban), was kept in due
time on the 14th day of the first month, at sunset (vv. 2–5), in accordance with the instructions given to Moses in Egypt (Ex. 12). There
were, however, certain persons who, for one reason or another, were
unable to participate in the celebration at the appointed time and a
new ruling was required regarding them (vv. 6–8). This new ruling is
given by God to Moses, and provides for a secondary Passover (פסח שני)
on the 14th day of the second month for those who could not observe
it in the first month (vv. 10–14).

This section appears to be out of place here, since the present book
begins with a command given in the second month of the second year,
while the law of this section must have been promulgated in the first
month. The Rabbis already noticed the difficulty and resorted in
explanation to the general principle that there is no strict chronological
sequence in the Torah (אין מוקדם ומאוחר בתורה, Sifre 64; Pes. 6b). It is,
however, possible to assume that this law was inserted here, although
out of place, in order not to interrupt the narrative of the events following upon the completion of the tabernacle, viz. the numbering of
the people and their arrangement in the camp, and the appointment
of the Levites and their consecration. All of this occurred at Sinai,
whence they did not depart until the twentieth day of the second
month (10.11).

1. *in the first month*] But the day of the month is not given. This
was the month preceding that in which the census was taken (1.1 ff.).
The offerings brought by the princes (ch. 7) also occurred during the
first month.

2. *Let the children of Israel keep*] This is rather an unusual form.
We should expect something like "Command the children of Israel
that they keep" (comp. 5.2; Lev. 24.2), or "Say" (as LXX, comp. 17.2),
or "Speak" (comp. Ex. 25.2; Lev. 16.2). The law about the observance

3 of Israel keep the passover in its appointed season. In the
fourteenth day of this month, at dusk, ye shall keep it in
its appointed season; according to all the statutes of it,
and according to all the ordinances thereof, shall ye keep
4 it.' And Moses spoke unto the children of Israel, that
5 they should keep the passover. And they kept the passover in the first month, on the fourteenth day of the
month, at dusk, in the wilderness of Sinai; according to
all that the LORD commanded Moses, so did the children
6 of Israel. But there were certain men, who were unclean
by the dead body of a man, so that they could not keep

of the Passover is repeated here because of the exception to be recorded
later. The Rabbis say that the repetition of the law here is intended
to indicate that the paschal offering should be brought also in the
wilderness and not only in Egypt and in Canaan (Ex. 12.35; ibn Ezra;
Ramban; comp. Ehrlich). Now that the tabernacle was set up and
dedicated there was no obstacle in the way of observing the Passover
in all its details. See Keil, p. 50, note, for a detailed discussion of the
number of paschal lambs offered at that time.

keep the passover] I. e. prepare the paschal offering.

in its appointed season] As given in the following verse.

3. *at dusk*] Lit. between the two evenings, i. e. between sunset
and dark (R. V. "at even"; Leeser, "toward evening"). The rabbinic
phrase is בין השמשות (Targum, בין שמשיא), between the two suns,
i. e. the sun and the moon, estimated at about one hour before the stars
become visible (cf. Shab. 34b).

according to all the statutes] Referring to the details of the law in
Ex. 12.1–20, 43–49.

6. *unclean by the dead body*] Ritually unclean because of having
come in contact with a dead body, which makes them unfit to participate in a sacrificial feast such as the paschal offering (Lev. 7.20, 21),
until after they have gone through the process of purification prescribed in ch. 19 (comp. Suk. 25a).

the passover on that day; and they came before Moses
and before Aaron on that day. And those men said unto 7
him: 'We are unclean by the dead body of a man; wherefore are we to be kept back, so as not to bring the offering
of the LORD in its appointed season among the children of
Israel?' And Moses said unto them: 'Stay ye, that I may 8
hear what the LORD will command concerning you.'

And the LORD spoke unto Moses, saying: 'Speak unto 9-10
the children of Israel, saying: If any man of you or of your
generations shall be unclean by reason of a dead body, or

and before Aaron] When they were together, although the question
was directed to Moses only (v. 7) and the decision was rendered by
him alone (Rashi).

7. *kept back*] From the rest of the congregation on this very important occasion, since this was not due to our fault but to accident.

8. *stay ye*] Wait until I hear what God will say. Ibn Ezra renders
this, "stand outside of the door of the tabernacle", while Moses would
enter the tabernacle and obtain the divine revelation.

10. The law is laid down here in general terms and without reference to the particular case under consideration. Besides those prevented from observing the Passover on account of ritual defilement,
those who may be away on a journey at the time are also included and
according to rabbinic law any one prevented from observing the Passover in its season, whatever the reason may be, should observe it in
the second month (Pes. 9.1; and 92a, 93a; Yer. Pes. 9.1; Sifre 69).
In II Chron. 30, a description is given of the observance of the delayed
Passover in the second month. Rabbinic opinion, however, differs
as to whether the observance then took place in the second month or
whether Hezekiah caused the previous year to be an intercalated
(מעברת) year, regarding Nisan as the second Adar (Sanh. 12b).

or of your generations] Any time in the future, making the law
general.

be in a journey afar off, yet he shall keep the passover unto
11 the LORD; in the second month on the fourteenth day at
dusk they shall keep it; they shall eat it with unleavened
12 bread and bitter herbs; they shall leave none of it unto the
morning, nor break a bone thereof; according to all the
13 statute of the passover they shall keep it. But the man
that is clean, and is not on a journey, and forbeareth to
keep the passover, that soul shall be cut off from his people;
because he brought not the offering of the LORD in its

in a journey afar off] The exact limitations of the phrase "afar off"
have been discussed by the Rabbis in detail (Pes. 93b; see Rashi and
Ramban).

he shall keep] Joined with the next verse. Mendelssohn makes the
phrase part of the condition "and he would keep", then they shall
make it, etc. as in v. 11.

11. *unleavened bread*] As in the case when the offering is brought
in the proper time (Ex. 12.8).

12. *they shall leave none of it*] Ex. 12.10; 34.25; more specifically
Deut. 16.4.

nor break a bone] Ex. 12.46.

all the statutes] Comp. Ex. 12.43. After specifying the three laws
pertaining to the paschal offering, there is the general injunction that
this Passover is to follow all the laws prescribed for the first. The
Rabbis, however, say that while the offering of the paschal lamb in
the second month differed in no respect from that of the first, the
second Passover is not observed as a holiday, nor need the leaven be
removed from the house, nor is one obliged to eat *Mazzot* except at
the time when the paschal lamb is partaken of, on the evening of the
14th (Sifre 69 end; Pes. 95a).

13. *forbeareth*] Without a legitimate excuse.

shall be cut off] Death by a divine agency. It has been suggested
that the punishment of *Kareth* may have meant banishment (Sulzberger, *The Law of Homicide*, p. 126).

appointed season, that man shall bear his sin. And if a **14**
stranger shall sojourn among you, and will keep the passover unto the LORD: according to the statute of the passover, and according to the ordinance thereof, so shall he
do; ye shall have one statute, both for the stranger, and
for him that is born in the land.'

And on the day that the tabernacle was reared up the **15**
cloud covered the tabernacle, even the tent of the testi-

bear his sin]   The consequences of the sin, the punishment that will
follow it (comp. 18.22; Lev. 20.20).
    14.   *And if a stranger*]   A resident foreigner (Ex. 12.48, 49; see
Sulzberger, *Status of Labor*, p. 4 ff.).
    and will keep]   If he desires to keep the Passover, he must conform
to all the regulations laid down both with regard to the first and the
second passover.

15–23.   THE MARCH REGULATED BY THE CLOUD.

The description of the march through the wilderness is now resumed.
The march was regulated by divine direction, expressed through the
cloud of glory resting upon the tabernacle. This cloud is described
as a column resting over the tabernacle, although in Ex. 33.7–11 it is
described as standing in front of the tabernacle. At night, the cloud
assumed a fiery appearance. As long as the cloud rested, the Israelites
remained in camp; when it rose, it was regarded as a signal for them
to depart. Before the tabernacle was erected, the cloud is mentioned
as preceding the Israelites on the journey (Ex. 13.21), but after the
tabernacle was set up, the cloud appeared before the tabernacle (or
over it) to serve as a guide for the journey (Ex. 40.34–38).   Before
departing from Mt. Sinai, the people were given detailed instructions
preparatory for the journey.
    15.   *even the tent of the testimony*]   Testimony is used in a technical
sense in connection with the tablets on which the Ten Commandments
were engraved (Ex. 31.18), denoting the solemn divine charge. It is
also used in connection with the ark which contained the tables (Ex.
25.22); also the tabernacle as containing the ark of the testimony

mony; and at even there was upon the tabernacle as it
16 were the appearance of fire, until morning. So it was
alway: the cloud covered it, and the appearance of fire by
17 night. And whenever the cloud was taken up from over
the Tent, then after that the children of Israel journeyed;
and in the place where the cloud abode, there the children
18 of Israel encamped. At the commandment of the LORD
the children of Israel journeyed, and at the commandment

(Ex. 38.21; Num. 1.50, 53; 10.11), or the tent, as here and 17.22, 23;
18.2, denoting the part of the tabernacle which contained the ark.
The cloud rested on that part of the tabernacle in which the holy place
and the holy of holies were situated (Ramban). Our version apparently
considers the term "tent of the testimony" to stand in apposition to
"tabernacle" (see Koenig, III, 289g).

and at even] In the evening the cloud assumed the appearance of
fire, and maintained this appearance until the morning (Ex. 40.38).
All the verbs in this section are used in the frequentative sense.

16. *and the appearance of fire*] The same cloud assuming the
appearance of fire (comp. v. 21; Luzzatto), and it is therefore unnecessary to add the word "by day" after "covered it", as do LXX, Syr.
and Vulg. When they departed from Egypt, a pillar of cloud preceded
them by day and a pillar of fire by night (Ex. 13.21), but after the
tabernacle was set up the cloud rested on it even when they were not
on the journey.

17. *and whenever*] Leeser (also Mendelssohn) has "as", perhaps
to indicate not only time but also direction. The word לפי often means
"in accordance with" (Gen. 16.16; Lev. 25.16) and it may be interpreted here to mean that the Israelites traveled "in accordance with"
the direction towards which the cloud was lifted (Sforno, Malbim).

18. *At the commandment*] Implied in the movement of the cloud
guided by divine order, so that no other directions were necessary
(comp. Gray, who maintains that besides the movement of the cloud
there was also a divine commandment each time given to Moses as to
the time of breaking up camp and the direction of the journey; see
Malbim).

of the LORD they encamped: as long as the cloud abode
upon the tabernacle they remained encamped. And when 19
the cloud tarried upon the tabernacle many days, then the
children of Israel kept the charge of the LORD, and journeyed not. And sometimes the cloud was a few days upon 20
the tabernacle; according to the commandment of the
LORD they remained encamped, and according to the
commandment of the LORD they journeyed. And some- 21
times the cloud was from evening until morning; and when
the cloud was taken up in the morning, they journeyed;
or if it continued by day and by night, when the cloud
was taken up, they journeyed. Whether it were two days, 22
or a month, or a year, that the cloud tarried upon the

19. *kept the charge of the Lord*] The order implied in the tarrying
of the cloud. Here the general statement is made, which is illustrated
by several specific examples in the following verses (ibn Ezra); or,
both vv. 19 and 20 contain the general statement, i. e. that whether
the cloud tarried for a long period or for a few days they remained in
camp, and vv. 21-22 contain the specific illustration (*Biur*).

20. *a few days*] Lit. numerable days, that can easily be numbered,
i. e. few (Deut. 33.6).

21. *And sometimes the cloud*] Which had the appearance of
fire in the evening (v. 16) rested only over night, when the march began
in the morning when the cloud was lifted, or it rested a day and a night,
or two days, or a month, or a year. In any case they encamped when
the cloud rested and proceeded on the march when it was lifted. Even
though they may have been fatigued and wanted more rest, or even
if they were displeased with the place and wanted to proceed further,
they disregarded their own wishes and regulated the march by the
movements of the cloud (Ramban, Sforno).

by day] The adverbial sense of יוֹמָם (comp. 10.34; Ex. 13.21), referring to the verbs "taken up" and "journeyed".

22. *a year*] The word ימים, meaning days, may denote any indefinite

tabernacle, abiding thereon, the children of Israel remained
encamped, and journeyed not; but when it was taken up,
23 they journeyed. At the commandment of the LORD they
encamped, and at the commandment of the LORD they
journeyed; they kept the charge of the LORD, at the commandment of the LORD by the hand of Moses.

10 2   And the LORD spoke unto Moses, saying: 'Make thee
two trumpets of silver; of beaten work shalt thou make

period of time (Gen. 40.4), but it may also mean a year (Lev. 25.29;
I Sam. 27.7; comp. Targum).

23.   *At the commandment*]   See note to v. 18.

CHAPTER 10.

1–10.   THE SILVER TRUMPETS.

In addition to the cloud which guided the Israelites on their journey,
Moses is commanded to prepare two trumpets, the sounding of which
would announce to the people when they were to march or to encamp
(Sifre 72). No further description of these trumpets is given except
that they were made of silver. According to Josephus (*Ant.* iii.12.6)
each trumpet was "in length a little less than a cubit. It was composed
of a narrow cube, somewhat thicker than a flute, but with so much
breadth as was sufficient for the admission of the breath of a man's
mouth; it ended in the form of a bell, like common trumpets". Repre-
sentations of trumpets are found on the Arch of Titus and on a Bar
Kokeba coin. It was distinguished from the *Shofar*, which was originally a ram's horn, and probably always retained that shape. The
trumpets were also used for the purpose of convening the assembly in
case of war and on new moons and festivals. In the wilderness, the
trumpets were used either to assemble the whole congregation or only
the princes or as a signal for the march.

2.   *of beaten work*]   Cf. 8.4 and note.

them; and they shall be unto thee for the calling of the
congregation, and for causing the camps to set forward.
And when they shall blow with them, all the congregation 3
shall gather themselves unto thee at the door of the tent
of meeting. And if they blow but with one, then the princes, 4
the heads of the thousands of Israel, shall gather themselves
unto thee. And when ye blow an alarm, the camps that lie 5
on the east side shall take their journey. And when ye 6
blow an alarm the second time, the camps that lie on the

3. *all the congregation*] Including also the princes (ibn Ezra). Comp.
Sulzberger, *Am Haaretz*, p. 8, who makes this term include the two
houses of the national assembly, the "lower house" (*Zekenim*) and the
"upper house" (*Nesiim*).

at the door of the tent] Where also the trumpeters stood (Sifre 73).

4. *if they blow but with one*] "They" is used here in the impersonal
sense, "any one" (Luzzatto, who explains this in the following manner:
The two trumpets were for the two sons of Aaron, Eleazar and Ithamar
(v. 8), so as not to arouse any jealousy between them, since one trumpet
would otherwise have answered all purposes. When the whole congregation was to be assembled, one sounded one trumpet, as a signal for
the princes to get ready, and the other sounded the other trumpet, as
a signal for the rest of the congregation. The same process was followed in case of breaking up camp, the two brothers sounding the
trumpets alternately).

heads of the thousands of Israel] This is a military term (comp. 1.15;
Ex. 18.21), but may also be rendered "families" or "inmates of a tent"
(Petrie, *Researches in Sinai*, 207–17).

5. *an alarm*] Possibly louder than the sound understood in vv. 3, 4,
and also different in quality, although in what the difference consisted
is not indicated here. According to tradition, the *Teki'ah* (vv. 3, 4)
was a long single sound, while the *Teru'ah* (vv. 5, 6) consisted of a series
of short, staccato sounds (BDB, p. 348b).

the camps] The three tribes, Judah, Issachar and Zebulun (2.3–9)
encamped on the east.

south side shall set forward; they shall blow an alarm for
7 their journeys. But when the assembly is to be gathered
together, ye shall blow, but ye shall not sound an alarm.
8 And the sons of Aaron, the priests, shall blow with the
trumpets; and they shall be to you for a statute for ever
9 throughout your generations. And when ye go to war in
your land against the adversary that oppresseth you,
then ye shall sound an alarm with the trumpets; and ye
shall be remembered before the LORD your God, and ye

6. *for their journeys*] I. e. also for the camps stationed on the west
and on the north (*Baraita de Meleket ha-Mishkan*, ed. Friedman, ch.13,
note 1, p. 83; Ramban). LXX repeats the same phrases for the western
and northern camps. Ibn Ezra is of the opinion that no blasts were
sounded for the start of the western and northern camps, since the
priests who blew the trumpets followed the southern camp (2.17; see
Sifre 73).

7. *assembly*] Apparently referring to the same body included in
v. 3 under עדה, the congregation or its representatives.

8. *shall blow*] On either occasion, when the assembly is convoked
or when the start for the march is announced.

throughout your generations] This, of course, can apply only to the
convocation of the assembly, and to the procedure followed when
going out to war, as explained in v. 9 (ibn Ezra).

9. *ye go to war*] After they settled in Canaan the trumpets were
to be used when they went out to war, whether defensive or offensive.
According to the opinion of R. Akiba, they were used on any occasion
of national distress like pestilence, famine, etc. (Sifre 76).

ye shall be remembered] The blowing of the trumpets was regarded
as a form of prayer, causing divine attention to be directed towards
them. For the efficacy of the trumpet blasts in battle, see II Chron.
13.12–16. In the case of the siege of Jericho, the *Shofar* was used with
similar results (Josh. 6).

shall be saved from your enemies. Also in the day of your 10
gladness, and in your appointed seasons, and in your new
moons, ye shall blow with the trumpets over your burnt-
offerings, and over the sacrifices of your peace-offerings;
and they shall be to you for a memorial before your God:
I am the LORD your God.'

10. *day of your gladness*] Any public festival or the celebration
of a victory on the battle-field (ibn Ezra). Some of the Rabbis make
this phrase refer to the Sabbath (Sifre 77), but the meaning here plainly
has reference to the celebration of any special occasion of joy (comp.
I Chron. 15.24; 16.5, on the occasion of the removal of the ark by
David; II Chron. 5.12; 7.6, on the occasion of the dedication of Solomon's Temple; Ezra 3.10, on the occasion of the laying of the foundation of the second Temple; Neh. 12.35, 41, on the occasion of the consecration of the walls of Jerusalem; II Chron. 29.27, on the occasion
of the purification of the Temple by Hezekiah).

appointed seasons] Festivals enumerated in ch. 28 and Lev. 23.

new moons] Cf. Ps. 81.3; Suk. 53a, 55b.

over your burnt-offerings] Together with the sacrifices offered on
such occasions.

for a memorial] Cf. v. 9, and Ex. 28.29.

10.11–22.1. WANDERINGS BETWEEN THE WILDERNESS OF SINAI
AND THE PLAINS OF MOAB.

10.11–28. DEPARTURE FROM THE WILDERNESS OF SINAI.

The Israelites arrived in the wilderness of Sinai at the beginning
of the third month (Ex. 19.1), about a month and a half after the
exodus. There they stayed for eleven months and nineteen days, the
period during which the Law was given to them, the tabernacle was
erected and all the preparations for the march were made. On the
twentieth day of the second month of the second year of the exodus,
they departed from the wilderness of Sinai and encamped in the wilderness of Paran. The order followed the detailed instructions given in
the previous chapters.

11   And it came to pass in the second year, in the second
month, on the twentieth day of the month, that the cloud
was taken up from over the tabernacle of the testimony.
12 And the children of Israel set forward by their stages out
of the wilderness of Sinai; and the cloud abode in the
13 wilderness of Paran.—And they took their first journey,
according to the commandment of the LORD by the hand
14 of Moses. And in the first place the standard of the camp
of the children of Judah set forward according to their
hosts; and over his host was Nahshon the son of Ammi-
15 nadab. And over the host of the tribe of the children of
16 Issachar was Nethanel the son of Zuar. And over the

11. *the cloud was taken up*] The cloud rested on the tabernacle
since the first day of the first month of the second year, when the
tabernacle was completely set up (9.15; Ex. 40.17, 34), altogether for
one month and nineteen days.

12. *by their stages*] The various places which they traversed
(33.2; Ex. 17.1). The word may also refer to the camp arrangement
while traveling (Rashi, ibn Ezra, comp. Keil).

the wilderness of Paran] There were three large divisions of the
desert which they passed through: Sinai, Paran and Zin. There was
also a large number of smaller areas or settlements, lying within these
districts, where they encamped from time to time, as described in ch.
33, so that the journey between Sinai and Paran was interrupted by
a number of stops. The wilderness of Paran lies between Sinai and
Edom and was known as the dwelling place of Ishmael (Gen. 21.21).
It probably corresponds to the modern desert of Et-tih.

13. *their first journey*] The first time that they followed all the
instructions given to them by Moses, as detailed in the following
verses.

commandment of the Lord] As indicated by the lifting of the cloud
(Dillmann).

14. *over his host*] The prince acting as the leader to the host
(Ramban). The order follows closely upon that described in ch. 2.

host of the tribe of the children of Zebulun was Eliab the
son of Helon. And the tabernacle was taken down; and 17
the sons of Gershon and the sons of Merari, who bore the
tabernacle, set forward. And the standard of the camp 18
of Reuben set forward according to their hosts; and over
his host was Elizur the son of Shedeur. And over the host 19
of the tribe of the children of Simeon was Shelumiel the
son of Zurishaddai. And over the host of the tribe of the 20
children of Gad was Eliasaph the son of Deuel. And the 21
Kohathites the bearers of the sanctuary set forward, that
the tabernacle might be set up against their coming.
And the standard of the camp of the children of Ephraim 22
set forward according to their hosts; and over his host
was Elishama the son of Ammihud. And over the host of 23
the tribe of the children of Manasseh was Gamaliel the
son of Pedahzur. And over the host of the tribe of the 24
children of Benjamin was Abidan the son of Gideoni. And 25

17. *was taken down*] In its component parts. When the camp of
Judah began the journey, Aaron and his sons took off the curtains
and covered the ark, and the Gershonites and Merarites took the parts
consigned to each and placed them on the wagons and proceeded, while
the holy objects were placed on their poles in the keeping of the Kohathites ready to be carried after the camp of Reuben departed (Rashi,
comp. *Baraita de Meleket ha-Mishkan*, ch. 13, p. 81). The verbs used
in this section have a frequentative sense, indicating that this was the
practice also on subsequent journeys.

21. *the sanctuary*] The holy objects, such as the ark, the table,
the candlestick, etc. (4.4 ff.).

that the tabernacle might be set up] By the Gershonites and Merarites
who preceded them. When the Kohathites came with the holy objects
they found the tabernacle set up, ready to receive the sacred objects
in their appointed places (Rashi, ibn Ezra).

the standard of the camp of the children of Dan, which
was the rearward of all the camps, set forward according
to their hosts; and over his host was Ahiezer the son of
26 Ammishaddai.   And over the host of the tribe of the
27 children of Asher was Pagiel the son of Ochran.   And over
the host of the tribe of the children of Naphtali was Ahira
28 the son of Enan.   Thus were the journeyings of the children
of Israel according to their hosts.—And they set forward.
29   And Moses said unto Hobab, the son of Reuel the
Midianite, Moses' father-in-law: 'We are journeying

25.   *rearward*]   מאסף is the military term for rearguard, opposed to
חלוץ, meaning vanguard (Josh. 6.9, 13; Isa. 52.12).

28.   *the journeyings*]   The arrangements while on the journey
(see note to v. 12). The description here indicates that the four camps
journeyed one *after* the other and not one alongside of the other, in
the manner in which they were encamped (Luzzatto, *Biur*; see note
to 2.34).

29–34.   Hobab Requested to Act as Guide.

This section is inserted here, after the march is described as having
commenced, although the incident must have occurred before they
set out (v. 33). Hobab, the Midianite, the father-in-law of Moses, who
was well acquainted with the land, is asked by Moses to accompany
the Israelites as a guide on their journey. Moses' father-in-law (Jethro)
is mentioned as having given some good advice to Moses even before
the Revelation (Ex. 18.1 ff.), but he afterwards returned to his home
in Midian (ib. v. 27). That he paid Moses another visit before the
latter finally departed from the vicinity is not unlikely. Hobab's reply
to Moses' repeated request is not recorded here. From references elsewhere it appears that members of the family of Moses' father-in-law
entered Canaan (Judg. 1.16). Comp. note to v. 29.

29.   *Moses' father-in-law*]   I. e. Reuel (Ex. 2.18), also known as
Jethro (ib. 3.1), so that Hobab was Moses' brother-in-law. In Judg.
4.1, however, Hobab is spoken of as the father-in-law of Moses, hence
the Rabbis identified Hobab with Jethro who, they said, was known

unto the place of which the LORD said: I will give it you;
come thou with us, and we will do thee good; for the LORD
hath spoken good concerning Israel.' And he said unto 30
him: 'I will not go; but I will depart to mine own land,

by seven different names: Reuel, Jether, Jethro, Hobab, Heber, Keni
and Putiel (Mek. Jethro, Amalek 1; Sifre 78; Ex. R. 27.7). Rashi and
Ramban are of the opinion that Hobab was Moses' father-in-law and
was the same person as Jethro, while Reuel was the father of Hobab,
interpreting Ex. 2.18, where Reuel is mentioned as the father of the
seven daughters of the priest of Midian, as meaning *grandfather*, who
may also be referred to as father (comp. Gen. 32.10, where Jacob refers
to Abraham as "my father"; comp. Gray, p. 93, who suggests that
Reuel may have been the clan name). Ibn Ezra favors the interpretation which makes Hobab Moses' brother-in-law, so that he is forced
to assume that the word חתן in Judg. 4.11 means brother-in-law (comp.
R. V. there).

According to the narrative in Ex. 18.1 ff., Jethro went to Moses
soon after the crossing of the Red Sea, when he brought with him
Moses' wife, Zipporah, and her two sons, and advised Moses regarding
the appointment of judges. Although there it is recorded (v. 27) that
he later returned to his home in Midian, it is possible that he came
back again to bid them farewell before they departed for their goal,
Canaan, or that the account of his return there is anticipatory of what
happened afterwards; although, as already indicated, it appears that
after this request Hobab did accompany them to Canaan.

unto the place] Comp. Ex. 33.1. Moses speaks here in the hope
that the entrance into the land of Canaan was only a short while off
(Rashi, three days), not knowing then that they would have to linger
in the wilderness thirty-eight years more and that he himself would
never enter the promised land (Sifre 78; comp. Luzzatto).

we will do thee good] And we shall be able to do it, because "the
Lord hath spoken (to bring, Targum) good concerning Israel", and
He will surely keep His promise.

30. Hobab refuses to go, because he would rather go back to his
native land and to his kindred. The indication here is that the home
of the Midianites lay in a different direction from that which the Israelites took in their journey. "The route of the Israelites to Kadesh would
lie in the N.W., that of Hobab to the E." (Gray).

31 and to my kindred.' And he said: 'Leave us not, I pray
thee; forasmuch as thou knowest how we are to encamp
in the wilderness, and thou shalt be to us instead of eyes.

32 And it shall be, if thou go with us, yea, it shall be, that
what good soever the LORD shall do unto us, the same will
we do unto thee.'

33   And they set forward from the mount of the LORD three
days' journey; and the ark of the covenant of the LORD

31. *how we are to encamp*] You know where we might encamp
and where we might not, since you are familiar with the wilderness.
The places where they should encamp were indicated by the cloud,
but after encamping, Hobab's knowledge as to the location of springs
or the dangerous places would be of great value to them (Keil). Some,
however, refer this to the past: since you know all that happened to
us on the way and how God has protected us, you should also share
in the good reserved for us in the future (Targum, LXX, Rashi, ibn
Ezra, Rashbam, Luzzatto).

instead of eyes] To guide us in our travels (comp. Job 29.15).

32. *will we do unto thee*] Evidently a promise of a share in the land
(Sifre 81; cf. Ramban). While it is not indicated here whether Hobab
followed Moses or not, the passages in Judg. 1.16; 4.11 show that the
descendants of Hobab settled in Canaan together with the children
of Israel.

33. *mount of the Lord*] Sinai (Targum, the mountain on which
the glory of the Lord was revealed), elsewhere called the mount of
God (Ex. 3.1; 4.27). The same name was later applied to Mount Zion
(Isa. 2.3; 30.29; Mic. 4.2; Ps. 24.2).

three days' journey] Which brought them to one of the stopping-
places in the wilderness of Paran (v. 12), either Taberah (11.3), or
Kibroth-hattaavah (11.34, 35), or Hazeroth (ib.; comp. 33.16).

and the ark of the covenant] The difficulty in this passage, which
implies that the ark preceded the camp, while in the description of
the journey the ark is referred to as being carried by the Kohathites
who marched after the standard of Reuben (v. 21), has given rise to
various conjectures and interpretations. Ibn Ezra is of the opinion

went before them three days' journey, to seek out a resting-place for them. And the cloud of the LORD was over them 34 by day, when they set forward from the camp.

that while usually the ark was in the midst of the camp, carried by the Kohathites together with the other holy objects, an exception was made in this their first journey when the ark was allowed to precede the camp, because of the dangers of the wilderness, to which they were not as yet accustomed (comp. Josh. 3.6). Some of the Rabbis believe that the ark here was not the ark of the covenant, but another ark which contained the fragments of the tablets which Moses broke when he saw the Israelites worship the golden calf (Ex. 32.19), and it was this ark that they took with them whenever they went to battle (Sifre 82). Luzzatto interprets the phrase here figuratively, that the ark which in reality was in the midst of the camp, "went before them", was their protection and guide (comp. Keil). None of these explanations, however, is quite satisfactory. The difficulty is further aggravated by v. 34, where the cloud is said to have rested over them, while in the former narrative the cloud is supposed to have rested over the tabernacle (9.15 ff.). It is possible that this is a fragment of another description of the wilderness journey, which was introduced here without a real connection with the preceding. It is not, however, necessary to assume that the ark is understood here to have moved by itself (Gray). In Josh. 3.3, 6, 13, it is said distinctly that the priests carried the ark.

three days' journey] The same three days mentioned before (ibn Ezra). Some take it that the ark preceded the camp a distance of three days' journey (Rashi). It is rather difficult to understand why the ark, which is here intended to serve as a guide to the people, should be so far removed from them. In Josh. 3.4, the distance between the ark and the people is given as 2000 cubits only. Some regard these three words as a dittograph, accidentally repeated from the first half of the verse.

34. *over them*] Apparently over the Israelites (see previous note), but it may also mean over those who carried the ark (cf. McNeile). Since the ark served as the guide here, the service of the cloud was confined to that of protection and therefore did not have to precede the people, but rested over them as a symbol of watchfulness (Sforno).

from the camp] The place where they were encamped (Rashi).

35   And it came to pass, when the ark set forward, that Moses said: 'Rise up, O LORD, and let Thine enemies be scattered; and let them that hate Thee flee before 36 Thee.' And when it rested, he said: 'Return, O LORD, unto the ten thousands of the families of Israel.'

35–36. PRAYER WHEN THE ARK STARTED AND WHEN IT RESTED.

These two verses contain the prayers which Moses uttered when the ark set out on a journey and when it rested. It has no connection with what preceded or with what follows, since the prayer was not confined to this first journey, but was recited every time that the ark was taken on an expedition and when it returned. These two verses are, in most manuscripts and in the masoretic text, enclosed by inverted Nuns (ɿ—ɿ), probably to indicate that this is a parenthetical paragraph. According to some of the Rabbis, it really belongs after 2.17 (Sifre 83; Shab. 115a). For a paraphrase of these verses see Ps. 68.2; 132.8.

Rise up, O Lord] The ark was the symbol of God's presence in the midst of Israel. When the ark started, the prayer was uttered that God also might rise and come to the aid of Israel, with the full assurance that when God rises, Israel's enemies, who are also God's enemies, will flee and be scattered. Targum paraphrases: "Reveal Thyself".

36. *he said*] He was accustomed to say.

Return] Some translate this word "give rest" (ibn Ezra quoting Hayyuj, and Rashi quoting Menahem ben Saruk), for the reason that the verb שוב to return is intransitive and cannot be used without a preposition. This, however, is not conclusive (comp. II Chron. 14.14), especially in poetry (Jer. 29.14; Ps. 126.1; Nah. 2.3).

families] Clans, comp. v. 4 and note. "Myriads of thousands" would fit here just as well, implying very large numbers (Deut. 33.17; comp. Ehrlich). These two verses are still used in the synagogue when the Torah is taken out of the ark and when it is returned to the ark respectively.

CHAPTER 11.

1–3. THE INCIDENT AT TABERAH.

The people are wearied because of the hardships of the road which they had to travel (Rashbam, comp. 21.4–6), or because of what they foresaw to be in store for them in the great wilderness which they had

And the people were as murmurers, speaking evil in **11**
the ears of the LORD; and when the LORD heard it, His
anger was kindled; and the fire of the LORD burnt among
them, and devoured in the uttermost part of the camp.
And the people cried unto Moses; and Moses prayed unto 2
the LORD, and the fire abated. And the name of that place 3

to traverse (Ramban), and begin to complain. God's anger is aroused
against the people who were showing such lack of faith in Him and
caused a fire to break out among them. In response to .Moses' prayer
the fire subsided. The place was named Taberah (burning) in com-
memoration of this event.

1. *as murmurers*] Those who find fault with everything, who are
on the lookout for some reason for their dissatisfaction (Sifre, 85, also
Targum). Luzzatto renders the verse "as soon as they complained,
the anger of the Lord was kindled against them" (comp. Gen. 38.29).

speaking evil] "Speaking" is not in the text, but is implied in the
word murmurers, furnishing a reason for the punishment that follows.
Some render "what was evil", their dissatisfaction and grumbling
was evil in the ears of the Lord (Luzzatto, Ehrlich), but in this case
the idiom would require here "eyes" instead of "ears" (comp. v. 10).

the fire of the Lord] Perhaps in the form of lightning, or actual fire
that appeared as coming down from heaven (comp. 16.35; Lev. 10.2;
II Kings 1.10).

uttermost part of the camp] The fire started at one end of the camp
and was about to spread through the camp, when its progress was
arrested through the intercession of Moses. There is no mention here of
any casualties and some believe that the fire caught only on some bushes
or some of the tents. The Rabbis interpret the expression "uttermost
part" as referring to certain people and differ in their opinions as to
whether it refers to the most distinguished or the most common of the
people (Sifre 85 end).

2. *cried*] Out of fear or pain, begging Moses to intercede in their
behalf (Sifre 86).

and Moses prayed] In behalf of them, comp. Gen. 20.7, 17; Num.
21.7; Deut. 9.20, 26.

abated] Lit. sank down, died out.

was called Taberah, because the fire of the LORD burnt among them.

4   And the mixed multitude that was among them fell a lusting; and the children of Israel also wept on their part, and said: 'Would that we were given flesh to eat!

3. *Taberah*] The name of the place where the fire started, but not of any settlement or encampment, hence not mentioned in 33.16. The name of the encampment itself was Kibroth-hattaavah (v. 34). The name Taberah is again mentioned in Deut. 9.22, as one of the places where the people aroused God's anger.

4–6. DISSATISFACTION WITH THE MANNA
AND THE DESIRE FOR FLESH

The "mixed multitude", probably foreigners who joined the camp, became dissatisfied with the manna and longed for meat food. Some of the Israelites joined them in their protest and recalled the good food which they had in Egypt.

4. *mixed multitude*] The camp followers, some Egyptians and possibly some slaves who escaped with them from Egypt. The Hebrew word אספסוף has been rendered well by "riff-raff" (McNeile). In Ex. 12.38, another expression is used (ערב רב) which may be similarly rendered (comp. Sifre 86).

fell a lusting] Used in connection with physical appetites.

also wept] The cry was first raised by the "mixed multitude", and incited by them the children of Israel also wept (Ibn Ezra, Luzzatto), but not "again" (R. V.; Leeser), which would make it refer back to the murmuring of v. 1, or to Ex. 16.2, 3.

would that we were given flesh to eat] R. V., "who shall give us flesh to eat?" is more literal. Although they took with them a large number of cattle (Ex. 12.38; comp. Num. 32.1), this was apparently not sufficient to provide food for all of them (Sifre 86), and the poorer classes were probably deprived of meat food.

We remember the fish, which we were wont to eat in Egypt 5
for nought; the cucumbers, and the melons, and the leeks,
and the onions, and the garlic; but now our soul is dried 6
away; there is nothing at all; we have nought save
this manna to look to.'—Now the manna was like 7

5. *We remember*] We can only recall it now, because of its absence
since we have been away from Egypt.   While they may have had some
meat in the wilderness, they were hardly able to procure fish there,
which was plentiful in Egypt (comp. Isa. 19.8).

the fish] The article used collectively for the species.

we were wont to eat] The use of the impf. here indicates duration
(comp. Targum).

for nought] For no money (Ramban, see Luzzatto) or for very little
money (ibn Ezra). Fish was very plentiful in Egypt and served as a
staple article of food for the poorer classes. Malbim ingeniously makes
"for nought" refer back to "we remember", rendering it "we recall
in vain", i. e. the recollection does us no good, but the Hebrew idiom
would not permit of such interpretation. The various vegetables
enumerated here give a clear presentation of the diet of the lower
classes in Egypt. The working classes in Egypt, according to the
description given by Lane in his "*Modern Egyptians*", ch. VII (quoted
by Gray), lived mainly on "bread (made of millet or of maize), milk,
new cheese, eggs, small salted fish, cucumbers and melons, and gourds
of a great variety of kinds, onions and leeks, beans, chick-peas, lupins,
the fruit of the black egg plant, lentils, dates and pickles". Their cry
was indeed for flesh, but in their complaint they also indicated the
lack of variety in their diet.

6. *dried away*] Our soul (appetite) is dried up for want of fresh,
juicy food (BDB). "The appetite is 'empty' for want of food and 'dry'
when it has bread but no soup or vegetables to go with it" (Ehrlich).

to look to] Lit. "our eyes". Even the manna is not in our possession.
We have to raise our eyes to heaven whence it comes (ibn Ezra), and
we are not always certain whether we shall find it or not (Ramban,
Biur).

coriander seed, and the appearance thereof as the appear-
8 ance of bdellium. The people went about, and gathered
it, and ground it in mills, or beat it in mortars, and seethed it
in pots, and made cakes of it; and the taste of it was as the
9 taste of a cake baked with oil. And when the dew fell
upon the camp in the night, the manna fell upon it.—

7–9. Description of the Manna.

This is a parenthetical paragraph, describing the manna and the
way in which it was used by the people. It contains, so to say, a decla-
ration to the outside world as to the kind of food which God provided
for them and therefore how baseless their complaint was (Sifre 88).

7. *coriander seed*] In Ex. 16.31, it is described as white. Josephus
(*Ant.* iii.1.6) says that it was so white that the people would have
mistaken it for snow had not Moses told them that it was food.

bdellium] A kind of gum resin, gelatinous, transparent and generally
pale yellowish in color. The word means elsewhere (Gen. 2.18) a precious stone or a pearl, the product of the land of Havilah.

8. *went about*] And picked it up, without any trouble or exertion
(Sifre 89).

beat it in mortars] The handmill was probably a more expensive
article and not as common as the mortar, which could be found also
in the households of the poor.

seethed it] After it was ground (comp. Ex. 16.23).

a cake baked with oil] In Ex. 16.31, the taste is compared to "a
wafer made with honey" (comp. Rashbam). The term לשד probably
means a juicy or dainty bit (BDB). The LXX rendering apparently
refers to a cake made with both oil and honey. Targum has "something
kneaded in oil". The rendering "like the juice of the olive tree" (Gordon) is not tenable, since the word שמן is never used for the tree or for
the fruit (עץ זית).

9. *upon it*] The manna fell upon the dew, which gave it a peculiar
sparkle (Ex. 16.14). Some commentators find in the description given
here of the manna and of the mode of its preparation a detailed reply
to the complaint of the people:

> 1. "The people went about and gathered it", obtained it for
> nothing, as they obtained fish in Egypt (v. 5).

And Moses heard the people weeping, family by family, 10
every man at the door of his tent; and the anger of the
LORD was kindled greatly; and Moses was displeased.

2. "They ground it .... seethed it and baked it", indicating
   that they had a variety of it in the manner of preparation.
3. "Its taste was as the taste of a cake baked with oil", over
   against "our soul is dried away" (v. 6).
4. They were certain of its coming every morning upon the dew
   which fell during the night (see *Biur*).

10–15. MOSES COMPLAINS TO GOD.

The narrative is now continued from v. 6, after the parenthetical
paragraph 7–9. Moses hears the complaints and the weeping of the
people and is distressed because their dissatisfaction was the cause
of God's anger. There is no manifestation of God's anger recorded
here until after the descent of the quails (v. 33), but Moses knew that
such complaints, exhibiting lack of faith, would arouse the anger of
God and this caused the outburst of his discontent with the burden
of his office. He does not complain to the people, he does not even
imply that their demands are unjust. His complaint is directed against
God, who has imposed the heavy burden upon him. In his despair,
he prays that God slay him so that he might thus be rid of the responsibility which was becoming entirely too onerous for him.

10. *family by family*] Making of it a public mourning (Rashi) as
was the custom in the case of a burial (ibn Ezra). The phrase may also
indicate that the weeping was widespread, embracing all the families
of the nation (Ehrlich).

at the door of his tent] To attract attention and make it more public,
so that Moses might see it (ibn Ezra).

and Moses was displeased] The position of this phrase would indicate
that the displeasure of Moses was caused by the fact that God's anger
was aroused, and not by the people's weeping. Some suggest that the
phrase "and the anger of the Lord was kindled greatly" is out of place
here, so that the cause of Moses' displeasure was his overhearing the
people weeping. It is, however, possible that the narrative aims to

11 And Moses said unto the LORD: 'Wherefore hast Thou
dealt ill with Thy servant? and wherefore have I not
found favour in Thy sight, that Thou layest the burden
12 of all this people upon me? Have I conceived all this
people? have I brought them forth, that Thou shouldest
say unto me: Carry them in thy bosom, as a nursing-father
carrieth the sucking child, unto the land which Thou
13 didst swear unto their fathers? Whence should I have
flesh to give unto all this people? for they trouble me with
their weeping, saying: Give us flesh, that we may eat.

indicate that Moses was disturbed because of God's anger, knowing
its dire consequences, or perhaps because he felt that the demand of
the Israelites was not entirely unreasonable.

11. *have I not found favour in Thy sight*] When I pleaded to be
relieved of the burden to bring them out of Egypt (Ex. 4.10–13).

the burden of all this people] Comp. Ex. 32.34; 33.1–3, 12–16, where
the burden was imposed on Moses, but he was then promised that an
angel, and later that God Himself would aid him in this work.

12. *Have I conceived*] The emphasis is on the pronoun "I". Not
Moses but God is the parent of this people (Ex. 4.22; Deut. 32.18),
and therefore Hê is responsible for them.

have I brought them forth] Both phrases are figurative of motherhood.
Leeser has "begotten them", referring the first phrase to motherhood
and the second to fatherhood (following ibn Ezra and Rashbam).
Targum makes both phrases refer to fatherhood (comp. Adler ad loc.,
also Ramban).

as a nursing-father] Used parenthetically to illustrate the manner
of carrying, implying both training and nourishment. The male nurse
was a common institution among the wealthier families (II Kings
10.1, 5; Isa. 49.23).

which Thou didst swear] Should be "I", since it is the continuation
of the direct discourse, but on account of the interruption of the parenthetic phrase the person is changed.

13. *they trouble me with their weeping*] Lit. they weep around me
(Leeser, comp. Judg. 14.16, 17).

I am not able to bear all this people myself alone, because 14
it is too heavy for me. And if Thou deal thus with me, 15
kill me, I pray Thee, out of hand, if I have found favour
in Thy sight; and let me not look upon my wretchedness.'

And the LORD said unto Moses: 'Gather unto Me 16

14. *alone*] Without Thy assistance, or without the assistance of
others (see Deut. 1.12, 13; comp. Ramban).

it is too heavy] That is, the burden of the people is too heavy.

15. *if Thou deal thus with me*] If you leave the whole matter to
me and give me no assistance.

kill me, I pray Thee, out of hand] Or "at once" (Leeser). If you insist
upon my carrying the whole burden myself, when I am unable to supply
their needs (v. 13), then it would be better that I meet with instant
death so that I may be spared these constant troubles (comp. Ex. 32.32;
I Kings 19.4; Jonah 4.3).

if I have found favour] If you would listen to my prayers.

my wretchedness] Caused by my helplessness to do what is expected
of me. The Rabbis read here "in their wretchedness", that is the evil
that is destined to come upon them in consequence of their disobedience (Sifre 91). The Masorah (*Ochlah we-Ochlah*, ed. Frensdorf, 113a)
regards this as one of the eighteen places where a change was made
by the scribes in the text with a view of avoiding disrespect.

16–17. APPOINTMENT OF SEVENTY ELDERS.

In reply to Moses' complaint that he is unable to bear the burden
of the people alone (v. 14), God tells him to appoint seventy elders,
who will assist him in the conduct of affairs, and to whom an emanation
of the spirit of Moses would be imparted. Mention of the appointment
of certain individuals to assist Moses in administering the affairs of
the nation is made in Ex. 18 in case of judicial procedure, while definite
reference to an institution of seventy elders is found in Ex. 24.1, 9.
The manner of the appointment of these elders is interrupted here
by the rebuke administered to the people (vv. 18–23). On the institution of the elder in ancient Israel, see *J. E.* s. v. Elder.

seventy men of the elders of Israel, whom thou knowest
to be the elders of the people, and officers over them; and
bring them unto the tent of meeting, that they may stand
17 there with thee. And I will come down and speak with
thee there; and I will take of the spirit which is upon thee,
and will put it upon them; and they shall bear the burden
of the people with thee, that thou bear it not thyself alone.
18 And say thou unto the people: Sanctify yourselves against

16. *of the elders of Israel*] The elders were the prominent men in
the various tribes and families (Ex. 4.29; 12.21), and out of these Moses
was to select seventy who would form a permanent body.

whom thou knowest] Who have exercised the double function of
elders (or advisers) and of officers in the sense of civil or judicial func-
tionaries vested with executive power (ibn Ezra; comp. Gray regarding
the exact meaning of *Shoter*).

with thee] To impress the people with the fact that the authority
given to them is derived from the divine source (Rashi).

17. *And I will come down*] As described in Ex. 33.9, 11.

there] In the tent of meeting, where the elders were assembled, so
that they also might hear (ibn Ezra, but comp. Ramban).

and I will take of the spirit] Lit. withdraw, reserve (cf. Gen. 27.36).
The spirit of Moses is here conceived of as quantitative, from which a
portion may be withdrawn (comp. Ehrlich, who interprets, "of the
kind of spirit"). In later Hebrew the word אצל is used in the sense of
emanation (like the cabalistic אצילות). The Rabbis illustrate this by
the simile of the candle light from which many other candles may be
lighted without diminishing its light (Rashi).

bear . . . with thee] Take part, associate themselves (cf. Ex. 18.22).
thyself alone] In reply to Moses' complaint in v. 14.

18–25. THE PROMISE OF FLESH FOOD.

18. *And say thou*] The continuation of the story, which was
interrupted by vv. 16–17, and a reply to Moses' outcry in v. 13.

Sanctify yourselves] Consecrate yourselves through ritual purification (Ex. 19.10; Josh. 3.5), or simply be prepared, ready (Targum,
Leeser).

to-morrow, and ye shall eat flesh; for ye have wept in the
ears of the LORD, saying: Would that we were given flesh
to eat! for it was well with us in Egypt; therefore the
LORD will give you flesh, and ye shall eat. Ye shall not   19
eat one day, nor two days, nor five days, neither ten days,
nor twenty days; but a whole month, until it come out   20
at your nostrils, and it be loathsome unto you; because
that ye have rejected the LORD who is among you, and
have troubled Him with weeping, saying: Why, now,
came we forth out of Egypt?' And Moses said: 'The   21
people, among whom I am, are six hundred thousand men
on foot; and yet Thou hast said: I will give them flesh,

against to-morrow] Sanctify yourselves to-day so that you may be
prepared by to-morrow to witness the miracle that is to be enacted
(comp. Josh. 3.5).

ye have wept] Taking the most objectionable phrases of their complaint: "Would that we were given flesh to eat" (v. 4), doubting the
power of God, and "it was well with us in Egypt" (v. 5), regretting
the days of slavery (v. 20; 14.3; Ex. 14.12).

20. *until it come out at your nostrils*] Until you become disgusted
with it (Targum). The reference may be to violent vomiting.

who is among you] Whose kindness and favor have been so plainly
manifested to you.

Why, now, came we forth out of Egypt] Which in itself was the greatest manifestation of God's favor (comp. Rashbam and *Biur*).

21. *Six hundred thousand*] In round numbers, omitting the additional 3,000 (1.46; comp. Ex. 12.37).

on foot] The Hebrew word רגלי was originally a military term,
denoting footmen, foot-soldiers (Judg. 20.2), but it is here used collectively for all Israel over the age of 20.

and yet Thou hast said] Moses expresses his astonishment at the
promise made by God to feed them with meat for a whole month.
The Rabbis endeavored in various ways to explain Moses' apparent
incredulity and lack of faith in the power of God (Sifre 95, also Rashi,
Rashbam, Ramban).

22 that they may eat a whole month! If flocks and herds
be slain for them, will they suffice them? or if all the fish
of the sea be gathered together for them, will they suffice
23 them?' And the LORD said unto Moses: 'Is the LORD's
hand waxed short? now shalt thou see whether My word
shall come to pass unto thee or not.'

24   And Moses went out, and told the people the words of
the LORD; and he gathered seventy men of the elders of
25 the people, and set them round about the Tent. And the
LORD came down in the cloud, and spoke unto him, and
took of the spirit that was upon him, and put it upon the
seventy elders; and it came to pass, that, when the spirit

22. *If flocks and herds*] Such as are within reach.

be gathered together] Since the word "gather" is used here instead
of "slain", used in connection with flocks and herds, the Rabbis deduce
the law that fish do not require to be slaughtered for food in the manner
prescribed for cattle (Hul. 27b).

23. *Is the Lord's hand waxed short*] Is His power limited? (Comp.
Isa. 50.2; 59.1), a rebuke to Moses for his lack of faith.

My word shall come to pass] God's word, once uttered, must become
realized (Isa. 55.11).

24. *And Moses went out*] From the tent of assembly, where he
probably laid his complaint before God (v. 11).

the words of the Lord] That they get themselves ready for the event
that will happen on the next day.

and he gathered seventy men] Description of the ceremony of the
appointment of the leaders is now resumed from v. 17.

round about the Tent] In front of the door of the tent, where God
would speak to Moses from within the cloud (comp. Ex. 33.9; Num.
12.5).

rested upon them, they prophesied, but they did so no
more. But there remained two men in the camp, the name 26

25. *they prophesied*] They came into a state of ecstasy (comp. I
Sam. 10.10–12; 18.10, et al.). The nature of their prophecy is not
indicated here, but it may be assumed that they realized the great
wrong in the complaints of the people and rebuked them for their
lack of faith and warned them against the impending punishment
(comp. Luzzatto).

but they did so no more] They exercised the power of prophecy only
on this occasion (Sifre 95, Rashi). Targum has "and they did not
stop", i. e. they continued to function as prophets (also Vulgate).

26–29. ELDAD AND MEDAD.

Eldad and Medad, two of those invited to come to the tent, for some
reason remained in the camp and began to prophesy, possibly at the
same time when the other elders standing near the tent prophesied.
This extraordinary event aroused the astonishment of the people and
the report was brought to Moses. Joshua, jealous of the authority of
his master, asks that they be prevented from doing so, to which Moses
replies: Would that all the people were possessed of the gift of prophecy,
thus again demonstrating his unselfishness and deep concern for the
welfare of the people.

From the text as it stands we are unable to tell whether Eldad and
Medad were of the seventy selected elders and by some mishap (or
because of their modesty, Sifre 95, Sanh. 17b) did not come to the tent,
so that there were actually only 68 elders present; or that they were
not of the 70 and still the spirit of prophecy rested on them. Either
supposition presents several difficulties. According to some of the
Rabbis, Moses selected six elders from each tribe, making a total of 72.
He then wrote the word "elder" on seventy pieces of paper and left
two ballots blank. The seventy-two elders, including Eldad and Medad,
were told to draw the lots and Eldad and Medad drew the blanks, so
that they were not invited to come to the tent. However, because they
were of those originally chosen by Moses, they also received of his
spirit and they also prophesied (Sifre 95; Sanh. 17b, comp. Malbim).
Other Rabbis were of the opinion that these two were of the seventy
invited elders, but they failed to come to the tent (ib.; comp. Luzzatto).

of the one was Eldad, and the name of the other Medad;
and the spirit rested upon them; and they were of them
that were recorded, but had not gone out unto the Tent;
27 and they prophesied in the camp. And there ran a young
man, and told Moses, and said: 'Eldad and Medad are
28 prophesying in the camp.' And Joshua the son of Nun,
the minister of Moses from his youth up, answered and
29 said: 'My lord Moses, shut them in.' And Moses said
unto him: 'Art thou jealous for my sake? would that all

26. *Eldad*] "God has loved," the same as Jedidiah and probably
identical with Elidad mentioned (34.12) as the prince of Benjamin.

Medad] Not found elsewhere in the Bible, although mentioned in
some Babylonian contract tables (Gray).

that were recorded] Enrolled among those who were to serve as
elders (comp. 1.17).

27. *a young man*] One of the young men attending on Moses
(ibn Ezra). Rashi quotes an opinion which identifies him with Gershom,
son of Moses.

28. *the minister of Moses*] Although not one of the seventy elders,
Joshua was present at the tent, where he always was (Ex. 33.11),
attending on Moses.

from his youth up] So also Targum, taking the word בחורים as an
abstract noun (Eccl. 11.9; 12.1 comp. Rashbam). Others (LXX,
Vulgate, R. V., comp. ibn Ezra and Luzzatto) translate "one of his
chosen ones", of his most trusted servants. Ehrlich's interpretation,
"from the time that God had chosen him (Moses)", is not convincing.

shut them in] Implying imprisonment (Targum), because they
dared prophesy without direct instructions (Ramban). Another
possible rendering is "forbid them" or "restrain them" (R. V., Leeser,
Biur, following Targum Jonathan).

29. *Art thou jealous for my sake?*] Do you expect to enhance my
glory by shutting out all possible competition? The Rabbis say that
the burden of their prophecy was that Moses would die in the wilderness and that Joshua would bring the Israelites into the promised land
(Sifre 95).

the LORD's people were prophets, that the LORD would
put His spirit upon them!' And Moses withdrew into the 30
camp, he and the elders of Israel.

And there went forth a wind from the LORD, and brought 31
across quails from the sea, and let them fall by the camp,
about a day's journey on this side, and a day's journey

would that all the Lord's people were prophets] This is not merely an
indication that such a state would be entirely agreeable to Moses, but
also expresses a prayer and a wish that this might really happen.

that the Lord would put His spirit upon them] In further explanation
of the term "prophets". It may also be rendered "if the Lord", i. e.
if it is agreeable to the Lord to place His spirit upon them.

31–34. THE QUAILS.

This is the continuation of v. 23, where Moses is assured by God
that He would satisfy the desire of the people for flesh. The quail,
spoken of here and in Ex. 16.11–13 (comp. Ps. 78.27; 105.40), is a
migratory bird belonging to the partridge family. Quails migrate in
vast flocks across the Arabian Desert, in the spring northward and in
the autumn southward. Their bodies are so heavy that they become
exceedingly fatigued from the flight and become an easy prey when
they land anywhere. A sea wind would bring them in immense numbers in the spring of the year to the Israelitish camp at night and they
could be gathered up in the morning without any difficulty. The miracle
here consisted in their being directed to the proper place at the proper
time (see Hastings, *Dictionary of the Bible*, s. v.). The Rabbis speak
of four kinds of quail: the feldfare, the partridge, the thrush and the
quail proper, and also refer, in a rather exaggerated manner, to its
fatness and its possibility of expansion in the process of baking (Yoma
75b).

31. *went forth a wind*] The quail always flies with the wind, represented here as coming from God (comp. Gen. 8.1; Ex. 10.13, 19; 14.21).

quails from the sea] Probably the Gulf of Akabah. The quail,
spoken of here as *salvim*, is still known both in Egypt and Syria as
Salwa (Gray).

about a day's journey] The quails were scattered over the camp and
also over an area of about a day's journey on either side of the camp.

on the other side, round about the camp, and about two
32 cubits above the face of the earth. And the people rose
up all that day, and all the night, and all the next day,
and gathered the quails; he that gathered least gathered
ten heaps; and they spread them all abroad for themselves
33 round about the camp. While the flesh was yet between
their teeth, ere it was chewed, the anger of the LORD was
kindled against the people, and the LORD smote the people

about two cubits above the face of the earth] The quails were hovering
about above the ground, as is their custom, at a height of about two
cubits, approximately one yard, so that they were easily caught (Sifre
97, Rashi). The more probable meaning is that the quails fell to the
ground exhausted one on top of the other, so that they formed a heap
of about two cubits in height (ibn Ezra).

32. *gathered ten heaps*] "*Homer*" (A. V., Leeser after Mendelssohn),
is a dry measure, equaling about 393.9 liters, or about 10 bushels. Our
translation implies no definite measure (as also in Ex. 8.10; comp.
Luzzatto).

and they spread them] For the purpose of drying them in the sun
and then eating them without cooking (Gray, quoting Herodotus,
mentions the custom also among the Egyptians). LXX and Sam., by
the transposition of the last two letters of the root, וישחטו שחוט, the
technical expression for the ritual slaughter of animals, render "and
they slaughtered" (comp. Sifre 98, Yoma 75b).

33. *ere it was chewed*] Indicating the rapidity with which the punishment came upon them. Another rendering is "ere it came to an end",
before the supply was exhausted (LXX, Targum, comp. Gray), i. e.
before the end of thirty days as promised in v. 20 (Reggio). The rabbinic interpretation is that the plague attacked some immediately
and others later, so that the food as well as the resultant plague continued for one month (Yoma 75b).

and the Lord smote the people] Although the plague may have been
the natural result of gluttonous eating of flesh or of the poisonous stuff
on which quails sometimes feed, this is seen here as divine punishment
of the people for their lack of faith (comp. Gray).

with a very great plague. And the name of that place was 34
called   Kibroth-hattaavah,   because   there   they   buried
the people that lusted.   From Kibroth-hattaavah the 35
people journeyed unto Hazeroth; and they abode at
Hazeroth.

34. *Kibroth-hattaavah*] The graves of lust, one of the encampments
mentioned in 33.17, part of which was also called Taberah (see note to
v. 3). Ehrlich's explanation that this name implies the burial of their
lust, indicating that after this plague they desired flesh no more, is
ingenious but not convincing.

35. *and they abode*] Were detained there, on account of Miriam's
leprosy, as related in the next chapter (v. 15).

Hazeroth] Mentioned here and in 12.15; 33.17, 18; Deut. 1.1. The
place has not been identified with any degree of certainty.   The suggestion has been made and followed by a number of scholars that
Hazeroth was identical with the modern 'Ain el-Huderah, about 40
miles north-east of Jebel-Musa and not quite half way between Jebel-
Musa and Akabah. Other places have been mentioned as identical
with Hazeroth (see Driver in Hastings, *Dictionary of the Bible*, s. v.;
Gray, Keil).

CHAPTER **12.**

1–16. AARON AND MIRIAM JEALOUS OF MOSES.

In this narrative, the exalted position of Moses among other prophets, or those upon whom God causes His spirit to rest, is further
emphasized. Miriam and Aaron become jealous of Moses and claim
equal authority with him. Moses hears of their murmurings, but says
nothing. God, however, would not permit this to pass unpunished.
First the rebuke is administered and then, in the presence of Moses,
both are told by God of the great difference in kind between the prophecy of Moses and that of other prophets. Miriam is further punished
with leprosy, from which she is healed only after Moses is induced by

12   And Miriam and Aaron spoke against Moses because

Aaron to intercede with God in her behalf. During the seven days of Miriam's leprosy the people tarried at Hazeroth.

While the charge against Miriam and Aaron here is obviously on account of their desire to be considered as equal in station with Moses, another incident is referred to in v. 1, which is made to stand out as the cause of their complaint, viz. "because of the Cushite woman whom he had married". The offence itself is not made clear and therefore gave rise to numerous interpretations. Some identify this woman with Zipporah, whom Moses married in Midian (Ex. 2.21), while others refer this to a more recent marriage which Moses contracted with a woman from Ethiopia. In the former case, the offence is regarded as consisting in that Moses had dismissed Zipporah, so that he might devote himself more freely to the service of God. In the latter case, the offence was that he married a foreign woman (see note to v. 1). In either case, the offence is rather trivial and may have been introduced here as the immediate occasion rather than as the cause of the complaint of Aaron and Miriam.

The fact that Aaron escaped punishment also gave rise to many fanciful interpretations, as indicated further in the notes. The main burden of the story, however, is perfectly obvious and naturally follows the description of the appointment of the seventy elders upon whom the spirit of Moses was allowed to rest.

Sulzberger ('*Am Haaretz*, p. 8), suggests, but does not elaborate his suggestion, that the complaint of Aaron and Miriam against Moses was due to the exclusion of the tribe of Levi from representation on the Council of Elders (11.16 ff.).

1. *spoke against*] Miriam is here mentioned first, possibly because she was the main instigator and Aaron was only a silent participant (comp. Sifre 99). Ehrlich's suggestion that the words here should be translated "and Miriam spoke *with* Aaron" is as usual novel but farfetched. Some suggest the insertion here of the word אחות before Aaron, so that Miriam would be the only offender. This would also account for the fact that she alone was punished (Kahana, comp. Gray).

of the Cushite woman whom he had married; for he had
married a Cushite woman. And they said: 'Hath the 2
Lord indeed spoken only with Moses? hath He not spoken

Cushite woman] Cush has been identified as the southern Nile
valley, or Upper Egypt, extending from Syene indefinitely to the
South, commonly called Ethiopia (BDB). This would indicate that
Moses had married an Ethiopian woman, of whom we hear nothing
further in the Bible, although a great deal in legend (Jos., *Ant.*, ii.10;
"*Dibre ha-Yamim le-Mosheh*", in *Ozar ha-Midrashim*, p. 359); and the
additional phrase, "for he had married, etc." (regarded by some as an
editorial gloss and omitted in the Vulgate) would point to the fact
that this happened close to the time when the incident occurred.
Others believe that Cush here is identical with a place in Northern
Arabia, so that it may refer to Zipporah whom Moses married in Midian
(*J. E.*, s. v. Cush), and therefore are forced to explain the displeasure
of Miriam and Aaron on different grounds (Sifre 99). R. Nathan connects this incident with the story of Eldad and Medad (11.26–29) in
the following way: Miriam was in the company of Zipporah when the
report came that Eldad and Medad were prophesying in the camp.
Zipporah then said to Miriam: "Woe to their wives if they become
prophets, since their husbands will then separate themselves from
them, even as Moses separated himself from me". This provoked
Miriam, who told it to Aaron, and both of them then spoke dispara-
gingly of Moses (Sifre 99, quoted in Rashi, comp. Targum). Another
rabbinical suggestion is that Cushite here means beautiful (Targum,
Sam., Sifre, ib.), a euphemism: "she was as beautiful as the Ethiopian
is black", or because the numerical value of כושית (730) is the same as
that of יפת מראה (Sifre, ib.).

for he had married] This apparently unnecessary addition points
to the interpretation which implies that the marriage was a recent one
and had no reference to Zipporah (Rashbam, comp. Gray).

2. *Hath the Lord indeed spoken only*] This was the main offence
of Aaron and Miriam in that they wished to assert that they were of
equal rank with Moses. Admitting that inspiration was granted to
Moses, they still insisted that they also had been vouchsafed the prophetic gift and were therefore on an equal footing with Moses.

3 also with us?' And the LORD heard it.—Now the man
Moses was very meek, above all the men that were upon
4 the face of the earth.—And the LORD spoke suddenly
unto Moses, and unto Aaron, and unto Miriam: 'Come
out ye three unto the tent of meeting.' And they three
5 came out. And the LORD came down in a pillar of cloud,
and stood at the door of the Tent, and called Aaron and
6 Miriam; and they both came forth. And He said: 'Hear

and the Lord heard it] Took note of it (11.1), although Moses himself paid no attention to it (Sifre 100).

3. *Now the man Moses*] This is placed here parenthetically to
show the absurdity of the charge contained in v. 2, which implies that
Moses boasted of the fact that God spoke to him. The Rabbis connect
this with v. 2b. Moses would not heed their grumblings because of
his extreme humility, but God heard it and took his part.

Those who believe in the Mosaic authorship of the whole Torah
find it difficult to ascribe this statement to one who is represented as
the meekest of men. Keil regards this merely as a "statement which
was indispensable to a full and correct interpretation of all the circumstances, and which was made quite objectively, with reference to
the character which Moses had not given to himself but had acquired
through the grace of God", and quoting Calmet, he further says, "as
he praises himself here without pride, so he will blame himself elsewhere with humility, a man of God whose character is not to be meas-
ured by the standards of ordinary men". For the Jewish believer who
holds that the Torah is not the work of Moses, but the work of God,
transmitted through Moses, the difficulty disappears.

4. *suddenly*] Immediately, while they were still speaking about Moses
(Targum, Rashbam), or without their expecting it (ibn Ezra, Ramban).
come out] Lit. "Go out", each one out of his or her tent (ibn Ezra)
and come to the tent of meeting.

5. *And the Lord came down*] Comp. 11.25. All three of them were
in the tent when the Lord summoned Aaron and Miriam to come out
of the tent and receive their rebuke, while Moses was to remain inside
(ibn Ezra), so that he should not hear his praise (Sifre 102).
Aaron and Miriam] Should be in quotation marks, direct discourse (Ehrlich).

now My words: if there be a prophet among you, I the
LORD do make Myself known unto him in a vision, I do
speak with him in a dream. My servant Moses is not so; 7

6–8. God rebukes Aaron and Miriam for their presumption. Grant-
ing that revelations are sometimes made to other prophets, there is a
great difference in the kind of revelation and in the form of transmission
in the case of other prophets from that of Moses. No prophet can
boast of such direct and intimate intercourse with God as that which
Moses enjoyed. The form of these three verses is rhythmical, in the
manner of an oracle.

6.   *If there be a prophet among you*]   In the Hebrew text the reading
is "your prophet", which gives no adequate sense. The reading which
would correspond to our translation would be נביא בכם (comp. Targum),
although the rendering is permissible even as the word stands (comp.
Ps. 115.7; see Luzzatto).

I the Lord]   "I" is not in the Hebrew text and is supplied, as in
Targum, and suggested by the cantillation marks. Ibn Ezra translates, "If there is among you a prophet of the Lord", implying a reading
נביאכם נביא ה׳, and disregarding the cantillation marks, according to
which ה׳ is separated from נביאכם (see Ramban, Luzzatto). Another
rendering makes of נביאכם an abstract noun, thus reading "if your
prophecy", i. e. your power of prophecy (Rashbam), but this is rather
strained. There are also several other interpretations and emendations, but our rendering, following the traditional interpretation, seems
the most acceptable.

in a vision]   Parallel to "in a dream", meaning a vision while asleep
(ibn Ezra); or, "vision" may refer to a day vision while awake, and
"dream" to a vision while asleep and unconscious.

with him in a dream]   Lit. "in him" (comp. Keil, "inasmuch as a
revelation in a dream fell within the inner sphere of soul life").

7.   *My servant Moses*]   A term of affection and trust (Deut. 34.5;
Ex. 14.31; Josh. 1.1 et al.), also applied to Abraham (Gen. 26.34), to
Isaac (Gen. 24.14), to Jacob (Ezek. 28.25), and to other worthy characters (see BDB), also in a special sense to the prophets (II Kings 9.7)
and to Israel (Isa. 41.8).

is not so]   My relations to Moses are not the same as to other prophets.

8 he is trusted in all My house; with him do I speak mouth
to mouth, even manifestly, and not in dark speeches; and
the similitude of the LORD doth he behold; wherefore then
were ye not afraid to speak against My servant, against
9 Moses?' And the anger of the LORD was kindled against
10 them; and He departed. And when the cloud was removed

he is trusted in all My house] He can approach Me at any time and
need not wait for a vision or a dream (ibn Ezra, *Biur*). Luzzatto
renders: "He is more trusted than all the other servants of My household", he stands higher than all the other prophets.

8. *mouth to mouth*] His revelation is direct (ibn Ezra), and while
he is fully conscious (Sforno, *Biur*). Comp. the expression "face to
face" in Ex. 33.11; Deut. 34.10.

even manifestly] In personal presence, not in a vision (BDB as
against Ewald, who identifies מַרְאָה with מִרְאֶה, and is forced to emend
ולא במראה ובחידות; see Szanto and Ehrlich).

and not in dark speeches] In riddles, in obscure phraseology that
requires explanation (Ezek. 17.2).

and the similitude of the Lord] Not the form of God, which is invis-
ible (Ex. 33.18–24), but the likeness that most closely resembles Him
(Sifre 103). Many attempts have been made to harmonize the various
references in the Bible to God's form with the notion of the incor-
poreality of God, a subject much discussed by the philosophers of the
middle ages. We shall, however, find less difficulty if we assume that
the ideas about the nature of God underwent a gradual development
in the Bible and became more refined with the advance of time.

were ye not afraid] In view of his great superiority over you, you
should have been afraid that you would arouse God's anger by attempting to compare yourselves with him.

9. *and He departed*] Having declared to them their guilt, God
departed in anger from them, allowing the punishment to come in His
absence (see Keil; comp. Sifre 105, the simile of the king who orders
the master to punish the young prince, but not in the king's presence,
because it would cause him pain to see his child punished).

10. *And when the cloud*] With God's departure, the cloud also
was removed from the tent.

from over the Tent, behold, Miriam was leprous, as white
as snow; and Aaron looked upon Miriam; and, behold,
she was leprous. And Aaron said unto Moses: 'Oh my 11
lord, lay not, I pray thee, sin upon us, for that we have
done foolishly, and for that we have sinned. Let her not, 12
I pray, be as one dead, of whom the flesh is half consumed

from over the Tent] I. e. the door of the tent (ibn Ezra), since the
cloud remained outside the tent while the rebuke was administered
(v. 5).

leprous, as white as snow] See Ex. 4.6. Leprosy is a chronic skin-
disease, characterized by ulcerous eruptions and successive falling off
of dead skin. Here probably a mild form of it is meant (comp. Lev.
13.13).

11. *lay not, I pray thee, sin upon us*] Aaron begs forgiveness for
both of them, although the punishment was inflicted upon Miriam
alone. To "lay sin" is to allow the consequences of sin to take effect,
as opposed to "take away sin" (Ex. 10.17; 32.33), which means to
withhold punishment.

we have done foolishly] We have acted out of ignorance (Jer. 5.4),
not knowing the high position which Moses held.

12. *be as one dead*] The leper, because he had to be removed from
the camp and from all contact with society (5.3; Lev. 13.45, 46) and
because of the loathsomeness of his disease, is regarded as one dead
(Sanh. 47a; 'Ab. Zarah 5a). Aaron implores Moses to intercede in
behalf of Miriam so that she should not remain leprous, and become
like one born with his flesh half consumed. Targum paraphrases:
"Let her not be removed from us, for she is our sister. Pray now that
this dead flesh that is on her be healed again" (see Rashi, following
Sifre and Pesikta ad loc., and comp. ibn Ezra). Targum Jonathan
paraphrases still more elaborately: "Let not Miriam our sister remain
leprous and thus defile as does a corpse and be like an infant fully
developed in its mother's womb but wasting away at birth, so that it
has to be taken out in pieces from the mother. Miriam our sister took
part in our wanderings and suffered with us in our troubles, and now
when the time has come for us to inherit the promised land, she should
be taken away from us". Rashbam renders the verse: "Be *thou* not
like one dead; inasmuch as all who come from the same mother's womb

13 when he cometh out of his mother's womb.' And Moses
cried unto the LORD, saying: 'Heal her now, O God, I
beseech Thee.'

14   And the LORD said unto Moses: 'If her father had but
spit in her face, should she not hide in shame seven days?
let her be shut up without the camp seven days, and after
15 that she shall be brought in again.' And Miriam was
shut up without the camp seven days; and the people
16 journeyed not till Miriam was brought in again. And

partly die (when any brother or sister dies)", i. e. Moses himself would
be like one dead, since half of his own flesh (his own sister) would be
consumed (comp. Sforno).

13. *Heal her now, O God, I beseech Thee*] A brief, but expressive
prayer, which Moses cries out on beholding his sister in her wretchedness. The suggested emendation: "Nay, now, heal her, I pray" (אֵל
for אֵל, BDB, p. 42, Gray et al.), has already been declared unnecessary
by Haupt (see Holzinger). Sforno suggests that the prayer emphasized
that the healing should be immediate, so that she should not be put
to the disgrace of having to be removed from the camp, as is required
by law.

14. *spit in her face*] A sign of contempt (Deut. 25.9; Isa. 50.6;
Job 30.10). Targum paraphrases: "rebuked her", possibly referring
to such a punishment for misconduct (comp. McNeile). Ehrlich's
suggestion that the spitting was for the purpose of healing, referring
to Mark 8.23 and to Yer. Sota 1, does not fit in with the text.

should she not hide in shame] Even if she is healed, as Moses had
prayed, she should not escape the public disgrace of being shut up for
the minimum period prescribed for the segregation of the leper (Lev.
13.4).

brought in again] Back to the camp.

15. *and the people journeyed not*] Out of regard for Miriam (Rashi,
quoting Sotah 9b: because she waited at the bulrushes when Moses
was placed there by his mother (Ex. 2.4), therefore she was rewarded
that the whole nation waited for her). The removal of the cloud from
over the tent (v. 10), which was usually the sign for breaking up camp

afterward the people journeyed from Hazeroth, and pitched in the wilderness of Paran.

(9.16–22), was interpreted in this instance as a sign of displeasure rather than as a signal for departure (Sforno, comp. *Biur* and Herxheimer).

16. *wilderness of Paran*] Which lies to the North of the Sinaitic peninsula (10.12). The name covers a large area, within which they made their encampments at different times. Among these places of encampment were Hazeroth, Rithmah (33.18) and Kadesh-barnea (Deut. 1.19, 22), whence the spies were sent out (13.26; comp. Ramban, Sforno).

13–14. THE SPIES.

During the period of their encampment at Kadesh, in the wilderness of Paran, Moses sent out twelve spies, one from each tribe, to investigate the land of Canaan. Included among the spies were Joshua and Caleb. On their return, the spies brought a glowing report of the productivity of the land, and as evidence brought some clusters of grapes, pomegranates and figs. Ten of them, however, contended that it would be impossible for them to conquer the land, the cities of which were strongly fortified and the inhabitants powerful men, including the "children of Anak" (giants). Joshua and Caleb, while agreeing with the description given by the other spies, insisted that with the help of God they would prevail and conquer the land. The people, on hearing the report of the spies, were greatly distressed and murmured against Moses for taking them out of Egypt. God's anger was aroused against Israel and dire punishment was obviated only through the intercession of Moses. However, because of their lack of faith, the present generation would not enter the promised land. For forty years they would wander in the wilderness, until all those above the age of twenty have died. Joshua and Caleb alone of those who came out of Egypt would be permitted to enter Canaan. When this decree was made known to the people, they became very sad and repentant and wanted to show their faith in the promise of God by beginning an attack on the outlying tribes, the Amalekites and the Canaanites, against the advice of Moses. In this they met with defeat and with considerable loss of life.

13 2 And the LORD spoke unto Moses, saying: 'Send thou men, that they may spy out the land of Canaan, which I give unto the children of Israel; of every tribe of their fathers shall ye send a man, every one a prince among 3 them.' And Moses sent them from the wilderness of Paran

CHAPTER **13.**

1–24. SPIES SELECTED AND SENT OFF.

The spies are selected and given instruction as to the points which they should investigate and report on.

2. *Send thou men*] The Rabbis interpreted the apparently super-fluous preposition "thee" (לך, although a perfectly legitimate use of the word grammatically, BDB, 515) to mean that this was not given in the form of a command to Moses, but rather of a permission or con-cession to the will of the people (Sotah 34b). Thus, the narrative here is made to harmonize with the text in Deut. 1.22, where it is implied that the spies were sent by Moses in response to a demand on the part of the people, who wished to be convinced of the good qualities of the land (Rashi, Ramban). The Samaritan version prefaces this narrative by introducing here, with a few changes, the verses from Deut. 1.20–23.

that they may spy out] Explore, seek the qualities of the land. Mal-bim distinguishes this from the term רגל used in Josh. 2, making the latter refer to the act of reconnoitering and finding the weak points of a land for the purpose of attack. The two verbs, however, are used interchangeably (see Luzzatto).

of every tribe] Excepting the tribe of Levi, which was not to have a portion in the land.

shall ye send] Including Moses and Aaron and perhaps also the whole congregation (v. 26), although the command was given to Moses alone (v. 1). LXX, Syr. and Sam. have "shalt thou send".

every one a prince among them] "Prince" here is not used in the technical sense, the head of the tribe (as 1.5–15), but in a general sense, an important personage, one distinguished among his clansmen (comp. Rashbam).

according to the commandment of the LORD; all of them
men who were heads of the children of Israel. And these   4
were their names: of the tribe of Reuben, Shammua the
son of Zaccur. Of the tribe of Simeon, Shaphat the son   5
of Hori. Of the tribe of Judah, Caleb the son of Jephunneh.   6
Of the tribe of Issachar, Igal the son of Joseph. Of the   7-8
tribe of Ephraim, Hoshea the son of Nun. Of the tribe   9
of Benjamin, Palti the son of Raphu. Of the tribe of   10
Zebulun, Gaddiel the son of Sodi. Of the tribe of Joseph,   11
namely, of the tribe of Manasseh, Gaddi the son of Susi.
Of the tribe of Dan, Ammiel the son of Gemalli. Of the   12-13
tribe of Asher, Sethur the son of Michael. Of the tribe of   14
Naphtali, Nahbi the son of Vophsi. Of the tribe of Gad,   15
Geuel the son of Machi. These are the names of the men   16
that Moses sent to spy out the land. And Moses called

3. *according to the commandment of the Lord*]   Rashi renders "with
the consent of the Lord", in agreement with the rabbinic interpretation
quoted above (note on v. 2). Others make the phrase "by the mouth
of" to refer to a choice by lot (Kahana, quoting *Bet Talmud*, I, 169).
Rashbam suggests that Moses called for volunteers to undertake the
task, and out of those who offered themselves he selected twelve.

4. *And these were their names*]   The order followed here is neither
that of the seniority of the tribes nor of the manner in which the camps
were arranged (1.5–15; 7.12–83). It is suggested that possibly the
order is according to the rank of the individuals selected (Ramban;
comp. 34.19–28). Another suggestion is that the lines here have been
misplaced and that originally the order of the seniority of the tribes
was followed here also (see Gray). With the exception of the names of
Joshua and Caleb, none of the other names are found elsewhere in the
Torah.

16. *and Moses called*]   With reference to v. 8, to indicate that
Hoshea mentioned there was the same whom Moses named Joshua
when he became his servant. It was customary for masters to change

17 Hoshea the son of Nun Joshua. And Moses sent them to spy out the land of Canaan, and said unto them: 'Get you up here into the South, and go up into the mountains; 18 and see the land, what it is; and the people that dwelleth therein, whether they are strong or weak, whether they 19 are few or many; and what the land is that they dwell in, whether it is good or bad; and what cities they are that

the names of their servants as a mark of special affection and favor (Gen. 41.45; Dan. 1.7). According to the Rabbis, Moses named him Joshua on this occasion, implying the prayer "God save thee from the wicked council of the spies" (Sotah 34b).

17. *Get you up here*] As though Moses pointed in the direction which they were to take. The word זה may be used as an enclitic, "go up then". Ibn Ezra (also A. V. and R. V.) supplies דרך, "this way".

into the South] Of Canaan, although north from the place where they were then encamped. Negeb (South), from a root meaning to be dry, parched (BDB), is the name given to the district south of Hebron to Kadesh in Judah and from the Dead Sea westward to the Mediterranean. Although not well supplied with water, lying between the cultivated land and the desert, the Negeb was a fertile district, especially good for pasture. It was inhabited by the Amalekites (v. 29) and the Canaanites (Judg. 1.9). It included 29 cities, besides villages, and was originally assigned to Judah, but later a part of it was given to Simeon (Josh. 15.21–32; 19.1–8). The Rabbis explain that Moses sent the spies first to the Negeb, the poorest part of Palestine, after the custom of the traders, who first show their ordinary wares and then the more valuable (Tan. Shelah, 12).

into the mountains] The mountainous region, as opposed to the plain, referring to the hilly country of the Amorites (Deut. 1.20; comp. Num. 14.40, 44).

18. *and see the land*] A general statement, followed by specific data. The "land" includes both the soil and the inhabitants of the country. The specific statements cover: a) the people; b) the climate; c) the fortifications of the towns; d) the fertility of the soil (Luzzatto).

they dwell in, whether in camps, or in strongholds; and 20
what the land is, whether it is fat or lean, whether there
is wood therein, or not. And be ye of good courage, and
bring of the fruit of the land.'—Now the time was the
time of the first-ripe grapes.—So they went up, and spied 21
out the land from the wilderness of Zin unto Rehob, at
the entrance to Hamath. And they went up into the 22
South, and came unto Hebron; and Ahiman, Sheshai,
and Talmai, the children of Anak, were there.—Now

19. *in camps*] Whether the cities are open villages or hamlets
(not necessarily nomadic camps, ibn Ezra) or fortified with walls.

20. *of good courage*] Courage may be needed since the suspicion of the inhabitants may be aroused. The word, however, may
signify simply exertion, effort (Gen. 48.2) or care (Deut. 12.23).

time of the first-ripe grapes] Probably about the middle of July.

21. *from the wilderness of Zin*] Part of the wilderness of Paran,
although some regard this as a district outside of Paran, part of the
country which they were to investigate. The spies, according to this
description, traversed practically the whole of Canaan, from south
(wilderness of Zin) to north. Rehob or Beth-rehob is in the north of
Palestine in the province of the tribe of Asher (Josh. 19.28; Judg. 1.31;
18.28). Hamath is identified with the northern limit of the Israelitish
territory (34.8; Josh. 13.5; Amos 6.14) and "the entrance of Hamath"
has been identified by some with a well-known pass, formed by a
depression between Lebanon and Hermon, described as "a vast and
lofty mountain-cleft 8 or 9 miles wide" (Gray, and references given
there).

22. *And they went up*] Some critics regard this as part of a different
version of the story, because of the several variations (see Holzinger,
Gray).

and came] The Hebrew text has "he came" (also Targum, but not
other versions). The Rabbis make it refer to Caleb (with reference to
Deut. 1.36), to whom the district was subsequently assigned (Josh.
15.13–19).

the children of Anak] Anak was a gentilic name, borne by a tribe
of "long-necked" men, an early giant people living about Hebron and

Hebron was built seven years before Zoan in Egypt.—

23 And they came unto the valley of Eshcol, and cut down

in Philistia (BDB). The descendants of these people were scattered
among the various principalities of Canaan and did not form an independent state. The three names mentioned here were probably names
of families or clans (Luzzatto) of the tribe which inhabited Hebron at
that time (see Hastings, *Dictionary of the Bible*, s. v.). Targum has
"children of the powerful".

Now Hebron was built seven years before Zoan in Egypt] To indicate
the antiquity of Hebron, that it was built even before the ancient city
of Zoan in Egypt. Zoan has been identified with the ancient Tanis
(see Targum) and the modern San, in the eastern part of the Delta,
near the coast of Lake Menzaleh. The date of the first building of
Tanis is given as earlier than 2000 B.C.E. Some think that the reference here is to the rebuilding of the town in the 19th dynasty, which
would coincide with the period preceding the Exodus (Gray).

Hebron, famous in biblical history, is about 17 miles southwest of
Jerusalem. Its ancient name was Kiriath-arba (Gen. 23.2), "the city
of Arba", the progenitor of the Anakim, or possibly "the city of the
four," referring to Arba and his three sons, mentioned here. Modern
critics explain the name as "Four-towns" (Tetrapolis), implying that
the city had four quarters, occupied by four confederate clans, which
may also be the meaning of Hebron (confederacy; Selbie in Hastings,
Dictionary of the Bible, s. v.). The Rabbis see in the "four" a reference
to Adam and the three patriarchs, said to be buried in the Cave of
Machpelah in Hebron.

The antiquity of the city, which is here emphasized, is also mentioned
by Josephus (*Ant.* i.8.3), who says in another place (*B. J.* iv.9.7)
that it was the oldest city in Palestine, older even than Memphis in
Egypt, and that its age, in his days, was 2300 years. Abraham bought
there a plot of ground for the burial of Sarah (Gen. 23.2). The sons of
Anak were driven out from Hebron and its environs by Caleb to whom
the district was given (Josh. 14.12; 15.14).

Ehrlich suggests a novel rendering here: "Now Hebron took seven
years to build, and it was built before Zoan in Egypt", indicating that
it was a large town, since it took such a long period to build, and also
that it was an ancient town, having been built before the ancient city
of Tanis in Egypt.

23. *the valley of Eshcol*] This valley or wady has not been identi-

from thence a branch with one cluster of grapes, and they
bore it upon a pole between two; they took also of the
pomegranates, and of the figs.—That place was called 24
the valley of Eshcol, because of the cluster which the
children of Israel cut down from thence.—And they 25
returned from spying out the land at the end of forty
days. And they went and came to Moses, and to Aaron, 26
and to all the congregation of the children of Israel, unto
the wilderness of Paran, to Kadesh; and brought back

fied, but it must have been in the vicinity of Hebron, known for its
rich vines and orchards (comp. Gen. 14.13 where Eshcol is mentioned
as the brother of Mamre and Aner, the allies of Abraham). The word,
the etymology of which is uncertain, means cluster, usually of grapes
(BDB). LXX adds here "and they spied it out".

and they bore it] Because of its weight; although there was only one
cluster of grapes on the branch, it required two persons to carry it
between them on a pole (comp. Sotah 34a, an exaggerated speculation
as to the weight of the cluster of grapes).

24. *was called*] Not passive but impersonal, "any one called". The
name may have been given to the place because of Eshcol (Gen. 14.13),
even as the neighboring grove was called the grove of Mamre, but
now an additional significance was given to the name on account of
this incident.

25–33. RETURN OF SPIES AND THEIR REPORT.

The spies return and deliver their report to Moses, Aaron and the
congregation of Israel. The land, they say, is indeed all that they were
told about it, but it is difficult to subdue because of the great power
of its inhabitants and the strong fortifications around the cities. Caleb's
attempt at silencing them is of no avail. They persist in expressing
their fear of the great and terrible men whom they saw there.

26. *to Kadesh*] Kadesh-barnea (32.8), identified with 'Ain Kadish,
50 miles south of Beer-sheba (see Trumbull's *Kadesh Barnea*, Phila.,
1884, for a full description of this place).

word unto them, and unto all the congregation, and
27 showed them the fruit of the land. And they told him,
and said: 'We came unto the land whither thou sentest
us, and surely it floweth with milk and honey; and this
28 is the fruit of it. Howbeit the people that dwell in the
land are fierce, and the cities are fortified, and very great;
29 and moreover we saw the children of Anak there. Amalek

unto them] I. e. Moses and Aaron.

27. *And they told him*] Turning to Moses who had sent them and
to whom they felt responsible.

and surely] Your (Moses') description of the land (Ex. 3.17) is
quite correct and agrees with the facts as we have seen them, and here
is the evidence, pointing to the fruit which they brought with them.
The phrase "flowing with milk and honey" is often used to denote the
promised land, denoting fertility and natural resources.

28. *Howbeit*] Ramban makes the use of this qualifying expression
the real sin of the spies. Their statements in themselves were quite
true, but the emphasis which they laid upon the difficulties, slurring
over the attractive features of the land in a few words, constituted
their main offence (comp. Luzzatto).

fierce] Implying both great strength and great cruelty.

very great] Although there were hardly any large towns in Canaan
at that time, they appeared very large to the Israelitish nomads (Herxheimer).

29. This verse may be the continuation of the report, in illustration
of the many obstacles that were in the way (Ramban), or it may be a
parenthetical sentence added by the chronicler in further explanation
of v. 28 (Gray). The enumeration of the various tribes that dwelt at
every point of entry, begins with the nearest point, the Negeb, where
the Amalekites dwelt, "an Arabian Nomad tribe, occupying the vast
desert region between Sinai on the South and the southern borders of
Palestine on the north" (Hastings, *Dictionary of the Bible*, s. v.), of
whose prowess they already had evidence at Rephidim (Ex. 17.8–11).
The other tribes mentioned here as living in the mountainous part of
the land are frequently confused with one another in the Bible, the
Amorites apparently being the most powerful and the largest among
them. The Canaanites dwelt on the coastland of Phoenicia and in the

dwelleth in the land of the South; and the Hittite, and
the Jebusite, and the Amorite, dwell in the mountains;
and the Canaanite dwelleth by the sea, and along by the
side of the Jordan.' And Caleb stilled the people toward 30
Moses, and said: 'We should go up at once, and possess
it; for we are well able to overcome it.' But the men that 31
went up with him said: 'We are not able to go up against
the people; for they are stronger than we.' And they 32

valley of the Jordan (comp. 14.25, 45). No mention is made of the
people occupying the north, since this was too far and inaccessible
(Ramban).

30. *And Caleb stilled the people*] ויהס is a denominative verb from
the interjection הס (hush), "and Caleb said to them: Hush!" (ibn
Ezra).

toward Moses] In respect to the complaints against Moses, or he
silenced the people so that they might listen to Moses (Sforno).

We should go up at once] We shall succeed in going up and crossing
the border even though it be surrounded by powerful tribes and fortified by natural defenses; and having entered, we shall indeed conquer
the land, even though its inhabitants are such powerful men (Malbim).

overcome it] The land, or "them", the inhabitants. Joshua took no
part in this first report because, being so closely associated with Moses,
he thought that his testimony would be discredited (Luzzatto, Ehrlich).

31. *We are not able*] To prevail against the people inhabiting the
land; or, we are not able even to go up and cross the border, much less
to conquer the land.

32. After they presented their report to Moses, Aaron and the
congregation of the children of Israel (v. 26), and gave their own
opinion as to the feasibility of an attack, the spies turned to the masses
of the people and aroused their fears by elaborating still further on
the extraordinary strength of the inhabitants of Canaan and on the
unsuitability of the land for a people like the Israelites. Modern biblical scholars discover in this a different version of the same narrative,
containing a number of important variations, which has been fused
with the former by a later editor.

spread an evil report of the land which they had spied
out unto the children of Israel, saying: 'The land, through
which we have passed to spy it out, is a land that eateth
up the inhabitants thereof; and all the people that we
33 saw in it are men of great stature. And there we saw the
Nephilim, the sons of Anak, who come of the Nephilim;
and we were in our own sight as grasshoppers, and so we
were in their sight.'

an evil report]   The expression מוציא דבה used here is usually applied
to a false report, while the expression מביא דבה (Gen. 37.2) refers to a
true report (Ramban, ibn Ezra, BDB, p. 179).

that eateth up the inhabitants thereof]   Does not produce enough to
support them, hence in contradiction to v. 27, the statement they
made to Moses (Gray).   The fact that this is followed immediately by
the statement that the people there are strong and large has led to the
explanation that only the very powerful are able to subsist there,
while the weak cannot survive in the pestilential climate (Sforno,
Luzzatto, comp. Ramban).   Another interpretation is that the land is
indeed very fruitful and highly desirable, but that for this very reason
it is so dangerous to settle there, because it is an apple of discord among
the surrounding tribes, "and as the different nations strove for its
possession, its inhabitants wasted away" through constant warfare
(Keil and references given by him).   For the idiomatic expression,
comp. Lev. 26.38; Ezek. 36.13.

33.   *the Nephilim*]   In still further exaggeration of the description
of the terrible inhabitants of the land, the spies add that the children
of Anak, mentioned before (vv. 22, 28), were really Nephilim, i. e.
demigods (Gen. 6.4), supernatural beings, not merely men of great
strength (Ramban).   LXX omits "the sons of Anak who come from
the Nephilim".   The exact meaning of the term Nephilim and its
etymology are very uncertain, and different interpretations and conjectures have been suggested by modern scholars.   It is possibly a relic
of ancient folklore as is suggested by the only other passage in which
it is found (Gen. 6.4).

as grasshoppers]   In comparison with them we appeared to ourselves
as grasshoppers, and from their contemptuous treatment of us, it

And all the congregation lifted up their voice, and **14**
cried; and the people wept that night. And all the children 2
of Israel murmured against Moses and against Aaron;
and the whole congregation said unto them: 'Would
that we had died in the land of Egypt! or would we had
died in this wilderness! And wherefore doth the LORD 3

appeared that they also regarded us as such (cf. Isa. 40.22). It is suggested that the phrase is intended to explain why the giants permitted
them to leave the land unhurt, because they looked upon them as
insignificant and unworthy of notice (Sforno).

CHAPTER 14.

1–6. THE PEOPLE DISCOURAGED BY THE REPORT OF THE SPIES.

On hearing the report of the spies, the people become discouraged
and begin to complain against Moses and Aaron for taking them out
of Egypt to become a prey to the inhabitants of Canaan. They even
plan to return to Egypt and subject themselves again to Pharaoh.
Moses and Aaron are dismayed, while Joshua and Caleb try to reassure
the people, but the people will not listen to them and even attempt
violence against Joshua and Caleb.

1. *lifted up their voices, and cried*] In the Hebrew text, "their
voices" is the object of both verbs (נתן קול means to cry, Gen. 45.2;
ibn Ezra).

and the people wept] The larger unit, as opposed to עדה, which may
refer to the representatives of the people (Rashi).

2. *murmured*] Expressed vehement dissatisfaction (Ex. 15.24;
17.3).

the whole congregation] Perhaps the chosen representatives, who
dared speak openly to Moses and Aaron, while the others murmured
by themselves.

Would that we had died] All this trouble and privation that we had
gone through was all for nought. We should rather have met death in
Egypt or in the wilderness than be delivered into the hands of these

bring us unto this land, to fall by the sword? Our wives
and our little ones will be a prey; were it not better for
4 us to return into Egypt?' And they said one to another:
'Let us make a captain, and let us return into Egypt.'
5 Then Moses and Aaron fell on their faces before all the
assembly of the congregation of the children of Israel.
6 And Joshua the son of Nun and Caleb the son of Jephunneh,
who were of them that spied out the land, rent their clothes.
7 And they spoke unto all the congregation of the children
of Israel, saying: 'The land, which we passed through to
8 spy it out, is an exceeding good land. If the LORD delight

terrible giants. In other places (Ex. 14.11; Num. 20.4) the preference
is made for death in Egypt to death in the wilderness, but here they
express their preference for death in either place rather than at
the hands of the Canaanites whom they were led to believe that they
would easily conquer.

3. *to fall by the sword*] Comp. Deut. 1.27, "Because the Lord
hateth us, He hath brought us forth out of the land of Egypt to deliver
us into the hand of the Amorites to destroy us."

were it not better] If this be the purpose of God, it would be better
if we escape now, while there is yet time, and return to Egypt. Moses
and Aaron are, of course, held responsible for the design which God
had concerning the people.

4. *Let us make a captain*] Other than Moses, who would agree to
take us back to Egypt (comp. Neh. 9.27). Ehrlich translates: "Let
us turn our heads and return to Egypt".

5. *fell on their faces*] In supplication before the people, entreating
them not to carry out their evil plan (Deut. 1.29; cf. 50.18; Ramban),
or out of sheer despondency and helplessness, realizing that argument
would accomplish nothing (Sforno), or indicating a desire to speak
and explain matters (as in 16.22; Luzzatto), or in prayer to God, asking
Him to intercede (Keil).

6. *rent their clothes*] In grief and distress. Tearing of garments
was a mark of grief and is still preserved in the custom of *Keri'ah* in
the case of the death of a near relative.

in us, then He will bring us into this land, and give it unto
us—a land which floweth with milk and honey. Only 9
rebel not against the LORD, neither fear ye the people of
the land; for they are bread for us; their defence is removed

7–9. REPORT OF JOSHUA AND CALEB.

Joshua and Caleb endeavor to pacify the people by refuting the
chief objections raised by the other spies. They emphasize the assertion
made by the spies themselves in their first report to Moses (13.27)
about the good qualities of the land and add that if they will only show
the proper confidence and faith in God, they will surely succeed in
taking possession of the land.

9. *only rebel not against the Lord*] The very expression of your
fear constitutes rebellion against God, as if you expected to conquer
the land by your own powers. After you have seen the wonders that
He did for you in connection with the exodus from Egypt, you ought
to know that He would help you in case of need (Ramban). The reference may also be to their threat to return to Egypt, against the plan
of God for them.

neither fear ye] Leeser, following Mendelssohn, has: "and then ye
need not fear", i. e. if you do not rebel against God, you need not fear
the people of the land.

for they are bread for us] We can consume them as easily as one eats
bread (Ps. 14.4; 53.4). Targum paraphrases: "Behold, they are delivered into our hands".

their defence is removed] Lit. "their shadow" (Leeser). In a hot
climate, the shadow is regarded as the greatest protection and when
the shadow is removed one remains exposed to all dangers (Luzzatto;
comp. Targum, "their strength"). It may also imply that the gods of
the Canaanites have removed their protection from them, while our
God is with us (Deut. 32.30, 31; Gray, McNeile). Frazer connects this
phrase with the superstition in vogue during the middle ages that the
fate of a person is sealed if his shadow lacks the head. The meaning
here would then be that their fate is already sealed (*Golden Bough*, I,
285–292). This superstition has survived in the popular notion about
seeing one's headless shadow on *Hosha'ana Rabba*. Abarbanel ingeniously connects this with the manna, of which it is said "as the sun

from over them, and the LORD is with us; fear them not.'
10 But all the congregation bade stone them with stones,
when the glory of the LORD appeared in the tent of meeting
unto all the children of Israel.

11   And the LORD said unto Moses: 'How long will this
people despise Me? and how long will they not believe
in Me, for all the signs which I have wrought among them?
12 I will smite them with the pestilence, and destroy them,

waxed hot, it melted" (Ex. 16.21), and renders this verse: "for they
are like unto our bread (manna) when the shadow is removed from it",
i. e. when the sun shines upon it.

10. *bade stone them*]   Contemplated to stone Joshua and Caleb,
and perhaps also Moses and Aaron.

when the glory of the Lord]   The cloud of glory, usually a fiery appearance, which indicated the presence of God (Ex. 24.16, 17).

11–38.   GOD'S ANGER AROUSED.   MOSES INTERCEDES.

Angered at the rebelliousness of the people, God threatens to destroy
them all in a pestilence and make of Moses a great nation. Moses
intercedes in their behalf, first on the ground that it would reflect
unfavorably on the glory of God among the nations and then on the
ground of God's mercy and forgiveness. God relents and pardons,
but the generation of the Exodus who saw God's wonders and still
had no faith, must die in the wilderness. Only their children will be
permitted to enter the promised land. The spies themselves are condemned to die in a plague forthwith.

11. *How long*]   An expression of impatience and indignation
(Ex. 10.3; 16.28).

despise Me]   Leeser:"provoke", better perhaps would be "contemn"
(as in Isa. 1.4), spurn.

for all the signs]   In spite of all the signs and wonders which I have
worked in their midst.

12. *and destroy them*]   R. V. has "disinherit them", but our rendering is more acceptable (as in Ex. 15.9; BDB, p. 440).

and will make of thee a nation greater and mightier than
they.' And Moses said unto the LORD: 'When the Egyp-   13
tians shall hear—for Thou broughtest up this people in
Thy might from among them—they will say to the inhabi-   14
tants of this land, who have heard that Thou LORD art in
the midst of this people; inasmuch as Thou LORD art seen
face to face, and Thy cloud standeth over them, and
Thou goest before them, in a pillar of cloud by day, and
in a pillar of fire by night; now if Thou shalt kill this people   15
as one man, then the nations which have heard the fame

and will make of thee]   And thereby fulfill the promise made to the
patriarchs (Gen. 12.2; 18.18, Rashi). The same thought is also expressed
in Ex. 32.10 and Deut. 9.14. LXX and Sam. have "thee and thy
father's house".

13.   *shall hear*]   That Thou hast destroyed the Israelites (Rashi).

for Thou broughtest up]   A parenthetic phrase. Rashi, followed by
other Jewish commentators, renders: "from the midst of whom Thou
hast brought up with Thy might this people", a phrase explanatory
of "the Egyptians". The broken construction of this verse is ascribed
by some to the great emotion which stirred Moses on hearing God's
verdict.

14.   *they will say*]   The Egyptians, who have *seen* all of God's
wonders in behalf of Israel, will say to the Canaanites, the inhabitants
of this land, who have *heard* what God has done for Israel, what follows
in v. 16 (Luzzatto).

who have heard]   "Who" is not in the Hebrew text.

face to face]   Plainly, lit. eye to eye.

standeth]   When they encamp.

goest]   When on the march.

Vv. 13 and 14 are not very clear and are regarded by modern scholars
as composed of a series of glosses, while the main plea of Moses really
begins with v. 15.

15.   *as one man*]   Without exception (Judg. 6.16), or, suddenly,
all at one time (Rashi).

the nations]   The Egyptians as well as the Canaanites and other
nations.

16 of Thee will speak, saying: Because the LORD was not
able to bring this people into the land which He swore
unto them, therefore He hath slain them in the wilderness.
17 And now, I pray Thee, let the power of the LORD be great,
18 according as Thou hast spoken, saying: The LORD is
slow to anger, and plenteous in lovingkindness, forgiving
iniquity and transgression, and that will by no means

16. *because the Lord was not able*] Those nations who have heard
of the manifestations of God's love for Israel, when they see that He
suddenly destroys them all, will naturally conclude that it is not because of His dislike for them, but because of His inability to carry out
the promise which He made to them (Rashbam, Luzzatto; comp.
Deut. 9.28).

He hath slain them] שחט is usually applied to the slaughter of animals,
but also to the wanton slaughter of human beings (Judg. 12.6).

17. *let the power of the Lord be great*] By the exercise of the quality
of mercy and forgiveness, through which His name and His power
will become great among the nations. The power of complete forgiveness is peculiar to God alone (Ps. 130.4), because men even if they
forgive an offence against them are unable to forget entirely (Ehrlich).
Leeser, following Mendelssohn, renders: "Let the greatness of the
power of the Lord be manifest".

according as Thou hast spoken] Ex. 34.6, 7, here somewhat abbreviated, comp. Ex. 20.5.

18. Moses did not ask for complete forgiveness of the people's
sin, which he also regarded as most reprehensible. If summary punishment is not to be meted out to them, it will be only because the glory
of God's name may suffer (comp. Ezek. 36.18–28; 39.21–29). Justice
will be attained and God's glory preserved if the punishment which
they rightly deserve is postponed and is not summarily carried out at
one time. The first phrase in Ex. 34.6, "merciful and gracious", is
therefore omitted here, and the quotation begins with "slow to anger",
i. e. long-suffering, to indicate that he prayed only for the postpone-
ment of the punishment and not for its entire removal. The response
(v. 20) is thus in accord with the prayer (Ramban).

clear the guilty; visiting the iniquity of the fathers upon
the children, upon the third and upon the fourth generation. Pardon, I pray Thee, the iniquity of this people 19
according unto the greatness of Thy lovingkindness, and
according as Thou hast forgiven this people, from Egypt
even until now.' And the LORD said: 'I have pardoned 20
according to thy word. But in very deed, as I live—and 21
all the earth shall be filled with the glory of the LORD—
surely all those men that have seen My glory, and My 22
signs, which I wrought in Egypt and in the wilderness,
yet have put Me to proof these ten times, and have not

19. *Thy lovingkindness*] Even though they be unworthy of forgiveness.

even until now] Leeser has "hitherto". The word הנה may be used
in a temporal as well as a spatial sense (ibn Ezra; BDB).

20. *according to thy word*] In agreement with thy pleading. God
thus promises that He will not smite the people at one time (v. 12),
but will be long-suffering with them, although the guilt must be expiated (Ramban).

21. *as I live*] The usual expression is "as the Lord liveth" (Judg.
8.19, et al.), but this form is also found (Deut. 32.40; Isa. 49.18 et al;
comp. Gen. 22.16).

and all the earth shall be filled] Parenthetical clause, meaning the
whole earth shall be filled with the glory of the Lord and this demands
the punishment of these men, so that the standards of justice be maintained (Luzzatto). The more usual rendering makes this clause a
second part of the oath, "as I live and as the glory of the Lord, etc."
(Rashi, ibn Ezra, R. V., Leeser, et al.), but the grammatical construction favors our rendering (comp. Ramban).

22. *surely*] Introducing the following statement regarding which
the oath is taken. A. V. and R. V., "because"; Leeser, "that".

put Me to proof] Tested Me, because of lack of faith. A. V., R. V.
and Leeser have "tempted".

these ten times] Many times, a round number (Gen. 31.41; Lev.
26.26; Job 19.3). The Rabbis ('Arak. 15a) enumerate ten instances

23 hearkened to My voice; surely they shall not see the land
which I swore unto their fathers, neither shall any of them
24 that despised Me see it. But My servant Caleb, because
he had another spirit with him, and hath followed Me
fully, him will I bring into the land whereinto he went;
25 and his seed shall possess it. Now the Amalekite and the

when Israel tested God: twice at the Red Sea (Ex. 14.11; Ps. 106.7);
twice in demanding water (Ex. 15.23; 17.2); twice, food (Ex. 16.20, 27);
twice, flesh (Ex. 16.3; Num. 11.4), once in the case of the golden calf
(Ex. 32), and once in the present instance of the spies.

23. *surely they shall not see*] After an oath, expressed or merely
implied, אם becomes an emphatic negative and אם לא an emphatic
affirmative (II Sam. 11.11; Gen. 14.32; Rashi, Sforno, BDB, p. 50).

that despised Me] Spurned Me (v. 11), even though they belong to
the second generation (ibn Ezra, Sforno, see Ramban). LXX adds
before this phrase: "but as for their children who are here with Me, as
many as have not known good and evil, every one that is young and
inexperienced, to them will I give this land" (v. 31; Deut. 1.39).

24. *My servant Caleb*] See note to 12.7.

because] Leeser has "as a reward". The word עקב means in consequence of, as a result of, but may also mean reward, gain (Ps. 19.12;
Prov. 22.4; BDB).

another spirit with him] Different from that actuating the other
spies (cf. 27.18). The Rabbis explain that Caleb had made the other
spies believe that he was with them in their plot, while he had "another
spirit with God", i. e. he wished to learn of their plans so as to be able
to frustrate them more intelligently (Num. R. 16.11; Sotah 34b).

whereinto he went] The land which he spied out, i. e. Hebron and
the neighboring country, which was later given to him by Joshua
(Josh. 14.6–14).

shall possess it] As if it were written יְרִשֶׁנָּה (BDB, comp. 33.53), or
he shall transmit it to his seed (Kimhi). The omission of Joshua here is
explained by modern critics on the ground that this belongs to a version in which Caleb alone took up the defense of the land. Ramban
explains the omission on the ground that since Joshua was destined
to take the place of Moses, no special mention of him was deemed
necessary.

Canaanite dwell in the Vale; to-morrow turn ye, and get you into the wilderness by the way to the Red Sea.'

25. The first clause of this verse seems to be inserted here for the purpose of indicating the difficulties that they would encounter should they attempt to proceed in opposition to God's will. The presence of these tribes as an obstacle in the way of the invaders was mentioned before by the spies themselves (13.29 and note). This clause is omitted in Deut. 1.40, where the rest of the narrative is repeated.

The difficulty lies also in the fact that while here both the Amalekites and the Canaanites are described as dwelling in the valley, according to 13.29 the Amalekites occupied the Negeb, while the Canaanites dwelt along the sea and the Jordan. On the other hand, according to vv. 43, 45, both the Amalekites and the Canaanites dwelt in the mountains. The suggestion is made that עמק here does not mean a broad valley, but a deep place, a declivity in the mountain, and הר in 43, 45 denotes a hilly country rather than a mountain (Gray). Ehrlich suggests the emendation here of ובהר instead of מחר, so that the passage would indicate that they dwelt both in the valley and on the hill (see Kahana and note to v. 45). Keil says: "The valley is no doubt the broad Wady Murreh, including a portion of the Negeb, in which the Amalekites led a nomad life, whilst the Canaanites really dwelt upon the mountain, close up to Wady Murreh".

to-morrow turn ye] They are advised to turn back into the wilderness in the direction of the Red Sea, a southeasterly route, and not to attempt any rash attack upon the inhabitants of the land, while God's favor was not with them.

26–38. PUNISHMENT DECREED UPON THE PEOPLE.

After having replied to Moses' plea in a general way, God directs Moses and Aaron to deliver to the people the detailed message regarding the punishment decreed upon them. All are condemned to wander about in the wilderness for a period of forty years, until all those above the age of twenty, with the exception of Caleb and Joshua, have died. Their children will be permitted to enter the promised land. The spies themselves are condmened to die in a plague at once. Some critics regard this section as belonging immediately after v. 10, while 11–25 is regarded as an insertion from another account of the narrative.

26 And the LORD spoke unto Moses and unto Aaron,
27 saying: 'How long shall I bear with this evil congregation,
that keep murmuring against Me? I have heard the
murmurings of the children of Israel, which they keep
28 murmuring against Me. Say unto them: As I live, saith
the LORD, surely as ye have spoken in Mine ears, so will
29 I do to you: your carcasses shall fall in this wilderness,
and all that were numbered of you, according to your
whole number, from twenty years old and upward, ye
30 that have murmured against Me; surely ye shall not

27. *How long shall I bear*] The verb is not expressed but is to be
supplied from v. 19. Some such word as אשא or אסלח should be understood here. Another interpretation is "How long shall this evil congregation murmur against Me" with impunity (see Gray, note).
Delitzsch suggests the insertion of לי before לעדה and translates: How
long will I have to bother with this wicked congregation! (comp. Hos.
14.9).

this evil congregation] Referring to the whole of Israel and not
merely to the spies (Luzzatto, as against Rashi).

that keep murmuring] Some critics omit this clause, regarding it a
dittography from the second half of the verse (Delitzsch, Gray). For
the expression, comp. Ex. 16.8, 9, 12.

28. *Say unto them*] Sing. referring to Moses, although the revelation is made to both Moses and Aaron.

As I live] Introducing an oath, as in v. 21.

saith the Lord] An expression frequently found in the prophetic
books. In the Torah it is found only here and in Gen. 22.16.

as ye have spoken] Vv. 2, 3.

29. *your carcasses*] A contemptuous term when applied to men
(Lev. 26.30; Ezek. 6.5); A. V. and R. V. "dead bodies".

all that were numbered] In the census described in ch. 1, excluding
the Levites who were not included in that census (1.47), but were
numbered in a later census (3.40).

30. *surely ye shall not come*] See note to v. 23.

come into the land, concerning which I lifted up My
hand that I would make you dwell therein, save Caleb
the son of Jephunneh, and Joshua the son of Nun. But 31
your little ones, that ye said would be a prey, them will
I bring in, and they shall know the land which ye have
rejected. But as for you, your carcasses shall fall in this 32
wilderness. And your children shall be wanderers in the 33
wilderness forty years, and shall bear your strayings,
until your carcasses be consumed in the wilderness. After 34
the number of the days in which ye spied out the land,
even forty days, for every day a year, shall ye bear your

I lifted up My hand] I swore. The expression points to a custom
of raising the hand towards heaven while taking an oath (Ex. 6.8;
Deut. 32.40).

31. *that ye said*] V. 3, comp. Deut. 1.39.

them shall I bring] Into the land.

which ye have rejected] We do not find in the report of the spies or
in the complaints of the people any aspersion against the land, with
the possible exception of 13.32. (See note ad loc.; cf. Ps. 106.24).

33. *wanderers*] Following LXX and Vulgate, suggesting perhaps חועים
or נעים (Geiger, *Urschrift*, p. 283). The Hebrew text has רעים shepherds,
i. e. they will live as nomads in the wilderness, wandering about with
their flocks from place to place (Rashbam, ibn Ezra; comp. Targum).

shall bear your strayings] Leeser has "backslidings"; R. V. has
"whoredoms", a figure often used by the prophets to indicate dis-
loyalty to God. A word such as "the result of" or "consequence of"
your strayings is understood here (comp. Targum, "your guilt").
Their children, although they will enter the land, will also suffer in
so far as they will have to wait for forty years for the happy moment
when they might enter the land of promise.

until your carcasses be consumed] Or, until the number of your
dead is completed (Mendelssohn).

34. *ye spied out*] Through your representatives, the spies.

iniquities, even forty years, and ye shall know My dis-
35 pleasure. I the LORD have spoken, surely this will I do
unto all this evil congregation, that are gathered together
against Me; in this wilderness they shall be consumed,
36 and there they shall die.' And the men, whom Moses
sent to spy out the land, and who, when they returned,
made all the congregation to murmur against him, by
37 bringing up an evil report against the land, even those
men that did bring up an evil report of the land, died by
38 the plague before the LORD. But Joshua the son of Nun,
and Caleb the son of Jephunneh, remained alive of those

My displeasure] You will then experience what it means when I
am displeased and remove My protection from you. Rashi renders:
"Ye shall know what it means when you incite people to oppose Me";
Targum and Syr. have: "your murmurings against Me"; LXX, "My
anger"; Vulgate, "My vengeance"; R. V., "My alienation" (the revok-
ing of My promise). BDB," My opposition".

35. *gathered together*] By appointment, in opposition to God
(comp. 16.11; 27.3).

consumed . . . . die] Both words meaning the same thing. The
Rabbis infer from the repetition that the generation of the wilderness
will have no portion in the world to come (Sanh. 108a; 110b).

36. *made all the congregation to murmur*] Following the *Kere*; the
Ketib is ילונו, "and they murmured together with the whole congregation".

an evil report] Comp. 13.32.

37. *by the plague*] All at one time (ibn Ezra); the expression is
used of a sudden infliction of death ascribed to the direct intervention
of God (17.13–15).

before the Lord] Possibly in front of the tabernacle (Luzzatto), or
decreed by the Lord (Mendelssohn, following Rashi).

38. Joshua is mentioned here before Caleb, also in v. 6; while in
other places (v. 30; 26.65; 32.12; Deut. 1.36, 38) Caleb is mentioned

men that went to spy out the land. And Moses told these 39
words unto all the children of Israel; and the people
mourned greatly. And they rose up early in the morning, 40
and got them up to the top of the mountain, saying: 'Lo,
we are here, and will go up unto the place which the LORD
hath promised; for we have sinned.' And Moses said: 41
'Wherefore now do ye transgress the commandment of

first. There is probably no particular significance in this transposition
(Kaspi, *Mishneh Kesef*, II, p. 259).

39. *these words*] The decree passed upon them, vv. 27–35.

40–45. PEOPLE REPENTANT. DEFEAT AT HORMAH.

The people, dismayed by the severe punishment decreed upon them,
seek to obtain God's favor by a display of faith in an attempt to attack
the border tribes. In spite of the warning given them by Moses, they
make the attack and meet with defeat at the hands of the Amalekites
and the Canaanites by whom they are driven back to Hormah. The
incident is also given in Deut. 1.41–44, but there the Amorites are the
people who drive the Israelites back. These terms were probably
used interchangeably to indicate the pre-Israelitish occupants of the
land.

40. *early in the morning*] As they were told to do (v. 25), but
instead of going backward in the direction of the Red Sea they proceeded forward toward the hilly country to some height in that region.
The "top of the mountain" here cannot refer to the summit of some
definite mountain, for in v. 44 they are said to have made the *attempt*
to go up and in v. 45 the Amalekites and the Canaanites are said to
have "come down" to them. It probably means in the direction of the
mountain, i. e. they made the attempt to proceed in the direction of
the hilly country, the road leading to Canaan (Rashi), when Moses
delivered the warning to them.

Lo, we are here] Prepared to follow the command of God and to
go, with faith in His protection, to the place which He promised to
give to us (comp. 10.29).

we have sinned] In allowing ourselves to be influenced by the spies.

41. *transgress*] Since the order was that they turn back (v. 25).

42 the LORD, seeing it shall not prosper? Go not up, for the
LORD is not among you; that ye be not smitten down
43 before your enemies. For there the Amalekite and the
Canaanite are before you, and ye shall fall by the sword;
forasmuch as ye are turned back from following the LORD,
44 and the LORD will not be with you.' But they presumed
to go up to the top of the mountain; nevertheless the ark
of the covenant of the LORD, and Moses, departed not out
45 of the camp. Then the Amalekite and the Canaanite,
who dwelt in that hill-country, came down, and smote
them and beat them down, even unto Hormah.

  it shall not prosper] Your present scheme will not succeed, although
it would have met with success had you not sinned in rebelling against
God.
  42. *is not among you*] Explains the reason why the present attempt
will not prosper.
  43. *For there*] In the mountain country whither you attempt to
go are the Amalekites and the Canaanites ready to smite you with
the sword.
  forasmuch as] Since you have turned away from the Lord you
cannot expect His protection.
  44. *But they presumed*] Showed presumption in attempting to go
up (Targum, Rashi, Luzzatto, cf. Deut. 1.43). Another rendering is:
"and they went up heedlessly", they manifested lightheadedness and
a sense of irresponsibility in going up (BDB; comp. Ehrlich).
  the ark of the covenant] Omitted in the narrative in Deut. (cf. 10.33).
  45. *in that hill-country*] Comp. note to v. 25. When the tribes
dwelling in the hilly region saw the Israelites approach, they assembled
to give battle.
  Hormah] A royal city of the Canaanites, in the south of Judea, in
the possession of the tribe of Simeon. It is frequently mentioned in
the Bible, but the exact site has not yet been established. According
to 21.3 the name was given to the place when Israel conquered the
Canaanites of Arad and consigned them to destruction. It was originally called Zephath and the name was changed to Hormah when

And the LORD spoke unto Moses, saying: Speak unto ₂ **15**
the children of Israel, and say unto them:

Judah and Simeon (after the death of Joshua) devoted its inhabitants
to destruction (Judg. 1.17; BDB). The word itself probably means
sacred or devoted place and occurs with the article only here. Because
of the article, some take this not as a proper name but as meaning "to
utter destruction" (ibn Ezra). In Deut. 1.44 the pursuit after the
Israelites is described as "from Seir unto Hormah". LXX and Sam.
add here "and they returned to the camp".

Palmer (*Desert of the Exodus*, II, 1, 379) identifies Hormah with
Sebaita or Esbeita, about 25 miles N.N.E. of Kadesh, simply on account of the resemblance in sound between Zephath and Esbeita. This
is opposed by Wooley and Lawrence (*The Wilderness of Zin*, London,
1936, p. 107), who seem inclined to follow ibn Ezra in taking the word
as a common rather than a proper noun.

Harold M. Wiener (*Posthumous Essays*, Oxford, 1932, pp. 37–47)
regards this incident as having occurred subsequent to that related in
21.1–3, where a victory of the Israelites over the King of Arad is
recorded, and the name of Hormah is said to have been given to that
place by the Israelites. He holds that the two incidents were misplaced,
the present attempt at a conquest of Canaan having come subsequent
to the first victory. After the crushing defeat they were obliged to
evacuate the district and wander around Edom to reach Canaan from
a point further north.

CHAPTER 15.

1–41. COLLECTION OF LAWS.

This chapter contains five distinct regulations, not connected in any
way either with the story of the spies preceding it or with the story
of Korah following it. These laws are: 1) 1–16, the exact quantities
of meal, oil and wine that should accompany various animal sacrifices;
2) 17–21, the offering of the *Hallah*, or the first part of the dough;
3) 22–31, offerings to be made by the community or by an individual
to atone for inadvertent sins; 4) 32–36, the penalty for the man who
gathered sticks on the Sabbath day; 5) 37–41, the law about wearing
fringes on the corners of garments.

When ye are come into the land of your habitations,
3 which I give unto you, and will make an offering by fire

1–16. MEAL, OIL AND WINE ACCOMPANYING SACRIFICES.

This section deals with the quantities of meal, oil and wine that are
to be offered in connection with all animal sacrifices. A fixed quantity
of each is prescribed in the case of either a burnt or a peace-offering,
varying with the nature of the sacrifice whether it be a lamb, a ram or
a bullock. In the case of a lamb, the offering shall include 1/10 of an
ephah of flour, 1/4 of a hin of oil and the same quantity of wine; of a
ram, 2/10 of an ephah of flour and 1/3 of a hin of oil and of wine; of a
bullock, 3/10 of an ephah of flour, 1/2 of a hin of oil and of wine. Ezekiel,
in describing the ideal Temple service of the future, has a similar scale,
but the amounts are much larger (see Ezek. 46.5–7, 11, 14). There,
however, the reference is made to the offering of the Prince only, while
here private offerings as well as communal sacrifices are included.
There is no relation between the prescriptions here and in Lev. 2,
where the meal-offering as such is discussed, without any reference to
the oil and wine (Gray as against Kuenen).

W. R. Smith (*Religion of the Semites*, p. 222) says: "When the Hebrew ate flesh, he ate bread with it and drank wine, and when he offered
flesh on the table of his God, it was natural that he should add to it
the same concomitants which were necessary to make up a comfortable
and generous meal".

2. *When ye are come*] I. e. when you begin to lead an agricultural
life, settled in your own land, you shall add to your animal sacrifices
also of the produce of the field and of the orchard, which you could not
do as long as you led a nomad life. This introductory phrase is often
found in connection with laws that presumed a settled, agricultural
life (Lev. 23.10; 25.2; Deut. 12.1; 19.1; comp. Sifre 107). Rashi and
ibn Ezra connect this phrase with the preceding story of the spies.
In order to assure them of the continued relationship between them
and God in spite of their sins, they are given these laws which assume
that the next generation will inherit the land promised to them (cf.
Keil).

habitations] Permanent dwelling places and not camps.

3. *and will make*] Continuation of the condition implied in the
previous verse and not a command (Rashi).

an offering by fire] A general term used for all kinds of sacrifices

unto the LORD, a burnt-offering, or a sacrifice, in fulfilment
of a vow clearly uttered, or as a freewill-offering, or in
your appointed seasons, to make a sweet savour unto the
LORD, of the herd, or of the flock; then shall he that bring-   4
eth his offering present unto the LORD a meal-offering of
a tenth part of an ephah of fine flour mingled with the

burnt on the altar, but more especially in connection with animal
sacrifices.

a burnt-offering, or a sacrifice]   The burnt-offering was burned entirely
on the altar, while of the sacrifice or peace-offering only a portion of
the fat was burned on the altar, and the rest of the animal, after a
portion was given to the priest, could be eaten by the person who
offered the sacrifice (Lev. 1.2–17; 3.1–17).

in fulfilment of a vow clearly uttered]   "In fulfilment of" is not expressed in the Hebrew text. Leeser has "in performing a pronounced vow".
The term לפלא נדר is rendered "to make a votive offering" (BDB;
comp. 6.2; Lev. 27.2). Others render it "to set aside a sacrifice vowed
for or freely offered" (Targum, ibn Ezra).

in your appointed seasons]   Sacrifices offered on Sabbaths and holidays (chs. 28, 29). All kinds of sacrifices are included here except the
thank-offering (Lev. 7.12; 22.29), but even this is not meant to be
excluded from the prescriptions that follow (Sifre 107; Men. 90b).

sweet savour]   An expression often used in connection with sacrifices
and meaning a soothing, tranquilizing odor, which makes them acceptable to God.

of the herd, or of the flock]   Excluding birds (Lev. 5.7; 12.8; Sifre 107;
Men. 90b).

4. *then shall he*]   The conclusion of the condition of vv. 2, 3. When
one offers such a sacrifice as described, he shall bring with it the meal-
offering and the libation, as given below.

tenth part of an ephah]   Or one Omer (Ex. 16.36), about seven pints.
An ephah is a dry measure, containing 3 Seahs; 1 Seah = 6 Kabs;
1 Kab = 4 Logs; 1 Log = 4 quarters (רבע), or the capacity of 6 eggs.
The ephah would be approximately one bushel. The tenth of an ephah
(Ex. 29.40), called עשרון or עמר, was used in the offerings here (Hastings,
Dictionary of the Bible, s. v. Weights and Measures).

5 fourth part of a hin of oil; and wine for the drink-offering,
the fourth part of a hin, shalt thou prepare with the burnt-
6 offering or for the sacrifice, for each lamb. Or for a ram,
thou shalt prepare for a meal-offering two tenth parts
of an ephah of fine flour mingled with the third part of a
7 hin of oil; and for the drink-offering thou shalt present
the third part of a hin of wine, of a sweet savour unto the
8 LORD. And when thou preparest a bullock for a burnt-
offering, or for a sacrifice, in fulfilment of a vow clearly

fourth part of a hin] Hin is a liquid measure containing 12 Logs or
about 1½ gallons, so that one quarter of a hin, or 3 Logs, would be
about 3 pints. The oil was mingled with the flour and burned entirely
upon the altar.

5. *for the drink-offering*] The wine was not poured upon the altar,
according to rabbinic tradition, but placed in silver bowls arranged on
the top of the altar, which were perforated at the bottom, so that the
wine passed through them into corresponding perforations in the altar
and sank into the ground under the altar (Suk. 4.9). Josephus (*Ant.*,
iii.9.4) says that the wine was poured "about the altar" (cf. Ecclus.
50.15, "at the foot of the altar").

for each lamb] Every sacrifice required the stipulated amount.

6. *Or for a ram*] If any of the sacrifices enumerated in v. 3 is
brought in the form of a ram, its meal-offering and libation shall be as
follows. Some of the Rabbis define "lamb" as a male sheep less than
one year old, and "ram" as a male sheep 13 months and one day old,
while others say that a lamb should be one year old and a ram two years
old (Parah 1.3).

7. *thou shalt present*] This rendering is not in accordance with the
traditional cantillation signs. Leeser has: "shalt thou bring, as a sweet
savour", preserving the cantillation signs and at the same time making
it refer to the first half of the verse.

of a sweet savour] Although this expression is usually employed in
connection with animal sacrifices, it may also be used in regard to
wine, which produces a pleasant odor (cf. Ecclus. 50.15).

uttered, or for peace-offerings unto the LORD; then shall ⁹
there be presented with the bullock a meal-offering of
three tenth parts of an ephah of fine flour mingled with
half a hin of oil. And thou shalt present for the drink- ¹⁰
offering half a hin of wine, for an offering made by fire, of
a sweet savour unto the LORD. Thus shall it be done for ¹¹
each bullock, or for each ram, or for each of the he-lambs,
or of the kids. According to the number that ye may ¹²
prepare, so shall ye do for every one according to their
number. All that are home-born shall do these things ¹³
after this manner, in presenting an offering made by fire,
of a sweet savour unto the LORD. And if a stranger sojourn ¹⁴

8. *for   peace-offerings*] Corresponding   to   "freewill-offering"   of
v. 3.

10. *an offering made by fire*] Referring to the meal-offering only
(v. 9) and not to the wine (Rashi), or to the sacrifice as a whole.

11. A general summary of the preceding, enumerating the three
kinds of animals in inverse order — ox, ram, lamb.

he-lambs, or of the kids] Leeser renders more literally: "or for a
lamb, be it of the sheep or of the goats". שׂה is the name given to a
small animal of the sheep or of the goat kind.

12. *according to the number*] The libation and meal-offerings should
be in accordance with the number of sacrifices, each animal requiring
the prescribed measure of flour, oil and wine.

13. *home-born*] I. e. a native Israelite.

14. *a stranger*] "A designate dweller in Israel, possessing certain
conceded, not inherited rights" (BDB). "A man of another tribe or
district who, coming to sojourn in a place where he was not strengthened
by the presence of his own kin, put himself under the protection of a
clan or of a powerful chief" (W. R. Smith, *Religion of the Semites*, 75 ff.).
Comp. Sulzberger, *The Status of Labor in Ancient Israel*, for suggestions as to the origin of the institution of *Ger*.

with you, or whosoever may be among you, throughout
your generations, and will offer an offering made by fire,
of a sweet savour unto the LORD; as ye do, so he shall do.
15 As for the congregation, there shall be one statute both
for you, and for the stranger that sojourneth with you, a
statute for ever throughout your generations; as ye are,
16 so shall the stranger be before the LORD. One law and one
ordinance shall be both for you, and for the stranger that
sojourneth with you.

among you] I. e. if a stranger sojourn with you temporarily or if
he remain with you for the future (*Biur*). Bertholet (quoted by Gray)
renders the two phrases here as follows: If any one sojourn with you
or if any one who does not enjoy the status of the *Ger* be in your midst
at any future time.

15. *As for the congregation*] Leeser has: "Congregation!" regarding
the ה as vocative (I Sam. 17.55, 58; I Kings 18.26; II Kings 9.5; Jer.
2.31; Saadia, Kimhi, followed by Luzzatto and Mendelssohn). Ibn
Ezra, however, takes the ה as a definite article and denies the existence
of a vocative ה in Hebrew (comp. Sifre 109, where this expression is
made to include also women; also Targum-Jonathan קהלא כולא). These
passages, declaring the absolute equality of the native and the stranger
and making the stranger share on an equal footing with the native in
all civil laws and in most of the ceremonial laws, are often repeated in
the Bible (Ex. 12.19, 48; Lev. 16.29; 17.8, 10, 12, 13, 15; 18.26; 20.2;
22.18; 24.16, 22; Num. 15.26, 30; 19.10; 35.15), and indicate the
lofty humanity of the biblical Law.

before the Lord] In the eyes of God all are equal (*Biur*, comp.
Luzzatto).

17–21.   FIRST PART OF DOUGH FOR THE PRIEST.

This section deals with the law regarding the portion of dough that
is to be given to the priest. The law is not very clear here, nor is any
additional light thrown upon it by the two other passages in which
reference is made to it (Ezek. 44.30; Neh. 10.38). The origin of the
term עריסה has not been definitely established, although it is certain

And the LORD spoke unto Moses, saying: Speak unto 17-18 the children of Israel, and say unto them:

When ye come into the land whither I bring you, then 19 it shall be, that, when ye eat of the bread of the land, ye shall set apart a portion for a gift unto the LORD. Of the 20 first of your dough ye shall set apart a cake for a gift; as that which is set apart of the threshing-floor, so shall ye set it apart. Of the first of your dough ye shall give unto 21 the LORD a portion for a gift throughout your generations.

that it is connected with some sort of porridge or paste. The law here would therefore indicate that the first bread of some definite kind of dough, generally used by the Israelites, should be given to the priest. Tradition, however, makes the law apply to all kinds of dough prepared of any of the five species of grain growing in Palestine, namely: wheat, barley, spelt, oats and rye (Hal. 1.1). The portion given to the priest is designated as *Hallah* (cake) and the Rabbis limited the obligation of *Hallah* to a dough of the size of one Omer, enough to fill a vessel of $10 \times 10 \times 3\frac{1}{4}$ inches (Hal. 2.5), of which 1/24 part should go to the priest in the case of private households and 1/48 part in the case of a bakery ('Eduy. 1.7). A whole treatise of the Mishna (Hallah) is devoted to the discussion of the laws that have grown up around this provision.

20. *the first of your dough*] The first part separated from it, before anything is done with it. Some translate "the first of your kneading trough" (BDB).

as that which is set apart of the threshing-floor] See 18.11. This is to be given to the priest, even as the portion of the grain was to be given to him. Rashi interprets: Just as there was no limit set to the portion of the grain that was to be given to the priest, so no limit is set for the *Hallah*.

21. *throughout your generations*] While settled in the land of Canaan (v. 18). This law, however, has been observed in a symbolic manner also after the exile from Palestine, when all agricultural laws fell into desuetude, even to the present time. The Rabbis prescribed that when dough is being prepared for baking, a small portion of it should be thrown into the fire, while a blessing is pronounced, symbolic of this priestly prescription (Hal. 4.8–11).

22   And when ye shall err, and not observe all these com-
     mandments, which the LORD hath spoken unto Moses,
23   even all that the LORD hath commanded you by the hand

22–31. SACRIFICES FOR SINS COMMITTED IN IGNORANCE.

This section deals with the sacrifices that were to be offered in the
case of the inadvertent breaking of any of the laws, either by the whole
congregation (24–26) or by an individual (27–28). This law also applies
equally to the native and to the stranger (29). A deliberate transgression, however, cannot be atoned for by a sacrifice, but the offender
must bear the punishment for his sin (30–31). A more elaborate statement regarding the sacrifices to be offered in case of sins committed
through ignorance or by inadvertence is found in Lev. chapters 4 and 5,
and there are also some differences in the details of the sacrifices. While
here we have only two cases, of an individual and of the congregation,
there two more are given, namely of the high-priest and of the prince.
Another variation is found in the kinds of sacrifices prescribed. While
here the congregation is required to offer a bullock for a burnt-offering
and a he-goat for a sin-offering, in Leviticus no mention is made of a
he-goat and the bullock is ordered to be brought as a sin-offering (Lev.
4.14). Again, in the case of the individual, the prescription here is a
she-goat for a sin-offering, but there either a she-goat or a female lamb
may be brought (Lev. 4.28, 32). The Rabbis try to explain the discrepancy by making the law in Leviticus refer to any kind of sin outside
of idolatry, and the law here to idolatry only (Sifre 113, 114; Hor. 8a).
Some commentators explain the variation by making the law in Leviticus
refer to sins of commission (Lev. 4.2, 13, 22, 27) and the law here (22)
to sins of omission. The whole tenor of this section, however, implies
no such distinction (comp. Ramban, Luzzatto, Keil, Gray).

22. *all these commandments*] This cannot refer to the preceding
two laws of this chapter, but must refer to some collection of laws, to
which this may have been an appendix. This is the view of modern
Bible commentators, by which they explain also the abrupt manner
in which this section is introduced (as compared with vv. 1–2, 17–18).
The Rabbis make this refer to the sin of idolatry, for "he who worships
idols is regarded as if he violated all the laws of God" (Sifre 111).

of Moses, from the day that the LORD gave commandment,
and onward throughout your generations; then it shall be, 24
if it be done in error by the congregation, it being hid from
their eyes, that all the congregation shall offer one young
bullock for a burnt-offering, for a sweet savour unto the
LORD—with the meal-offering thereof, and the drink-
offering thereof, according to the ordinance—and one
he-goat for a sin-offering. And the priest shall make 25
atonement for all the congregation of the children of Israel,

23. *that the Lord gave commandment*] Referring to the revelation
at Mt. Sinai (Rashbam, Sforno) and also all other laws that may in
the future be promulgated by the prophets (Sifre 111, comp. *Biur*).

24. *then it shall be*] The conclusion of vv. 22, 23. In the case of
inadvertent transgressions, a distinction shall be made between communal and individual transgressions.

it being hid] Not expressed in the Hebrew text, but implied by the
context (comp. Lev. 4.13).

according to the ordinance] As prescribed in vv. 9–10. The sin-
offering, however, did not require either meal-offering or libation.

It is rather difficult to conceive of a case when the whole community
should be led astray to transgress *all the laws* of God, or even, as the
Rabbis understood it, to be induced to worship idols without knowing
that they were acting contrary to the will of God. Some make it refer
to a period when the people, led astray by wicked rulers, follow certain
idolatrous customs, which they have come to regard as Jewish because
of the example set before them by their leaders (Keil, comp. Ramban).
The suggestion that עדה here refers to a constituent assembly who
made an error in judgment (Sulzberger, *Law of Homicide*, 15) appears
quite plausible (comp. Rashi).

a sin-offering] Usually the sin-offering comes before the burnt-
offering (as in 6.11, 16; Lev. 5.7), "it being necessary that the sin should
be expiated before the congregation can sanctify its life and efforts
afresh to the Lord in the burnt-offering" (Keil, comp. Rashi; Hor. 13a;
Zeb. 90a, accounting for the defective לחטת).

25. *the priest*] Who happens to officiate at this ceremony.

and they shall be forgiven; for it was an error, and they
have brought their offering, an offering made by fire unto
the LORD, and their sin-offering before the LORD, for their
26 error. And all the congregation of the children of Israel
shall be forgiven, and the stranger that sojourneth among
them; for in respect of all the people it was done in error.
27 And if one person sin through error, then he shall offer
28 a she-goat of the first year for a sin-offering. And the
priest shall make atonement for the soul that erreth, when
he sinneth through error, before the LORD, to make atone-
29 ment for him; and he shall be forgiven, both he that is
home-born among the children of Israel, and the stranger
that sojourneth among them: ye shall have one law for
30 him that doeth aught in error. But the soul that doeth
aught with a high hand, whether he be home-born or a
stranger, the same blasphemeth the LORD; and that soul

shall be forgiven] First because it was an error and then because in
offering the prescribed sacrifices they have indicated their regret and
their desire to return to the worship of God.

26. *in respect of all the people*] Even though the error was made by
the leaders only, the rest of the people, including even the stranger who
followed their example, also needed atonement.

27. *through error*] This also is made to refer to the sin of idolatry
committed by an individual inadvertently, since any other sin in such
a case is atoned for by the offering of a she-goat or of a female sheep
(Lev. 4.27–35, comp. Rashi).

28. *when he sinneth through error*] An explanatory phrase: God
will forgive because it was done through error (v. 25).

30. *with a high hand*] Indicating open and deliberate defiance.
The phrase is also used in the sense of boldness and courage (33.3;
Ex. 14.8). Targum renders בריש גלי, openly, publicly (comp. ibn.
Ezra).

blasphemeth the Lord] He does this in defiance of the Lord and His

shall be cut off from among his people. Because he hath 31
despised the word of the LORD, and hath broken His
commandment; that soul shall utterly be cut off, his
iniquity shall be upon him.

And while the children of Israel were in the wilderness, 32
they found a man gathering sticks upon the sabbath day.

law and therefore cannot atone for his sin except with his life. Because
of the enormity of the sin and the evil example set to others, when
committed in a defiant and open manner, even repentance will not be
accepted in atonement (see Sforno). For the punishment of *Karet*
see note to 9.13.

31. *his iniquity shall be upon him*] The guilt attaching to his
iniquity is upon him, i. e. he brought the punishment upon himself
(ibn Ezra, *Biur*). Others interpret this phrase to mean that he shall
be cut off with the iniquity still attaching to him and unatoned for
(McNeile, but see Rashi).

32–36. INCIDENT OF SABBATH VIOLATION.

This section relates an incident in illustration of a sin committed
with "a high hand". While wandering in the wilderness, the Israelites
came across a man who flagrantly violated the Sabbath by gathering
sticks on that day. Although it was known that Sabbath breaking was
a capital offence (Ex. 31.14, 15; 35.2), Moses and Aaron and the leaders
of the congregation before whom the offender was brought were uncertain as to the exact mode of punishment. The man was placed in
custody until Moses received a message from God ordering the culprit
to be stoned to death. The sentence was carried out without delay
(comp. Lev. 24.10–23, where a similar instance is recorded).

32. *in the wilderness*] No definite place is mentioned (the wilderness of Sinai according to ibn Ezra), nor any specific time given (Iyar
16 or 21 of the first year after the Exodus, Sifre Zuta 32, see Horovitz's
note ad loc. and Malbim).

a man] The Rabbis identified him with Zelophehad (27.3; Sifre
113; Shab. 96b).

gathering sticks] This was considered a violation of the Sabbath
since it implied the breaking up of branches (Shab. 96b).

33 And they that found him gathering sticks brought him
unto Moses and Aaron, and unto all the congregation.
34 And they put him in ward, because it had not been declared
35 what should be done to him. And the LORD said unto
Moses: 'The man shall surely be put to death; all the
congregation shall stone him with stones without the
36 camp.' And all the congregation brought him without

33. *they that found him*] Who caught him in the act and arrested
him on the spot.
all the congregation] The representatives of the community, who
possessed the judicial power (Sifre 113; cf. 9.6).
34. *in ward*] The guard-house in camp (Lev. 24.12). For imprisonment as a mode of preliminary punishment see Sulzberger, *Law of
Homicide*, 131 ff.
it had not been declared] They knew that Sabbath violation was a
capital offence (Ex. 31.14), but they did not know the exact form of
execution in this case (Sifre 114; Sanh. 78b).
35. *shall stone him*] The infinitive alone is used here without the
customary addition of the finite verb (as in Lev. 24.16), and has here
the force of an imperative (Ex. 20.8; Deut. 5.12; comp. Rashi).
without the camp] All executions were carried out outside of the
camp (Lev. 24.14) or outside of the town or village (Sanh. 42b).
36. *all the congregation*] It was a general custom in antiquity to have
the whole community participate in a capital punishment, so as to
have them all share in the responsibility (W. R. Smith, *Religion of the
Semites*, 285). The Rabbis render "in the presence of the whole congregation", the witnesses were to act as the executioners, while the
whole congregation was present (Sifre 114).

37–41. FRINGES (*Zizit*) TO BE ATTACHED TO GARMENTS.

The law about having fringes attached to the four corners of a garment is mentioned in Deut. 22.12, but here the reason is given in detail
that they should serve as constant reminders of the consecration of
Israel to God and to His commandments, while there the reason is not
given. The *Zizit* (fringes) were to serve as a symbol, reminding the
Jew of his affiliation with God and emphasizing his sense of loyalty.

the camp, and stoned him with stones, and he died, as the
LORD commanded Moses.

And the LORD spoke unto Moses, saying: 'Speak unto 37-38
the children of Israel, and bid them that they make them
throughout their generations fringes in the corners of
their garments, and that they put with the fringe of each
corner a thread of blue. And it shall be unto you for a 39
fringe, that ye may look upon it, and remember all the

This section was regarded of such great importance that it was included
in the *Shema‘*, which Jews are to recite morning and evening daily.
It is possible, as some modern critics assume, that this custom of wearing the fringes was of great antiquity and originally had an entirely
different reason, but was later invested with this lofty religious significance (Hastings, *Dictionary of the Bible*, s. v. Fringes). This custom is
mentioned in the N. T. (Mat. 14.36; 9.20; Mark 6.56; Luke 8.14) and
has persisted among the Jews to the present day (see *J. E.* s. v. Arba‘
Kanfot; Fringes). A small garment (*Arba‘ Kanfot*, lit. Four Corners),
with the fringes attached to its four corners, is still worn by many Jews
under the upper garments, while during the morning prayers a larger
scarf (*Tallit*), also having the fringes attached to its four corners, is
worn over the outer garb (comp. ibn Ezra to v. 39, suggesting that
since this law is intended to keep Israel away from sin, the *Tallit* should
be worn all the time and not only during services, when the temptation
to sin is much less).

38. *fringes*] Tassels attached to the flowing ends of garments.
In Deut. 22.12, a different word is used (גדילים), translated "twisted
cords", which is the actual practice to the present day.

a thread of blue] Or violet (BDB), to keep the fringes together (cf.
Ex. 28.28, 37). Because of the difficulty of obtaining the correct shade
of blue required, it was later permitted to use a white thread to twist
the other threads together (Men. 4.1 and ib. 38a; for the present custom, see *J. E.* s. v.).

39. *And it shall be unto you for a fringe*] The thread of blue, after
it is used to fasten the threads, shall itself become one of the fringes,
included in their number. Some take the word here in a different sense
from that of v. 38 and regard it as denoting an ornament, an object

commandments of the LORD, and do them; and that ye
go not about after your own heart and your own eyes,
40 after which ye use to go astray; that ye may remember
and do all My commandments, and be holy unto your
41 God. I am the LORD your God, who brought you out of
the land of Egypt, to be your God: I am the LORD your
God.'

to look at (Saadia, Rashbam), hence Mendelssohn "*Schaufaeden.*"
The tassel is not to serve the superstitious purpose that it had served,
but is to be a reminder of God and His laws (Gray, McNeile). Delitzsch,
99a, suggests the reading לאות instead of לציצת. It is quite possible
that the word *Zizit*, originally meaning fringe, became a technical
expression later, denoting the entire ceremony, and the expression
here may mean that this tassel shall be the *Zizit* that you know of in
connection with your religious ceremonies.

    and remember all the commandments] It should remind you of God's
laws and not of the superstitious fears that it recalled to you before
(Gray, comp. *Biur*).

    to go astray] R. V. "ye use to go a whoring", the phrase usually
employed to refer to some improper cult or superstition (Lev. 17.7;
20.5 et al.; comp. ibn Ezra).

    40. *ye may remember*] Apparently an unnecessary repetition of
v. 39, but it may mean that when you do remember and fulfill God's
commandments then will you be holy to your God, an ideal set for
Israel in many places in the Bible. Holiness will be the result of your
devotion to the observance of God's laws.

    41. *to be your God*] The purpose of the exodus was to make you
realize your relationship with God, as is indicated in the phrase which
Moses was told to repeat to Pharaoh: "Send out My people so that
they may serve Me" (Ex. 4.22, 23; 5.1; 6.7; 7.16, 26; 8.16; 9.1, 13; 10.3).

16–18. REBELLION OF KORAH.

The choice of the Levites to be the ministers in the sanctuary and to
assume the functions previously exercised by the first-born (3.12–13,
40–51; 8.16–18) was displeasing to the members of the tribe of Reuben,
the first-born son of Jacob, who may have expected that this distinc-

tion would be conferred upon them. On the other hand, the elevation of the house of Aaron over the rest of the Levites and the assignment to them of the most sacred functions in connection with the service, making the other Levites subservient to them (3.5–10; 8.19), was distasteful to some of the members of that tribe. Besides this, there were other malcontents in the camp of Israel who were opposed to the leadership of Moses and Aaron. All these elements are here recorded to have combined in open rebellion against their leaders. This revolution was regarded as an offence against God, and the rebels received their due punishment. The leaders are swallowed up by the earth (16.32), the more important followers are burned to death (16.35), while a large number of other followers die in a plague (17.14). In order to impress the people still further with the fact that the appointments were sanctioned by God, the miraculous blossoming of the staff of Aaron amidst the staves of the other tribes is related (17.16–28). This is followed in ch. 18 by a series of regulations, setting forth the relation of the Levites to the priests on one hand and to the rest of Israel on the other, the portions that the people have to give to the Levites and to the priests and what the Levites, in their turn, have to give to the priests out of their portions.

The story as recorded here presents a number of difficulties, some of which have already been noticed by the Rabbis. Modern critics, following Kuenen, discovered in this narrative two distinct stories, which were later combined by an editor — one story relates the incident of a civil rebellion, led by Dathan and Abiram, against the authority of Moses, and the other story is about the rebellion of Korah and his 250 followers against the tribe of Levi, claiming to possess an equal degree of holiness and therefore entitled, like the Levites, to exercise the functions in the tabernacle. Another version of the latter story was that Korah and his followers opposed the assumption of priesthood by Aaron and his sons. The separation of the story of Dathan and Abiram from the story of Korah is supported by the fact that in Deut. 11.6 and Ps. 106.17 mention is made of Dathan and Abiram and not of Korah, while in Num. 27.3 Korah alone is mentioned.

The two stories here amalgamated by an editor, according to the critics, belonged to two different sources. The story of Dathan and Abiram and their lay followers, expressing dissatisfaction with Moses' leadership in civil matters, comes from JE, while the other version,

representing a rebellion against the superiority of the Levites, and
another incident of a rebellion by the Levites against the priesthood,
fused here together, is traced to the P source. The later editor, in
combining the two stories, added some phrases here and there, but
left the main narratives in the original form in which he found them
in the sources. Thus the sources are separated in the following manner:

JE   (Dathan and Abiram Story), 16.1b, 2a, 12–15, 25–26, 27b–34.

P   (Korah protesting against the superiority of the Tribe of
     Levi), 16.1a, 2b–7a, 18–24, 27a, 32b, 35, 41–50 and ch. 17.

D   (Korah the Levite opposing Aaron and the priestly family),
     16.7b–11, 16–17, 36–40.

Thus JE speaks only of Dathan and Abiram, while P speaks only of
Korah. In the former Moses deals with Dathan and Abiram and in
the latter with Korah and his followers. In each instance, the interests
are different and the personalities are different. The 250 men represented as following Korah were not all of the tribe of Levi, as is evident
from the reference in 27.3, where the daughters of Zelophehad stress
the fact that their father, a member of the tribe of Manasseh, was not
among those who plotted with Korah. See Driver, *Introduction to
the Literature of the Old Testament*, 63–65; Gray, 186–193; but comp.
Orr, 358–9.

Those holding to the traditional view that the story forms one single
unit and relates of a rebellion in which several elements combined,
endeavor to solve the difficulties and repetitions in the story in various
ways. Contrary to the popular view that Korah was swallowed by the
earth, ibn Ezra, Luzzatto and others insist that only Dathan and Abiram
and Korah's possessions were swallowed up by the earth, while Korah
and the 250 men were consumed by the fire. This opinion is based on
the fact that, according to the narrative, Korah was not at his tent but
at the sanctuary, ready to offer up the incense, when the catastrophe
of the earth opening its mouth is assumed to have occurred. The
expression in 26.10, where Korah is mentioned as having been swallowed up by the earth, is interpreted to refer to Korah's tent and its
inhabitants, but not to Korah himself. Some of the Rabbis suggest
that Korah was first burned to death and then his ashes were swallowed
up by the earth, while others say that he was neither burnt nor swallowed up by the earth, but that he died in the plague (Sanh. 110a).

Now Korah, the son of Izhar, the son of Kohath, the **16**
son of Levi, with Dathan and Abiram, the sons of Eliab,
and On, the son of Peleth, sons of Reuben, took men;
and they rose up in face of Moses, with certain of the 2

CHAPTER 16.

1–2. THE LEADERS OF THE REBELLION.

Korah, a Levite, Dathan, Abiram and On of the tribe of Reuben,
and 250 prominent men of the congregation of Israel, rise against
Moses and against Aaron.

1. *Korah, the son of Izhar*] The Rabbis explain the reason for
Korah's rebellion to have been the appointment of Elizaphan, the son
of Uzziel, as the head of the Kohathite family (3.30). Korah maintained
that since the sons of Amram, the eldest son of Kohath, took unto
themselves the priesthood (Aaron) and the leadership of the people
(Moses), the position of head of the family should by right go to himself, the son of the second son of Kohath, Izhar, and not to the son of
the youngest son of Kohath, Uzziel (Tan., Korah, 3, comp. Rashi here).

On, the son of Peleth] Not mentioned again here or in any other
place in the Bible, possibly because he played but a minor part in the
incident, or because he later withdrew from the conspiracy (Keil).
Some make this name a corrupt repetition of the last three letters of
Eliab and also change Peleth into Pallu, so that the verse would read:
"and Dathan and Abiram, sons of Eliab, son of Pallu, son of Reuben"
(26.8, 9; see Gray and references there given).

took men] The word "men" is not in the Hebrew text, but is supplied
from the context (ibn Ezra, Luzzatto, A. V.). Some do not translate
the word ויקח at all, taking it to indicate merely preparation for action
(cf. II Sam. 18.18; Ramban, *Biur*). Leeser, following Mendelssohn,
renders "was presumptuous". LXX rendering indicates a reading
ויאמר. Targum, followed by Rashi, translates "separated himself"
(comp. Adler). Some modern commentators suggest the emendation
ויקם "and he arose" (BDB), while others connect it with the following
verse, "took and rose up against Moses with 250 men" (Keil, quoting
Gesenius).

2. *in face of Moses*] In open revolt, in the presence of Moses.

children of Israel, two hundred and fifty men; they were
princes of the congregation, the elect men of the assembly,
3 men of renown; and they assembled themselves together
against Moses and against Aaron, and said unto them:
'Ye take too much upon you, seeing all the congregation
are holy, every one of them, and the LORD is among them;
wherefore then lift ye up yourselves above the assembly
4 of the LORD?' And when Moses heard it, he fell upon his
5 face. And he spoke unto Korah and unto all his company,

princes of the congregation] Prominent persons, but not the appointed
princes of the tribes (7.2).

elect men of the assembly] Also in 1.16; 26.9; men usually summoned
to meetings of the assembly (LXX, see Rashbam).

men of renown] Lit. men of name, having a good reputation, as
opposed to "nameless" ignoble persons (Job 30.8).

3–7. KORAH'S ARGUMENT.

Korah and his followers, in the presence of Moses and Aaron, maintain the equal holiness of all the people and accuse Moses and Aaron
of assuming superiority over the people. Moses, angered at the presumption, tells them to appear the next morning with censers filled
with fire and incense, when God Himself will indicate whom He has
chosen.

3. *and they assembled themselves together*] In open hostility and
revolt, all prepared to carry out the plot which they hatched some
time before.

ye take too much upon you] "Ye assume too much" (Leeser, following Rashi), lit. "enough!" (Deut. 1.6; 2.3).

all the congregation are holy] Why then set up the tribe of Levi
above them, and still further, why do you take the highest offices
unto yourselves? (Comp. Ex. 19.6).

lift ye up yourselves] Consider yourselves above the rest of the
congregation.

4. *he fell upon his face*] In grief and anger (comp. 14.5; note
Ehrlich's emendation, after Gen. 4.5, ויפלו פניו "and his countenance

saying: 'In the morning the LORD will show who are His,
and who is holy, and will cause him to come near unto
Him; even him whom He may choose will He cause to
come near unto Him. This do: take you censers, Korah, 6
and all his company; and put fire therein, and put incense 7

fell"), or in supplication (*Biur*). The Rabbis interpret the phrase as
denoting helplessness and dismay. After he succeeded in averting
the anger of God on several previous occasions, Moses felt that it
would be too much to ask again for God's pardon of this act of rebellion
(Tan., Korah 9; Rashi). Moses alone is mentioned here, although in
two other instances in this narrative (16.22; 17.10) Aaron is coupled
with him. The suggestion has been made (Ramban) that Aaron did
not wish to enter into the controversy since he was more intimately
concerned in it.

5. *In the morning*] The time when the incense was offered in the
sanctuary (Ex. 30.7; comp. 16.7).

will show who are His] Which of the tribes was meant to do the
service of God (comp. 3.12), in answer to the Reubenites. LXX paraphrases: "The Lord has investigated (בָּקַר) and knows those who are
His".

and who is holy] Who of the Levites shall perform the priestly
duties (comp. I Chron. 23.13), in answer to Korah.

to come near unto Him] To do service before God (comp. Ps.65.5).

even him whom He may choose] LXX renders this whole phrase in
the negative: "and him whom He will not choose He will not cause to
come near before Him", apparently because of the unnecessary repetition. Ramban suggests that this refers to the future. The one whom
God will designate as His choice in the morning shall for all future
time be the functionary in the sanctuary.

6. *This do*] Here is the test which will determine whether any one
not chosen by God could engage in the service of the sanctuary with
impunity. The offering of incense was one of the priestly functions
and was thus made the test for both the Levites and the others associated with them (comp. the incident of Nadab and Abihu, Lev. 10.1, 2).

censers] Bronze dishes in which live coals were placed and the
incense burned (Lev. 10.1; 16.12).

upon them before the LORD to-morrow; and it shall be
that the man whom the LORD doth choose, he shall be
8 holy; ye take too much upon you, ye sons of Levi.' And
Moses said unto Korah: 'Hear now, ye sons of Levi:
9 is it but a small thing unto you, that the God of Israel
hath separated you from the congregation of Israel, to
bring you near to Himself, to do the service of the tabernacle of the LORD, and to stand before the congregation

7.   *before the Lord*]   At the door of the tent of assembly, as indicated
in v. 18.

ye take too much upon you, ye sons of Levi]   To lead in a rebellion
against those appointed by God, after you have been singled out by
Him above the rest of the community. The address is directed to
Korah and his Levitic followers, who were apparently the chief insti-
gators in the sedition, although among their followers there were many
non-Levites. The same phrase was used by them against Moses and
Aaron (v. 3).

8–11.   MOSES REPUDIATES KORAH'S CLAIM.

The rebuke is further elaborated by Moses and the claim of the
Levites to be regarded as equal in holiness with Aaron is repudiated
and regarded as an affront to God. It was by divine decree that the
Levites were singled out of the rest of the congregation to perform
the services of the sanctuary and it was by the same divine decree that
Aaron and his household were given the priesthood. You are thus
rebelling against God and not against Aaron, when you seek for yourselves the higher office which God has withheld from you.

8.   *ye sons of Levi*]   This address is directed to Korah as the ringleader and as the representative of the Levites and not as the representative of the whole group of rebels, upon whom the test of vv. 6, 7
was to be made. Korah, the Levite, and his Levitic followers surely
have no cause for complaint.

9.   *the God of Israel*]   Although the God of all Israel, He singled
you out for the honor of performing His services.

the service of the tabernacle]   As described in ch. 4.

to minister unto them; and that He hath brought thee 10
near, and all thy brethren the sons of Levi with thee?
and will ye seek the priesthood also? Therefore thou and 11
all thy company that are gathered together against the
LORD—; and as to Aaron, what is he that ye murmur

to minister unto them] When they bring their sacrifices, the Levites
are to prepare the offerings and then chant hymns while the offering
is being made by the priests (Rashi, ibn Ezra).

10. *brought thee near*] To the service from which the rest of Israel
is excluded (Rashi, comp. Ehrlich). Ibn Ezra interprets: "and *now*
that he brought thee near" (comp. *Biur*).

the priesthood also] Targum renders "high-priesthood", perhaps
implying the selfish desire of Korah to become high-priest himself
(comp. Adler).

11. *Therefore thou*] Leeser, following Mendelssohn, has "beware!",
indicating a threat, the nature of which is not explained (see *Biur*,
quoting Gen. 4.15). This, however, is not necessary, since the word
לכן is often used in the sense of "according to such conditions", "this
being so" (BDB), after the statement of the facts.

that are gathered together against the Lord] Ibn Ezra suggests that
the ה of הנועדים is superfluous, so that the rendering would be "thou and
all thy company, against the Lord ye are gathered". Ehrlich emends
in the same sense עדתכה נועדים (also Kahana). Luzzatto quotes the
opinion of one of his pupils, who proposed the reading הנועדים נועדים.
In any case, the emphasis should be placed on the words "against the
Lord", in contrast to Aaron (see Rashbam).

and as to Aaron] Aaron did not usurp the priesthood, but is acting
in accordance with the command of God (cf. Ex. 16.8).

12–15. MOSES INVITES DATHAN AND ABIRAM, but THEY REFUSE TO COME.

Moses then summons Dathan and Abiram to come before him and
present their complaints. They refuse to come and boldly accuse
Moses of being responsible for all the troubles that have befallen the
nation and also of assuming an overbearing attitude toward the people.
This angers Moses and he appeals to God for redress.

12 against him?' And Moses sent to call Dathan and Abiram,
the sons of Eliab; and they said: 'We will not come up;
13 is it a small thing that thou hast brought us up out of a
land flowing with milk and honey, to kill us in the wilderness, but thou must needs make thyself also a prince over
14 us? Moreover thou hast not brought us into a land flowing
with milk and honey, nor given us inheritance of fields
and vineyards; wilt thou put out the eyes of these men?
15 we will not come up.' And Moses was very wroth, and
said unto the LORD: 'Respect not Thou their offering;

12. *sent to call*] Possibly by messenger, inviting them to come
before him at the tabernacle (cf. 22.5).

we will not come up] The term עלה is often used in connection with
the appearance at a holy place or before a court of justice, even when
no actual ascent is implied (Deut. 25.7; Judg. 4.5; ibn Ezra, Rashbam).

13. *is it a small thing*] Using Moses' expression (v. 9) derisively.
Is it nothing to you that you fooled us in taking us out from such a
land as Egypt, which is the real "land flowing with milk and honey",
to kill us in the wilderness, according to the decree pronounced against
us (14.29), that you also dare to set yourself up as a prince over us
and to order us about (20.4)?

14. *Moreover*] You did not keep your promise to bring us to a
land flowing with milk and honey (Ex. 3.17), nor did you even supply
us with the possession of an ordinary field and vineyard.

wilt thou put out the eyes of these men?] Do you think that you can
continue to hoodwink us as you did until now? The expression is similar
to the English idiom "throw dust in the eyes of" (Gray). "These men"
may refer to themselves (Rashi, Sforno), or to their followers (Rashbam, ibn Ezra).

we will not come up] Concluding with the same words with which
they began, making their defiance more emphatic.

15. *Respect not Thou their offering*] The phrase means to regard
graciously (Lev. 26.9), to accept with favor. Moses prays that God
shall not heed any offering that they may desire to make in the capacity
of priests, the office to which they aspire (Ramban); or that He may

I have not taken one ass from them, neither have I hurt
one of them.' And Moses said unto Korah: 'Be thou and 16
all thy congregation before the LORD, thou, and they,
and Aaron, to-morrow; and take ye every man his fire-pan, 17
and put incense upon them, and bring ye before the LORD
every man his fire-pan, two hundred and fifty fire-pans;
thou also, and Aaron, each his fire-pan.' And they took 18
every man his fire-pan, and put fire in them, and laid

not accept with favor the incense which they are about to offer (Rashi).
It is also possible that no special sacrifice is in the mind of the writer
but a general reference to any sacrifice that they may wish to offer.

I have not taken one ass from them] Leeser, following Targum, Rashi
and Mendelssohn, has "an ass of any one of them", making חמור a construct (cf. I Sam. 12.3). LXX apparently had a reading חמוד, "a desirable object" (cf. Meg. 9b). Their charge was that Moses was seeking
to exercise dominion over them, to which the reply is made that he
did not take from them even an ass for service, which would be within
the right of any ruler (see Targum and Adler, Ramban, Tan. Korah,
19, quoted also by Rashi).

hurt one of them] Mendelssohn has "insulted"; Leeser, "done wrong".

16–17. This is a repetition of vv. 6–7, with the addition of a few
details. Korah and his company, the 250 men of various tribes, are to
bring their censers and offer up incense. This will be the test as to
whom God had chosen to act in the capacity of priest. Aaron is mentioned here but not in v. 6, where it may have been implied in the
phrase "him whom He may choose will He cause to come near to Him"
(see ibn Ezra and Ramban).

18–22. CONTENDING PARTIES ASSEMBLE BEFORE THE TABERNACLE.

18. Korah and his company agree to Moses' proposition and prepare to go through with the test as prescribed. They prepare their
censers and come before the door of the sanctuary, perhaps on the
same day, without waiting for the morrow (Luzzatto), in their eager-
ness to establish their claim. Moses and Aaron also come.

incense thereon, and stood at the door of the tent of meet-
19 ing with Moses and Aaron. And Korah assembled all the
congregation against them unto the door of the tent of
meeting; and the glory of the LORD appeared unto all the
congregation.

20 And the LORD spoke unto Moses and unto Aaron, saying:
21 'Separate yourselves from among this congregation, that I
22 may consume them in a moment.' And they fell upon their
faces, and said: 'O God, the God of the spirits of all flesh,

19. *assembled all the congregation*] He induced also others who had
abstained from open rebellion to come and witness the ceremony,
whereby he expected to establish his claim that Moses and Aaron
usurped the power which did not belong to them (Tan. Korah, 19;
Rashi). The very presence there of the assembled multitude, who
should have had more faith in Moses, was interpreted as their being
against Moses and Aaron, and it was for this reason that they were
all regarded as rebels, deserving of punishment (see Ramban to v. 21,
comp. Gray).

the glory of the Lord] See note to 14.10.

20–22. God, in His anger, threatens to destroy the whole congregation, but Moses and Aaron intercede in their behalf, arguing that
the guilt lay with the ringleaders, who alone should be punished, while
the masses of the people who were led astray should not suffer the
severe penalty.

21. *that I may consume them*] As if God would not harm them as
long as Moses and Aaron were in their midst. Leeser has "and I shall
consume them" (comp. 17.10).

22. *And they fell upon their faces*] In prayer, see note to v. 4.

of the spirits of all flesh] The spirit residing in all flesh, both men
and animals, parallel to נפש (BDB). *El* is used here as a divine proper
name, while in 27.16 *Adonai* is used in a similar phrase (BDB). God
of the spirits of all flesh, the creator of all beings, may indeed do what
seems proper to Him and no one dares question His wisdom. Still, is
it right that the whole congregation should be destroyed because of
the sins of one man? (ibn Ezra). The God of the spirits surely knows

shall one man sin, and wilt Thou be wroth with all the congregation?'

And the LORD spoke unto Moses, saying: 'Speak unto 23-24 the congregation, saying: Get you up from about the dwelling of Korah, Dathan, and Abiram.' And Moses 25 rose up and went unto Dathan and Abiram; and the

what is in the soul of man and knows who is guilty and who is not (Rashi, Rashbam).

shall one man sin] Referring to Korah, the ringleader, or the whole phrase may have been a popular saying and is used here in the sense of a "few". Comp. Gen. 18.23–32, the arguments advanced by Abraham against the destruction of Sodom and Gomorrah. The ה is used here as an interrogative *He* and should be punctuated with a *patah* (Ges.-K. 100m; Delitzsch, 72c). Leeser, following Rashi and Mendelssohn, translates this as a definite article, giving the verse an interrogative sense nevertheless.

23–34. MOSES AND THE ELDERS IN FRONT OF THE DWELLINGS OF DATHAN AND ABIRAM.

Moses, followed by the loyal elders of Israel, goes to the tents of Dathan and Abiram, not to plead or argue with them (comp., however, Sanh. 110a), but to warn the people in that vicinity against the impending danger. When the people remove from the neighborhood, Moses proposes the test which will prove that his appointment came from God. If the rebels die a natural death, his appointment is not from God, but if the earth open its mouth and swallow them alive, then the appointment came from God. Moses' threat is realized and the earth swallows up the rebels and all their possessions. The Israelites, on beholding the sight, flee in terror. See introductory note to this chapter.

24. *the dwelling of Korah, Dathan and Abiram*] The expression here would indicate that Korah, Dathan and Abiram all occupied one tent, which is impossible. The suggestion has been made that the word "dwelling" here refers to "neighborhood" or "district", since the Kohathites to whom Korah belonged and the Reubenites were stationed in the camp near one another to the south of the Tabernacle (2.10; 3.29; comp. ibn Ezra). Those who regard this to be a composite story (see introductory note) believe that in the original narrative the phrase

26 elders of Israel followed him. And he spoke unto the congregation, saying: 'Depart, I pray you, from the tents of these wicked men, and touch nothing of theirs, lest ye
27 be swept away in all their sins.' So they got them up from the dwelling of Korah, Dathan, and Abiram, on every side; and Dathan and Abiram came out, and stood at the door of their tents, with their wives, and their
28 sons, and their little ones. And Moses said: 'Hereby ye shall know that the LORD hath sent me to do all these works, and that I have not done them of mine own mind.

read למשכן ה' (to the tabernacle of the Lord), and the later editor supplied the last three words (see Gray).

25. *the elders of Israel*] Perhaps the seventy elders of 11.16.

26. *unto the congregation*] The assembled multitudes who had no direct share in the rebellion.

of these wicked men] Dathan and Abiram. The Rabbis include four classes of people under the designation of *Rasha'* (wicked): Those who attempt to do physical violence to others; those who refuse to pay their debts; those who are insolent and have no respect for their superiors; those who incite to strife and sedition. Dathan and Abiram belong to the last class (Tan. Korah, 21).

in all their sins] In the punishment that will come to them as a consequence of their sins (comp. Gen. 13.15).

27. *they got them up*] The people removed themselves (v. 24).

came out, and stood] In front of their tents in defiance of Moses' warning, and did not move with the other people (Tan. ib. 22; Rashi).

28. *Hereby*] By what is going to happen. Moses proposes to the assembled people the following test, speaking of Dathan and Abiram in the third person (comp. Gen. 42.33; Ex. 7.17).

all these works] Referring to the appointment of Aaron and the Levites, which was the cause of the rebellion (Rashi, ibn Ezra); or it may refer to all the works accomplished by Moses in his capacity as leader of the people, against which Dathan and Abiram complained (vv. 13, 14; Ramban, *Biur*).

of mine own mind] Lit. my own heart (Mendelssohn, Leeser, comp. Targum), because of my desire to lord it over you.

If these men die the common death of all men, and be 29
visited after the visitation of all men, then the LORD hath
not sent me. But if the LORD make a new thing, and the 30
ground open her mouth, and swallow them up, with all
that appertain unto them, and they go down alive into
the pit, then ye shall understand that these men have
despised the LORD.' And it came to pass, as he made an 31
end of speaking all these words, that the ground did cleave
asunder that was under them. And the earth opened her 32
mouth, and swallowed them up, and their households,
and all the men that appertained unto Korah, and all

29. *after the visitation of all men*] In a natural way, and not through
an extraordinary catastrophe.

30. *make a new thing*] Lit. "create a creation", something that
did not exist before (cf. Jer. 31.22).

into the pit] Sheol, the underworld, somewhere beneath the earth,
the place where departed spirits dwell (cf. Gen. 37.35; Ps. 55.66).

then ye shall understand] This will be proof to you that the work
that I have done was directed by God and that these men who oppose
me thereby despise God. The new creation was not that the earth
swallowed them up, since earthquakes occurred also in the course of
nature (ibn Ezra). It consisted in the fact that the catastrophe occurred
just then, at the command of Moses (*Biur*), or in that the earth returned
afterwards to its former shape (v. 32; Ramban).

the Lord] Not me.

32. *their households*] Comp. Targum, "the people of their houses",
i. e. their wives and children and other persons belonging to them
(ibn Ezra; Adler).

the men that appertained unto Korah] Referring to his slaves and
members of his household, but not to his followers in this rebellion
who are represented as being at the tabernacle at that time. Those
who regard the account as composed of different narratives take this
phrase to be the work of the editor in his attempt to combine the narratives into one story (see introductory note). The fate of Korah

33 their goods. So they, and all that appertained to them,
   went down alive into the pit; and the earth closed upon
34 them, and they perished from among the assembly. And
   all Israel that were round about them fled at the cry of
35 them; for they said: 'Lest the earth swallow us up.' And
   fire came forth from the LORD, and devoured the two
   hundred and fifty men that offered the incense.

himself is not given here (nor in Deut. 11.6), although in 26.10 he is
included among those who were swallowed up by the earth (comp.
Tan. Korah 23; Sanh. 110a). The sons of Korah are distinctly mentioned there as having survived the catastrophe.

   34.   *fled at the cry of them*]   At the outcry produced by them (Ramban, Rashbam), or at the sound produced by the destruction of the
tents and all that were in them (Rashi, Luzzatto).

   Lest the earth swallow us up]   Although they were at a safe distance
from the place where the miracle occurred (vv. 26, 27), they were
alarmed when they heard the noise and fled still further.

35.   THE TWO HUNDRED AND FIFTY MEN DESTROYED

   And fire came forth]   Comp. Lev. 10.2, where the same expression
is used in connection with the similar sin committed by Nadab and
Abihu, the sons of Aaron. This verse is a sequel to v. 19. According
to ibn Ezra, Korah also was burned by the fire that consumed the
250 men.

CHAPTER 17.

1–5.   THE CENSERS MADE INTO A MEMORIAL

   The censers used by the 250 men are declared to be holy, unfit for
ordinary use, and Moses is told to order Eleazar to make out of these
censers a covering to the altar, which shall serve as a memorial for all
future generations that none but the descendants of Aaron may offer
incense upon the altar. In Ex. 27.2 it is recorded that the altar was
overlaid with bronze at the time when it was first constructed. The
LXX adds there (Ex. 38.2, parallel to LXX, Ex. 38.22), "he made the

And the Lord spoke unto Moses, saying: 'Speak unto 2 **17**
Eleazar the son of Aaron the priest, that he take up the
fire-pans out of the burning, and scatter thou the fire
yonder; for they are become holy; even the fire-pans of 3
these men who have sinned at the cost of their lives, and
let them be made beaten plates for a covering of the
altar—for they are become holy, because they were offered
before the Lord—that they may be a sign unto the children

bronze altar out of the bronze censers which belonged to the men who
revolted with the congregation of Korah", apparently in an attempt
at reconciling the origin of the bronze covering as given here and in
Ex. 27.2. It is, however, quite possible to assume that while the altar
already had a bronze covering given to it at the time of its construction,
another layer of bronze was added to it out of the 250 censers (cf.
Gray). In the LXX and in A. V. and R. V., ch. 16 continues to v. 50,
corresponding to 17.15 of our version.

2. *Speak unto Eleazar*] The order was given to Eleazar and not
to Aaron, perhaps because Aaron was more directly concerned in the
controversy (Ehrlich), or because Aaron as the high priest had to be
more careful even than the ordinary priests to avoid contact with
dead bodies (comp. Lev. 10.4; 21.10).

out of the burning] From among the people who were burned (Targum, LXX).

scatter thou the fire yonder] Beyond the altar. The fire refers to the
live coals that were placed upon the censers (16.7, 18). LXX has
"and the strange fire scatter" (הַזָּרָה זְרֵה).

for they are become holy] The censers have become holy because
they were intended to be used in the service of the altar and therefore
should not be left for profane use (see Rashi, ibn Ezra and especially
Ramban). For the ancient conception of holiness, see Hastings, *Dictionary of the Bible*, s. v.; *J. E.*, s. v.; Gray, pp. 209–211.

3. *even the fire-pans*] In further explanation of preceding verse.

at the cost of their lives] Who have forfeited their lives through their
sin (II Sam. 23.17; II Kings 2.23).

because they were offered] Referring back to the last phrase of v. 2.

a sign] A warning, as explained in v.5.

4 of Israel.' And Eleazar the priest took the brazen fire-pans,
which they that were burnt had offered; and they beat
5 them out for a covering of the altar, to be a memorial
unto the children of Israel, to the end that no common
man, that is not of the seed of Aaron, draw near to burn
incense before the LORD; that he fare not as Korah, and
as his company; as the LORD spoke unto him by the hand
of Moses.

6   But on the morrow all the congregation of the children
of Israel murmured against Moses and against Aaron,

5. *common man*] Usually either a non-priest or non-Levite (3.10),
hence it is necessary to specify here that this refers to the non-priest,
even though he be a Levite.

as the Lord spoke unto him] Going back to v. 4. Eleazar
followed the order which was given to him by God through Moses
(Rashbam, Ramban). Some render לו, "concerning him", referring to
Aaron and the sanctity of the priesthood (Rashi, ibn Ezra).

6–15. PLAGUE DESTROYS PEOPLE WHO MURMURED AGAINST THE PUNISHMENT OF KORAH.

The people, distressed at the destruction of Korah's followers, accuse
Moses and Aaron of having caused the death of so many of their leaders
and representatives. God is angered at this display of insubordination
and is about to cause the destruction of the whole community, when
Moses intercedes in their behalf. He orders Aaron to take a censer
and place upon it fire from the altar and proceed with it among the
people, where the plague already started. Aaron succeeds in staying
the plague, only after 14,700 of the people had already perished. Thus
the same censer which had brought death to the 250 men, when offered
by the person appointed by God, is the means of averting death.

6. *on the morrow*] After the destruction of the 250 men by fire
(16.35).

saying: 'Ye have killed the people of the LORD.' And it 7
came to pass, when the congregation was assembled
against Moses and against Aaron, that they looked toward
the tent of meeting; and, behold, the cloud covered it,
and the glory of the LORD appeared. And Moses and 8
Aaron came to the front of the tent of meeting. And the 9
LORD spoke unto Moses, saying: 'Get you up from among 10
this congregation, that I may consume them in a moment.'
And they fell upon their faces. And Moses said unto 11

Ye have killed]   You have caused the death (Targum) of these people,
since it was at your suggestion that they brought the incense (ibn Ezra,
Ramban and Rashbam).

the people of the Lord]   The 250 men who are described as the representatives and leaders of the people (16.2).

7.   *that they looked toward the tent of meeting*]   Lit. turned toward
(cf. Ex. 16.10). They looked at the tabernacle, where the cloud always
rested (9.16; Ex. 40.38), and saw the glory of the Lord there, which
was a sign that God wished to communicate a message to the people
through Moses (Gray). Hence, Moses and Aaron came near to the
tabernacle (v. 8).

9.   *unto Moses*]   LXX adds "and Aaron", which is supported by
the plural in the following verse.

10.   *Get you up*]   Parallel to 16.21, except that there a different verb
is used. Moses and Aaron are told to remove themselves from the
midst of the congregation so that they may be spared the fate that is
impending over the people. Some explain this order as intended to
save them from the sight of beholding the terrible misfortune that was
to come, to prevent them from interfering in the execution of the
punishment with their prayers (Ramban).

And they fell upon their faces]   In prayer, as in 16.22, where the
prayer is expressed, but here it is omitted.

Aaron: 'Take thy fire-pan, and put fire therein from off
the altar, and lay incense thereon, and carry it quickly
unto the congregation, and make atonement for them;
for there is wrath gone out from the LORD: the plague is
12 begun.' And Aaron took as Moses spoke, and ran into the
midst of the assembly; and, behold, the plague was begun
among the people; and he put on the incense, and made
13 atonement for the people. And he stood between the
14 dead and the living; and the plague was stayed. Now

11. *Take thy fire-pan*] "*Thy*" is not in the Hebrew text, although
it may be implied in the definite article used, *the fire-pan*, the one which
you always use (ibn Ezra).

from off the altar] Fire which has already been consecrated, while in
16.7 plain fire was apparently intended.

lay incense thereon] To indicate that the same incense which caused
death when used by unauthorized persons, has the power to check
destruction when used by God's appointed minister (Rashi, Rashbam).

and make atonement for them] With the same object which was the
cause of the sin (comp. the incident of the bronze serpent, 21.6–9).
The Rabbis deduce from this expression that the incense possessed an
atoning power (Yoma 44a, comp. Shab. 89a).

for there is wrath gone out] The wrath of God, as implied in His
words (v. 10), has already begun the execution of the punishment.
The "wrath of God" is represented here as an independent emanation,
capable of doing evil as soon as it proceeds from God, similar to the
conception of the Angel of Death in rabbinic literature (see Rashi;
Shab. 89a; cf. Luzzatto).

13. *And he stood between the dead and the living*] When Aaron
reached the place where the people were assembled, the plague had
already started and many had already died. He then placed himself
in the midst of the assembly and checked the plague with the incense
which he offered. Aaron, though the high-priest, deliberately comes
here in contact with dead bodies, which he is forbidden to do (Lev.
21.11), in order to save the lives of the people. It was also for the
same reason that he permitted himself to take the incense out of the
tabernacle (Ehrlich).

they that died by the plague were fourteen thousand and seven hundred, besides them that died about the matter of Korah. And Aaron returned unto Moses unto the door of the tent of meeting, and the plague was stayed. 15

And the LORD spoke unto Moses, saying: 'Speak unto the children of Israel, and take of them rods, one for each fathers' house, of all their princes according to their fathers' 16-17

14. *besides them that died*] The 250 men who were burned when about to offer incense on the altar (16.35).

15. *and the plague was stayed*] Leeser, following Mendelssohn, has "after the plague was stayed"; others have "the plague having been stayed" (Gray), both of which indicate that Aaron did not return to the tent until after the plague was checked. Our rendering, following R. V., makes the sense obscure. Ibn Ezra takes this whole verse as introductory to the following section: When Aaron returned, after the plague was stayed, God spoke unto Moses, etc. (also *Biur*).

16–28. BLOSSOMING OF AARON'S ROD.

Another proof is here given of God's choice of the tribe of Levi to be the ministers in the sanctuary, to the exclusion of the other tribes. The princes of the twelve tribes (Ephraim and Manasseh being regarded as two) are ordered to bring each a rod, inscribed with the name of the prince, while the rod of the tribe of Levi should bear the name of Aaron, the representative of that tribe. The rods are deposited in the tent of assembly before the ark. The following morning, the rod of Aaron is found to have blossomed forth and to bear ripe almonds. This was to be conclusive evidence of the selection of the tribe of Levi. All the rods are then returned to their owners, but the rod of Aaron is placed back again in front of the ark and kept there as a sign and warning to future malcontents who may question the rights of the Levites to the position occupied by them. The people are frightened by this miraculous manifestation and express their alarm at the possibility of their being destroyed any time that they may come near to the sanctuary. There follows then in ch. 18 a description of the laws regulating the relation among the various classes: the priests, the Levites and the Israelites.

17. *one for each fathers' house*] One of the original twelve tribes,

houses, twelve rods; thou shalt write every man's name
18 upon his rod. And thou shalt write Aaron's name upon
the rod of Levi, for there shall be one rod for the head of
19 their fathers' houses. And thou shalt lay them up in the
tent of meeting before the testimony, where I meet with
20 you. And it shall come to pass, that the man whom I shall
choose, his rod shall bud; and I will make to cease from
Me the murmurings of the children of Israel, which they

as is clearly explained here (comp. 1.2 and note). The rod or staff may
have been part of the official insignia carried about by the princes as a
mark of their office, or the ordinary cane usually carried by people in
antiquity (comp. note to 21.18; Gen. 38.18, 25; I Sam. 14.43).

every man's name] The names of the princes and not the names of
the tribes.

18. *for there shall be one rod*] The three divisions of the tribe of
Levi, Gershonites, Kohathites and Merarites (4.34 ff.), shall be represented by only one rod, on which the name of Aaron is inscribed. This
is intended to emphasize that both the priestly and the Levitic orders
were to be represented by one rod, the rod of Aaron (Rashi, Ramban,
ibn Ezra). There were thus thirteen rods altogether, the twelve rods
of the twelve princes of the secular tribes and the rod of Aaron representing the tribe of Levi. Some, however, believe that there were only
twelve rods altogether, including the rod of Aaron, while the tribes of
Ephraim and Manasseh were represented by one rod, the rod of Joseph
(Ramban, Keil, Ehrlich, comp. Deut. 27.12).

19. *before the testimony*] I. e. the ark containing the testimony
(4.5; 7.89), the tablets with the Ten Words engraved upon them.

where I meet with you] With the children of Israel, in whose behalf
the meetings were held with Moses (comp. Ex. 29.42, 43). LXX has
"with thee", referring to Moses (comp. Ex. 25.22; 30.6, 36). The
phrase indicates habitual action (ibn Ezra), "I am wont to meet you"
(Gray).

20. *the man whom I shall choose*] The man representing the tribe
that God has chosen.

murmur against you.' And Moses spoke unto the children 21
of Israel; and all their princes gave him rods, for each
prince one, according to their fathers' houses, even twelve
rods; and the rod of Aaron was among their rods. And 22
Moses laid up the rods before the LORD in the tent of the
testimony. And it came to pass on the morrow, that 23
Moses went into the tent of the testimony; and, behold,
the rod of Aaron for the house of Levi was budded, and
put forth buds, and bloomed blossoms, and bore ripe
almonds. And Moses brought out all the rods from before 24

against you] Which they murmur to me against you (Mendelssohn,
Biur), i. e. God will be relieved from listening to these constant complaints.

21. *was among their rods*] Included in the twelve, see note to v. 18;
or it may mean that the thirteen rods were stuck in the ground, Aaron's
rod standing in the middle (McNeile).

22. *in the tent of the testimony*] Perhaps the holy of holies (also
in v. 19), or it may refer to the tabernacle as a whole (comp. **9.15**
and n.).

23. *for the house*] Representing the tribe of Levi.

budded, and put forth buds] "Budded" is here used as a general term
for growth, which is further more definitely described in the three
stages of growth — budding, flowering and producing fruit — the complete process having been accomplished overnight. Rashbam explains
that when Moses first saw it, it had only budded. He then took it up
to show it to the people, and while he held it in his hands the bud
turned into a flower and the flower into a fruit, in the sight of the
people. This interpretation explains the difficulty that if the ripe fruit
was first seen, the earlier processes could not have been seen and could
only be conjectured. Luzzatto, quoting one of his pupils, says that it
was possible that the rod had sprouted in several places and when
discovered some of the sprouts were in bud, others in flower and still
others as ripe almonds. See Gray, p. 217, who quotes instances of
miraculous vegetation of dried sticks in the folklore of other nation-
alities.

the LORD unto all the children of Israel; and they looked,
and took every man his rod.

25 And the LORD said unto Moses: 'Put back the rod of
Aaron before the testimony, to be kept there, for a token
against the rebellious children; that there may be made an
end of their murmurings against Me, that they die not.'

26 Thus did Moses; as the LORD commanded him, so did he.

27 And the children of Israel spoke unto Moses, saying:
'Behold, we perish, we are undone, we are all undone.

28 Every one that cometh near, that cometh near unto the
tabernacle of the LORD, is to die; shall we wholly perish?'

24. *and they looked*] Examined them for the names written on
each; or they looked to see what happened to Aaron's rod.

25. *Put back*] After it was shown to the people, God tells Moses
to put back the rod of Aaron.

to be kept there] Comp. Ex. 16.32, 34.

rebellious children] Of future generations.

that they die not] The consequence of rebellion is death, hence it
will be for their own benefit to have this rod serve them as a reminder
so that they fall not into such dangerous sins.

27–28. Impressed by the several miraculous signs by which the
superiority of the Levites is established and their selection as the
exclusive ministers of the sanctuary confirmed, the people become
thoroughly frightened lest through an oversight one of them make a
step beyond the limits of the sanctuary and thereby forfeit his life
(Rashi). The exclamations in v. 27 are apparently induced by a dread
of the fate that may be in store for any of them. The Targum paraphrases: "Behold some of us were killed by the sword (14.45), some
were swallowed up by the earth (16.32), while others died in the plague
(17.14)". This may be our fate, if one of us should take a step nearer
to the tabernacle than is permitted. The repetition of the phrase
"cometh near" (v. 28, LXX only once, "who toucheth") may be
distributive, "any one who comes near", or may be emphatic, "that
cometh near at all" (Leeser), in the slightest degree (A. V., comp.
Luzzatto).

And the LORD said unto Aaron: 'Thou and thy sons **18**
and thy fathers' house with thee shall bear the iniquity

CHAPTER 18.

1–32. PRIESTLY AND LEVITICAL REGULATIONS.

The fear of the people of coming in close contact with the sanctuary,
inspired by the story of Korah and expressed by them in 17.27–28,
called forth a series of regulations, governing the relation of the priests
and the Levites to the people. Punishment will come to those only
who wantonly defy the will of God, but the Israelite who unwittingly
trespasses the sacred precincts will not be held to account for it. The
responsibility of the sanctuary rests entirely upon Aaron and the tribe
of Levi. The laws are told directly to Aaron, the head of the tribe,
and include regulations governing the relation of the priests and the
Levites to the sanctuary, as well as those pertaining to the special
portions that the Israelites were to give to the priests and the Levites
and the portion that the Levites were to give to the priests out of their
shares.

1–7. PRIESTS AND LEVITES ALONE TO MINISTER
IN THE SANCTUARY.

The sanctuary is to be entirely in charge of the priests, in which
they shall have the assistance of the Levites. The latter, however, are
not to come in direct contact with the sacred objects and the altar.
This arrangement is designed especially to prevent the common Israelite from coming too close to the sanctuary, by which he might incur
punishment of the severest kind. Similar regulations are found also
above, 1.50–53; 3.5–10, 38.

1. *unto Aaron*] Usually instructions given to Aaron are given
through Moses (6.23; 8.2; Lev. 8.2; 16.2; 21.1), except in this chapter
(vv. 1, 8, 20) and in Lev. 10.8, where the instructions are said to have
been given directly to Aaron. The Rabbis interpret this also as having
been imparted to Aaron through Moses, rendering the word אֶל "concerning" or "pertaining" to Aaron (Sifre Zuta, Rashi, ibn Ezra; comp.
Sifre 116 and Horovitz's note, also Malbim).

and thy father's house] The family of Kohath (Rashi, ibn Ezra),
or better the whole tribe of Levi (Mendelssohn, Gray).

shall bear the iniquity] The consequence of the iniquity (comp.

of the sanctuary; and thou and thy sons with thee shall
2 bear the iniquity of your priesthood. And thy brethren
also, the tribe of Levi, the tribe of thy father, bring thou
near with thee, that they may be joined unto thee, and
minister unto thee, thou and thy sons with thee being
3 before the tent of the testimony. And they shall keep
thy charge, and the charge of all the Tent; only they shall
not come nigh unto the holy furniture and unto the altar,

14.34). The priests and the Levites shall be responsible for any sin
committed by an Israelite, either by entering the sanctuary behind
the curtain or by touching anything that he is forbidden to touch.

the iniquity of your priesthood] Aaron and his sons, the priests, are
held responsible for any transgression committed either by a Levite
or by a common Israelite in matters pertaining to the priesthood.
They are to guard against non-priests performing such services in the
sanctuary as only priests may perform (comp. Luzzatto).

2. *And thy brethren also, the tribe of Levi*] In further explanation
of the term "thy fathers' house" in v.1. Rashi, who understands by
"thy fathers' house" the Kohathites only, makes the phrase "thy
brethren" refer to the Gershonites and Merarites.

and minister unto thee, thou and thy sons, etc.] The service of the
Levites is not to be given to the priests in a personal way, but only in
connection with the tabernacle service. A. V. and R. V. have "but
thou and thy sons". Leeser has "while thou and thy sons" (comp.
Mendelssohn, Gray, Sifre 116 and Horovitz's note).

the tent of the testimony] Cf. 17.22. This refers to any of the priestly
duties in the sanctuary or in the court of the sanctuary (comp. Sforno,
who restricts the phrase here to "the holy of holies which serves as
the tent for the ark in which the testimony is kept").

3. *And they shall keep thy charge*] The Levites shall attend to the
various duties assigned to them in the tabernacle, but they must not
come near to the holy vessels, the table of showbread, the candlestick,
the altar or even the bronze altar which is outside of the holy place, to
do service there, since these services may be performed by the
priests only (cf. 3.7; 4.15).

that they die not, neither they, nor ye. And they shall 4
be joined unto thee, and keep the charge of the tent of
meeting, whatsoever the service of the Tent may be; but
a common man shall not draw nigh unto you. And ye 5
shall keep the charge of the holy things, and the charge
of the altar, that there be wrath no more upon the children
of Israel. And I, behold, I have taken your brethren the 6
Levites from among the children of Israel; for you they
are given as a gift unto the LORD, to do the service of the
tent of meeting. And thou and thy sons with thee shall 7
keep your priesthood in everything that pertaineth to the
altar, and to that within the veil; and ye shall serve; I

neither they, nor ye] The Levites guilty of such a transgression as
well as the priests who allow it are guilty of a capital offense (Sifre
116; 'Ar. 11b).

4. *and they shall . . . keep the charge*] The Levites alone may do the
work of the tabernacle, but the "common man", the lay Israelite, may
not come near to do any of the service assigned either to the priests
or to the Levites. This is an order not to the "common man" but to
the priests that they should not permit it (Rashi), although the punishment is to be meted out also to the transgressor (see 1.51).

5. *And ye shall keep*] Referring to the priests who are in charge
of the sacred objects (v. 3; Sforno).

that there be wrath no more] See 17.11.

6. *as a gift unto the Lord*] They are given to the priests as a gift,
but only to do such service as pertains unto the Lord (cf. v. 2; Rashi;
see 3.9; 8.16, 19).

7. *And thou and thy sons*] The priests shall perform their duties
in connection with the service pertaining to the altar and the service
"without the veil", i. e. in the holy of holies (Ex. 26.33), where the
high priest performed his services on the Day of Atonement (Lev.
16.12, 13). Other priestly services in the holy place, where the table of
showbread, the candlestick and the golden altar were placed, are also
included, although not expressed (Yoma 24b, see Hirsch).

give you the priesthood as a service of gift; and the common man that draweth nigh shall be put to death.'

a service of gift] Not a drudgery, but a service of honor and dignity
(Ramban). The expression is rather strange and unusual. Some take
it to refer to the gifts which the priests were to receive from the laity
and from the Levites, as explained further in this chapter, and render
the phrase "a service that carries a gift with it" (Ehrlich), but this is
rather strained. Another suggestion is that the priests are endowed
with these privileges not because they deserve it, but as a free gift
from God (McNeile).

and the common man] Whether an Israelite or a Levite, who "draweth near" to do any of the duties assigned to the priests, shall be put
to death (comp. 1.53).

8–20. Gifts Due to the Priests.

As a compensation for the services expected from the priests, to
whom no share in the land was given (v. 20), certain definite revenues
are prescribed to be given to them out of the "holy things" which the
Israelites are commanded to give to the sanctuary. These include:
1) All the meal-offerings, the sin-offerings and the guilt-offerings,
excepting those parts which are burned on the altar. These must be
eaten by the male members of the priestly families "in a most holy
place" (v. 10), i. e. in the court of the tabernacle (Lev. 6.9, 19; 7.6).
2) "The heave-offerings of their gifts", i. e. the breast and the leg of
all peace-offerings and anything else that is waved on the altar. These
may be eaten by both the male and female members of the priestly
families, when in a state of ritual cleanliness. 3) All the gifts of the
first-fruits, including the first-fruits of oil, wine and corn. These also
may be eaten by both males and females when ritually clean. 4) All
"devoted" things, dedicated by individuals to the sanctuary. 5) The
first-born of both men and beasts. The first-born of clean animals
belong to the priest and may be eaten by him after the blood and fat
had been offered on the altar. The first-born of unclean animals had
to be redeemed and the redemption-money given to the priest. The
first-born of man also had to be redeemed and the redemption-money
(five shekels) given to the priest.

And the LORD spoke unto Aaron: 'And I, behold, I 8
have given thee the charge of My heave-offerings; even
of all the hallowed things of the children of Israel unto
thee have I given them for a consecrated portion, and to
thy sons, as a due for ever. This shall be thine of the most 9
holy things, reserved from the fire: every offering of theirs,
even every meal-offering of theirs, and every sin-offering
of theirs, and every guilt-offering of theirs, which they
may render unto Me, shall be most holy for thee and for

8. *And I*] All the gifts enumerated below belong in the first
instance to God and it is God who assigns them to the priests.

the charge of My heave-offerings] The charge of the gifts made to
God by the Israelites, so that they be not profaned or used improperly
(Rashi). Another possible rendering is "that which is kept of the contributions made to Me", the part of the offering which is not burned
on the altar (Gray, comp. Ehrlich).

for a consecrated portion] Cf. Lev. 7.35. A. V. has "by reason of the
anointing"; Leeser, "as an official portion" (comp. Gray, phil. n., p. 233).
Both these renderings are also found in Sifre 117, and both are apparently derived there from the same root משח, "to anoint". The
idea of the phrase is that this is not to be considered as a wage, but as
a gift presented to high dignitaries (Targum, Rashi).

9. *reserved from the fire*] After the portions that are to be offered
on the altar have been offered (Targum, Rashi). Every meal-offering,
after a handful of the flour was burnt on the altar (Lev. 2.3; 5.13; 6.9),
and every sin and guilt-offering, after the fat has been offered and the
blood sprinkled and poured out on the altar (Lev. 4.25, 26; 7.2–5). In
the case of the burnt-offerings, the skin only was given over to the
priests (Lev. 7.8).

which they may render unto Me] Lit. "return unto Me", or "make
restitution unto Me", since the guilt-offering is connected with the
idea of compensation for wrongs done to individuals (5.8; I Sam. 6.3;
Rashi, Luzzatto, Ehrlich). Our translation may intend to include also
all the forms of sacrifices mentioned here (Herxheimer).

10 thy sons. In a most holy place shalt thou eat thereof;
every male may eat thereof; it shall be holy unto thee.
11 And this is thine: the heave-offering of their gift, even all
the wave-offerings of the children of Israel; I have given
them unto thee, and to thy sons and to thy daughters
with thee, as a due for ever; every one that is clean in thy
12 house may eat thereof. All the best of the oil, and all the

10. *In a most holy place*] Inside of the curtain in the court of the
tabernacle (Rashi, after Lev. 6.19). The phrase קדש הקדשים usually
denotes the holy of holies, a place where no one was permitted to enter,
except the high priest on the Day of Atonement. The Rabbis have
therefore interpreted this phrase to mean the inside of the tent, an unusual meaning of the phrase (Sifre 117, comp. ibn Ezra). R. V. has "as
the most holy things", in the manner of the most holy things (so also
Ramban, *Biur*, Ehrlich; comp. Ezek. 42.13; 46.20), but the construction of the sentence will not allow this.

11. *the heave-offering of their gift*] The portions given to the
priest out of the peace-offerings (Lev. 7.30–34) and the Nazirite sacrifice (6.19, 20), consisting of the breast and the right thigh which, as
prescribed, were first waved over the altar (Rashi). The peace-offerings
are usually designated as שלמים and the Rabbis class them as קדשים
קלים to distinguish them from the קדשי קדשים of v. 9.

even all the wave-offerings] This is not meant to include all the
objects that were waved over the altar, but only the part of the peace-
offering (the breast) that was so waved.

and to thy daughters with thee] Including also the wives of the priests,
even though not of priestly families themselves, as well as other members of the priest's household, including his slaves (Zeb. 5.6, 7). On
the other hand, the daughters of a priest who are married to common
Israelites lose their right to partake of these portions (Lev. 22.12;
comp. Ehrlich, who derives this law from the expression "with thee",
as long as they are in thy charge).

that is clean] Ritually, a condition that was a necessary prerequisite
for partaking of a sacrificial meal (Lev. 22.3–7).

12. *All the best*] Lit. fat, a term often used for the best (Deut.
32.14; Ps. 81.17; 147.14).

best of the wine, and of the corn, the first part of them
which they give unto the LORD, to thee have I given them.
The first-ripe fruits of all that is in their land, which they 13
bring unto the LORD, shall be thine; every one that is
clean in thy house may eat thereof. Every thing devoted 14
in Israel shall be thine. Every thing that openeth the 15
womb, of all flesh which they offer unto the LORD, both
of man and beast, shall be thine; howbeit the first-born
of man shalt thou surely redeem, and the firstling of unclean

the first part of them]   The choice part, in explanation of "the best"
(comp. Deut. 18.4). The usual interpretation is that this refers to the
priestly portion of the produce of the field, the "first" gift put aside ·
after the harvest (Sifre 117; Rashi). No definite amount is fixed here,
but the Rabbis declared that the generous would give 1/40 of the crop
(or according to Bet Shammai 1/30), the average person 1/50 and the
parsimonious 1/60 (Ter. 4.3; comp. Hirsch).

13. *The first-ripe fruits*] Referring to the ceremony described in
Deut. 26.2–10, known as the offering of the *Bikkurim*, i. e. the first
ripe fruits that one notices in his field or orchard and designates as
Bikkurim are brought to Jerusalem with elaborate ceremony and
deposited with the priest, after the owner recites the prescribed formula
(Mishna, Bik. I; comp. Gray's discussion of the whole subject,
pp. 225–229).

of all that is in their land] The seven species of vegetation for which
Palestine is known, viz. wheat, barley, vine, fig, pomegranate, oil and
honey (Bik. 1.3).

14. *Every thing devoted*] Everything that an individual of his own
free will devotes to the service of the sanctuary (cf. Lev. 27, 28, 29).

15. *Every thing that openeth the womb*] All first-born by right belong
to God (Ex. 13.2; 12–15) and are by Him given to the priests. The
first-born of man and of unclean animals shall be redeemed and the
redemption-money given to the priest, while the first-born of clean
animals should be given to the priest outright.

the firstling of unclean beasts shalt thou redeem] According to the
rabbinic interpretation, this refers only to the first-born of the ass and
not to that of any other unclean animal, as the horse or the camel,

16 beasts shalt thou redeem. And their redemption-money—
from a month old shalt thou redeem them—shall be,
according to thy valuation, five shekels of silver, after
the shekel of the sanctuary—the same is twenty gerahs.
17 But the firstling of an ox, or the firstling of a sheep, or the

since in Ex. 13.13 the ass only is mentioned (Sifre 117; Bek. 5b, 6a).
There, however, the redemption appears to be optional, since the
owner could kill the ass if he so desired, while here the redemption
seems to be obligatory. Hirsch maintains that here also the redemption of the ass is optional and finds a support in the fact that in the
case of the first-born of man, the expression is פדה תפדה, "shalt thou
surely redeem", while in the case of the unclean animal the word תפדה,
"thou *mayest* redeem", is used (comp. Gray, p.230).

shalt thou redeem] I. e. accept the redemption-money, the whole
section being addressed to Aaron.

16. *And their redemption-money*] Of the first-born among men,
although the plural here might indicate that it refers also to the first-
born of unclean animals. The rendering "his" (McNeile) or "its"
(Gray) would be more correct, since the first-born of unclean animals
are to be redeemed according to their valuation by the priest (Lev.
27.11, 27) or, in the case of an ass, by a sheep, presumably of equal
value (Ex. 13.13). R. V. has: "And those that are to be redeemed of
them from a month old shalt thou redeem" (comp. Holzinger's suggestion that both the first-born of man and of unclean cattle were to
be brought to the priest to be valued).

from a month old] On reaching the age of one month. In the case
of clean animals, the law prescribes that they be given to the priest
after the eighth day of their birth (Ex. 22.29). The redemption of the
first-born of unclean animals may take place immediately at birth
(Bek. 12b).

according to thy valuation] Leeser's rendering, "according to the
usual estimation", is perhaps more correct, since the suffix ך should
not be taken here as the pronominal ending for 2nd masc. sing., but
as belonging to the root (Ehrlich to Lev. 5.15). Targum has "his
estimate" (comp. Koenig, *Lehrgeb.*, II, 277c, 303a).

five shekels] Cf. 3.47 and note.

17–18. The first-born of clean animals cannot be redeemed but
must be given to the priest and are to be treated in the same manner

firstling of a goat, thou shalt not redeem; they are holy:
thou shalt dash their blood against the altar, and shalt
make their fat smoke for an offering made by fire, for a
sweet savour unto the Lord. And the flesh of them shall 18
be thine, as the wave-breast and as the right thigh, it
shall be thine. All the heave-offerings of the holy things, 19
which the children of Israel offer unto the Lord, have I
given thee, and thy sons and thy daughters with thee, as
a due for ever; it is an everlasting covenant of salt before
the Lord unto thee and to thy seed with thee.'

And the Lord said unto Aaron: 'Thou shalt have no 20

as the peace-offerings, i. e. the blood is poured out against the altar
and the fat burned on the altar (Lev. 3.2–5). The flesh of the first-
born, however, is not like the flesh of the peace-offering, which may be
eaten by any one who is ritually clean (Lev. 7.19–21), but may be
eaten only by the priest, even as the breast and the thigh of the peace-
offering (cf. v. 11 and n.).

19. A summary of the laws enumerated above, forming a proper
conclusion to the introduction in v. 8 (Sifre 118).

covenant of salt] An everlasting covenant that cannot be broken
(Rashi, Rashbam, see II Chron. 13.5; comp. Gray, quoting W. R.
Smith and Wellhausen, about the institution of the covenant of salt
among the Arabs; comp. Trumbull, *Covenant of Salt*, N. Y., 1899).

20. *And the Lord said unto Aaron*] This apparently is the beginning of a new section, although in the Hebrew text the new section
begins with v. 21. Aaron is addressed here as the representative of the
priests and not of the whole tribe of Levi, although the fact is true also
with regard to the whole tribe (vv. 23, 24). Because no landed property
was assigned to the priests in Canaan, these offerings are to be given
to them for their maintenance. The Rabbis explain the terms "portion"
and "inheritance", the latter to refer to a portion in the land at the
time of the division and the former to a share in the booty taken from
the enemy (Sifre 119). See 35.1–8 regarding the 48 towns that were
set aside for the priests and the Levites, and the notes there.

inheritance in their land, neither shalt thou have any
portion among them; I am thy portion and thine inherit-
21 ance among the children of Israel. And unto the children
of Levi, behold, I have given all the tithe in Israel for an
inheritance, in return for their service which they serve,
22 even the service of the tent of meeting. And henceforth
the children of Israel shall not come nigh the tent of meet-
23 ing, lest they bear sin, and die. But the Levites alone shall

I am thy portion]   Targum has "the gifts which I give you are thy
portion", which is of course a paraphrase (see Adler). The reference
is here primarily to the material benefits that the priests derive out
of the gifts which the Israelites offer to God, although it may also
have a spiritual connotation, indicating that God is the portion of the
priests in the sense of Ps. 16.5 (comp. Deut. 10.9; 18.2; Josh. 13.14–23).

21–24.   GIFTS DUE TO THE LEVITES.

The Levites are to receive the tithe, i. e. one tenth of the produce
of the fields of the Israelites, in remuneration for their services in the
tabernacle. Thus, while they have no portion in the land, they are
given a portion in the produce of the land
  21. *all the tithe*] I. e. the tenth part of all the produce of the field
(comp. Deut. 14.22–29; 26.12–15). In Lev. 27.30–33 reference is also
made to the tithe of cattle, but both here and in Deut. the reference
is apparently exclusively to the tithe of the produce of the field (comp.
Neh. 10.38).
  in return for their service] An actual wage and material reward
(comp. v. 31) as distinguished from the "consecrated portion" (v. 8
and note) applied to the priestly gifts (Ehrlich).
  22. *lest they bear sin, and die*] The Levites are given this remuneration for their work in the tabernacle, so that the Israelites should not
come near to the sanctuary and thereby suffer penalty. The Levites
are thus saving the Israelites from sin and from its consequent results,
as was demonstrated in the incident of Korah (17.28; *Biur*).
  23. *the Levites alone*] The word הוא is well rendered here "alone"
in antithesis to "the children of Israel" in v. 22 (ibn Ezra).

do the service of the tent of meeting, and they shall bear their iniquity; it shall be a statute for ever throughout your generations, and among the children of Israel they shall have no inheritance. For the tithe of the children of 24 Israel, which they set apart as a gift unto the LORD, I have given to the Levites for an inheritance; therefore I have said unto them: Among the children of Israel they shall have no inheritance.'

And the LORD spoke unto Moses, saying: 'Moreover 25-26 thou shalt speak unto the Levites, and say unto them: When ye take of the children of Israel the tithe which I have given you from them for your inheritance, then ye

and they shall bear their iniquity] The Levites will be responsible for sins committed by the Israelites in connection with the tabernacle, since the Levites have the charge to keep the Israelites away from it (v. 1; Rashi, *Biur*; but comp. Kahana).

they shall have no inheritance] In the division of the land, although certain towns were assigned to them (v. 20 and note).

24. *as a gift unto the Lord*] The tithe also is a gift that the Israelites set apart for God and by Him is given to the Levites. The term תרומה is ordinarily applied to the heave-offering given to the priest, and it is used here, according to the Rabbis, because when the tithe is given to the Levite it still contains within it the tenth part of it which is due to the priest (Sifre 119).

25–32. GIFTS DUE TO THE PRIESTS FROM THE LEVITES.

From the tithe that the Israelites give to the Levites, the latter are told to set aside one tenth for the priests. Although this belongs to the priestly dues and should follow v. 19, it is inserted here because it is dependent on the Levitical tithe of 21–24 (see Neh. 10.39).

25. *unto Moses*] Rather than to Aaron as in vv. 1, 8, 20, because the following law applies to the relation between the priests and the Levites, in which Aaron is concerned (ibn Ezra).

shall set apart of it a gift for the LORD, even a tithe of
27 the tithe. And the gift which ye set apart shall be reckoned
unto you, as though it were the corn of the threshing-floor,
28 and as the fulness of the winepress. Thus ye also shall
set apart a gift unto the LORD of all your tithes, which ye
receive of the children of Israel; and thereof ye shall give
the gift which is set apart unto the LORD to Aaron the
29 priest. Out of all that is given you ye shall set apart all
of that which is due unto the LORD, of all the best thereof,
30 even the hallowed part thereof out of it. Therefore thou
shalt say unto them: When ye set apart the best thereof

27. *And the gift which ye set apart*] I. e. the tenth part of the tithe
which the Levites give to the priests shall be regarded with the same
sanctity as the heave-offering which the Israelites give to the priests
directly (v. 12; Rashi). Others take the word תרומתכם to refer not to
the gift which the Levites are to give to the priests, but to the tithe
which the Israelites give to the Levites (v. 24; in antithesis to תרומת ה׳
in v. 28), and understand the passage in the sense that after the Levites
received their tithe they were to regard it as their own, just as the
Israelites regarded the flour spread out on the threshing-floor and
the wine produced by the wine press, from which they have set aside
the heave-offering, as their own (Herxheimer, Ehrlich). The difficulty
with this interpretation is that while the amount of the heave-offering
is not specified, here a tenth is specifically mentioned. Luzzatto renders:
"and it shall be accounted unto you as if you had given out of your
own threshing-floor and wine press".

29. *of all the best thereof*] Out of the best of the tithe given to you,
you shall set aside the tenth part (the hallowed part) for the priest
(cf. v. 12).

30. *thou shalt say*] Referring to Moses.

When ye set apart] After you have taken off the tenth part of your
tithe and given it to the priest, you may use the remainder in the same
manner as the Israelites use their produce after the hallowed portions
have been separated, as is explained in the following verse (see v. 27
and note).

from it, then it shall be counted unto the Levites as the
increase of the threshing-floor, and as the increase of the
winepress. And ye may eat it in every place, ye and your 31
households; for it is your reward in return for your service
in the tent of meeting. And ye shall bear no sin by reason 32

31. *in every place*] Not like the priestly gifts which may be eaten
only in a holy place (v. 10), or the heave-offering of the priest which
may be eaten only in a place which is ritually clean (Sifre 122).

32. *And ye shall bear no sin*] The Levites who set aside the tenth
part of their tithes for the priest shall be clear of all sin in respect to
it. On the other hand, if they consume the tithe without giving up the
tenth, which is included among the "holy things of the children of
Israel", they are guilty of a capital offence. The Rabbis also stress the
phrase "the best thereof" and rule that it is sinful for the Levite not
to set aside for the priest the best part of the tithe given to him (Sifre
122; Yeb. 89b).

Note.— The Rabbis classified all the priestly gifts under the following
24 headings, 12 of which constitute gifts made on the Temple precincts
and 12 those presented outside of the Temple. The following are the
gifts assigned to the priests in the Temple: 1) Sin-offerings; 2) Guilt-
offerings; 3) The congregational peace-offering brought on Shabuot
(Lev. 23.20); 4) The skin of the burnt-offering; 5) The remainder of
the oil that accompanied the offerings of the leper; 6) The remainder
of the Omer of barley offered on the second day of Passover; 7) The
two loaves offered on Shabuot; 8) The showbread; 9) The remainder
of all meal-offerings; 10) The heave-offering that accompanied the
thank-offerings, consisting of loaves of four kinds (Lev. 7.12–14);
11) The breast and the thigh of individual peace-offerings; 12) The
shoulder of the ram offered by the Nazirite, together with the loaves
that go with it. The twelve gifts that the priests received outside of
the Temple, are: 1) The heave-offering (*Terumah*, about 1/50 of the
produce of the field); 2) The tenth part of the tithe given to the
Levites; 3) First part of the dough; 4) The first-fruits (*Bikkurim*);
5) The first part of the wool after shearing; 6) The shoulder, the two
cheeks and the maw, known as *Mattanot* (Deut. 18.3); 7) The first-
born of men; 8) The first-born of clean animals; 9) The first-born of

of it, seeing that ye have set apart from it the best thereof; and ye shall not profane the holy things of the children of Israel, that ye die not.'

19   And the LORD spoke unto Moses and unto Aaron, saying:

the ass; 10) All devoted things; 11) The field that was devoted and not redeemed at the time of the jubilee (Lev. 27.21); 12) Property taken by violence from one who died without heirs (a *Ger*) and returned by the repentant robber (Num. 5.8; Sifre 119 and Horovitz's notes; with some variations found Hul. 133b; B. K. 110b; Tosefta Hal. 2.8; Yer. Hal. 60a).

CHAPTER 19.

1–22. PROCESS OF RITUAL PURIFICATION.

This chapter deals with a peculiar form of purification prescribed for those who have come in contact with a dead body. The first part (1–13) describes the method of purification, the second part (14–22), the laws concerning the impurity. The whole chapter apparently has no connection with the preceding or with the following chapters, but forms a distinct unit by itself. Ibn Ezra finds a connection between this and the preceding chapter in that both contain statutes that pertain to the priests, since the whole work of preparing the ashes was to be done by the priest (vv. 3, 4, 5, 7). On the other hand, the connection between this and the following chapter, where the death of Miriam is recorded, is suggested by Josephus. The people who busied themselves with the burial of Miriam were purified by the ashes of the first red heifer prepared by Moses (*Ant.* iv.4.6). There is no reference to the ceremony described here in any other part of the Bible except in the section 31.19–24 (comp. Heb. 9.13), which obviously assumes this ceremony, although impurity caused by contact with a dead body is frequently referred to (Lev. 21.1–4, 10; 22.4–7; Num. 5.2; 6.6–13; 9.6, etc.). See Gray, 241–248, where parallels are quoted from primitive cults and different interpretations of this ceremony are presented.

This is the statute of the law which the LORD hath 2
commanded, saying: Speak unto the children of Israel,
that they bring thee a red heifer, faultless, wherein is no

1–13. PURIFICATION BY THE ASHES OF THE RED HEIFER.

The prescription here is as follows: A red cow, without blemish,
which has never borne a yoke, is to be slain outside the camp. Eleazar
takes some of its blood and sprinkles it seven times in the direction of
the tabernacle. The cow is then burned, together with some cedar-
wood, hyssop and a scarlet thread. The ashes are then gathered together and preserved outside of the camp to be used, after being mixed
with water, in the process of purification. Any person who has become
defiled through contact with a dead body shall have these "waters of
impurity" sprinkled upon him on the third and seventh days after he
became impure, and on the completion of the seventh day his impurity
is declared removed. The priest who prepares the offering, the one
who burns the cow and the one who gathers the ashes, are all rendered
unclean for a period of one day.

1. *unto Moses and unto Aaron*] The verb in the next verse is in
the singular, referring to Moses, who was to deliver the message to the
children of Israel (Ramban), or perhaps to Aaron only (as in 18.1, 8, 20).

2. *the statute of the law*] Cf. 31.21. These are the only two places
where this combination חקת התורה is used, and both deal with this
manner of purification. The Rabbis apply this expression to laws the
reason for which is not apparent, or such as present contradictions
like the ceremony of the red heifer, the ashes of which remove impurity
and yet those who are engaged in its preparation themselves become
impure thereby (Num. R. 19.1, 4; Tan. Hukkat, 4, 26).

a red heifer] The more common Hebrew term for heifer is עגלה
(Gen. 15.9), while the word פרה usually denotes a full-grown animal
(Gen. 32.16). There is a difference of opinion among the Rabbis as
to the exact age limit of the red heifer, R. Meir maintaining that it
may be five years old or more (Sifre 123; Parah 1.1). It must be a
female, as in the case of the sin-offering (6.14; Lev. 4.27; 5.6; 14.10)
and entirely red. The Rabbis explain that the red heifer was to serve
as an atonement for the sin of the golden calf, hence it had to be a
female like the sin-offering and it must be red, which is symbolic of
sin (Isa. 1.18).

faultless, wherein is no blemish] A. V., "without spot", Leeser,

3 blemish, and upon which never came yoke. And ye shall
give her unto Eleazar the priest, and she shall be brought
forth without the camp, and she shall be slain before his
4 face. And Eleazar the priest shall take of her blood with

"a completely red cow" (cf. Mendelssohn), following the rabbinic
interpretation (Sifre 123; Parah 2.5) that "faultless" here modifies
"red", to indicate that it must be perfectly red, so that if it had two
hairs of a different color it would be invalidated for use in this ceremony.
This explains the apparent redundancy of "faultless" and "without
blemish", although this use is not uncommon (Lev. 22.19–21).

upon which never came yoke] This provision is also required in
the case of the heifer brought by the inhabitants of a town in the
vicinity of which a dead body was found (Deut. 21.2), and the cows
that brought the ark back from the Philistines (I Sam. 6.7), but in
other cases where cows are offered as sacrifices this requirement is
not necessary. Here it is required that no profane work should have
been done by the heifer.

3. *and ye shall give her*] The pl. used here, referring back to v. 1,
Moses and Aaron.

unto Eleazar the priest] Under whose direction the ceremony shall
be performed. Since the work connected with the ceremony causes
impurity, the high-priest Aaron was not allowed to do it (comp. Ramban). In later times the ceremony could be performed by any priest
(Sifre 123; Parah 4.1; Yoma 42b).

she shall be brought out and .... slain] In the Hebrew text both
verbs are in the active form, hence Leeser translates the first, "he shall
bring forth", i. e. Eleazar, and the second, "some one shall kill it",
as impersonal, in accordance with the traditional rendering (Rashi,
ibn Ezra). LXX translates both in the plural.

without the camp] Since this was not to be treated as a sacrifice
and caused ritual pollution, it should be taken out of the camp, which
should always be kept clean. There are other instances too where a
sacrifice, especially that of an anointed prince or of the congregation,
has to be burned outside the camp (Lev. 4.11, 21; 8.17; 9.11; 16.27),
but in those cases certain parts were first offered on the altar.

his finger, and sprinkle of her blood toward the front of
the tent of meeting seven times. And the heifer shall be 5
burnt in his sight; her skin, and her flesh, and her blood,
with her dung, shall be burnt. And the priest shall take 6
cedar-wood, and hyssop, and scarlet, and cast it into the

4. *with his finger*] The forefinger of the right hand (BDB; Sifre
123).

and sprinkle] As in the case of the sin-offering of the prince or of
the congregation (Lev. 4.6, 17), or of the sacrifices offered by the high-
priest on the Day of Atonement (Lev. 16.14, 19).

5. *shall be burnt*] See note to v. 3.

in his sight] In the sight of Eleazar (comp. Rashbam, "in the sight
of Aaron").

with her dung] The fecal matter that is in the intestines at the time
of burning. The entire cow was burnt, as in the case of the sin-offering
of the prince and of the congregation (Lev. 4.11, 20). In the case of
the whole-offering, the skin was not burnt but given to the priest
(Lev. 1.6).

6. *And the priest*] Eleazar or any other priest (Targ. Jon.; Yoma
43a).

cedar-wood, and hyssop] A piece of the cedar tree (Sifre 124) and
the hyssop, the strongest and the weakest respectively of the vegetable
kingdom (cf. I Kings 5.13). It is possible that the latter was taken for
its medicinal value and cleansing properties (Ps. 51.9).

and scarlet] Lit. scarlet-worm (*caccus ilicis*, which attaches itself
to leaves and twigs of *quercus coccifera*, the dried body of the female
of which yields coloring matter, BDB). Mendelssohn and Leeser have
"scarlet thread". In Lev. 14.4 ff., the same three objects are used in
the process of the purification of a leper, but while there the thread is
tied around the cedar-wood and the hyssop and then the combination
is dipped in the blood of the sacrifice and sprinkled on the leper, here
they are thrown into the pyre made by the burning of the heifer. The
hyssop is also used elsewhere as a brush with which blood is sprinkled
on a person or on objects (v. 18; Ex. 12.22; comp. ibn Ezra on Lev.
14.4).

7 midst of the burning of the heifer. Then the priest shall
wash his clothes, and he shall bathe his flesh in water,
and afterward he may come into the camp, and the priest
8 shall be unclean until the even. And he that burneth
her shall wash his clothes in water, and bathe his flesh in
9 water, and shall be unclean until the even. And a man
that is clean shall gather up the ashes of the heifer, and
lay them up without the camp in a clean place, and it
shall be kept for the congregation of the children of Israel
for a water of sprinkling; it is a purification from sin.
10 And he that gathereth the ashes of the heifer shall wash
his clothes, and be unclean until the even; and it shall be

7.   *Then the priest*]   Who threw the objects into the fire (ibn Ezra).
he may come into the camp]   Rashi suggests that this phrase belongs
after "and the priest shall be unclean until the even". Another explanation is that after the burning, Eleazar's work was done so that he
might return to the camp, although he continues unclean until the
evening in respect to partaking of holy food (*Biur*, cf. ibn Ezra). However, the expression "he may come into the camp" is technical in the
sense that the impurity is entirely removed (cf. Lev. 16, 26, 28).
9.   *a man that is clean*]   One who was not in any way connected
with the ceremony until now and not necessarily a priest (Sifre 124).
it shall be kept]   Lit. it shall be for a keeping (cf. 17.25; Ex. 16.32,
34), i. e. the ashes. The Rabbis say that part of the ashes was actually
stored away in the Temple (Sifre 124; Sifre Zuta; Parah, 3.11).
for a water of sprinkling]   So also Rashi; R. V., "water of separation",
margin, "water of impurity", water that removes impurity (BDB).
The phrase presupposes the mingling of the ashes with water, although
this is not expressed until later (v. 17). Herxheimer has "water of
the unclean", water used for those who are unclean (comp. note there).
it is a purification from sin]   The water serves the purpose of purification (Rashi, comp. Sifre 124). R. V., "it is a sin-offering", has no
point when applied to the ashes (comp. 8.7). Leeser's "it is a purification offering" is no improvement.

unto the children of Israel, and unto the stranger that
sojourneth among them, for a statute for ever. He that 11
toucheth the dead, even any man's dead body, shall be
unclean seven days; the same shall purify himself there- 12
with on the third day and on the seventh day, and he shall
be clean; but if he purify not himself the third day and
the seventh day, he shall not be clean. Whosoever toucheth 13
the dead, even the body of any man that is dead, and
purifieth not himself—he hath defiled the tabernacle of
the LORD—that soul shall be cut off from Israel; because
the water of sprinkling was not dashed against him, he
shall be unclean; his uncleanness is yet upon him. This 14

11. *any man's dead body*] Whether Jew or non-Jew (ibn Ezra;
Yeb. 61a), but not that of an animal, in which case the period of defilement concludes with the sunset of the same day (Lev. 11.24, 25, 27 ff.).

shall be unclean] This phrase may also be regarded as the protasis
of the following verse: Any one who touches . . . . and thereby becomes
unclean for seven days, shall go through this process of purification
(ibn Ezra, Luzzatto).

12. *shall purify himself therewith*] With the ashes of purification
(Targum, Rashi).

and he shall be clean] At the end of the seventh day. There is no
punishment prescribed for the one who refuses to submit to this process
of purification, except that he remains unclean.

13. *he hath defiled the tabernacle of the Lord*] If the same person,
while unclean, entered the tabernacle, he was guilty of an offence that
carried with it the punishment of *Karet* (v. 20; Lev. 15.31; Sifre 129;
comp. 9.13 and note).

his uncleanness is yet upon him] As long as the water of purification
was not sprinkled upon him as prescribed. Our translation is careful
to distinguish between הזה sprinkle and זרק dash, both here and in
vv. 18, 19, 20. This would imply that first the water was sprinkled
upon the person or object that has become unclean and then it was

is the law: when a man dieth in a tent, every one that
cometh into the tent, and every thing that is in the tent,
15 shall be unclean seven days. And every open vessel,

dashed against him or it (cf. Gray and BDB, s. v. זרק). Many of the
other versions make no such distinction and render both words "sprinkle".

14–22. PURIFICATION FROM DEFILEMENT BY CONTACT WITH THE DEAD.

In this section more detailed regulations are given with regard to
the impurity caused by contact with a dead body. Not only actual
contact (11–13), but the mere presence of a person or of an uncovered
vessel in a tent where a death occurred causes defilement (14–15).
Similarly contact in the open field with the body of a person who suffered a violent death, or with a bone of a dead person or with a grave
causes the same degree of defilement (16). The mode of purification
is then described in greater detail than in 12–13 (17–20), with the
addition that the one who sprinkles the water or touches it also becomes
defiled (21). Everything that the person so defiled touches also
becomes unclean, although such impurity is of a lesser degree, the
period of uncleanness lasting only one day (22).

14. *when a man dieth in a tent*] The usual dwelling place in the
wilderness, but the law applies also to a house or any other habitation
(LXX has here also "house"). The Rabbis extended this law to include
anything that overhangs or forms a covering over a dead body (Sifre
126). Nor is it necessary that the person should die in the tent or under
that covering. Even if the death occurred elsewhere and the body
was brought into the tent, the degree of defilement for any one who
entered the tent would be the same (ib.; ibn Ezra; Ramban).

every one that cometh into the tent] While the dead body is there, even
though he did not come in direct contact with it.

everything that is in the tent]   Including the tent itself (Ramban).

15. *every open vessel*]   The Rabbis understood by this vessels made
of clay only, viz. earthenware, which become impure only through
contact with the inside surface (Lev. 11.33), and when they become
defiled they cannot be cleansed but must be destroyed (Sifre **126**;
Targum, Rashi).

which hath no covering close-bound upon it, is unclean.
And whosoever in the open field toucheth one that is 16
slain with a sword, or one that dieth of himself, or a bone
of a man, or a grave, shall be unclean seven days. And 17
for the unclean they shall take of the ashes of the burning
of the purification from sin, and running water shall be
put thereto in a vessel. And a clean person shall take 18
hyssop, and dip it in the water, and sprinkle it upon the
tent, and upon all the vessels, and upon the persons that

---

covering close-bound] The words פתיל צמיד are found only here in
this sense. According to rabbinic interpretation, צמיד means the covering and פתיל the clay which fastens the cover to the vessel (Sifre 126).
Other interpretations have been given to this phrase (ibn Ezra, Kimhi,
cf. Gray, phil. note), but they are all of the same significance, indicating
a vessel that is well covered (Saadia takes פתיל as a modifying passive
participle, "no cover is tied thereto"; Kohut 62).

is unclean] Remains unclean and cannot be purified.

16. *in the open field*] Cf. II Sam. 11.11. In the open, where there
is no covering, impurity is communicated only through direct contact
(Rashi).

17. *of the ashes*] Lit. dust, but it may mean anything pulverized
(=אפר, comp. Hul. 88b).

the purification from sin] Comp. v. 9.

running water] Fresh water from a running stream.

shall be put thereto in a vessel] Following Targum, but contrary to
rabbinic tradition, which requires that the water be placed in the
vessel first and then the ashes (Sifre 128; Yoma 43b et al.; cf. Ramban
and Adler, who endeavor to find a means of reconciling Targum with
the rabbinic law).

18. *a clean person*] Perhaps a priest (ibn Ezra), although this is
not required by law (Sifre 129).

hyssop] A bunch of hyssop, distinct from that which was to be
burnt with the heifer (v. 6).

and sprinkle] Enumerating in a general way the cases mentioned
in vv. 14–16.

were there, and upon him that touched the bone, or the
19 slain, or the dead, or the grave. And the clean person
shall sprinkle upon the unclean on the third day, and on
the seventh day; and on the seventh day he shall purify
him; and he shall wash his clothes, and bathe himself in
20 water, and shall be clean at even. But the man that shall
be unclean, and shall not purify himself, that soul shall
be cut off from the midst of the assembly, because he
hath defiled the sanctuary of the LORD; the water of sprinkling hath not been dashed against him: he is unclean.
21 And it shall be a perpetual statute unto them; and he
that sprinkleth the water of sprinkling shall wash his
clothes; and he that toucheth the water of sprinkling
22 shall be unclean until even. And whatsoever the unclean
person toucheth shall be unclean; and the soul that toucheth
him shall be unclean until even.

19. *And the clean person*] In further explanation of v. 18.
he shall purify him] He shall declare him pure at the end of the
seventh day, after he has washed his clothes and bathed.
20. *But the man*] Repetition of v. 13.
the sanctuary] Comp. v. 13, where "tabernacle" is used, and see
Shab. 16b.
21. *and he that sprinkleth*] The water of purification brings to
those that come in contact with it impurity of a slight degree, lasting
only one day (comp. note on v. 2). The Rabbis, however, say that the
one who sprinkles the water does not become impure, and that this
law applies only to the one who carries it or the one who touches it
(Nid. 9a; Yoma 14a, cf. Sifre 129, Sifre Zuta and Malbim).
22. *And the soul that toucheth him*] Who touches the person who
has become unclean by contact with the dead body or was under the
same roof with the dead body. In rabbinic phraseology, the dead body
itelf is designated as אבי אבות הטומאה, the one coming in contact with it
as אב הטומאה, the one touching that person as ראשון לטומאה, and in some
cases also a שני לטומאה is mentioned.

And the children of Israel, even the whole congregation, **20**

20. HAPPENINGS DURING PERIOD OF WANDERING.

This chapter brings the narrative down to the close of the period of the forty years' wandering in the wilderness. The children of Israel arrive in the wilderness of Zin, where Miriam dies (v. 1). Scarcity of water again calls forth the dissatisfaction of the people and results in the sin of Moses and Aaron, on account of which they are condemned to die in the wilderness and not to enter the promised land (2–13). In preparing for the conquest of Canaan, the Israelites ask the Edomites to permit them to pass through their land, but the request is refused (14–21). Aaron then dies at Mount Hor and Eleazar is appointed his successor (22–29).

This chapter seems to follow upon ch. 14, where the Israelites, on account of their contemplated rebellion in connection with the incident of the spies, are doomed to wander in the wilderness for forty years, until the generation of the exodus entirely disappears (14.33). An attempt to enter Canaan at that time failed (14.44–45). The spies were sent out while the Israelites were in the wilderness of Paran, in the second year of the exodus, while the narrative begins here with the first month of the fortieth year (cf. 33.38), so that the intervening 38 years are not accounted for in this narrative. The wilderness of Zin lies between Paran and Canaan (but see note on 13.21), the district traversed by the spies, so that the intervening 38 years were spent somewhere between these two points, although in 14.25 the people were ordered to go to the wilderness by the way of the Red Sea, which would indicate a backward direction. In Deut. 2.14 it is related that the 38 years were spent in wandering from Kadesh to the borders of Moab, Kadesh denoting Kadesh-barnea in the wilderness of Paran. It is therefore established that only a short time was consumed in the journey toward the Red Sea, while the greater part of the 38 years was spent in wandering about in the wilderness of Paran, until they reached the wilderness of Zin, at the beginning of the fortieth year.

1. MIRIAM DIES AT KADESH.

even the whole congregation] The same combination is found again in v. 22. Rashi and ibn Ezra (comp. Num. R. 19.9) regard the repetition of the phrase as emphasizing the fact that "the whole congregation included all that were destined to enter the promised land after the generation of the exodus had died out" (cf. Ramban).

came into the wilderness of Zin in the first month; and
the people abode in Kadesh; and Miriam died there, and

into the wilderness of Zin]   From the wilderness of Paran, where the
years of wandering were spent (cf. note on 13.21).

in the first month]   Probably of the fortieth year (ibn Ezra, Rashbam,
but comp. Luzzatto המשתדל).

the people abode in Kadesh]   Described in Deut. 1.2 as being "eleven
days' journey from Horeb by the way of Mount Seir". Kadesh is also
found in the wilderness of Paran, whence the spies were sent out (13.26).
This fact led some to believe that there were two places by that name,
one in the wilderness of Paran and the other in the wilderness of Zin
(Ramban, comp. *Biur*). The more likely explanation is that the whole
district was known as the wilderness of Paran, of which the wilderness
of Zin formed the northern part. The Israelites entered Kadesh, which
was situated in the wilderness of Zin, early in their travels and stayed
there for many years (Deut. 1.46). Because of the doom pronounced
upon them in consequence of the incident of the spies, which occurred
while they were settled there, they were compelled to wander about in
a southerly direction, until they came back to Kadesh in the fortieth
year (Szanto, comp. Luzzatto המשתדל, Herxheimer).

The site of Kadesh was established in 1842 by John Rowlands, as
lying between El Arish and Mount Hor, the burial place of Aaron.
There is still a spring of water there which the Arabs call "Ain Kadeis".
The spot was again visited by Henry Clay Trumbull in 1882, who wrote
a glowing and detailed description of the territory (*Kadesh Barnea*,
New York, 1884). C. Leonard Wooley and T. E. Lawrence who ex-
plored the country in 1913 for other reasons, while discounting much
of Trumbull's enthusiastic description of the verdure and the attract-
iveness of the place, agree with the early identification, but extend the
term Kadesh to include a much larger territory, making the wilderness of Zin and Kadesh-barnea identical with the country now included
in Ain el Guderat, Kusseima Muweilleh, and Ain Kadeis, for "only in
the Kusseima district are to be found enough water and green stuffs
to maintain so large a tribe for so long". (*Wilderness of Zin*, London,
1915, new ed., 1936, ch. IV; see Barton, *Archaeology and the Bible*,
p. 95)

and Miriam died there]   If we assume that the date given at the
beginning of this verse refers also to the death of Miriam, her death
preceded that of Aaron by five months only (33.38).

was buried there. And there was no water for the congre- 2
gation; and they assembled themselves together against
Moses and against Aaron. And the people strove with 3
Moses, and spoke, saying: 'Would that we had perished
when our brethren perished before the LORD! And why 4

2–13. THE SIN OF MOSES AND AARON AT MERIBAH.

The people found themselves without water and began to quarrel
with Moses and Aaron, reproaching them for having brought them to
the wilderness, where they were destined to die of thirst. God ordered
Moses to speak to one of the rocks in the neighborhood, in the presence
of the congregation, saying that enough water would come out to
satisfy the people and their cattle. Moses and Aaron called the people
together in front of the rock, but instead of speaking to the rock, Moses
struck the rock twice and water flowed from it. Because of this disobedience, God told Moses and Aaron that they, too, would share
the fate of all those who perished in the wilderness and would not be
permitted to enter the promised land.

A similar incident is recorded in Ex. 17.1–7, as having occurred at
the beginning of their journey, when they were encamped at Rephidim.
There, however, Moses is told to strike the rock, which he did, and
there were no evil consequences. Modern students of the Bible regard
these two narratives as different versions of the same story (Gray,
p. 258; comp., however, Keil who opposes this).

2. *And there was no water*] The Rabbis connect this with the
preceding verse in which the death of Miriam is recorded. During
the life of Miriam, so they relate, a spring of water followed the people
wherever they went and at her death the spring disappeared, so that
there was no water for the people (Ta'an. 9a; comp. Abarbanel; Keil,
p. 131 note).

3. *strove with Moses*] Principally, although the complaint was
against both Moses and Aaron (comp. Ex. 17.2).

when our brethren perished] As a result of the rebellion of Korah
(16.33, 35; 17.14; Luzzatto), or it may have reference to the generation
of the exodus that died in the wilderness (ibn Ezra).

before the Lord] As a punishment from God. Hirsch is of the opinion
that this phrase denotes a natural death, in contradistinction to death

have ye brought the assembly of the LORD into this wilder-
5 ness, to die there, we and our cattle? And wherefore
have ye made us to come up out of Egypt, to bring us in
unto this evil place? it is no place of seed, or of figs, or of
vines, or of pomegranates; neither is there any water to
6 drink.' And Moses and Aaron went from the presence of
the assembly unto the door of the tent of meeting, and
fell upon their faces; and the glory of the LORD appeared
7 unto them. And the LORD spoke unto Moses, saying:
8 'Take the rod, and assemble the congregation, thou, and
Aaron thy brother, and speak ye unto the rock before

from thirst by which they were now threatened, but the phrase does
not have this connotation and often has the opposite meaning (cf.
note on 3.4).

5. *out of Egypt*] Where we lacked none of the necessities of life
(16.13).

neither is there any water to drink] Not only is this not the land of
plenty pictured to us, but it even lacks the most indispensable needs
of life, like water.

6. *from the presence of the assembly*] As if fleeing for fear that
they might do them bodily harm, they take refuge in the tabernacle
(cf. Gen. 7.7; ibn Ezra).

and fell upon their faces] In prayer (cf. 14.5; 17.10; ibn Ezra), or
from exhaustion (*Biur*).

8. *Take the rod*] This may refer either to the rod which was placed
in the sanctuary as an everlasting memorial of the selection of the
tribe of Levi and was known as the rod of Aaron (17.25; Rashbam),
or to the rod of Moses with which he had already performed many
miracles (Ex. 4.17, 20 et al.) and which was kept in the sanctuary
(v. 9; ibn Ezra).

and speak ye] At Rephidim the order was to strike the rock (Ex.
17.6).

unto the rock] A definite rock, lying in the vicinity (ibn Ezra; comp.
Trumbull, *Kadesh Barnea*, pp. 272–274, for a description of this place).

their eyes, that it give forth its water; and thou shalt
bring forth to them water out of the rock; so thou shalt
give the congregation and their cattle drink.' And Moses 9
took the rod from before the LORD, as He commanded
him. And Moses and Aaron gathered the assembly together 10
before the rock, and he said unto them: 'Hear now, ye
rebels; are we to bring you forth water out of this rock?'
And Moses lifted up his hand, and smote the rock with 11
his rod twice; and water came forth abundantly, and the
congregation drank, and their cattle. And the LORD said 12

its water] The water that is often found in the bed of rocks (cf.
Malbim).

10. *Hear now, ye rebels*] Called so because of their expressed fear
of perishing in the wilderness before God's promise to them is fulfilled and because of their complaint against having been taken out of
Egypt. Neither of these would constitute an act of rebellion and it is
therefore charged to Moses' anger which made him utter this harsh
expression and which, according to some (see note on v. 12), constituted his sin.

are we to bring you forth water] Is it possible for us to bring
forth water out of this rock in a natural way? And yet this will now
happen through the will of God (see following note).

12. The sin of Moses and Aaron is described here as lack of faith
in God, while in v. 24 it is designated as rebellion against God. The
exact nature of the sin, however, which appears to have been regarded
so heinous as to cause their exclusion from entering the land of promise,
is not stated explicitly and has been a source of perplexity to Bible
commentators from the oldest times to the present day. The Jewish
traditional explanation is that the sin consisted in that they *struck*
the rock instead of speaking to it, as they were told to do. A large
rock or hill may have springs of water within it, which, however, may
be clogged by stones or earth. If Moses had spoken to the rock, as he
was ordered to do, and the water had come forth, the miracle would
have been quite patent and the name of God would have been sanctified thereby. In obtaining water by striking the rock, Moses failed

unto Moses and Aaron: 'Because ye believed not in Me,

to sanctify the name of God, because the people might say that there
was nothing miraculous about it, as the obstruction was removed
when the rock was struck and the water came forth in a natural way.
Through this action, therefore, which was an act of disobedience,
contrary to the express command of God, Moses and Aaron missed a
great opportunity of causing the name of God to become sanctified
among the people. This explanation, while not entirely satisfactory,
appears to be more reasonable than many another put forth in ancient
or modern times. The objection of ibn Ezra that Aaron should not
have been included in the punishment, since it was Moses who struck
the rock, is not valid because Aaron seems to have been associated
with Moses throughout the entire incident.

Moses and Aaron, allowing themselves to be overcome by ill-will
and resentment against the constant murmurings of the people, committed an indiscretion which is unpardonable in leaders. In his anger
(comp. Ps. 106.32, 33), Moses speaks harshly to the assembled congregation of Israel and strikes the rock, instead of addressing it as he
was commanded, thereby frustrating the purpose which God had in
mind in the performance of this miracle — the sanctification of God's
name. They thus failed to establish greater faith in God among the
people, which was the expected result had the plan been carried out
(comp. Luzzatto and Malbim).

Some are of the opinion that the sin of Moses is purposely not stated,
in order to keep his memory free from blemish (Ehrlich). In Deut.
1.37, it appears from the context that Moses was forbidden to enter
Canaan because of the sin of the spies, when the whole congregation
of the exodus was condemned to die in the wilderness (but see Orr, 278).
Other explanations of the sin have been given by various authors
(comp. Abarbanel). Some find it in the fact that Moses and Aaron
had not the courage to stand up and rebuke the people, and acted in a
cowardly manner in "fleeing" for refuge to the tabernacle (*Biur*).
Others see it in the expression "are we to bring you forth water", as
if they could do it with their own power, without the help of God
(Ramban). Others again find it in the fact that they called the people
"rebels", an offensive name for the people chosen by God (cf. ibn Ezra,
end). Modern Bible critics see here a conscious attempt on the part
of the editor to mutilate the original text of the traditional narrative
in order to obscure the sin committed by the great leaders. They even

to sanctify Me in the eyes of the children of Israel, therefore ye shall not bring this assembly into the land which I have given them.' These are the waters of Meribah, 13 where the children of Israel strove with the LORD, and He was sanctified in them.

attempt to reconstruct the original version by having the question "are we to bring you forth water out of this rock?" addressed by Moses to God, when ordered to speak to the rock. The rebuke, "Hear now, ye rebels", was, according to them, not addressed by Moses to the people, but by God to Moses and Aaron, and then followed by the command to strike the rock, which they did (Gray, following Cornill; Kahana).

to sanctify Me] The sin of Moses and Aaron prevented the power of God from becoming manifest to the people in its entire glory.

which I have given them] Which I promised to give to them. God's promise is regarded so certain of fulfillment that it is spoken of as if it had already been carried out.

13. *These are the waters of Meribah*] I. e. strife. The place is also known as Meribath-kadesh (27.14; Deut. 32.51; Ezek. 48.28 and 47.19) and is to be distinguished from the place Massah and Meribah in Rephidim (Ex. 17.7).

and He was sanctified in them] In the waters, in spite of the fact that Moses and Aaron did not carry out the full intention of God (Rashbam, Luzzatto); or "through them" (Leeser), through Moses and Aaron, because of the punishment decreed upon them as a result of the incident, which was a vindication of God's justice (Rashi, *Biur*; comp. ibn Ezra, quoting Lev. 10.3); or "in them" may refer back to the children of Israel in whose midst God's name became sanctified (McNeile, cf. Ezek. 20.41; 28.25). In the Sam. Pentateuch, Deut. 3.26b–28 is inserted here.

14–21. EDOM REFUSES PASSAGE TO ISRAEL.

Moses appeals to the king of Edom on the ground of his blood-relationship with Israel, to permit the Israelites to pass through his land, as their journey would be greatly shortened if they could enter Canaan from the east. The request is refused by the Edomites and the Israelites are compelled to retreat and take a round about way to

14   And Moses sent messengers from Kadesh unto the
king of Edom: 'Thus saith thy brother Israel: Thou
15 knowest all the travail that hath befallen us; how our
fathers went down into Egypt, and we dwelt in Egypt a
long time; and the Egyptians dealt ill with us, and our
16 fathers; and when we cried unto the LORD, He heard our
voice, and sent an angel, and brought us forth out of Egypt;
and, behold, we are in Kadesh, a city in the uttermost of
17 thy border. Let us pass, I pray thee, through thy land;
we will not pass through field or through vineyard, neither
will we drink of the water of the wells; we will go along
the king's highway, we will not turn aside to the right

reach their goal (21.4, 12, 13). Comp. Gen. 32.4–33.16, Jacob's endeavor to find favor with his brother Esau, the eponymous ancestor
of Edom. In the Sam. Pentateuch, this section is preceded by Deut.
2.2–6.

14. *Thus saith*] The words that the messengers should deliver
to the king of Edom.

thy brother] Israel, the brother of Esau, the progenitor of Edom
(Gen. 25.25, 30). The close relationship between Israel and Edom
finds expression in a number of passages (Deut. 2.4; 23.8; Obad. 1.10,
12; Amos 1.11).

Thou knowest] It is assumed that the Edomites had learned of
the trouble that Israel had gone through in Egypt (Ex. 15.15), a brief
summary of which is given in v. 15, and on account of their relationship with Israel entertained feelings of sympathy with them. No
mention is made here of the hardships of the journey in the wilderness,
possibly because they could not be expected to know of these.

16. *an angel*] Ibn Ezra (Ex. 14.19; 23.20; Isa. 63.9); or "a messenger" (Mendelssohn, as in v. 14), perhaps referring to Moses (Rashi).

uttermost of thy border] On the western border of Edom.

17. *the king's highway*] A route passed by traders, with royal
permission. In more recent times, such through routes were known as
darb es-sultan, the Sultan's way. The promise is made that they would

hand nor to the left, until we have passed thy border.'
And Edom said unto him: 'Thou shalt not pass through 18
me, lest I come out with the sword against thee.' And 19
the children of Israel said unto him: 'We will go up by
the highway; and if we drink of thy water, I and my cattle,
then will I give the price thereof; let me only pass through
on my feet; there is no hurt.' And he said: 'Thou shalt 20

go by the regular road and not touch cultivated land, that they would
pay for all that they may require on the road and that they would
cause no inconvenience to anybody.

thy border]   The northern border of Edom, leading to Canaan.

18.   *Edom*]   The king or the people of Edom.

with the sword]   Comp. Gen. 27.40 (Rashi; see Sforno who regards
this not as a threat of war, but as an explanation for the refusal. The
king of Edom expresses the apprehension that their passage might
lead to squabbles with the people and then to bloodshed).

19.   *And the children of Israel said*]   A second group of messengers
is sent to try again to obtain peaceful passage through the land, perhaps endeavoring to remove any misapprehension that may have
arisen from the original request.

by the highway]   The public road, not through cities, the road followed by caravans, which would make it synonymous with "king's
highway" in **v. 17**. Ehrlich renders "king's highway" as the road for
the passage of armies, and when this was refused, they asked permission to proceed over the "trade route". LXX distinguishes between
the request here and in v. 17 by saying that there they asked to be
permitted to pass through the land, and when this was refused, they
asked to be allowed to pass along the border of the land, by way of the
hill (comp. Gray).

on my feet]   Not on horses and donkeys, which might cause damage
(Ehrlich).

there is no hurt]   There is no intention to do any harm (comp. I
Sam. 20.21), nor is there any possibility of harm coming to you through
our passage.

not pass through.' And Edom came out against him with
21 much people, and with a strong hand. Thus Edom refused
to give Israel passage through his border; wherefore Israel
turned away from him.

22 And they journeyed from Kadesh; and the children of
Israel, even the whole congregation, came unto mount
23 Hor. And the LORD spoke unto Moses and Aaron in mount
24 Hor, by the border of the land of Edom, saying: 'Aaron
shall be gathered unto his people; for he shall not enter
into the land which I have given unto the children of

---

20. *and Edom came out against him*]   To show that the refusal was
definite and final, although no war was precipitated. On the refusal
of Edom, Israel turned back (v. 21), not wishing to force the matter
(Deut. 2.5).

22–29.   DEATH OF AARON.

Refused by Edom to pass through their land, the Israelites leave
Kadesh and reach Mount Hor. There Aaron dies and Eleazar is in-
ducted into the office of the high-priesthood.

22. *even the whole congregation*]   Cf. note on v. 1; see Rashi and ibn
Ezra.

mount Hor]   Identified with the modern Jebel Nebi Harun, about
50 miles south of the Dead Sea, just south of Petra (BDB), held sacred
by the Arabs. A small mosque on the summit of the mountain marks
its site. This identification is supported by ancient authorities (Josephus, Jerome, Eusebius) and by local tradition, but is disputed by
modern critics on the ground that Petra is quite some distance from
the border of Edom, while Hor is described here (v. 23) as being on
the border of Edom. In recent times, Hor has been identified with
Jebel Madurah, northeast of Kadesh and a short distance south of
the Dead Sea (Trumbull, *Kadesh Barnea*, pp. 127–139; Wooley and
Lawrence, *Wilderness of Zin*, p. 80; see note to v. 29).

24. *gathered unto his people*]   A euphemism for death, as is also
the phrase "lie with one's ancestors" (BDB, s. v. אב 4).

Israel, because ye rebelled against My word at the waters
of Meribah. Take Aaron and Eleazar his son, and bring 25
them up unto mount Hor. And strip Aaron of his garments, 26
and put them upon Eleazar his son; and Aaron shall be
gathered unto his people, and shall die there.' And Moses 27
did as the LORD commanded; and they went up into mount
Hor in the sight of all the congregation. And Moses 28
stripped Aaron of his garments, and put them upon Eleazar
his son; and Aaron died there in the top of the mount;
and Moses and Eleazar came down from the mount. And 29
when all the congregation saw that Aaron was dead, they
wept for Aaron thirty days, even all the house of Israel.

ye rebelled against My word] Cf. note on v. 12; comp. 27.14 and
Deut. 32.51, where "trespassed" is used.

26. *And strip Aaron*] Remove the garments, which are the insignia of the high-priesthood (Lev. 8.7–9), and place them upon Eleazar,
symbolic of the transference of office (cf. Deut. 10.6).

27. *and Moses did*] Notwithstanding the pain that the process
must have caused him (Rashi; Num. R. 19.11).

29. *And when all the congregation saw*] Since Moses and Eleazar
came down without him. According to rabbinic legend, angels brought
down the bed with the body of Aaron in it and showed it to the people
(Num. R. 19.11). Malbim understands by the term "congregation"
here the representatives of the people (Sanhedrin) who came up to
prepare the body for burial.

even all the house of Israel] Cf. Deut. 34.8, "the children of Israel"
wept for Moses when he died. Tradition ascribes to Aaron the character
of peace-maker, whose influence was felt in the homes of the Israelites.
"House" is often applied by the Rabbis to the women of a household
(cf. Ex. 19.3, Rashi), and here also they say that the women took a
prominent part in the mourning for Aaron (Rashi).

In Deut. 10.6 it is recorded that Aaron died and was buried in Moserah, six stations before Mt. Hor, while here and in 33.38 the death of

Aaron is represented as having occurred at Mt. Hor. It has been suggested that the death occurred at Hor, but that when the Israelites were attacked by the Canaanites they retreated to Moserah, taking with them the body of Aaron and burying it there (Malbim). This, however, does not remove the difficulty, since in Deut. it says distinctly that Aaron *died* at Moserah. Another suggestion is that the place of encampment was Moserah and that Aaron was taken from Moserah to Hor, where his death occurred, while the people were encamped at Moserah (comp. Orr, 280; see Reider's note on Deut. 10.6). The exact locality of Moserah is not known.

CHAPTER 21.

21. FURTHER HAPPENINGS DURING PERIOD OF WANDERING.

This chapter relates the further movements of the Israelites, in the course of which they achieved three victories: over the King of Arad (1–3); over the King of the Amorites (21–31); and over the King of Bashan (33–35). In their journey from Mount Hor, they were again punished for their murmurings, when they were attacked by fiery serpents (4–9). In the course of the narrative regarding the various stages of their wanderings, the chronicler included several ancient poetic sayings connected with the places traversed (10–20). The geographical difficulties will be discussed in the notes.

1–3. VICTORY OVER KING OF ARAD.

The King of Arad, a Canaanitish city, attacks the Israelites and takes some of them captive. Israel is aroused to war against him and succeeds in battle and destroys the country and its inhabitants, giving to the district the name of Hormah.

The section seems out of place here if we assume that the incident occurred after the death of Aaron, when the Israelites were encamped near Mt. Hor, for in the next section (v. 4) we are told that they proceeded from Mt. Hor southward in the direction of the Red Sea, and not northward through the Negeb. For this reason, this section has been regarded as parenthetical here, having no relation to the preceding or the following narrative, but connected with the reference in Judg. 1.17, where it is related that the tribes of Judah and Simeon gained a victory at Hormah, placed there in conjunction with Arad (v. 16). The theory advanced is that the first attempt to fight against

And the Canaanite, the king of Arad, who dwelt in the **21**
South, heard tell that Israel came by the way of Atharim;

the Canaanites having proved unsuccessful (14.40–45), some of the
Israelites (Judah and Simeon) tried again a passage in the same place
and were successful and continued their march into Canaan. In this
manner the three references to the meaning of the name Hormah
(here; 14.45 and Judg. 1.17) would be connected with the same incident
(Gray). Ramban suggests that Arad was situated in the Negeb on the
west side of the Jordan, in the vicinity of Hebron, and that having
heard of Israel's advance in the direction of Canaan, the King of Arad
collected his army and proceeded to attack them, where they were
encamped at that time, near Mt. Hor, in the wilderness of Moab.
After the Israelites gained their victory over the king of Arad, they
called the place of battle Hormah. The land of Arad, however, was
conquered later by Joshua (Josh. 12.14) and entirely destroyed still
later (Judg. 1.17) by Judah and Simeon. The expression "them and
their cities" used here he explains to refer to the future destruction
of Arad and not to the present victory. Ibn Ezra suggests that there
were two places by the same name on either side of the Jordan and
that the present incident is quite distinct from the incident mentioned
in Joshua and Judges. Malbim believes that the king of Arad, a country
situated on the other side of the Jordan, also had possessions on this
side of the Jordan and that those mentioned here were in the wilderness of Moab, while Joshua destroyed his Canaanitish possessions
(also Luzzatto; comp. Keil).

1. *Arad*] The place has been identified with certain ruins on the
top of a hill, Tel 'Arad, about 17 miles south of Hebron, assigned to
the tribe of Judah (Josh. 12.14; Judg. 1.17; comp. introductory note).

in the South] The Negeb (south). Arad is mentioned in Judg. 1.16
as a place in the wilderness of Judah where the Kenites settled.

heard tell] "Tell" is not in the Hebrew text (Leeser omits it; Mendelssohn has *erfuhr*, i. e. learned). Comp. the rabbinic explanation
which connects this with the death of Aaron (R. H. 3a).

by the way of Atharim] Following LXX, Saadia and R. V. On the
other hand, Targum, Rashi, ibn Ezra, Kimhi, A. V., Mendelssohn
and Leeser, influenced by the resemblance of האתרים to התרים (BDB),
translate this "by way of the spies", the route taken by the spies
(13.21–25). Dillmann, quoted by Gray, following an Arabic root,
renders the phrase "by the caravan route".

and he fought against Israel, and took some of them
2 captive. And Israel vowed a vow unto the Lord, and
said: 'If Thou wilt indeed deliver this people into my
3 hand, then I will utterly destroy their cities.' And the
Lord hearkened to the voice of Israel, and delivered up
the Canaanites; and they utterly destroyed them and
their cities; and the name of the place was called Hormah.

2. *I will utterly destroy*] The verb חרם, used only in the Hiphil,
generally denotes to pronounce a thing sacred and inviolable, devoted
to God. When a city was "devoted", the inhabitants were put to death,
the spoils being destroyed or not, depending upon the occasion (contrast Josh. 6.17, 21; I Sam. 15.3 with Deut. 2.34 ff.; 3.6, 7; BDB; comp.
Ehrlich).

3. *and the name of the place was called Hormah*] "Place" here
probably means district, although the name Hormah was also applied
to a town (Josh. 12.14, as distinct from Arad; 15.30; and Judg. 1.17,
where the former name of the town is given as Zephath).

4–9. THE BRONZE SERPENT.

Wearied from the long journey, the Israelites speak "against God
and against Moses", complaining about the insufficiency of food and
water. For this they are punished with a plague of fiery serpents,
which destroys many of them. The people then repent of their sin and,
at the command of God, Moses constructs a bronze serpent and puts
it up on a pole; any one suffering from the bite of a serpent is healed
when he looks up to the pole.

In II Kings 18.4, it is related that Hezekiah destroyed the bronze
serpent which Moses had erected, because it became an object of worship to the Israelites at that time. The symbol erected by Moses was
used for idolatrous purposes in later times and Hezekiah, in his campaign for religious reform, removed it for this reason. Modern scholars
have found among many other ancient cults beliefs in the relation of
the serpent to healing (see Gray, 275–6).

And they journeyed from mount Hor by the way to 4
the Red Sea, to compass the land of Edom; and the soul
of the people became impatient because of the way. And 5
the people spoke against God, and against Moses: 'Wherefore have ye brought us up out of Egypt to die in the wilderness? for there is no bread, and there is no water; and our
soul loatheth this light bread.' And the LORD sent fiery 6
serpents among the people, and they bit the people; and

4. *by the way to the Red Sea*] This is connected with 20.21. In their
effort to avoid an encounter with Edom, they traveled backwards,
in the direction of the Red Sea (14.25) and then went in an easterly
direction towards the north, in the region where Moab was situated.

and the soul of the people became impatient] Lit. "was shortened"
(R. V. "much discouraged"), an idiomatic expression, signifying utter
depression and disgust (Zech. 11.8; Judg. 10.16; 16.16).

because of the way] Because they had to turn back after they were
almost within reach of their goal.

5. *against God, and against Moses*] This was not a manifestation
of doubt as to Moses' selection for leadership or his ability, as was the
case in several previous instances, but a complaint both against God
and against Moses, His minister, for the manner in which they were
treated (Hirsch; comp. Targum and Adler).

this light bread] Easily digestible, not satisfying, referring to the
manna (Targum, Rashi). The word may also have the meaning of
worthless, contemptible, vile (R. V. margin; Leeser; comp. 'Ab. Zarah
5a).

6. *fiery serpents*] Serpents whose bite produced an inflammation
of the skin, subsequently causing death (Rashi). In the Hebrew text
both words are nouns, "the serpents, the fiery ones", and some regard
the latter as the name of the species of serpent here meant (Mendelssohn, Herxheimer). However, it is possible to take השרפים here as an
adjective, modifying הנחשים, as implied in the present rendering (Rashi,
ibn Ezra, Kimhi).

they bit the people] The piel used here indicates the fatal results of
the bite (BDB; Ehrlich).

7 much people of Israel died. And the people came to Moses,
and said: 'We have sinned, because we have spoken
against the LORD, and against thee; pray unto the LORD,
that He take away the serpents from us.' And Moses
8 prayed for the people. And the LORD said unto Moses:
'Make thee a fiery serpent, and set it upon a pole; and it
shall come to pass, that every one that is bitten, when he
9 seeth it, shall live.' And Moses made a serpent of brass,
and set it upon the pole; and it came to pass, that if a
serpent had bitten any man, when he looked unto the
10 serpent of brass, he lived. And the children of Israel
11 journeyed, and pitched in Oboth. And they journeyed
from Oboth, and pitched at Ije-abarim, in the wilderness

8. *a fiery serpent*] Made of brass, as in v. 9, or, according to some,
of bronze, an alloy of copper and tin (Gray).
a pole] So that it might be seen by all.
shall live] The serpents were not removed as requested by the
people (v. 7), but their sting was made harmless by this device. The
Rabbis say that the mere gazing at the bronze serpent did not produce
the healing, but that when the one who was bitten looked up towards
heaven and uttered a sincere prayer to God, his prayer was heard and
the wound was healed (R. H. 3.8; comp. Wisdom of Solomon, 16.6, 7).

10–20. JOURNEY FROM MT. HOR TO THE PLAINS OF MOAB.

Here are enumerated the successive stages in the wanderings of the
Israelites from Mt. Hor until they reached the field of Moab.
10. *in Oboth*] In 33.41–43, Zalmonah and Punon are mentioned
as stations between Hor and Oboth. The site of Oboth has not been
identified.
11. *Ije-abarim*] Abarim is the name given to the mountainous
district of Moab, just northeast of the Dead Sea. The Ije of Abarim
is on the eastern border of Moab, before Dibon-gad (33.45), and is
also referred to as Ijim (33.45).

which is in front of Moab, toward the sunrising. From 12
thence they journeyed, and pitched in the valley of Zered.
From thence they journeyed, and pitched on the other 13
side of the Arnon, which is in the wilderness, that cometh
out of the border of the Amorites.—For Arnon is the
border of Moab, between Moab and the Amorites; where- 14
fore it is said in the book of the Wars of the LORD:

12. *the valley of Zered*] Perhaps identical with Dibon-gad (33.45),
the name given to the place after it became part of the possession of
the tribe of Gad (Malbim). On reaching this station, the 38 years of
wandering from Kadesh-barnea were completed (Deut. 2.14). The
identification of the place is disputed, although generally conceded
to be the Wadi Kerak, to the south of the Arnon. In the Sam. Pent.
this verse is preceded by Deut. 2.9 and followed by Deut. 2.17–19.

13. *on the other side of the Arnon*] I. e. north of the river Arnon,
the main stream of Moab, now known as Wadi el Mojib, about 13
miles east of the Dead Sea. The southern branch of it is the more
important, as it is formed by several streams at Aroer and flows thence
almost directly west for about 20 miles. It ranges from 40 to 100 feet
in width and from 1 to 4 feet in depth.

the border of the Amorites] The stream forms a natural boundary,
separating the territories of the Amorites and of Moab (cf. Judg.
11.13 ff.), and later those of Reuben and of Moab (Deut. 3.16; Josh.
13.16). Not wishing to encroach upon the territory of Moab (Deut.
2.9), the Israelites encamped on the other side of the river Arnon, i. e.
on the side of the Amorites.

14. *the book of the Wars of the Lord*] An ancient collection of war
songs from which the following is a quotation, indicating that Arnon
was on the border of Moab (ibn Ezra). The quotation here is in two
parts: the first (14–15) describes the boundary of Moab, which the
Israelites circumvented; and the second (17–20), the journeyings of
the people to other stations, which included also an ancient Song of
the Well (17–18). The meaning of these excerpts, taken out from the
context of another work, is not always clear. The verbs are missing
and have to be supplied by conjecture. Some of the Jewish commentators take the word ספר to denote not a book but a narrative. In nar-
rating the wars of the Lord to their children, the Israelites used to sing

Vaheb in Suphah,

And the valleys of Arnon,

15   And the slope of the valleys

That inclineth toward the seat of Ar,

And leaneth upon the border of Moab.—

16   And from thence to Beer; that is the well whereof the
LORD said unto Moses: 'Gather the people together, and
17   I will give them water.' Then sang Israel this song:

the following songs. In this manner they obviate the difficulty of
assuming the existence of other books contemporaneous with the
Torah (Rashi, Rashbam, Luzzatto et al.).

Vaheb in Suphah]   A verb, "we remember" (*Biur*), or "we passed"
(Gray), or "we captured" (McNeil), is to be supplied here. As it
stands, Vaheb is intended to be the name of a town, situated in a district by the name of Suphah. Neither of these names has been identified. Malbim identifies Vaheb with Mattanah (v. 18), because of a
possible similarity in meaning. Suphah has been identified by some
with Suph (Deut. 1.1). Some take Suphah as a common noun, meaning
storm, and make the phrase refer to God, who passed Vaheb in a storm
(Luzzatto; see Ashkenazi, and comp. Targum and Rashi).

the valleys of Arnon]   The wadis or streams which enter into the
river Arnon.

15.   *And the slope*]   (We also passed) the cliff or the bottom of the
ravine, which inclines towards Ar, forming the border of Moab.

seat of Ar]   Ar, a city in Moab, perhaps the capital (Isa. 15.1), or a
province of Moab, is here personified as having a seat or dwelling-place.

and leaneth]   A poetic expression for the cliff adjoining the boundary
of Moab. It is this phrase that illustrates the statement in v. 13 regarding the boundary of Moab.

16.   *And from thence to Beer*]   Continuing the narrative of v. 13,
interrupted by the quotation. Beer is found as the name of a place in
Judg. 9.21 and the plural Beeroth in II Sam. 4.2. It is possible that
this is an abbreviation of a compound name, perhaps Beer-elim, mentioned in Isa. 15.8, as situated in Northern Moab.

whereof the Lord said]   Apparently this gives the reason why the
place was called Beer, because at a time when the people needed water

Spring up, O well—sing ye unto it—
The well, which the princes digged,   **18**
Which the nobles of the people delved,
With the sceptre, and with their staves.

And from the wilderness to Mattanah; and from Mattanah **19**

a well was discovered there by Moses, through the help of God. This
has no reference to the well of Miriam or to the incident at Meribah,
but to an occurrence not recorded in the Torah, regarding which,
however, a popular song survived (ibn Ezra; comp. Sforno).

17–18.   The Song of the Well, quoted here, presents the picture of
people standing around a well, encouraging each other to join in the
song and exhorting the well to pour forth its refreshing waters, and
referring to the fact that the well was discovered for them by their
leaders, the nobles of their people. Although not so indicated, it is
possible that this song also is an excerpt from the book of the Wars
of the Lord mentioned before (v. 14).

18.   *With the sceptre*]   The commander's staff, the symbol of authority, referring to the "princes"; "with their staves", the symbol of
dignity, refers to the "nobles of the people". The suggestion made by
Budde well explains the use of these rather strange implements for
the digging of a well. He says that this is "an allusion to a custom by
which when a well had been discovered it was lightly covered over, and
then, on a subsequent occasion, solemnly opened with a symbolic
action of the sceptre-like staves of the Sheikhs of the clan, and formally
declared clan property" (quoted by Gray, p. 289). Here, of course,
the reference is to Moses and Aaron and to the princes of Israel.

And from the wilderness to Mattanah]   The last place of encampment
mentioned in v. 16 was Beer, hence LXX reads here "and from Beer
to Mattanah", regarding this last clause as the continuation of the
march from v. 16. Another suggestion is that this phrase is still the
continuation of the song: the well was a "gift from the wilderness",
omitting the conjunction "and" (Gray, quoting Budde). According
to this rendering it will be necessary to change in the following verse
"and from Mattanah" to "and from there" (as in v. 16). Targum takes
all these names as proper nouns, descriptive of the miraculous following of the well after the camp throughout their wanderings (Num.
R. 19.14; Tan. Hukkat, 47).

19.   *and from Mattanah to Nahaliel*]   A place by the name of Mat-

20 to Nahaliel; and from Nahaliel to Bamoth; and from
Bamoth to the valley that is in the field of Moab, by the
top of Pisgah, which looketh down upon the desert.

tanah is entirely unknown. Nahaliel, lit. the valley of God, also has
not been identified, although it is suggested that it may refer to the
modern Wady Zerka Ma'in, which possesses salubrious springs (G. A.
Smith, *Historical Geography of Palestine*, p. 562).

Bamoth] Lit. high places, possibly identical with Bamoth-baal
(22.41; Josh. 13.17), lying in the region north of Arnon, commanding
a view over the plain of Moab.

20. *the valley that is in the field of Moab*] Meaning the land of
Moab (Ruth 1.1, 2; comp. Gen. 32.4; Judg. 5.4), or possibly the name
of a district in Moab which was retained even after the territory came
into the possession of the Amorites. This valley has been identified
by some with the present Wadi 'Ayun Musa, "which runs into the
Jordan valley some four or five miles north of the northern end of the
Dead Sea, the torrent then flowing with a south-westerly curve into
the Sea" (McNeile).

by the top of Pisgah] The name given to the western edge of the
Moabite plateau, where it falls steeply into the Dead Sea and the
Jordan valley.

upon the desert] Possibly a proper name (Jeshimon) given to the
waste land in the Jordan valley, just north of the Dead Sea and east
of the river, where was situated Beth-jeshimoth (33. 49; comp. 23.28).

21–25.   THE WAR WITH SIHON.

This is the continuation of v. 13. When the Israelites encamped at
the river Arnon, they sent messengers to Sihon, King of Heshbon, as
they did before to the King of Edom (20.1 ff.), with the request that
they be permitted to pass through his land. Sihon refused the request
and came out with his army to war with Israel. He was defeated in
battle and his land was occupied by the Israelites.

Sihon is described here as the king of the Amorites, possibly meaning "mountain-dwellers", although the term Amorites is often applied
to all the inhabitants of Canaan. Sihon is also sometimes described
as the king of Heshbon, his principal city (Deut. 3.6 et al). The two
chief kingdoms of the Amorites, east of the Jordan, were those of Sihon

And Israel sent messengers unto Sihon king of the 21
Amorites, saying: 'Let me pass through thy land; we will 22
not turn aside into field, or into vineyard; we will not
drink of the water of the wells; we will go by the king's
highway, until we have passed thy border.' And Sihon 23
would not suffer Israel to pass through his border; but
Sihon gathered all his people together, and went out
against Israel into the wilderness, and came to Jahaz;
and he fought against Israel. And Israel smote him with 24
the edge of the sword, and possessed his land from the
Arnon unto the Jabbok, even unto the children of Ammon;

and of Og (Deut. 31.4; Josh. 2.10). "Og ruled in Bashan, Sihon more
to the south, where he had driven the Moabites from fertile land between the Jabbok and the Arnon" (Sayce in Hastings, *Dictionary of
the Bible*, s. v.). The same story of the war with Sihon is also found
in Deut. 2.24–36 and Judg. 11.9–22.

22. *the king's highway*] Comp. note on 20.17.

until we have passed thy border] The furthermost limit of the land.
The word נבול may also be rendered "territory" (BDB).

23. *into the wilderness*] Comp. v. 13. In Deut. 2.26, the name of
the place whence the messengers were sent to Sihon is given as "the
wilderness of Kedemoth".

Jahaz] The name of a city in the plain on the border of Moab, the
site of which has not been identified, probably on the eastern border
of the land of Sihon (Judg. 11.20; I Chron. 6.63). It is mentioned in
connection with Kedemoth, and on the Moabite stone of Mesha it is
referred to as being near Dibon (Gray).

unto the Jabbok] A river, now called Wadi Zarka, which empties
into the Jordan. "In its upper semicircular portion it forms a boundary
between East and West, while in its lower portion it forms a boundary
between North and South". Thus, in the present description of the
territory of Sihon, "the lower portion of the Jabbok formed the northern boundary, while the upper portion formed the eastern boundary
of Sihon's kingdom; and the verse may be made clear by inserting
'northward' after Jabbok and 'eastward' after Arnon. The upper por-

25 for the border of the children of Ammon was strong. And
Israel took all these cities; and Israel dwelt in all the cities
of the Amorites, in Heshbon, and in all the towns thereof.
26 For Heshbon was the city of Sihon the king of the Amorites,
who had fought against the former king of Moab, and
taken all his land out of his hand, even unto the Arnon.
27 Wherefore they that speak in parables say:

tion is referred to in Deut. 2.37, where the border of the children of
Ammon is described as 'all the side of the river Jabbok'. The river
Jabbok is also mentioned as a boundary in Deut. 3.16; Josh. 12.2;
Judg. 11.12, 22" (Chapman in Hastings, *Dictionary of the Bible*, s. v.).

for the border of the children of Ammon was strong] And therefore
was not penetrated by Sihon when he conquered Moab. This may
also be a reason why the Israelites did not extend their conquests
further (comp. Rashi). LXX reads Jazer instead of עז כי. Jazer was
the name of a city to which Moses sent spies and which he later subdued (v. 32; Josh. 13.25).

25. *in Heshbon*] Probably the capital city. It is identified with
the modern Heshban, situated about 18 miles east of the Jordan,
opposite Jericho.

the towns thereof] Lit. "the daughters thereof", the capital city
being regarded as the mother-city, and the provinces, the small towns
and villages round about it, as the daughter-towns.

26–30. OLD SONG IN CELEBRATION OF VICTORY OVER SIHON.

Heshbon, although formerly a Moabite city, was now the city of
Sihon, who captured it together with the adjacent territory north of
the Arnon from an earlier king of Moab. This explanation is followed
by an ancient song, apparently in illustration of this statement, although
the song itself presents many difficulties. According to rabbinic interpretation (Hul. 60b), this explains that although the Israelites were
forbidden to take any part of the territory of Moab (Deut. 2.9, 10),
they were allowed to appropriate Heshbon and its provinces, which
had been wrested from Moab by the Amorites before the Israelites
arrived there (Rashi, Ramban).

27. *they that speak in parables*] Who recite proverbs and maxims

Come ye to Heshbon!

Let the city of Sihon be built and established!

For a fire is gone out of Heshbon,   28

A flame from the city of Sihon;

It hath devoured Ar of Moab,

The lords of the high places of Arnon.

Woe to thee, Moab!   29

Thou art undone, O people of Chemosh;

as well as short poems and ballads. Who these *Moshelim* were is a matter of dispute. Jewish tradition assumes that they were Amorites and that the poem is an excerpt of an old Amorite war song which was composed at the time when Heshbon was captured by Sihon from Moab. The song has now become the song of the Israelites, because it emphasized the greatness of Israel's victory in wresting this important town from the Amorites (Num. R. 19.18; comp. Rashi and Ramban). Other explanations have been given by various commentators (see Gray, McNeile, Ehrlich, Kahana).

Come ye to Heshbon] An invitation extended by the king or by his generals to the Amorite people to come from different points and settle in the conquered city and make it a metropolis. Heshbon is called the city of Sihon, because Sihon was the outstanding hero in its capture.

28. *For a fire is gone out*] The conquest of Heshbon was like a fire that consumed the whole of Moab, and even reached its capital Ar. Not that Ar was captured, but that it suffered greatly from the loss of Heshbon. Ar may refer here, as in the following phrase, to the people of Moab rather than to the city (cf. note on v. 15).

the lords of the high places of Arnon] The proprietors of the heights, the Moabite chiefs. The "high places" are the lofty rocks on the border of the Arnon, or it may be taken as a proper name, the Bamoth of the Arnon, as in v. 19 (cf. Jer. 48.45, 46). Targum takes this word Bamoth as a high place of worship and renders: the priests who worshiped at their shrines on the heights of Arnon.

29. *O people of Chemosh*] Chemosh was the national deity of Moab (Judg. 11.24; I Kings 11.7), and the Moabites are also elsewhere spoken of as the people of Chemosh (Jer. 48.46).

He hath given his sons as fugitives,

And his daughters into captivity,

Unto Sihon king of the Amorites.

30   We have shot at them—Heshbon is perished—even
unto Dibon,

And we have laid waste even unto Nophah,

Which reacheth unto Medeba.

he hath given] Chemosh, in his anger against his own people, has given his children, i. e. the people of Moab, as fugitives.

30. *We have shot at them*] This verse presents many philological difficulties and has therefore given rise to many and widely differing renderings. The rendering adopted here, following R. V. (Leeser has "we have thrown them down"), considers ונירם as a verb from the root ירה, which means to shoot or throw (Kimhi). The form is grammatically difficult, as we should expect וַנִּירָם (see *Biur*). LXX apparently had a different reading here for it renders: and their seed (dynasty, comp. Targum, Rashi, *Biur*) is perished, Heshbon to Dibon, and women (נָשִׁים) extended the fire against Moab (instead of Medeba; comp. Ehrlich, who accepts this rendering, except that he retains Medeba instead of Moab). Several other renderings have been suggested, but none is quite satisfactory. The vocalization as well as the cantillation signs favor the rendering adopted by our version.

Heshbon is perished] These are still the words of the Amorite poet. We have fought against them until we laid Heshbon waste, even unto Dibon, i. e. the whole stretch of territory was taken away from Moab.

even unto Dibon] A city east of the Dead Sea and north of Arnon. It was part of the territory of Reuben (Josh. 13.9, 17), but it is mentioned as having been rebuilt by Gad (32.3, 34), hence also called Dibon-gad (33.45). Its modern name is Dhiban and it has become famous through the discovery there in 1868 of the Moabite Stone.

Nophah] Found only here and has not been identified. Some suggest that it is the same as Nobah (32.42; Judg. 8.11).

Which] In the Heb. text, the ר of אשר has a masoretic dot over it, indicating a doubt in the mind of the Masoretes whether the letter should not be omitted. In this case the LXX reading "fire" may be correct. The Syriac version has "Nobah which lies in the desert", reading מדבר instead of מידבא.

Medeba] A town about 1½ hours' journey south of Heshbon, on

Thus Israel dwelt in the land of the Amorites. And 31-32
Moses sent to spy out Jazer, and they took the towns
thereof, and drove out the Amorites that were there. And 33
they turned and went up by the way of Bashan; and Og
the king of Bashan went out against them, he and all his

the Roman road to Kerak. It was assigned to Reuben (Josh. 13.9–16),
but apparently taken away from them later by Moab (II Sam. 8.2).
LXX reads Moab here instead of Medeba. Many interesting objects
have of late been discovered on the site of Medeba (Chapman in
Hastings, *Dictionary of the Bible*, s. v.).

31–32. CONQUEST OF JAZER.

The narrative of v. 26 is continued here. While encamped in the
land of the Amorites, the Israelites extended their conquests further
to Jazer and the province around it.

32. *Jazer*] Its site is doubtful, although it is generally identified
with Khirbel Sar. It is mentioned as having been assigned to Gad
(32.35; Josh. 13.25). It is described as being about 15 miles from
Heshbon, lying on the way of the Israelites towards Bashan, and as
having been very fertile and thickly populated.

and drove out] Following the *Kere*. The *Ketib* ויירש would mean
and he inherited, took possession of (v. 35).

33–35. VICTORY OVER OG.

When the Israelites proceeded on their journey farther north, they
encountered Bashan, a fertile stretch of land, north of Gilead, extending from the Jabbok to Hermon, noted for its rich pasture land, fine
cattle and oak forests. There they met Og, the king of Bashan, who
waged war with them. Having been assured by God, through Moses,
of victory, the Israelites slew Og and his army and occupied his land.
The same story is told in greater detail in Deut. 3.1 ff. and references
to it are found in 32.33; Deut. 1.4; 4.47; 19.7; Josh. 9.10; 12.4; 13.30.

34 people, to battle at Edrei. And the LORD said unto Moses:
'Fear him not; for I have delivered him into thy hand,
and all his people, and his land; and thou shalt do to him
as thou didst unto Sihon king of the Amorites, who dwelt
35 at Heshbon.' So they smote him, and his sons, and all
his people, until there was none left him remaining; and
they possessed his land.

33.   *Edrei*]   A city in Bashan, assigned to Machir, son of Manasseh
(Josh. 13.31). It was situated on the southern border of Bashan (Deut.
3.1, 10), about 30 miles east of the Sea of Tiberias and about 30 miles
west of the Hauran range, and is identified with the modern Edreat
or Derat.

34.   *Fear him not*]   The encouragement here may have been necessary because of the reputed strength of Og, who was regarded to be
one of the Rephaim (Deut. 3.11; comp. Nid. 61a and Rashi and Ramban here).

35.   *and his sons*]   In the narrative in Deut. 3.3, this phrase is
omitted, and it is also omitted here in the Sam. version. The phrase,
however, is found in Deut. 2.33 in connection with the destruction of
Sihon (see Rashi there).

CHAPTER 22.

1. ISRAEL ENCAMPED IN PLAINS OF MOAB.

The Israelites encamped in the "plains of Moab", that part of the
large Arabah, or plain of the Jordan, which belonged to Moab before
Sihon had conquered Moab and taken a large portion of its territory.
The place of encampment is given as the region which faces Jericho,
on the western side of the Jordan. The camp is further defined in
33.49 as extending from Beth-jeshimoth to Abel-shittim (see note
there). The plain on the western side of the Jordan is called "the
plains of Jericho" (Josh. 4.13; 5.10).

And the children of Israel journeyed, and pitched in **22**
the plains of Moab beyond the Jordan at Jericho.

beyond]   I. e. on the east side of the Jordan opposite Jericho, which
is on the western bank of the river.

22.2–36.13.   INCIDENTS DURING STAY IN PLAINS OF MOAB.

22.2–24.25.   THE STORY OF BALAAM.

Balak, king of Moab, having heard of the defeat of the powerful
Amorite kings at the hands of the Israelites, becomes terrified at the
prospect of the same fate befalling him and his land. He consults with
the elders of Midian and together they decide to engage the services
of a famous heathen prophet, Balaam, who is noted for the effectiveness
of his curses and blessings, to come and curse Israel, so that the Moabites might find it easy to subdue them. The messengers of Balak come
to Balaam and endeavor to induce him to do the biddings of their
chief. Balaam refuses the invitation, claiming that God would not
permit him to curse the people of Israel. Balak then sends a more
important embassy, who promise Balaam wealth and distinction, if
he would agree to do as their master desires. Balaam at once disil-
lusions the noble ambassadors of the thought that any promise of
riches could induce him to do anything that was contrary to the wish
of God. This time, however, he receives God's permission to accompany the messengers of Balak, but with the distinct understanding
that he will do only that which God will tell him to do. When he sets
out on his journey, God manifests His displeasure with Balaam by sending an angel with a drawn sword to block the way before him. Balaam
does not see the angel, but the ass does and when in terror she tries
to step aside from the path in order to avoid the angel, Balaam strikes
her. The ass complains to Balaam of his cruelty and Balaam suddenly
sees the angel. The angel tells Balaam that his journey is displeasing
to God, but when Balaam offers to return home, the angel tells him
that he may proceed on his journey provided that he speak only
that which God puts in his mouth.

When he reaches the border of Moab, Balaam is met by Balak, to
whom he repeats the conditions by which he is bound. Balak leads

Balaam to high places from which the Israelitish camp can be seen
and entreats him to send his curse upon them. In each instance, however, Balaam is inspired to deliver a blessing rather than a curse.
This is repeated three times, when, disgusted and enraged, Balak orders
the prophet to go home. Before departing, Balaam delivers another
prophecy in which the doom of Moab and of Edom at the hands of
Israel is foretold. He then adds some other prophecies regarding the
fate awaiting other enemies of Israel. Then Balak and Balaam separate, each returning to his respective home.

The narrative as well as the four oracles which Balaam delivered
regarding Israel, may be regarded as a separate fragment and was so
regarded by the Rabbis, who call it "the Section (or Book, Munich
Ms. of Talmud) of Balaam" and attribute its authorship to Moses
(B.B. 14b). The purpose of this "section" or "book" is quite obvious.
It emphasizes the fact that Israel has always been under the special
protection of God and that God would not permit any harm to befall
His people. Even the greatest power for evil at that time, as Balaam
was apparently considered by his contemporaries, had to bend to the
will of God and instead of a curse he was forced to pronounce blessings
on the people of God. A striking parallel has been drawn between this
story placed at the end of Israel's wanderings and the story of Pharaoh
at the beginning of the wandering. Just as at the beginning Pharaoh
endeavors to oppose God's design for Israel and is made to suffer for
it, so now too Balak attempts to balk God's plan to bring Israel to
the promised land and suffers a similar fate. This similarity is alluded
to in Micah 6.4, 5, and the thought of God's interest in Israel is used
there as an appeal to Israel for greater loyalty (Kalisch, 63–64; Gray,
315–316).

The narrative as given here presents several difficulties, the most
striking of which is the contradiction between the statement in 22.20,
where it is expressly told that God gave Balaam permission to go,
and the incident on his journey when God appears to be angry with him
for going. For this and other reasons, modern Bible critics recognize
here at least two distinct accounts of the same story, varying in detail,
which have been combined by an editor into one. It is also because
of this combination that the character of Balaam has been given varying estimates by different commentators. From the general trend of

the narrative here and especially from the lofty expressions regarding
Israel used in Balaam's prophecies, it is inferred that Balaam was
regarded by the chronicler as an upright man and as a true follower of
the God of Israel, an estimate that is corroborated by the reference in
Micah 6.4 (comp. Num. R. 20.1). Other references to Balaam in the
Bible, however, regard him in a less favorable light (Deut. 23.5, 6;
Josh. 24.9, 10; Neh. 13.2), while in Num. 31.16 he is charged with the
crime of inducing the Israelites to consort with the Moabitish women,
a sin for which the Israelites were punished by a devastating plague,
in which 24,000 persons were destroyed (25.9). Jewish tradition pic-
tures Balaam in most unfavorable and lurid lights, attributing to him
many sins and vicious traits of character (Ab. 5.19; Sanh. 10.2; 106b;
comp. Kalisch, 22–38). Among modern writers, the ghastly picture
of the character of Balaam held up by the Rabbis has been consider-
ably modified, although many still look upon him as extremely vain and
avaricious. M. M. Kalisch, in an elaborate study of the whole subject
(*The Prophecies of Balaam, or The Hebrew and the Heathen*, London,
1877), goes to the other extreme, making of Balaam an admirable
personality, a true adherent of the God of Israel and a faithful follower
of His commands. The general impression one obtains from the perusal
of this episode is that Balaam, conceived here as a heathen prophet,
who practiced soothsaying and divination as an art, is made the mouthpiece of the Hebrew poet through which the magnificent picture of
Israel's prosperity and the close relation between God and Israel are
presented in a masterly form. With this object in view, the heathen
necromancer (Josh. 13.22) is pictured as obeying the commands of
the God of Israel and even as speaking in His name. The writer is not
always consistent in maintaining the picture of his hero as at first conceived, but he is careful to stress the point that even this powerful
person, with whose powers kings counted and whose reputation as an
effective wonder-worker was universally recognized, has to submit to
the will of God and do His bidding, even against his personal interests
and perhaps also against his personal inclinations. Balak's appeal to
his avarice and to his vainglory has no effect, because it was against
the people of God that he wanted the heathen prophet to direct his
curses and the people of God is already blessed (22.12). Further details
of the narrative will be referred to in the notes.

2 And Balak the son of Zippor saw all that Israel had
3 done to the Amorites. And Moab was sore afraid of the
people, because they were many; and Moab was overcome
4 with dread because of the children of Israel. And Moab

2-21. IN FEAR OF ISRAEL, BALAK SENDS FOR BALAAM TO CURSE THEM.

Balak, King of Moab, seeing the Israelites encamped near his territory, becomes frightened and tries to obtain the services of Balaam,
a noted heathen prophet, to curse the Israelites, so that he might
more easily vanquish them in battle. Balaam first refuses, but is later
persuaded to go with Balak's messengers, on condition that he will
say only that which God will order him to say.

2. *Balak the son of Zippor*] The name Balak comes from a Hebrew
root which means to lay waste, hence Balak would mean the devas-
tator (BDB). Zippor is the Hebrew word for bird, the feminine of
which, Zipporah, was the name of the wife of Moses (Ex. 2.21).

to the Amorites] Sihon, king of Heshbon, and Og, king of Bashan.
The former only is designated here as an Amorite (21.21, 25, 31), but
the latter is probably also included (Deut. 3.8; 4.47; 31.4; Josh. 2.10;
9.10; 24.12).

3. *And Moab*] "King of" or "people of" understood. Luzzatto
regards vv. 3-4 as parenthetic: "Balak saw . . . . that Moab was
afraid . . . . and that Moab said to the elders of Midian . . . . Balak
being king of Moab at that time . . . . hence he sent messengers, etc.".
This is rather ingenious but the construction would be most unusual.

was sore afraid] Cf. Ex. 15.15. The proximity of the Israelites to
Moab induced the fear of an attack by them. Balak was perhaps
unaware of Israel's offers of peace to Edom and to Sihon, or, if he knew
of them, he did not think that he would be similarly treated. The sad
experiences of Sihon and Og taught him not to engage in an offensive
war with them and he therefore resorts to magic and divination as a
possible means of exterminating the supposed enemy whom he feared.
It has also been suggested that Moab being a pastoral people (II Kings
3.4) were not really afraid of an attack by the Israelites, but feared
that they would devour all the pasturage around them (Gray).

overcome with dread] The term יקץ also includes the idea of loathing
(Ex. 1.12). The feeling of fear was combined with a feeling of loathing
and disgust.

said unto the elders of Midian: 'Now will this multitude
lick up all that is round about us, as the ox licketh up the
grass of the field.'—And Balak the son of Zippor was king

4. *the elders of Midian*] Of whom Moab sought counsel in this
matter (comp. ibn Ezra, who identifies the elders with the five kings
of Midian, 31.8; Ramban suggests that these were the judges and
administrators appointed by Sihon after his conquest of the land).
The Midianites are represented in Ex. 18.9–12 as a friendly people,
whose priest, Jethro, was willing to acknowledge the God of Abraham.
Here, however, they appear as a nation of idolaters, the enemies of
Israel (25.17), by whom they are finally destroyed (31.1 ff.; comp.
Num. R. 20.4; Sanh. 105a). It is therefore suggested that the name
of Midian was applied to a number of clans, spread over a large area,
extending from the peninsula of Sinai to the north, near the territory
of Moab (comp. Gen. 36.35), "a tract of country to the north of Arabia
and on the east shore of the Gulf of Akabah, with freedom to roam
northwards along the eastern boundary of Edom and Moab" (Chapman
in Hastings, *Dictionary of the Bible*, s. v.). In Gen. 37.25, 28 the terms
Midianites and Ishmaelites are used interchangeably. Balaam does not
refer to the Midianites at all, a fact that led some critics to assume that
the introduction of the Midianites here was for the purpose of connect-
ing this incident with other incidents where Balaam is found associated
with Midian (31.8, 16; Josh. 13.21). On the other hand, Josephus
(*Ant.* iv.6.2–13) makes it appear as if Balak was only a tool in the
hands of the Midianites, while Targ. Jon. makes Balak himself a
Midianite (see Kalisch, 84–87).
Now] Since they are in possession of the neighboring lands of
Sihon and of Og, there is nothing to prevent them from invading our
country (Sforno), or of attacking us frequently and spoiling our crops
and pasture lands.
lick up] A figure taken from pastoral life (II Kings 3.4).
And Balak] This clause, parenthetically inserted here, has been
regarded by some modern critics as a gloss by a later scribe to indicate
the relationship between Balak and Moab, which the author did not
think it necessary to explain. The Rabbis suggest that Balak was not
a hereditary king of Moab, but that he was himself a Midianite (comp.
Targ. Yer.) who was made king in this emergency (Num. R. 20.4;
comp. Kalisch, 87–89; but see Ramban who connects this with Judg.
11.25).

5 of Moab at that time.—And he sent messengers unto
Balaam the son of Beor, to Pethor, which is by the River,
to the land of the children of his people, to call him, saying:
'Behold, there is a people come out from Egypt; behold,
they cover the face of the earth, and they abide over

5. *Balaam the son of Beor*] Because of the similarity of this name
with that of Bela son of Beor, mentioned as a king of Edom (Gen.
36.32), some were led to identify the two names as belonging to one
person. The name Balaam (Heb. Bileam) has been associated by the
Rabbis with the expression בֹּלֵעָם, "destroyer of the people" (Sanh.
105a). Others connect it with בְּלִי־עָם, "without a people", or "Bel is
my kinsman". Beor may have the meaning of "torch" or "burning".

to Pethor, which is by the River] Identified with Pitru, situated on
the Sajur river, a tributary of the Euphrates, which is often designated
simply as "The River" (Gen. 31.21; Ex. 23.31; Josh. 24.2). In Deut.
23.5, Pethor is described as situated in "Aram-naharaim", i. e. Mesopotamia, the region between the Euphrates in its upper course and
the Khabour. The town Pitru is also mentioned in one of the inscriptions of Shalmaneser II (Gray, 325). This would make Balaam's home
a distance of about 400 miles from Moab, taking more than twenty
days to travel. The four journeys of the story would therefore have
required about three months.

the land of the children of his people] I. e. his native land, to indicate
that he was the product of his people, the Chaldeans, who were noted
in antiquity as soothsayers and magicians (Ramban). Some make
this refer back to Balak, who was a native of Aram, where he might
have heard of Balaam's powers (Rashi). Many of the old versions read
here "the land of the children of Ammon" instead of "his people". This
would make Balaam's home much closer to Moab and would explain
the use of the ass, which would be unfit for a long journey, requiring
camels and a regular caravan (comp., however, Kalisch, 112).

they cover the face of the earth] Heb. text has "the eye of the earth",
i. e. the visible surface of the earth (cf. Gen. 10.5, 15). Targum renders
"the eye of the sun of the earth", as if the sun were the eye of the earth,
and by covering the earth, they leave no room for the sun to shine
upon (*Biur*, Ehrlich).

against me. Come now therefore, I pray thee, curse me 6
this people; for they are too mighty for me; peradventure
I shall prevail, that we may smite them, and that I may
drive them out of the land; for I know that he whom thou
blessest is blessed, and he whom thou cursest is cursed.'

6. *curse me this people*] Balak hopes that through the curse pronounced by Balaam he would be assured of victory in his contemplated
attack upon the Israelites. The use of the word לי is regarded by some
as alluding to the ancient practice, evidenced by documents recently
unearthed, which required that the name of the person in whose behalf
an imprecation was made should be carefully given, so that the gods
may make no mistake (Kalisch, 113), but this is an unnecessary refine-
ment as the dative of reference is quite in consonance with Hebrew
idiom (Ges.-K. 119s; BDB, 515).

for they are too mighty for me] The word עצום carries the double
meaning of mighty and numerous (BDB). LXX has "for us".

I shall prevail, that we may smite them] The change from sing. to
plur. is rather strange, but the sense is quite clear. I shall be able, with
the help of my people, to overcome them. Ibn Ezra (also *Biur* and
possibly also Targum, Mendelssohn, Leeser) regards נכה as an infinit.
"I shall be able to smite him". Others (Sforno, Abarbanel) make
Balak associate Balaam with himself, that through warfare and curses
Israel might be overcome. The prep. ב (בו) is often used in a partitive
sense (BDB 88), "to smite some of them" (Ps. 78.31). Balak would be
satisfied with a qualified victory, if it would only make them depart
from his land (Luzzatto).

whom thou blessest is blessed] Balak pays tribute to Balaam's general
skill, although he sought not his blessing, but his curse. The belief in the
efficacy of the blessings and the curses of magicians and wizards was
common not only among the ancient peoples of the Orient, but also
among all peoples throughout the ages, even up to very recent days.
The Bible is full of references to such a belief (II Kings 2.23, 24; comp.
the curse written on a scroll in the case of the woman suspected of
infidelity, Num. 5.11–29; also the expression אררי יום, Job 3.8, possibly
referring to a professional guild of cursers; comp. Kalisch, 99–102;
Gray, 327–8, where references are given to classic and medieval literature).

7 And the elders of Moab and the elders of Midian departed
with the rewards of divination in their hand; and they
came unto Balaam, and spoke unto him the words of
8 Balak. And he said unto them: 'Lodge here this night,
and I will bring you back word, as the LORD may speak
unto me'; and the princes of Moab abode with Balaam.

7. *the rewards of divination*] As an earnest of the larger rewards
still awaiting him when his task is successfully accomplished (Herxheimer; comp. ibn Ezra, quoting Samuel ha-Nagid). The custom of
bringing a fee to a prophet or a soothsayer is often referred to in the
Bible (I Sam. 9.8; I Kings 14.3; II Kings 8.8), hence it does not imply a
reproach on Balaam's character, although the later prophets denounced
this practice (Micah 3.5, 11; Ezek. 13.19). Some take the word to
mean "the instruments of divination" (Rashi, Sforno, Mendelssohn,
comp. BDB and Ezek. 21.27), although it might have been taken for
granted that Balaam, the magician by trade, would have his tools
with him (Num. R. 20.7; Tan. Balak, 34). Others again render the
term in the sense that the messengers were themselves magicians
(with the power of divination in their hands), so that he would not
be able to offer an evasive excuse for not going (ibn Ezra, Rashi and
Num. R. ib.; see Kalisch, 108–110).

8. *as the Lord may speak unto me*] The heathen prophet here and
throughout the narrative is made to appear as a worshiper of the God
of Israel, whose behests he is ready to follow implicitly. This is not at
all strange, in the light of what is known of the attitude of the ancients
to their gods. The God of Israel is the one who had control of the
destinies of His adherents, even in the eyes of the heathen, and it is
therefore to Him that all appeals in their behalf, whether for good or
for evil, are to be made (Luzzatto). Kalisch endeavors to show (pp.
16–21) that Balaam is represented as a true believer in the God of
Israel. The rabbinic homilists explain this by saying that Balaam was
especially designated a prophet to the heathens so that they may have
no excuse for their wickedness by arguing that if they had prophets
to guide them, as did Israel, they also would have reached a higher
state of culture and morality.

the princes of Moab] The more important members of the commission, the elders of Midian merely accompanying them. The latter

And God came unto Balaam, and said: 'What men are 9
these with thee?' And Balaam said unto God: 'Balak the 10
son of Zippor, king of Moab, hath sent unto me [saying]:
Behold the people that is come out of Egypt, it covereth 11
the face of the earth; now, come curse me them; peradven-
ure I shall be able to fight against them, and shall drive
them out.' And God said unto Balaam: 'Thou shalt not 12
go with them; thou shalt not curse the people; for they
are blessed.' And Balaam rose up in the morning, and said 13

may either have left, not wishing to remain over night, or are not
mentioned because of their insignificant part in the narrative. (Comp.
note to v. 4).

9. *And God came unto Balaam*] In a dream or in a vision.

What men are these with thee?] Leeser, "Who are these men with
thee?" Although nothing is hidden from God, the question is asked
as introductory to the conversation that follows (ibn Ezra; comp. Gen.
3.9; 4.9). The wording of the question, as given in our rendering,
points not so much to the identity of the men as to their business in
the house of Balaam (Ehrlich).

10. [*saying*]] Not in the Heb. text, but is found in LXX, where
also the word "them" is added.

11. Balaam repeats Balak's message, with a few unimportant
variations (vv. 5, 6).

and shall drive them out] Not to exterminate them, but only to
engage them in battle so that they may be driven away from this
district (comp. Rashi, following the midrashic interpretation, by
which each of the variations is made to indicate Balaam's inveterate
hatred of Israel).

12. *for they are blessed*] And no curse can have an effect on them
(Gen. 27.33), hence there would be no use in your going with them.
The rabbinic homilists take the three clauses: thou shalt not go, thou
shalt not curse, for they are blessed, as answers to queries put by
Balaam. After he was told not to go, he asked whether he might curse
them from where he was, and when this also was forbidden, he asked
again whether he might bless them, but this also was denied him, and

unto the princes of Balak: 'Get you into your land; for
14 the LORD refuseth to give me leave to go with you.' And
the princes of Moab rose up, and they went unto Balak,
15 and said: 'Balaam refuseth to come with us.' And Balak
sent yet again princes, more, and more honourable than
16 they. And they came to Balaam, and said to him: 'Thus
saith Balak the son of Zippor: Let nothing, I pray thee,
17 hinder thee from coming unto me; for I will promote thee
unto very great honour, and whatsoever thou sayest unto
me I will do; come therefore, I pray thee, curse me this
18 people.' And Balaam answered and said unto the servants
of Balak: 'If Balak would give me his house full of silver

he was told: "we want neither your honey nor your sting" (Num. R.
20.9).

13. *refuseth to give me leave*] He does not give them the reason for
God's refusal as indicated in v. 12, perhaps because he did not expect
them to understand it fully, or because he did not wish to destroy
all their hope. The suggestion is made that he withheld the real reason
for the refusal, because he wanted Balak to send a more important
embassy whereby the honor given him would be enhanced (Rashi).

14. *Balaam refuseth*] Without mentioning that he was acting
under the direct orders from God.

15. *more*] In number, although the word רבים may also be translated great ones, chiefs (Esth. 1.8; ibn Ezra, *Biur*). Balak naturally
supposed that by sending a more important embassy Balaam might
be induced to come, interpreting the reason for his first refusal that
not sufficient respect was shown to him.

16. *Let nothing, I pray thee, hinder thee*] R. V. It is also possible to
take the verb here as a reflexive and to translate: "Hold not thyself
back from coming" (Gray, comp. Leeser).

17. *I will promote thee unto very great honour*] R. V. There is no
indication in the Heb. text of the idea of promotion to office, but simply
"I shall greatly honor thee" (Leeser, Kalisch).

and gold, I cannot go beyond the word of the LORD my
God, to do any thing, small or great. Now therefore, I 19
pray you, tarry ye also here this night, that I may know
what the LORD will speak unto me more.' And God came 20
unto Balaam at night, and said unto him: 'If the men
are come to call thee, rise up, go with them; but only the
word which I speak unto thee, that shalt thou do.' And 21
Balaam rose up in the morning, and saddled his ass, and

18. *I cannot go beyond*] Transgress (Mendelssohn, Leeser) or go
against (Kalisch). "Go beyond" implies that not only can he not do
anything against the will of God, but also that he cannot do anything
which God did not expressly tell him to do.

small or great] Comp. 24.13, "good or evil", idiomatic expressions,
meaning anything at all.

19. *tarry ye also here this night*] Even though he might have been
certain that God would not permit him to curse Israel(v. 12), still he
did not wish to dismiss the distinguished embassy without ascertaining
again whether there was any change in God's plans. He expected that
during the night he might again have an opportunity to learn whether
it would please God if he went with them.

20. *If the men are come to call thee*] If they are insistent upon your
going and are satisfied to take the chance, you may go with them, but
you may do only what I command you to do. There is no indication
here that God would tell him to bless Israel, although Balaam might
have inferred it. Still he might be useful in giving advice or in deliver-
ing to them a prophecy regarding their own future destinies. He then
went with them, but did not divulge to the messengers the full import
of the condition made by God, and it was for this reason that God was
angry with him (v. 22; Ramban followed by many other commentators; comp. ibn Ezra). God gave Balaam permission to go in order to
have him pronounce the blessings and praises, which might otherwise
have remained unsaid (comp. Kalisch, 119–124).

21. *saddled his ass*] The female ass, although the male ass was
also commonly used for riding, especially short distances. For longer
journeys, the camel would be the animal used (comp. note to v. 5).

22 went with the princes of Moab. And God's anger was
kindled because he went; and the angel of the LORD placed
himself in the way for an adversary against him.—Now
he was riding upon his ass, and his two servants were with
23 him.—And the ass saw the angel of the LORD standing in
the way, with his sword drawn in his hand; and the ass

22–35. BALAAM REBUKED BY HIS ASS.

God is angered at Balaam for going with the princes of Moab and
sends an angel to hinder him on the way. Balaam does not notice the
angel, but his ass does and tries to turn sideways in order to avoid
the angel. The perversity of the ass arouses Balaam's anger and he
strikes her with his stick. The ass complains to Balaam of his cruelty
and lack of consideration for his faithful beast. Balaam suddenly
perceives the angel, who explains to Balaam that it was he who stood
as a hindrance on the way and that the ass was entirely guiltless.
Full of contrition, Balaam is ready to turn back, but the angel permits
him to go on, on the condition that he say only that which God will
tell him to say.

22. *And God's anger was kindled*] Comp. note to v. 20. Modern
critics regard this section as a part of a different version of the story,
since they are unable to account for God's anger after He once gave
him permission to go with the messengers of Balak.

for an adversary] Satan is the word used here in the Heb. text, the
original meaning of which is adversary or hindrance; later it became
a proper name given to a distinct personality occupying the position
of accuser in the court of heaven (cf. Job 1.6 ff.; 2.1 ff.).

his two servants] Comp. Gen. 22.3. The princes of Moab, who are
represented in v. 21 as accompanying him on the road, are not mentioned again until v. 35. This is taken as an additional reason for
regarding this section as part of another version, although it is quite
possible to assume that Balaam and his servants became separated
from the party while this incident occurred and later joined them again.

23. *with his sword drawn*] A sign of God's anger (Josh. 5.13;
Gen. 3.24). On perceiving the angel, the ass turns from the open road

turned aside out of the way, and went into the field; and
Balaam smote the ass, to turn her into the way. Then 24
the angel of the LORD stood in a hollow way between the
vineyards, a fence being on this side, and a fence on that
side. And the ass saw the angel of the LORD, and she thrust 25
herself unto the wall, and crushed Balaam's foot against
the wall; and he smote her again. And the angel of the 26
LORD went further, and stood in a narrow place, where
was no way to turn either to the right hand or to the left.
And the ass saw the angel of the LORD, and she lay down 27
under Balaam; and Balaam's anger was kindled, and he
smote the ass with his staff. And the LORD opened the 28
mouth of the ass, and she said unto Balaam: 'What have

(דרך) to the cultivated land (שדה), and is then struck by Balaam in
order to bring her back to the open road.

24. *in a hollow way*] A road shut in between vineyards, fenced
about by walls of stone (Prov. 24.31) or of thorns (Isa. 5.5), so that
the ass could not turn to the open field as before.

25. *and she thrust herself*] Either out of fright or because she
sought to find room to pass. The niphal is used here in a reflexive
sense.

crushed Balaam's foot] From this reference arose the tradition that
Balaam was lame on one leg (Sanh. 105a; Rashbam, comp. 23.3).

26. *in a narrow place*] Completely blocking the way so that the
ass could do nothing but lie down on the place where she stood. The
angel appears three times and Balaam smites his ass three times,
while the ass speaks only twice, the third time the angel speaks and
reproves Balaam. The Rabbis interpret the repetition of the number
three here homiletically (Num. R. 20.11). The two servants of Balaam
were apparently not present at the time (Sforno), or if they were they
did not hear or see what was going on (Ramban).

28. *opened the mouth of the ass*] Gave her power of speech (Ezek.
3.27; 33.22). The miracle recorded here has its parallels in the folklore
of many ancient peoples (Gray, 334). The only parallel in the Bible

I done unto thee, that thou hast smitten me these three

29 times?' And Balaam said unto the ass: 'Because thou
hast mocked me; I would there were a sword in my hand,

30 for now I had killed thee.' And the ass said unto Balaam:
'Am not I thine ass, upon which thou hast ridden all thy
life long unto this day? was I ever wont to do so unto thee?'

31 And he said: 'Nay.' Then the LORD opened the eyes of

is the story of the serpent speaking to Eve in Gen. 3. The point of the
miracle here is apparently to show Balaam that God is the one who
gives speech and He can therefore control speech at His will (Ramban,
Sforno, Ehrlich). Maimonides (*Moreh Nebukim*, II.42) explains this
whole incident, including the speaking of the ass, as having taken
place in a prophetic vision vouchsafed to Balaam, and this view was
shared by other rationalists of the middle ages and of more modern
times, although it was sharply contested by others and was one of the
points that gave rise to the famous Maimunist controversy. The
traditional view is that this was a miracle, ordained by God at the
time of creation (Ab. 5.6) for the purpose of glorifying the name of
God and manifesting His great love for Israel (ibn Ezra; see Kalisch,
123–143).

29. *thou hast mocked me*] The word התעללת is used to express
severe treatment of another, in derision, for one's own pleasure (Ex.
10.2; Judg. 19.25). Balaam shows no surprise when he hears the ass
speak, or at least, the chronicler does not indicate that the strange
phenomenon appeared to him unusual (similarly in the case of the
serpent speaking to Eve, Gen. 3.4 ff.).

30. *all thy life long*] Lit. "ever since thou wast" (cf. Gen. 48.15),
indicating a long period of service. Leeser's rendering "from thy
commencement" is not clear. Perhaps "from the time that thou hast
learnt to ride" (*Biur*).

was I ever wont] Have I ever shown a habit of acting thus toward
thee? Hence, instead of beating her, Balaam should have tried to
investigate the cause of her strange and unusual behavior. The ass,
however, does not give the reason for her conduct.

31. *opened the eyes*] Made him see what was hidden from him
until now (comp. Ehrlich to Gen. 21.19; Ps. 119.18).

Balaam, and he saw the angel of the LORD standing in the
way, with his sword drawn in his hand; and he bowed his
head, and fell on his face. And the angel of the LORD said 32
unto him: 'Wherefore hast thou smitten thine ass these
three times? behold, I am come forth for an adversary,
because thy way is contrary unto me; and the ass saw me, 33
and turned aside before me these three times; unless she
had turned aside from me, surely now I had even slain
thee, and saved her alive.' And Balaam said unto the 34
angel of the LORD: 'I have sinned; for I knew not that

bowed his head]   In homage and submission.

32.   *Wherefore*]   The angel reproves Balaam for beating the ass,
declaring the ass not only innocent of any intention to mock at him,
but even instrumental in saving her master's life.

because thy way is contrary unto me]   The word ירט used here is
unusual. Leeser, following Mendelssohn, renders "because thy way
which is odious to me was too quickly begun". Another rendering is
"thou hast precipitated thy journey in front of me", i. e. rushed reck-
lessly in front me (BDB). Our translation follows the sense implied
in Targum and older versions, although it does not indicate the exact
meaning of the word ירט, which probably denotes to be precipitous
or destructive (Job 16.11). The expression לנגדי indicates opposition,
hence this is regarded as a censure of Balaam for his readiness to follow
the embassy, knowing that this would be displeasing to God.

33.   *unless*]   The Heb. text has here אולי, which means "perhaps",
and therefore an emendation לולי has been suggested, which means
"if not, unless" (BDB, but comp. Rashbam).

I had even slain thee]   Not only caused you the delay and the injury
to your leg (Rashi, Rashbam, *Biur*). Leeser has "not only have slain
thee but saved her alive", but the idiom in this case would require
גם in both clauses (comp. Ehrlich). The rabbinic tradition is that the
ass died after this incident, so that she might not become an object of
worship, or in order to save Balaam from ignominy (Num. R. 20.12;
comp. Lev. 20.15, 16).

34.   *I have sinned*]   Unwittingly, not knowing the cause of the

thou stoodest in the way against me; now therefore, if it
35 displease thee, I will get me back.' And the angel of the
Lord said unto Balaam: 'Go with the men; but only the
word that I shall speak unto thee, that thou shalt speak.'
36 So Balaam went with the princes of Balak. And when
Balak heard that Balaam was come, he went out to meet
him unto Ir-moab, which is on the border of Arnon, which
37 is in the utmost part of the border. And Balak said unto

action of the ass, and therefore striking her for no fault of hers. Realizing now that his going displeases God, he is ready to turn back.

35. This verse is practically a repetition of v. 20, except that here
the angel speaks in the name of God. The words "that I shall speak
unto thee" must be regarded as a direct quotation referring to God and
not to the angel.

36–41. BALAK WELCOMES BALAAM.

On hearing of Balaam's arrival, Balak goes out to meet him. He
first reproaches him for not responding to his first call, but Balaam
tells him that even now that he has come he can say nothing but what
God will direct him to say. On arriving at Kiriath-huzoth, Balak
arranges a sumptuous meal for Balaam and his company. They then
go up to an elevated plain from which Balaam can see part of the
Israelitish camp.　According to those who regard the narrative as
composed of two sources, v. 36 follows immediately upon v. 21 in one
of these sources.

36. *Ir-moab*] To be taken as a composite proper name (also
Leeser, Luzzatto, Ehrlich). Some take it as "a certain city of Moab"
(Targum, Mendelssohn, Herxheimer). Rashi renders it "the metropolis of Moab" (Num. R. 20.14), perhaps identifying it with Ar,
believed by some to be the name of the capital of Moab (Isa. 15.1),
which was to the north of Arnon (21.15, 28). The description of the
meeting-place given here indicates that it lay on the northern boundary
of Moab and on the eastern end of that part of the boundary.

Balaam: 'Did I not earnestly send unto thee to call thee? wherefore camest thou not unto me? am I not able indeed to promote thee to honour?' And Balaam said unto Balak: 38 'Lo, I am come unto thee; have I now any power at all to speak any thing? the word that God putteth in my mouth, that shall I speak.' And Balaam went with Balak, and 39 they came unto Kiriath-huzoth. And Balak sacrificed 40 oxen and sheep, and sent to Balaam, and to the princes that were with him. And it came to pass in the morning 41

37. *Did I not earnestly send*] The construction of the Hebrew here, the inf. abs. with the indic., signifies earnest and emphatic action, although it may also indicate repeated action and refer to the two embassies sent by Balak.

am I not able] Was it because you doubted my ability to reward you well for your services?

38. *Lo, I am come unto thee*] There would have been no use in my coming to you then, nor is there any use in my coming now, for I shall not be able to gratify your wish, as I am simply an instrument in the hands of God, and only what He puts in my mouth will I be able to say.

39. *Kiriath-huzoth*] This name is found here only and the place has not been identified (comp. 32.37). The literal meaning is "city of streets" (comp. Targum קרית מחווהי, city of his market places), which might indicate a populous city. The Rabbis say that Balak sought to appeal to the sympathies of Balaam, by pointing to the large number of men, women and children whom the Israelites came to destroy (Num. R. 20.14).

40. *And Balak sacrificed*] More accurately "slew" (Leeser), but among the ancient Hebrews, it appears, only such flesh was eaten as came from an animal that was previously brought as a sacrifice (comp. Hul. 17b).

and sent] Portions of the flesh to the distinguished guests, as a mark of respect and attention (Gen. 43.34; I Sam. 9.23 ff.).

that Balak took Balaam, and brought him up into Bamoth-baal, and he saw from thence the utmost part of the people.

23   And Balaam said unto Balak: 'Build me here seven altars, and prepare me here seven bullocks and seven rams.'

41. *Bamoth-baal*] Which lay near Dibon, possibly a sanctuary town (21.19; Josh. 13.17 comp. Targum), or, perhaps, identical with Bamoth-arnon (21.18; ibn Ezra), selected because of the sanctity of the place and because from it the object of the imprecation might be seen.

the utmost part of the people] The part nearest to them, while the rest of the camp was obscured from view (cf. 23.13).

CHAPTER 23.

1–6.   BALAK MAKES PREPARATIONS FOR CURSE.

Balaam orders Balak to erect seven altars and to arrange a sacrifice consisting of seven oxen and seven rams. Both officiate at the offering of the sacrifices, when Balaam bids Balak to remain near the altars, while he goes a little distance away in the expectation that he may receive a message from God. God appears to him and gives him a message. Balaam then returns to the place where Balak and the princes of Moab stood waiting for him.

Sacrifices were regarded as a necessary complement to divine worship and as a most efficient means of turning the divine favor towards the one who offered them, hence it was expected that Balak's desire might be granted and that God would allow Balaam to curse Israel. The sacred number seven is used in order to insure still further God's favor for the cause which Balak sought to achieve (cf. Job 42.8; see ibn Ezra).

1. *and prepare*] Make the animals ready for sacrifice (comp. Zeph. 1.7).

And Balak did as Balaam had spoken; and Balak and 2
Balaam offered on every altar a bullock and a ram. And 3
Balaam said unto Balak: 'Stand by thy burnt-offering,
and I will go; peradventure the LORD will come to meet me;
and whatsoever He showeth me I will tell thee.' And he
went to a bare height. And God met Balaam; and he said 4
unto Him: 'I have prepared the seven altars, and I have
offered up a bullock and a ram on every altar.' And the 5

2. *and Balak and Balaam offered*] Balaam is associated here in
making the offerings (cf. v. 4). LXX omits the two names here, making
Balak the subject of both clauses of the verse.

on every altar] The definite article here in the Hebrew text is regarded as distributive (following Targum, ibn Ezra).

3. *Stand by thy burnt-offering*] The word התיצב implies the idea
of standing quiet and passive, in the expectation of something that
is about to happen (Ex. 14.13; I Sam. 12.7, 16), and it might also
include the idea of prayer. Balak was to remain at prayer near his
sacrifices, while Balaam was seeking divine revelation in solitude.

will come to meet me] To impart a revelation (comp. Ex. 13.18).

to a bare height] A solitary place, where he would not be disturbed
(Isa. 13.2; 41.18; Jer. 3.2, 21). Targum has "thoughtfully alone"
(cf. Rashi; Zunz); Saadia has "he went calmly" (see Kohut, 202–4);
Rashbam, following the talmudic tradition (Sanh. 105a) that Balaam
became lame as a result of the ass crushing his foot against the wall
(note on 22.25), renders this word "limping". Some regard שפי as an
abbreviation (שאל פי ה "to ask for a revelation"; comp. LXX), while
others emend לכשפים "for enchantments" (see Gray, 343–344; Kalisch,
169–170; Ehrlich; Kahana).

4. *And God met Balaam*] Accidentally, indicating an inferior
degree of prophecy (Rashi, Ramban).

and he said] Balaam said: I prepared the altars and sacrifices and
now I am ready to receive a revelation. Comp. Rashi, who quotes the
midrashic interpretation that Balaam's seven altars were to balance
the seven altars erected by the three patriarchs: Abraham four (Gen.
12.7, 8; 13.18; 26.9), Isaac one (Gen. 26.25), and Jacob two (Gen.
33.20; 35.7). Comp. Tan. Balak 16 and Buber's note 97.

LORD put a word in Balaam's mouth, and said: 'Return
6 unto Balak, and thus thou shalt speak.' And he returned
unto him, and, lo, he stood by his burnt-offering, he, and
7 all the princes of Moab. And he took up his parable, and
said:

> From Aram Balak bringeth me,
> The king of Moab from the mountains of the East:
> 'Come, curse me Jacob,
> And come, execrate Israel.'

5. *put a word in Balaam's mouth*] Delivered the revelation to
him, or told him the exact words which he should say (Ramban).

7-10. BALAAM'S FIRST PROPHECY.

The first prophecy of Balaam, consisting of seven couplets, tells of
the purpose for which he was invited and declares that this purpose
was impossible of realization. He then speaks of Israel, a people separate and distinct from all other nations, large and powerful, and concludes with the prayer that his own end might be like the end prepared for them.

7. *his parable*] The word משל here means really a prophetic discourse, delivered in figurative language (BDB; comp. note on 22.5).

From Aram] The birthplace of Balaam (22.5), a shortened form of
Aram-naharaim (Hos. 12.13).

the mountains of the East] Cf. Deut. 33.15, where the same phrase
is rendered "ancient mountains". Here the reference may be to the
high ranges of the Syrian desert, visible from a distance (Gray) or, if
regarded as parallel to Aram (Mesopotamia), the reference may be to
the low ranges of the plain lying to the north (Kalisch).

execrate] R. V. and Leeser have "defy". The word זעם means to
be indignant, hence to express indignation in speech, denounce, curse
(BDB). The parallelism of Jacob and Israel, repeated here several
times, is also found in Isa. 40.55 (17 times) and in Micah 1-3 (4 times;
Gray).

How shall I curse, whom God hath not cursed?   8

And how shall I execrate, whom the LORD hath not
  execrated?

For from the top of the rocks I see him,   9

And from the hills I behold him:

Lo, it is a people that shall dwell alone,

And shall not be reckoned among the nations.

Who hath counted the dust of Jacob,   10

Or numbered the stock of Israel?

9. *For from the top of the rocks*] Referring to Bamoth-baal where
he was standing (22.41). As I look at him from this height, I realize
that God will not consent to have him cursed, for he is a people that
dwelleth alone, a peculiar treasure of God, whom He set aside for a
high purpose (Ex. 19.5; Deut. 7.6). Another rendering has been suggested: I see him (Israel) towering above the top of the rocks, and
above the hills; he stands alone in strength and is not to be counted
with other nations (Ehrlich).

shall not be reckoned] He does not partake of the fate of other
nations (Targum, Rashi), and is not subject to the ills that might
befall other nations (cf. Deut. 32.12, where a similar figure is used in
relation to God).

10. *Who hath counted*] Who is able to count? (Targum; R. V.).
Their strength is equaled by their superior numbers.

the dust] The great multitudes, reminiscent of the figure in Gen.
13.16; 28.14.

Or numbered] Adopting the reading ספר מי (LXX, Sam., see, however, Kalisch 182).

the stock] Cf. Rashi, from רבע to beget (BDB, Lev. 20.16; comp.
Nid. 13a), hence posterity. R. V., Mendelssohn, Leeser, Herxheimer
and others have "the fourth part", i. e. a small portion of them,
because Balaam could see only one of the four flanks of the Israelitish
camp (2.10) to which allusion is here made (Targum; ibn Ezra; Ramban). Some, following LXX (demos = common people), translate
"the myriads of Israel", assuming a reading רבבות (cf. 10.36; Deut.
33.17). Hertz takes the word to mean "ashes", thus producing a perfect parallelism.

Let me die the death of the righteous,
And let mine end be like his!

11 And Balak said unto Balaam: 'What hast thou done
    unto me? I took thee to curse mine enemies, and, behold,
12 thou hast blessed them altogether.' And he answered and
    said: 'Must I not take heed to speak that which the LORD
13 putteth in my mouth?' And Balak said unto him: 'Come,

the death of the righteous] Israel, a nation of upright men; possibly
a play on the name Jeshurun (Deut. 32.15; 33.26).

let mine end be like his] As happy as is the future reserved for
Israel. This has no reference to immortality or the future life, as is
assumed by some, but to the material blessings that are in store for
the righteous nation and for the individual members of such a nation.

11-17. BALAK, DISAPPOINTED, MAKES MORE
ELABORATE PREPARATIONS.

Balak is surprised and angered on hearing the prophetic utterance
regarding his enemies, but Balaam tells him again that he is powerless
in the matter and is not to be blamed. Believing that perhaps the
place was not well-chosen, Balak suggests a change and they proceed
to the top of Pisgah, where again seven altars are built and sacrifices
are offered. Balak remains with the sacrifices, while Balaam goes out
in search of a revelation. On receiving the revelation, he returns to
the place where Balak is and delivers his second prophecy.

11. *thou hast blessed them altogether*] R. V., "thou hast done nothing
but bless". Leeser has "thou hast even blessed them", i. e. not only
didst thou not curse, but thou didst even bless. He might have abstained from blessing, if he could not curse. There is really no actual
blessing in Balaam's words, except what is implied in the praise be-
stowed upon Israel. The word ברך has also the meaning of praise
(BDB).

12. *take heed*] Cf. Deut. 5.1; 6.25, implying moral obligation.
Balaam says that he can neither curse not bless. He is only the instrument of God and produces only what God puts in his mouth.

I pray thee, with me unto another place, from whence
thou mayest see them; thou shalt see but the utmost part
of them, and shalt not see them all; and curse me them
from thence.' And he took him into the field of Zophim, 14
to the top of Pisgah, and built seven altars, and offered
up a bullock and a ram on every altar. And he said unto 15

13. *unto another place*] A change of locality was believed to cause
a change in the divine decree concerning individuals or nations (R. H.
16b; B. M. 75b and the popular saying משנה מקום משנה מזל). Balak
hoped that he might still succeed in obtaining a curse for his enemies
by having the prophet view them from a different angle.

thou shalt see but the utmost part of them] Although at Bamoth-baal
he also saw only part of the people (22.41), Balak thought that the
sight inspired the prophet to utter his words of praise and therefore
desired that he should see now a much smaller portion of the people
than before (cf. Luzzatto). It is also possible to render it "thou shalt
look only on part of them" even though you may see all (see Kalisch,
190). Some suggest that Balak wished to take him to a spot from
which he could see the entire Israelitish camp and pronounce his curse
on them all at one time. Accordingly they render this verse: "from
which thou shalt see him (the whole of him, while now) thou seest
only part of him and not the whole of him" (Keil).

14. *the field of Zophim*] The ancient versions as well as many
modern commentators regard the word צופים as a common noun and
translate "the field of the watchmen" (also Targum, Rashi), a high
place where watchmen were stationed to espy the approach of an
enemy (comp. Koenig, *Messian. Weissagungen*, p. 12, who understands
by this a place from where the passing of clouds or the flight of birds
could be seen for the purpose of augury or divination).

the top of Pisgah] "The ridge of Pisgah, a part of the mountain-
chain of Abarim, stretches to the north and east of Mount Attarus,
on which was Bamoth-baal, the scene of the first prophecy. The
'Field of Seers' must, therefore, have been in close proximity to Mount
Nebo, which is likewise described as 'a summit of Pisgah' and is only
a short distance southwest of the ancient town of Heshbon" (Kalisch,
189).

Balak: 'Stand here by thy burnt-offering, while I go
16 toward a meeting yonder.' And the LORD met Balaam,
and put a word in his mouth, and said: 'Return unto Balak,
17 and thus shalt thou speak.' And he came to him, and, lo,
he stood by his burnt-offering, and the princes of Moab
with him. And Balak said unto him: 'What hath the
18 LORD spoken?' And he took up his parable, and said:

Arise, Balak, and hear;
Give ear unto me, thou son of Zippor:
19 God is not a man, that He should lie;
Neither the son of man, that He should repent:
When He hath said, will He not do it?
Or when He hath spoken, will He not make it good?

15. *Stand here*] Comp. Ex. 2.12.

go toward a meeting] With God, understood. The term is used throughout the narrative in the sense of receiving a revelation.

18–24. BALAAM'S SECOND PROPHECY.

In the second prophecy, consisting of eleven couplets, Balaam tells Balak that God will not change His mind concerning Israel. Free from trouble as they are and enjoying the protection of God, who brought them out of Egypt, no magic can prevail against Israel. Strong as a lion, Israel will subdue all his enemies.

18. *Arise*] Balak was standing at the time (v. 17) and therefore the phrase is an invitation merely to listen attentively (cf. Isa. 32.9).

Give ear unto me] LXX has "my witness" (עֵדִי) instead of "to me" (עָדַי).

19. *that He should lie*] Balak's hope that God might change His mind if the circumstances are changed cannot be realized, for God is not like man. He decreed blessings for Israel and will keep His promise to them.

Behold, I am bidden to bless;   20
And when He hath blessed, I cannot call it back.
None hath beheld iniquity in Jacob,   21
Neither hath one seen perverseness in Israel;
The LORD his God is with him,
And the shouting for the King is among them.
God who brought them forth out of Egypt   22

20. *I am bidden*] I received instructions to bless, God *took* me
to bless (comp. v. 11).

when He hath blessed] Another reading here is, "and I shall continue
to bless and I shall not recall it", emending ואברך.

I cannot call it back] The blessing once pronounced must take
effect, and surely cannot be turned into a curse.

21. *None hath beheld*] Impersonal, following LXX. Others make
God the subject of the verb (Rashi, Herxheimer). Luzzatto renders:
He cannot bear to see anyone practice iniquity against Jacob. Rashbam renders: He does not wish to see iniquity in Jacob, even when it
exists; He closes His eyes so as not to see it (comp. Num. R. 20.18).

iniquity] God may sometimes change His decrees if circumstances
change. In this case, however, there is no reason for God to change
His plan regarding Israel, since the people kept their purity and continued loyal to Him. The two words rendered here "iniquity" and
"perverseness" (עמל, און) are taken by some to denote "calamity" and
"trouble", descriptive of the external glory of Israel (as in vv. 9, 10;
Biur; see previous note).

And the shouting for the King] God; the constant rejoicing for their
God who is in their midst (cf. Deut. 33.5). The shouting for the King
is reminiscent of the sounding of the trumpets in connection with the
holy seasons and the sacrifices (10.1–10; Ps. 47.6; 89.16).

22. *God who brought them forth out of Egypt*] In contrast to Balak's
words (22.5), "a people has gone out of Egypt". This great event
occurred through the intervention of their God, who is mighty and
ready to protect and guard His people (Rashi).

Is for them like the lofty horns of the wild-ox.

23   For there is no enchantment with Jacob,
Neither is there any divination with Israel;
Now is it said of Jacob and of Israel:
'What hath God wrought!'

24   Behold a people that riseth up as a lioness,

lofty horns] The word תוֹעֲפוֹת is rare and the meaning obscure. It sometimes denotes mountain peaks (Ps. 95.4), but by comparison with Deut. 33.17 it is likely that the rendering given here is in accord with the original meaning of the word. It indicates both strength and protection.

of the wild-ox] The symbol of strength and fierceness, described in Job 39.9–12, probably identical with the *rimu* found in Assyrian inscriptions and denoting a huge bovine animal, now extinct.

23.   *there is no enchantment with Jacob*] The strength and prosperity of Israel are due to the direct interest of God in them and not to any intermediaries. Enchantment and divination may be necessary in the case of other peoples, but not of the people to whom God manifests Himself in a direct and intimate manner. This seems to be the meaning of this clause (Rashi, ibn Ezra), although many other interpretations have been given. Another rendering is offered by a number of Jewish commentators, who translate the word בְּיַעֲקֹב *against* Jacob, meaning that no enchantment will have an effect against Jacob (Targum, Ramban, Luzzatto). Others interpret this clause to indicate that Israel is free from such idolatrous practices as enchantment and divination (comp. I Sam. 15.23), and make it parallel to v. 21, where it speaks of the absence of sin and iniquity in Israel (comp. Kalisch, 208–209).

of Jacob and of Israel] Regarding Israel it will be said: What wonders hath God wrought! The rendering "to Jacob" (Leeser) agrees better with the context. Jacob is told beforehand what God intends to do for him or in his behalf (Rashi), contrasting prophecy with divination. Luzzatto offers an ingenious suggestion: Jacob and Israel will be given a third name, "Mah-Pa'al-El" (How wonderful are the things that God does!), i. e. Israel is destined for great things.

24.   *that riseth up as a lioness*] Through the protection of God

And as a lion doth he lift himself up;
He shall not lie down until he eat of the prey,
And drink the blood of the slain.

And Balak said unto Balaam: 'Neither curse them at 25
all, nor bless them at all.' But Balaam answered and said 26
unto Balak: 'Told not I thee, saying: All that the LORD
speaketh, that I must do?' And Balak said unto Balaam: 27
'Come now, I will take thee unto another place; peradventure it will please God that thou mayest curse me them
from thence.' And Balak took Balaam unto the top of Peor, 28

(v. 22) Israel becomes as a lion in strength (Gen. 49.9; Deut. 33.20;
Micah 5.8), proudly conquering his enemies (the Canaanites or the
Midianites; Rashi, ibn Ezra) and taking possession of their land (Tar-
gum).

23.25–24.2. BALAK, ANGERED, MAKES NEW PREPARATIONS.

Balak is angered at Balaam's words of praise of his enemy and tells
him that if he cannot curse, he should also forbear from blessing.
Balaam, however, reminds him that he is powerless to say anything
except what God has ordered him to say. Balak then makes another
attempt at a change of locality, hoping thereby to effect a change in
God's attitude towards Israel, so that He might permit Balaam to
curse Israel. He is willing to admit that Balaam is not at fault and
that God's consent is necessary and is therefore trying to obtain that
consent by having the prophet view the camp of Israel from another
place. There he again erects seven altars and prepares the sacrifices.
Balaam, however, realizing that it is pleasing to God to hear Israel
blessed, does not seek any new revelation and begins his third prophecy
without leaving the place.

28. *the top of Peor*] Apparently a mountain on the same ridge of
Pisgah where was also Sedeh-zofim (v. 14). The exact place has not
been identified. Beth-peor, a sanctuary where the Baal of Peor (25.3)

29 that looketh down upon the desert. And Balaam said
unto Balak: 'Build me here seven altars, and prepare
30 me here seven bullocks and seven rams.' And Balak did
as Balaam had said, and offered up a bullock and a ram
on every altar.

24   And when Balaam saw that it pleased the LORD to bless
Israel, he went not, as at the other times, to meet with
enchantments, but he set his face toward the wilderness.

was worshiped (Deut. 3.29; 4.46; 34.6; Josh. 13.20), was probably in
the vicinity of this summit (Targum has "the top of the elevation",
comp. Adler).

upon the desert] Cf. 21.20.

CHAPTER 24.

1. *as at the other times*] The previous two times (23.3, 15), when
he left Balak at the altar and went out to obtain a revelation.

to meet with enchantments] Which consisted chiefly of observing
signs or omens. This does not necessarily imply that Balaam sought
enchantments or omens in the first two instances, as there is no reference to such in the narrative before. The meaning simply is that he
did not proceed to obtain his revelation in the same manner as before,
when he appeared to have given the impression that certain spots or
conditions were more favorable than others for communion with God.
Certain that God desired him to bless Israel, he did not any more go
out to find a revelation by a chance inspiration from God, but proceeded
on his own account to bless Israel. This seems to be the plain meaning
of the phrase here, although it may have assumed a more sinister
meaning in later times (comp. Kalisch, 218 ff.). Modern critics regard
this as a gloss or as belonging to another source (Gray).

toward the wilderness] the plain called Arboth-moab (22.1; ibn
Ezra, comp. Targum), where the Israelites were encamped.

And Balaam lifted up his eyes, and he saw Israel dwelling 2
tribe by tribe; and the spirit of God came upon him. And 3
he took up his parable, and said:

The saying of Balaam the son of Beor,
And the saying of the man whose eye is opened;

2. *dwelling tribe by tribe*] In an orderly arrangement, as described
in chs. 2 and 10; comp. Targum Jon. The doors of their tents were so
arranged as to preclude the possibility for any of them to pry into the
family secrets of his neighbor (B.B. 60a).

the spirit of God] Distinguished from the revelations which he
previously received. Before, he was merely the mouthpiece of God,
now the spirit of God actuated him and became part of him (Ramban).

3–9. BALAAM'S THIRD PROPHECY.

The third prophecy of Balaam, consisting of nine couplets and two
triplets, begins with an introduction descriptive of himself as the
prophet of God, whose privilege it is to see visions and to obtain revelations emanating from the divine source. The prophecy itself (5–9)
begins with a poetic description of the Israelitish camp which he sees
from a distance and by the sight of which he is inspired to foretell the
glorious future awaiting that people. God has given them strength
to subdue their enemies, and this strength is the surety for their future
peace and prosperity. It is advisable for any other people to secure
the friendship of Israel, for those who bless them will be blessed, but
those who curse them will be cursed.

3. *The saying of Balaam*] The word נאם introducing a prophetic
utterance usually relates to God. There are only a very few instances
(here and v. 15, also II Sam. 23.1; Ps. 36.2; Prov. 30.1) where the term
is used before the name of a man.

whose eye is opened] Who is able to see what will happen in the
future (Targum). The word שתם is found here only, and the translation is conjectural. In the Talmud this root means to open ('Ab.
Zarah 5.3, 69a; see Levy, *Wörterbuch*, s. v.). Others make it identical
with the root שתם = סתם, which means to close, one who has hitherto
been blind to the revelation of God, or one who was physically blind
in one eye (Rashi, comp. Nid. 31a; see Kalisch, 231–232).

4   The saying of him who heareth the words of God,
     Who seeth the vision of the Almighty,
     Fallen down, yet with opened eyes:
5   How goodly are thy tents, O Jacob,
     Thy dwellings, O Israel!
6   As valleys stretched out,
     As gardens by the river-side;
     As aloes planted of the LORD,

4. *who heareth . . . . Who seeth*]   In the trance the prophet sees an apparition from whose mouth a message proceeds (cf. Job 4.13–16).

Fallen down]   While in the trance (I Sam. 19.24) and still with his eyes open (ibn Ezra). Targum has "while asleep He reveals Himself to him" (cf. 22.20). Verses 3 and 4 are repeated in vv. 15 and 16, except that there another phrase is added, "who knoweth the knowledge of the Most High". Some critics believe that our verse also contained this phrase but that it fell out by mistake.

5. *How goodly are thy tents*]   Leeser has "how beautiful". Viewing the camp of Israel with its numerous tents, Balaam is inspired to praise the people and foretell their future destiny (comp. note to v. 2).

6. *As valleys*]   Wadis, glens, through which a stream passes, a figure of prosperity. Some translate here "as streams" (Mendelssohn, Leeser), but this is out of harmony with the parallelism of the rest of the verse. Perles (*JQR*, XI, 688) translates "like palm trees stretched out", basing it on the Arabic (BDB), but this is no improvement on our rendering.

stretched out]   As they appeared from the height. Although the tents of v. 5 are the subject of the comparisons here, the prophet has in mind the people occupying the tents.

As gardens by the river-side]   Which are fruitful and flourishing (Isa. 58.11; comp. Isa. 1.30; Targum has "Euphrates" instead of river, comp. note on 22.5).

As aloes planted of the Lord]   The aloe is a sweet-smelling tree, used as a perfume (Ps. 45.9; Prov. 7.17; Cant. 4.14). LXX renders "like the tents" (cf. Dan. 11.45), and is followed by some early Jewish and Christian versions (see Rashi, comp. Kohut, 64), but besides the

As cedars beside the waters;

Water shall flow from his branches,   7

And his seed shall be in many waters;

etymological difficulty, this rendering would interfere with the symmetry of the similes introduced here.

As cedars beside the waters] Cedar trees, especially the cedars of Lebanon, do not grow in moist places, but rather seek elevated land. However, several species of trees were called by the name of ארז (cf. R. H. 23a, where one Rabbi mentions four, and another ten kinds; Post in Hastings, *Dictionary of the Bible*, s. v. mentions three kinds). The poet should not be pressed too hard because of a slip in the knowledge of botany. The cedar tree was regarded as the king of the trees and even if Balaam never saw one, he used the simile from his general knowledge and placed the cedar near the water, the source of all fruitfulness to the oriental (Post, ib., s. v. Aloes). It is therefore unnecessary to emend here or to transpose the verse to read: as palms beside the waters, as cedars which God hath planted (cf. Ps. 104.16 and Gray).

7. *Water shall flow*] Continuing the figure of the preceding verse. Water, so precious in the Orient, will be most abundant in Israel.

from his branches] The trees mentioned in v. 6 will be so well-watered that the water will flow down from their branches (ibn Ezra, Luzzatto; cf. Jer. 11.16; Ezek. 17.6, 7). The more common rendering, however, is that of R. V., following Rashi, "water shall flow from his buckets", which is not very clear. It may be interpreted as a figure for the abundance of wells and springs in the land of Israel (Kalisch; Gray).

And his seed shall be in many waters] The blessings vouchsafed to Israel of the present will also extend to his posterity, whose land will be abundantly watered. These two lines have caused much trouble to exegetes, and various renderings and emendations of the text have been suggested. The old versions, like LXX, Syr., Targum, give a rather free rendering which is more in the nature of a homily and leave us in the dark as to whether they had a text different from ours. On the basis of these, however, some very fantastic emendations have been made by modern commentators. One most generally adopted would yield a translation something like the following: "Nations will

And his king shall be higher than Agag,

And his kingdom shall be exalted.

8   God who brought him forth out of Egypt

Is for him like the lofty horns of the wild-ox;

He shall eat up the nations that are his adversaries,

And shall break their bones in pieces,

.   And pierce them through with his arrows.

9   He couched, he lay down as a lion,

---

tremble because of his strength and his arm shall be upon many peoples"
(ירגזו לאמים מחילו וזרעו על עמים רבים). The meaning of the verse as it
stands appears to be that the poet is stressing the prosperity of Israel
by using the figure of the tree which is so favorably planted, the seed
being near many waters, and the abundance of the water is shown by
the drippings from its branches (Rashi, ibn Ezra).

And his king] The king of Israel, whoever he may be. Some think
it refers to Saul, the first king of Israel, who will capture Agag, the king
of the Amalekites (I Sam. 15. 8, 32, 33); this would then be a prophetic
utterance (Rashi, ibn Ezra). The view advanced by ancient as well
as by some modern commentators that Agag was the name by which
all Amalekite kings were designated, as Pharaoh was the name given
to the kings of Egypt (Ramban, comp. Kalisch, 239), is not supported
by any other evidence. The meaning of the phrase is that Israel will
prevail against all his enemies, including the most hated, the Amalekites. LXX has Gog instead of Agag (comp. Ezek. 38.39), while some
modern critics (Cheyne) suggest the reading of Og here.

8.   *God who brought him forth*] Is the one who affords him this
protection and glory (a repetition of 23.22).

And pierce them through with his arrows] The arrows of Israel,
directed against his enemies, shall not fail to accomplish their purpose
(ibn Ezra, Luzzatto). The emendation of חלציו for חציו (and shatter
their loins) gives a better parallel to the preceding clause.

9.   *He couched*] In 23.24 the lion rises to obtain his prey; here the
triumphant lion, loaded with prey, lies down to rest and no one dares
disturb him. After Israel has vanquished all his enemies, he will settle
in peace in his land, Canaan (Targum), and no one will then disturb
him (comp. Gen. 49.9).

And as a lioness; who shall rouse him up?
Blessed be every one that blesseth thee,
And cursed be every one that curseth thee.

And Balak's anger was kindled against Balaam, and he 10
smote his hands together; and Balak said unto Balaam:
'I called thee to curse mine enemies, and, behold, thou
hast altogether blessed them these three times. Therefore 11
now flee thou to thy place; I thought to promote thee unto

Blessed be]   A fitting ending to this glorious prophecy (comp. Gen.
27.29; 12.3).

10–14.   Balak is Provoked and Balaam Explains.

The last utterances of Balaam provoked Balak so much that he
ordered him to go back to his land, having forfeited all claims to consideration and honor that were prepared for him. Balaam in reply
refers again to his earlier statements that he did not come under false
pretenses and that he was quite definite and explicit as to the limitations of his powers.

10.   *And Balak's anger was kindled*]   After the first prophecy,
Balak merely rebuked Balaam mildly (23.11). After the second prophecy, Balak became more impatient and said: "Neither curse them
at all, nor bless them at all" (23.25). Now, after the third prophecy,
Balak's anger is aroused to the highest degree, and he smites his hands,
as an expression of anguish and extreme annoyance. The clapping
of hands is often a sign of contempt and derision (Job 27.23; Lam.
2.15) and may indicate the king's contempt "for a magician who had
so little control over his gods as to be unable to secure a reward from
them".

and Balak said]   A repetition of 23.11.

11.   *flee thou*]   From before mine anger. The king, in his anger,
was ready to do violence to Balaam and was only restrained by Balaam's
high position and dignity. The same expression is also used in a similar
instance when Amaziah, priest of Baal, orders the prophet Amos to
flee from the northern kingdom (Amos 7.12; comp. Ehrlich).

great honour; but, lo, the LORD hath kept thee back from
12 honour.' And Balaam said unto Balak: 'Spoke I not also
to thy messengers that thou didst send unto me, saying:
13 If Balak would give me his house full of silver and gold, I
cannot go beyond the word of the LORD, to do either good
or bad of mine own mind; what the LORD speaketh, that
14 will I speak? And now, behold, I go unto my people; come,
and I will announce to thee what this people shall do to thy
15 people in the end of days.' And he took up his parable,
and said:

> The saying of Balaam the son of Beor,
> And the saying of the man whose eye is opened;
16   The saying of him who heareth the words of God,

the Lord hath kept thee back from honour] The same Lord in whose
name you blessed Israel withheld honor and wealth from thee.

12–13. Repetition of 22.18, with slight variations.

14. *I go unto my people*] Balaam is quite ready to go back, as
Balak suggested, but before he departs he gives Balak information
as to the future destiny of Moab and its relation to Israel.

I will announce to thee] Lit. I will advise thee (Leeser; R. V. "adver-
tise", old English term for "announce"). The Rabbis take this word
in its literal meaning and explain it in the light of 31.16: I will give
you advice how to bring about the destruction of Israel. Incite them
to sin and corruption, hateful to their God, and they will surely be
led to ruin (25.1–9; Sanh. 105b; Rashi, Sforno).

in the end of days] The indeterminate future.

15–25. FURTHER PROPHECIES OF BALAAM.

Balaam's prophecies regarding the conquest by Israel of both Moab
and Edom (15–19), the destruction of Amalek (20), the fate of the
Kenites (21–22), and of other nations (23–24). Balaam then proceeds
back to his home and Balak returns to his place.

And knoweth the knowledge of the Most High,
Who seeth the vision of the Almighty,
Fallen down, yet with opened eyes:
I see him, but not now;
I behold him, but not nigh;
There shall step forth a star out of Jacob,
And a sceptre shall rise out of Israel,
And shall smite through the corners of Moab,

17

15–17. The Doom of Moab.

15–16. Identical with vv. 3–4, except that there the phrase "and knoweth the knowledge of the Most High" is omitted (see note there).

16. *And knoweth the knowledge of the Most High*] Balaam, being God's trusted servant, knows all that God knows. This knowledge is imparted to him in the manner knowledge is imparted to the legitimate prophet and not by magical art (ibn Ezra).

17. *I see him*] Israel, but not as he is at present nor as near, in the place where he is at present encamped. The traditional interpretation applies this to the great king of Israel, king David, who is referred to as "the star" who subjugated Moab (II Sam. 8.2; Rashi, ibn Ezra, comp. Rashbam).

but not now] Referring to "the end of days" (v. 14), or "not as he is now", referring to the future glory of Israel.

There shall step forth a star] A figure for a great king (comp. Isa. 14.12), probably David, the ideal king of Israel. R. Akiba is said to have applied this verse to Bar Kokeba (or Bar Kozeba), who for a brief period succeeded in throwing off the Roman yoke from Israel (132–125 C.E.; Yer. Ta'an. 4.5; Lam. R. 2.5; Bacher, *Agada d. Tannaiten*, I, 284 note). Many commentators have taken this as a messianic prophecy (Targum; comp. Koenig, *Messian. Weissagungen*, pp. 107–118), and pious Christians have endeavored to find here a reference to the person of Jesus (see Kalisch, 248 ff.).

a sceptre] The symbol of royalty (Gen. 49.10).

And shall smite through the corners of Moab] Cut Moab through from one corner to the opposite corner. Leeser has: "the chiefs of Moab" (after Targum, LXX, Mendelssohn), possibly suggesting a

And break down all the sons of Seth.

18   And Edom shall be a possession,

Seir also, even his enemies, shall be a possession;

reading פחתי (governors, cf. Ezra 2.6; 8.4; Neh. 3.11) or interpreting the word פאתי in a figurative sense. Another rendering is: the two sides of the head of Moab, i. e. the two temples, Moab being personified. Israel's arrows will pierce the head of Moab through both his temples, thus completely destroying him (Gray).

And break down all the sons of Seth] Son of Adam (Gen. 4.25), a term intended to include all the nations of the earth (Targum, LXX, Rashi, ibn Ezra et al.). This interpretation is difficult because there is no reason why the nations of the world should be referred to as the sons of Seth rather than as the sons of Adam or Noah. Numerous other renderings have been offered for this word, but none is quite satisfactory. R. V. has "sons of tumult" (implying a slight emendation, שאת for שת; comp. Lam. 3.47). Some read here שאון instead of שת (after Jer. 48.45) and render it the same as R. V. (McNeile; comp. Hastings, *Dictionary of the Bible*, s. v. Sheth, where *Shaon* is taken as a proper name of a Moabite city, after Amos 2.2). It is also possible to assume that *Sheth* was an ancient name for Moab, as Seir was for Edom (comp. Szanto, Kautzsch, Holzinger), if there were any support for the assumption. Sayce (*Hebraica*, IV, 1–6) endeavors to establish that *Sheth* was the name of a Moabite deity, so that "the sons of *Sheth*" would denote the followers of that deity.

18–19. PROPHECY CONCERNING EDOM.

18. *And Edom shall be a possession*] Of Israel. If the preceding prophecy against Moab refers to king David, the prophecy against Edom follows here naturally, since Edom also was subjugated by David (II Sam. 8.14; ibn Ezra). Other commentators regard this verse as the first of a number of brief prophecies against different nations, later added to the "Book" of Balaam (Kalisch, 263 ff.).

Seir also] The ancient name for Edom (Judg. 5.4).

even his enemies] In apposition to Seir, the enemy of Israel or of Israel's king (comp. Ehrlich, who emends שער אויביו, "the gate of his enemies", after Gen. 22.17).

While Israel doeth valiantly.

And out of Jacob shall one have dominion,   19

And shall destroy the remnant from the city.

And he looked on Amalek, and took up his parable, 20
and said:

Amalek was the first of the nations;

But his end shall come to destruction.

doeth valiantly] In contrast with Edom. Targum has "acquireth
wealth".

19. *And out of Jacob shall one have dominion*] Possibly referring
to the king of v. 17, and implying that he will have world-wide dominion and destroy all his enemies.

the remnant from the city] To be taken in a collective sense, all the
cities (cf. Obad. v. 18; Amos 9.12). Leeser has: "whatever escapeth
out of the city," which practically has the same sense. Mendelssohn's
"and an avenger will destroy the remnant" (cf. Isa. 13.17) is far-
fetched. Some take the phrase "from the city" as a parallel to "out
of Jacob" and make it refer to Zion. The rendering would then be:
"Out of Jacob shall one have dominion and out of the city (of Zion)
shall he destroy the remnant" (comp. Kalisch, Holzinger, Gray).
Some refer this back to Moab and take עיר as the capital of Moab
(22.36; Ehrlich).

20. PROPHECY CONCERNING AMALEK.

And he looked on Amalek] Not necessarily in a vision (Rashi, ibn
Ezra), but in reality, seeing the nomadic tribe from the lofty elevation
where he stood, just as he saw the Israelites from there (Ramban).
The Amalekites are here assumed as wandering about on the eastern
side of the Jordan (13.29; 14.43, 45) and might be seen from certain
points of Pisgah.

the first of the nations] Not in point of time as the oldest nation, but
the choicest, the most powerful nation (Ramban; cf. Amos 6.1, where
the same expression is used for Israel). Targum paraphrases: Amalek
was the first among the nations to wage war against Israel (also Rashi,
ibn Ezra, Keil), but this is not warranted by the text.

But his end shall come to destruction] Antithetic to "first nation";

21   And he looked on the Kenite, and took up his parable,
and said:

Though firm be thy dwelling-place,
And though thy nest be set in the rock;
22   Nevertheless Kain shall be wasted;

his end shall be that he will be entirely destroyed. Amalek was attacked
by Saul at the order of Samuel (I Sam. 15, note especially v. 18, "until
they be consumed"), later by David (I Sam. 30.17) and finally destroyed in the time of Hezekiah (I Chron. 4.43). Amalek, like Edom,
was regarded as the arch-enemy of Israel (cf. Deut. 25.19), and by
popular tradition Haman, the Agagite, was assumed to be a descendant of this hateful tribe (Kalisch, 277 ff.).

21–22.   PROPHECY CONCERNING THE KENITES.

21. *And he looked on the Kenite*] The Kenites were a Bedouin
tribe, living among the Amalekites (I Sam. 15.6) and also scattered
among the Israelites (I Sam. 27.10; 30.29). In contrast to the Amalekites they appear to have lived in friendship with Israel, and Saul expressly refers to their kindness, on account of which he spared them
when he attacked Amalek (ib. 15.6). Hobab, the father-in-law of
Moses (cf. 10.29, note), is designated as a member of that tribe (Judg.
4.11), and Jael, a Kenite woman, helped in the defeat of Sisera by Barak
and Deborah (Judg. 4.17; 5.24). In all the biblical records there is no
mention of any hostility against Israel on the part of the Kenites.
This brief prophecy is therefore couched not in the vengeful spirit of
the prophecies against Moab, Edom and Amalek, but rather in a sym-
pathetic form. The prophet contemplates with sympathy the sad end
of a people that has always proved itself loyal and friendly to Israel.

Though firm be thy dwelling-place]   Comp. Obad. v. 3, 4; Jer. 49.16,
where similar expressions are used regarding Edom.

thy nest be set in the rock]   Assuring security against attack. The
figure is taken from the nest of the eagle and forms a perfect parono-
masia on the name Kain (קֵן).

22.   *Nevertheless*]   Used as a strong adversative, a rare use of the
phrase (comp. Job 42.8; BDB, 475a).

Kain shall be wasted]   His strongholds will be removed and he will
be laid open to attack and to injury (cf. Isa. 5.5). Kain is here pre-

How long? Asshur shall carry thee away captive.

And he took up his parable, and said: 23

Alas, who shall live after God hath appointed him?

sumed to be the ancestor of the tribe. The word Kain comes from a root meaning to forge and may mean spear (II Sam. 21.16), hence the Kenites are assumed by some to have been a guild of wandering smiths. This is corroborated by the description given of Tubal-cain as "the forger of every cutting instrument of brass and iron" (Gen. 4.22). They "probably first imparted to the Israelites information about the ore deposits in the 'Arabah" (Glueck, "Explorations in Eastern Palestine", II, p. 49, in *The Annual of the American School of Oriental Research*, vol. XV., New Haven, 1935). Oesterly and Robinson (*Hebrew Religion*, pp. 110 ff.) would make of Jethro a Kenite priest, whose religion was adopted by Moses when he was wandering in the neighborhood of Mt. Sinai, situated in the Kenite district of Midian. Yahweh was the tribal god of the Kenites, whose seat was on Mt. Sinai, and Jethro was his priest.

How long?] Until what time? (BDB, 554a). Leeser, following Mendelssohn, has: "whither". R. V. (also Kalisch), "until Asshur shall carry thee away captive". The meaning is very obscure and none of the renderings gives a satisfactory sense. The traditional interpretation is that the Kenites living among the Israelites will be secure and their fate will be similar to that of Israel. Even though they also will be removed from their secure position, they will suffer captivity at the hands of Asshur, together with the Israelites, but will not be utterly destroyed as will be the Amalekites (Ramban, Rashi, comp. Luzzatto).

23–24. PROPHECY CONCERNING ASSYRIA.

23. *Alas, who shall live after God hath appointed him*] Referring to Assyria, the instrument of God in meting out punishments to nations who have forsaken Him (cf. Isa. 10.5 ff.). At the mention of the name of Asshur, the prophet is reminded of the sufferings that Israel is destined to endure at the hands of Assyria and is therefore prompted to foretell the future destiny of that nation. Others regard אל as an abbreviation of אלה and translate: "Who shall live when He does these things?" (Geiger, *Urschrift*, 367; see Kohut, 79).

24 But ships shall come from the coast of Kittim,
And they shall afflict Asshur, and shall afflict Eber,
And he also shall come to destruction.

25 And Balaam rose up, and went and returned to his place;
and Balak also went his way.

24. *But ships shall come from the coast of Kittim*] Kittim is usually identified with a town, Kitim, in Cyprus (cf. Gen. 10.4, where Kittim is mentioned as a son of Javan, i. e. Greece), although it is sometimes used as a general name for western maritime nations (Jer. 2.10; Ezek. 27.6). The Targum renders it "Romans" (cf. Adler and Ramban).

and shall afflict Eber] A name used to designate the inhabitants of the other side of the Euphrates, or Mesopotamia (Gen. 10.24), perhaps referring here to the Babylonians. Asshur and Eber here are probably meant to include the great powers of the East, who would have to succumb to the advancing powers of the West, the Greeks and the Romans. "It is quite evident that here the term 'from the coast of Kittim' is used not to describe the island of Cyprus, or any other exactly defined territory, but as indicating quite generally some great western people which had made themselves a name, and became a terror among the nations. No doubt, Asshur and Eber stand for the great powers of the East collectively, and the prophecy is a foretelling of the utter overthrow of the sovereignty of the Eastern monarchies by the advancing powers of the great empires of the West. The beginning of the fulfilment was seen in the campaign of Alexander the Great, but it was much more truly and permanently realized in the development and growth of the Romans" (Macpherson, in Hastings, *Dictionary of the Bible*, s. v. Kittim).

And he also] Either refers to Asshur and Eber, regarded as a single idea (Gray), or more probably to the one who brought about their downfall, the people of Kittim or of the West (Ramban).

25. *And Balaam rose up*] Comp. Gen. 18.33; 32.1, 2. Ibn Ezra suggests that Balaam was prostrate on his face while prophesying (v. 4), and after he finished his prophecies, he rose up from the ground.

And Israel abode in Shittim, and the people began to **25**
commit harlotry with the daughters of Moab. And they 2
called the people unto the sacrifices of their gods; and the
people did eat, and bowed down to their gods. And Israel 3
joined himself unto the Baal of Peor; and the anger of the

CHAPTER 25.

1–5. ISRAEL LURED BY THE WOMEN OF MOAB.

While encamped at Shittim, the last station in the march of the
Israelites in the wilderness, they are allured to illicit intercourse with
the women of Moab, and through them are led to worship Baal-peor, the
local Moabite deity. This sinful act is promptly punished by Moses.

1. *in Shittim*] Lit. Acacias, a place in the plains of Moab, which
was taken from the Moabites by the Amorites and from the latter by
the Israelites. It was the last camping place of the Israelites in the
wilderness (33.49), whence Joshua sent out the spies (Josh. 2.1) and
whence the Israelites proceeded to cross the Jordan (Josh. 3.1). It is
also referred to as Abel-shittim (33.49). The site has not been identified. According to Josephus (*Ant.*, iv.8.1), it was situated 60 stadia
from the Jordan, and may be identical with the modern Abila (Gray).

to commit harlotry] According to the rabbinic interpretation, Balaam
gave that advice to Balak to allure the Israelites to sin and thus arouse
the anger of their God against them (note on 24.14). The young women
of Moab and of Midian were then ordered to entice the Israelites to
sin and then to serve their idols (Sanh. 106a; comp. Ramban to 31.16).

2. *And they called*] The women invited the people with whom they
had immoral relations to join them in their religious festivities. The
invitation was accepted by the Israelites and through the participation
in the Moabite festivals they were led to worship the gods of Moab
(cf. Ex. 34.15, 16).

3. *joined himself*] The word used here, צמד, means to attach
oneself, to join, and the noun צֶמֶד means a couple, a pair. It may therefore be rendered, they paired off, an Israelite and a Moabitess, in the
worship of Baal-peor (Ehrlich, cf. ibn Ezra).

the Baal of Peor] The local deity of Mt. Peor (23.28), although the

4 LORD was kindled against Israel. And the LORD said unto
Moses: 'Take all the chiefs of the people, and hang them
up unto the LORD in face of the sun, that the fierce anger
5 of the LORD may turn away from Israel.' And Moses said
unto the judges of Israel: 'Slay ye every one his men that

national god of Moab was Chemosh (21.29). From the many allusions
to Baal-peor in the Bible, it appears that its worship was of a licentious
character (31.16; Deut. 4.3; Josh. 22.17; Hos. 9.10; Ps. 106.28), and
in the opinion of the Rabbis it was of a most degrading kind (Sanh.
106a; Sifre 131; Num. R. 20.23).

4. *Take all the chiefs of the people, and hang them up unto the Lord*]
In propitiation of the sin committed by the people, and thus appease
the anger of the Lord (cf. II Sam. 21.1–5). Leeser translates: "and
(cause them to) hang (the guilty) up before the Lord". This is in harmony with the interpretation given by Targum ("and judge and kill
those who are found guilty of a capital offence"), the rabbinic tradition
(Sifre 131; Sanh. 35a; Num. R. 20.24), Rashi and most of the Jewish
commentators of the middle ages. According to this, v. 5 would be a
further elaboration of the present verse. The verse as it stands, however, by no means contains all this (cf. Adler to Targum), and it plainly
indicates that the punishment was to be inflicted upon the chiefs of
the people. The exact manner of execution intended here by "hang"
(הוקע) is not certain. The term is found only once more in the same
sense, in the case of the execution of the sons of Saul (II Sam. 21.6, 9),
and has been variously rendered as impale, crucify, throw down (BDB).
The Rabbis, in the light of later legislation, said that the punishment
meted out to one who worshiped idols was stoning, followed by hang-
ing the body in public view (Rashi, cf. Sanh. 34b).

in face of the sun] In public view (cf. Deut. 21.25).

5. *every one his men*] Every judge the men under his jurisdiction
(Ex. 18.25), who have been found guilty of the crime of idolatry
(cf. Ex. 32.27, where the Levites act as executioners in the case of the
golden calf). Although not mentioned here, the execution is assumed
to have been carried out (ibn Ezra).

have joined themselves unto the Baal of Peor.' And, 6
behold, one of the children of Israel came and brought
unto his brethren a Midianitish woman in the sight of
Moses, and in the sight of all the congregation of the
children of Israel, while they were weeping at the

6-15. PHINEHAS SLAYS AN OFFENDING ISRAELITE.
THE REWARD FOR HIS ZEAL.

Phinehas, the son of Eleazar the priest, seeing an Israelite, Zimri,
son of Salu, one of the heads of the tribe of Simeon, committing a sin
with a Midianite woman, kills them both in his zeal for God. As a
reward, he is promised that the priesthood will for all time remain in
his family.

6. *one of the children of Israel*] Zimri, the son of Salu, a Simeonite,
as given in v. 14.

brought unto his brethren] Introduced to his family (ibn Ezra). Until
now, the Israelites consorted with the foreign women in their own
homes, but this was a case where the foreign woman was brought to
the Israelitish camp, and with her perhaps the worship of the foreign
god, which defiled the camp. Luzzatto suggests that he showed them
boastfully the prize that he acquired, a daughter of one of the chiefs
of the Midianites.

a Midianitish woman] Whose name is given in v. 14 as Cozbi, the
daughter of Zur.

in the sight of Moses] Without shame, defiantly (cf. Sanh. 82a).

while they were weeping] The reason for their weeping is not given
here, but in v. 8 it appears that a plague had broken out among the
Israelites in consequence of their sin and that it was stayed only after
Phinehas's zealous act was performed. According to some of the old
Jewish commentators, the plague broke out in consequence of their
worship of Baal-peor, which aroused God's anger (v. 3). In order to
appease God's anger (v. 4), the elders were told to execute summary
punishment on the offenders, and they in turn commissioned the judges
to carry out the order (v. 5). The plague would not be stayed until
all the guilty were punished, but their number was very large and the
people wept (in prayer, ibn Ezra) to avert the plague. Through the
act of Phinehas the plague was stayed and the executions also were

7 door of the tent of meeting. And when Phinehas, the son
of Eleazar, the son of Aaron the priest, saw it, he rose up
from the midst of the congregation, and took a spear in
8 his hand. And he went after the man of Israel into the
chamber, and thrust both of them through, the man of Israel,
and the woman through her belly. So the plague was stayed

stopped, but all those who worshiped Baal were finally punished (Deut.
4.3, 4) and could not enter the promised land (see Ramban).

at the door of the tent] Weeping in prayer before God to stop the
plague.

7. Phinehas, the son of Eleazar, whose mother was one of the
daughters of Putiel (Ex. 6.25), plays an important part in Jewish
history and legend. His religious zeal, demonstrated in the present
act, was greatly extolled in later ages and held up as an example of
devotion and loyalty to the God of Israel (Ps. 106.30, 31; Ecclus. 45.23;
I Macc. 2.26). He is mentioned as the one who led the Israelites against
Midian (31.6 ff.), headed a commission to plead with the tribes that
settled on the east side of the Jordan with regard to the altar which
they erected there (Josh. 22.13), and delivered a divine message to
the Israelites at the time of the war with the Benjamites (Judg. 20.28).
At the time of the distribution of the land, he was given a hill in Mt.
Ephraim where his father Eleazar was buried (Josh. 24.33). The Rabbis
have preserved many legends about him (Sifre 131; Sanh. 82a), and
some identified him with the prophet Elijah (see Friedman's Introd.
to *Seder Eliyahu*).

from the midst of the congregation] Who were sitting at the entrance
of the tabernacle weeping, at a loss to know what to do (Sifre 131;
Sanh. 82a).

8. *into the chamber*] The meaning of the word קֻבָּה, found only
here, is uncertain. It may be related to an Arabic word meaning a
vault or a tent, and thus a tent of honor, occupied by a chief or by his
harem. R. V. has "pavilion".

through her belly] Following Targum, Rashi and others. Ibn Ezra
suggests the rendering "in her tent" (comp. Luzzatto).

So the plague was stayed] See note on v. 6.

The Rabbis found difficulty in justifying Phinehas's act, which was
illegal, since Zimri was not tried by a court and found guilty of a capital

from the children of Israel. And those that died by the ₉
plague were twenty and four thousand.

And the LORD spoke unto Moses, saying: 'Phinehas, the ₁₀₋₁₁
son of Eleazar, the son of Aaron the priest, hath turned
My wrath away from the children of Israel, in that he was
very jealous for My sake among them, so that I consumed
not the children of Israel in My jealousy. Wherefore say: ₁₂
Behold, I give unto him My covenant of peace; and it ₁₃
shall be unto him, and to his seed after him, the covenant
of an everlasting priesthood; because he was jealous for

offence. They refer to an emergency law according to which one who
had intercourse with an Aramean (gentile) woman, although not subject
to legal prosecution, might be killed by a zealot who witnessed the
commission of the crime (Sanh. 82a). However, the zeal of Phinehas
in this case was aroused not so much because of the crime of adultery
committed by an Israelite, but because the act of adultery carried with
it idolatry, hence "jealous for My sake" (v. 11), "for his God" (v. 13;
comp. Ehrlich).

11. *he was very jealous for My sake*] Taking God's part. Leeser
has "in My stead", doing what I should have done (see Rashi, ibn
Ezra), so that My anger was appeased.

among them] Causing the name of God to be sanctified among the
people.

12. *Wherefore say*] Proclaim it among the people (Ramban).

My covenant of peace] Carrying with it the assurance of God's
friendship and favor (Mal. 2.4 ff.; Isa. 54.10; Ezek. 34.25; 37.26) and
perhaps thereby making him immune against the possible revenge
that Zimri's relatives may seek to inflict upon him (ibn Ezra).

13. *the covenant of an everlasting priesthood*] If all the descendants
of Aaron were assumed to act as priests, there would be no special gift
in confirming the priesthood to the family of Phinehas. The old Jewish commentators, therefore, make this promise refer to the high-
priesthood (ibn Ezra, Luzzatto). According to the rabbinic tradition,
when Aaron was initiated into the priesthood, only his sons were
initiated with him (Lev. 8–10), but not his grandchildren. Now, the

his God, and made atonement for the children of Israel.'

14 Now the name of the man of Israel that was slain, who was slain with the Midianitish woman, was Zimri, the son of Salu, a prince of a fathers' house among the Simeonites.

15 And the name of the Midianitish woman that was slain was Cozbi, the daughter of Zur; he was head of the people of a fathers' house in Midian.

16-17   And the LORD spoke unto Moses, saying: 'Harass the
18 Midianites, and smite them; for they harass you, by their wiles wherewith they have beguiled you in the matter of

priesthood was confirmed in the family of Phinehas by a special decree (Zeb. 101b; Rashi). Comp. Gray for the modern critical theory and see Curtiss, *The Levitical Priests*, p. 27 ff.

14. *Now the name*] The names and pedigrees of the victims are given in detail in order to enhance the heroism of Phinehas, who was not afraid to attack two such prominent persons (Rashi).

a prince of a fathers' house] See note on 1.2; one of the five families of the tribe of Simeon (26.12, 13; Gen. 46.10; Ex. 6.15; see Rashi).

15. *head of the people*] Tribal division. Zur was one of the five chiefs or kings of Midian (31.8; Josh. 13.21).

16–18. ORDER TO PREPARE FOR ATTACK ON MIDIANITES.

God tells Moses to prepare for an offensive war against the Midianites for plotting the destruction of Israel in connection with the worship of Baal-peor and because of the possibility of an attack in revenge for the death of Cozbi. This is in anticipation of the narrative of the offensive war against the Midianites in 31.1 ff.

17. *Harass*] Show hostility, start war, in contradistinction to Deut. 2.9, "be not at enmity with Moab, neither contend with them in battle" (comp. B. K. 38a).

18. *for they harass you, by their wiles*] To incite you to sin and thereby arouse God's anger against you. The elders of Midian are mentioned as being associated with Balak in his desire to have Israel cursed (22.4, 7), and now in connection with the immoralities practiced at Baal-peor (see Ramban).

Peor, and in the matter of Cozbi, the daughter of the prince of Midian, their sister, who was slain on the day of the plague in the matter of Peor.'

And it came to pass after the plague, that the LORD **26** spoke unto Moses and unto Eleazar the son of Aaron the

and in the matter of Cozbi] An additional reason to anticipate a possible attack by them in revenge for the killing of Cozbi by Phinehas (ibn Ezra). The intention may also be here to connect the incident of Cozbi with the worship of Baal-peor, which was the real offense (note on v. 8).

CHAPTER 26.

25.19–26.51. THE SECOND NUMBERING OF THE PEOPLE.

After the plague—the last and heaviest penalty suffered by the Israelites in the wilderness — Moses and Eleazar, Aaron having died (20.23–29), are ordered to take a census of the people. They were counted before, in the second year of the exodus (1.1 ff.), and now, in the last year of their sojourn in the wilderness, they are counted again, perhaps in order to determine who is entitled to a share in the promised land (v. 53; ibn Ezra), or in anticipation of the war with the Midianites. The Rabbis use here the parable of the shepherd who counts the sheep of his flock after a wolf entered the fold and consumed some of them; so here also after the plague Moses is told to count the Israelites. Another simile used by them is that of the shepherd who undertakes the care of the flocks of his master. He counts the sheep entrusted to him on entering upon his work and he counts them again when the term of his ministry is concluded. Moses, to whose care the Israelites were entrusted, also counted them soon after the exodus and now, when he was about to die and give up the post of leader, he counts them again (Tan. Phinehas, 6).

The words, "And it came to pass after the plague", are designated here, according to the masoretic text, as v. 19 of ch. 25. In other versions, and also in R. V., they begin the first verse of ch. 26. That they were connected with the following chapter is shown by the masoretic mark, known as *Pesik*, placed here.

2 priest, saying: 'Take the sum of all the congregation of
the children of Israel, from twenty years old and upward,
by their fathers' houses, all that are able to go forth to
3 war in Israel.' And Moses and Eleazar the priest spoke
with them in the plains of Moab by the Jordan at Jericho,
4 saying: '[Take the sum of the people,] from twenty years
old and upward, as the LORD commanded Moses and the
children of Israel, that came forth out of the land of Egypt.'
5   Reuben, the first-born of Israel: the sons of Reuben: of
Hanoch, the family of the Hanochites; of Pallu, the family
6 of the Palluites; of Hezron, the family of the Hezronites;
7 of Carmi, the family of the Carmites. These are the families

3.   *with them*]   The heads of the tribes who should proceed with
the taking of the census, as in v. 4 ff. Our rendering assumes a reading
אֹתָם (comp. ibn Ezra), although even such a reading would be unusual,
as the preposition most frequently used in such phrases is אליהם. Some
emend ויפקד (comp. Targum) instead of וידבר and omit the לאמר at
the end of the verse, so that the translation would be as follows: And
Moses and Eleazar the priest numbered them . . . . from twenty years,
etc. LXX omits אתם.

4.   *Take the sum of the people*]   Inclosed in brackets, because not
in the Heb. text, but found in 1.2 (comp. Rashi).

as the Lord commanded]   In 1.3, to number those who were twenty
years old and over. The suggestion that "and the children of Israel"
is to be joined with the following verse (comp. ibn Ezra; LXX adds
here "*you* and the children of Israel who went out of Egypt were Reuben,
etc.") is untenable, since according to v. 64 there were included in this
census also those who were born in the wilderness or who were less than
twenty years old at the time of the exodus. The suggested emendation
of לבני instead of ובני (Paterson, Kahana), "concerning", does not
improve matters.

5.   *the sons of Reuben*]   I. e. the clans of the tribe of Reuben were
four, the names being the same as those given in Gen. 46.9; Ex. 6.14;
I Chron. 5.3.

of the Reubenites; and they that were numbered of them were forty and three thousand and seven hundred and thirty. And the sons of Pallu: Eliab. And the sons of 8-9 Eliab: Nemuel, and Dathan, and Abiram. These are that Dathan and Abiram, the elect of the congregation, who strove against Moses and against Aaron in the company of Korah, when they strove against the LORD; and the 10 earth opened her mouth, and swallowed them up together with Korah, when that company died; what time the fire devoured two hundred and fifty men, and they became a sign. Notwithstanding the sons of Korah died not.   11

8. *And the sons of Palu: Eliab*] Although only one name is mentioned, still the pl. is used, as is also the case elsewhere (v. 36; Gen. 46.23; I Chron. 1.41). The pl. may be understood here in the sense of descendants, the clan of Eliab. Malbim suggests that Palu may have had other sons also, but Eliab's name was singled out because of the Korah incident in which his sons were implicated.

9. *elect of the congregation*] Cf. notes on 1.16 and 16.2.

who strove] Rashi renders "who incited to strife". The word נצה in the Niphal means to strive with one another, when two are engaged in a fight, and in Hiphil it means to begin a quarrel, but also to cause a quarrel (BDB). Targum, "gathered against", has the same meaning (comp. ibn Ezra).

10. *what time the fire devoured*] At the time when the fire devoured. The two outstanding events in connection with the rebellion of Korah are thus referred to here, although the main object is to tell that of the issue of Eliab only one family, that of Nemuel, remained to take a portion in the land.

and they became a sign] A warning to future generations (cf. 17.3, where the fire-pans, made into a covering for the altar, are designated to serve as a sign, although the word used there is אות).

11. *Notwithstanding the sons of Korah died not*] Possibly because they did not take part in the plot, while the descendants of Dathan and of Abiram were destroyed with the others (ibn Ezra, Malbim; comp. Sanh. 110a). A family of Korah is mentioned in v. 58 and a

12 The sons of Simeon after their families: of Nemuel, the family of the Nemuelites; of Jamin, the family of the
13 Jaminites; of Jachin, the family of the Jachinites; of Zerah, the family of the Zerahites; of Shaul, the family of the
14 Shaulites. These are the families of the Simeonites, twenty and two thousand and two hundred.

15 The sons of Gad after their families: of Zephon, the family of the Zephonites; of Haggi, the family of the
16 Haggites; of Shuni, the family of the Shunites; of Ozni, the family of the Oznites; of Eri, the family of the Erites;
17 of Arod, the family of the Arodites; of Areli, the family of
18 the Arelites. These are the families of the sons of Gad according to those that were numbered of them, forty thousand and five hundred.

19 The sons of Judah: Er and Onan; and Er and Onan
20 died in the land of Canaan. And the sons of Judah after their families were: of Shelah, the family of the Shelanites;

---

number of Psalms are ascribed to the Levitic guild known as the sons of Korah. The apparent contradiction between this verse and 16.32 is explained by assuming that the phrase "the men that appertained to Korah" refers to his slaves and not to his children (see note there).

12. *Nemuel*]   In Gen. 46.10 and Ex. 6.15 the name is Jemuel.

Jachin]   In I Chron. 4.24 the name is Jarib.

13. *Zerah*]   In Gen. and Ex. the name here is Zohar. There is also mentioned a sixth clan by the name of Ohad, which is omitted here and in I Chron. 4.24, possibly because it was entirely extinct at that time (Rashi).

15. *Zephon*]   In Gen. 46.16 the name is Ziphion.

16. *Ozni*]   In Gen. 46.16 the name is Ezbon (cf. Rashi).

19. *Er and Onan died in the land of Canaan*]   During the lifetime of their father (Gen. 38.7, 10; 46.12).

of Perez, the family of the Perezites; of Zerah, the family
of the Zerahites. And the sons of Perez were: of Hezron, 21
the family of the Hezronites; of Hamul, the family of the
Hamulites. These are the families of Judah according to 22
those that were numbered of them, threescore and sixteen
thousand and five hundred.

The sons of Issachar after their families: of Tola, the 23
family of the Tolaites; of Puvah, the family of the Punites;
of Jashub, the family of the Jashubites; of Shimron, the 24
family of the Shimronites. These are the families of 25
Issachar according to those that were numbered of them,
threescore and four thousand and three hundred.

The sons of Zebulun after their families: of Sered, the 26
family of the Seredites; of Elon, the family of the Elonites;
of Jahleel, the family of the Jahleelites. These are the 27
families of the Zebulunites according to those that were
numbered of them, threescore thousand and five hundred.

The sons of Joseph after their families: Manasseh and 28
Ephraim. The sons of Manasseh: of Machir, the family 29
of the Machirites—and Machir begot Gilead; of Gilead,
the family of the Gileadites. These are the sons of Gilead: 30
of Iezer, the family of the Iezerites; of Helek, the family
of the Helekites; and of Asriel, the family of the Asrielites; 31

24. *Jashub*] In Gen. 46.13 the name is Iob.

29. *sons of Manasseh*] Only one son is mentioned here, but the
pl. reference is to his descendants (note on v. 8; comp. Hastings, *Dictionary of the Bible*, s. v. Manasseh, for a full discussion of the genealogy
given here).

30. *Iezer*] In Josh. 17.2 the name is Abiezer, the ancestor of
Gideon (Judg. 6.11, 24, 34).

32 and of Shechem, the family of the Shechemites; and of Shemida, the family of the Shemidaites; and of Hepher,
33 the family of the Hepherites. And Zelophehad the son of Hepher had no sons, but daughters; and the names of the daughters of Zelophehad were Mahlah, and Noah, Hoglah,
34 Milcah, and Tirzah. These are the families of Manasseh; and they that were numbered of them were fifty and two thousand and seven hundred.

35 These are the sons of Ephraim after their families: of Shuthelah, the family of the Shuthelahites; of Becher, the family of the Becherites; of Tahan, the family of the
36 Tahanites. And these are the sons of Shuthelah: of Eran,
37 the family of the Eranites. These are the families of the sons of Ephraim according to those that were numbered of them, thirty and two thousand and five hundred. These are the sons of Joseph after their families.

38 The sons of Benjamin after their families: of Bela, the family of the Belaites; of Ashbel, the family of the Ashbel-
39 ites; of Ahiram, the family of the Ahiramites; of Shephu-pham, the family of the Shuphamites; of Hupham, the

---

33. *the names of the daughters of Zelophehad*] Mentioned here in anticipation of the law passed as a result of their claim (27.1 ff.).

35. *Becher*] In I Chron. 7.20 the name is Bered.

38. *Ahiram*] In Gen. 46.21 the name is Ehi (see Rashi) and in I Chron. 8.1 it is Aharah. In Gen. three more names are mentioned: Becher (cf. v. 35), Gera and Rosh which are omitted here. The name Gera is found among the families of Benjamin (Judg. 3.15, Ehud son of Gera; II Sam. 16.5, Shimei son of Gera), and in I Chron. 8.3 ff. several other names not mentioned here are found (see Gray).

39. *Shephupham*] In Gen. 46.21 the name is Muppim.

Hupham] In Gen. the name is Huppim.

family of the Huphamites. And the sons of Bela were 40
Ard and Naaman; [of Ard,] the family of the Ardites; of
Naaman, the family of the Naamites. These are the sons 41
of Benjamin after their families; and they that were
numbered of them were forty and five thousand and six
hundred.

These are the sons of Dan after their families: of Shuham, 42
the family of the Shuhamites. These are the families of
Dan after their families. All the families of the Shuham- 43
ites, according to those that were numbered of them, were
threescore and four thousand and four hundred.

The sons of Asher after their families: of Imnah, the 44
family of the Imnites; of Ishvi, the family of the Ishvites;
of Beriah, the family of the Beriites. Of the sons of Beriah: 45
of Heber, the family of the Heberites; of Malchiel, the
family of the Malchielites. And the name of the daughter 46
of Asher was Serah. These are the families of the sons of 47

40. *sons of Bela*] In Gen. 46.21 Ard (cf. I Chron. 8.3, Addar) and
Naama are counted among the sons of Benjamin (see Rashi to v. 13).

42. *Shuham*] In Gen. 46.23 the name is Hushim.

45. See Hommel, *Ancient Hebrew Tradition as Illustrated by the
Monuments*, 234 ff.

46. *And the name of the daughter of Asher was Serah*] The reason
for including here and in Gen. 46.17; I Chron. 7.30 the name of a
daughter of Asher is not clear. Many legends have grown up around
her name because of the fact that this is the only feminine name included in the genealogical lists. (See *J. E.*, s. v. Serah, Ispahan). Rashi,
influenced by these legends, suggests that the reason for mentioning
her name was because of her remarkable old age. Ramban, quoting
a version of the Targum which reads here, "the name of the daughter
of the wife of Asher", not found in our text of the Targum, suggests
that she was a step-daughter of Asher, whose father died without
male issue, and she was therefore in the same category as the daughters

Asher according to those that were numbered of them, fifty and three thousand and four hundred.

48 The sons of Naphtali after their families: of Jahzeel, the family of the Jahzeelites; of Guni, the family of the
49 Gunites; of Jezer, the family of the Jezerites; of Shillem, the
50 family of the Shillemites. These are the families of Naphtali according to their families; and they that were numbered of them were forty and five thousand and four hundred.

of Zelophehad, having inherited the portion of her father, and it is for this reason that her name is mentioned here, as are also the names of the daughters of Zelophehad (v. 33; comp. Luzzatto).

COMPARATIVE TABLE OF THE CENSUS OF THE SECOND YEAR AND OF THE FORTIETH YEAR.

TRIBES	CENSUS OF 2nd YEAR	CENSUS OF 40th YEAR	INCREASE	DECREASE
1. Reuben	46,500	43,730		2,770
2. Simeon	59,300	22,200*		37,100*
3. Gad	45,650	40,500		5,150
4. Judah	74,600	76,500	1,900	
5. Issachar	54,400	64,300	9,900	
6. Zebulun	57,400	60,500	3,100	
7. Ephraim	40,500	32,500		8,000
8. Manasseh	32,200	52,700	20,500	
9. Benjamin	35,400	45,600	10,200	
10. Dan	62,700	64,400	1,700	
11. Asher	41,500	53,400	11,900	
12. Naphtali	53,400	45,400		8,000
TOTAL	603,550	601,730	59,200	61,020

a total decrease of 1820.

*The great drop in the tribe of Simeon was probably due to the great losses which that tribe suffered in the plague following the Rebellion of Korah (17.14) and that following the incident at Baal-peor (25.9). In the apportionment of the land, Simeon was given territory with Judah (Josh. 19.9), with which tribe it may have become amalgamated later on (cf. Judg. 1.3).

These are they that were numbered of the children of 51
Israel, six hundred thousand and a thousand and seven
hundred and thirty.

And the LORD spoke unto Moses, saying: 'Unto these 52-53
the land shall be divided for an inheritance according to
the number of names. To the more thou shalt give the 54
more inheritance, and to the fewer thou shalt give the less
inheritance; to each one according to those that were
numbered of it shall its inheritance be given. Notwith- 55
standing the land shall be divided by lot; according to

52–56. DIVISION OF THE LAND AMONG THE TRIBES.

Moses is told that the promised land is to be divided among the
clans enumerated above, in accordance with the number of persons
in each clan. The division of the land, however, as to the districts
that should go to each tribe, was determined by lot.

53. *Unto these*]   The tribes and families enumerated above.

according to the number of names]   I. e. the persons in each tribe
who are over the age of twenty.

54. *To the more*]   To the larger tribe.

thou shalt give]   From this it would appear that the land was divided
among the tribes before the conquest of Canaan (as is also implied in
Judg. 1.1–3), but in other places it appears that the division did not
take place until after the conquest (Josh. 13.15–14.5). It is possible
to take the phrase in a more general sense, that Moses shall order the
land to be allotted in that manner (McNeil).

to each one]   Each tribe as well as each division of a tribe (B.B. 122a).

55. *Notwithstanding the land shall be divided by lot*]   Although the
land is to be apportioned to tribes in accordance with their population,
the lot shall decide the tract of land which is to go to each tribe,
without, however, limiting its boundaries (see Ramban).

the names of the tribes of their fathers they shall inherit.
56 According to the lot shall their inheritance be divided
between the more and the fewer.'

57 And these are they that were numbered of the Levites
after their families: of Gershon, the family of the Gershonites; of Kohath, the family of the Kohathites; of Merari,
58 the family of the Merarites. These are the families of
Levi: the family of the Libnites, the family of the Hebron-

according to the names of the tribes of their fathers] Individuals shall
get their share through the tribe to which they belong and within
the limits of the portion given to each tribe. There is a difference of
opinion among the Rabbis as to the manner of the division. One
opinion is that the division was made on the basis of the first census
(יוצאי מצרים), while another opinion is that the division was on the
basis of the second census (באי הארץ), while still another opinion is
that both censuses were taken into consideration. The difference
would be in the case of two brothers included in the first census, one
leaving one son and the other three sons grown to manhood at the
time of the second census. According to the first opinion these four
would obtain two portions, while according to the second opinion four
portions would be assigned to them (B.B. 117a, b).

56. *According to the lot*] The division of the land among the various
households within the tribe shall also be in accordance with the size
of each family, while the lot will decide the site to be apportioned to
each family, as in the case of the division among the tribes.

their inheritance] Following LXX and R. V. The Heb. text has
"his inheritance", or "the inheritance of each" (Mendelssohn, Leeser).

57–62. SEPARATE CENSUS OF THE LEVITES.

The Levites, who were not to share in the division of the land, were
counted separately, as in the first census (1.47 ff.).

57. *after their families*] The three chief clans of the tribe of Levi
(3.17).

58. *These are the families of Levi*] In existence at that time. The
Libnites belonged to the clan of Gershon, while Shimei, another son

ites, the family of the Mahlites, the family of the Mushites, the family of the Korahites. And Kohath begot Amram. And the name of Amram's wife was Jochebed, the daughter 59 of Levi, who was born to Levi in Egypt; and she bore unto Amram Aaron and Moses, and Miriam their sister. And 60 unto Aaron were born Nadab and Abihu, Eleazar and Ithamar. And Nadab and Abihu died, when they offered 61 strange fire before the LORD. And they that were num- 62 bered of them were twenty and three thousand, every male from a month old and upward; for they were not numbered among the children of Israel, because there was no inheritance given them among the children of Israel.

of Gershon (Ex. 6.17), is omitted here. The Hebronites and Korahites belonged to the clan of Kohath. Kohath, according to Ex. 6.18, had four sons: Amram, Izhar, Hebron and Uzziel. Of these the only ones mentioned here are Hebron and Korah, who was a son of Izhar, while Amram is treated separately. Uzziel is entirely omitted and of the sons of Izhar only Korah is mentioned, while his other two sons, Nepheg and Zichri, are omitted here. The Mahlites and Mushites belonged to the clan of Merari (Ex. 6.19). Those omitted here are supposed to have left no issue (ibn Ezra), although descendants of Shimei are referred to in I Chron. 23.9.

And Kohath begot Amram] This is introductory to the following verses, descriptive of the priestly branch of the Levitic tribe.

59. According to this Amram was a nephew of Jochebed and their marriage would be considered incestuous (Lev. 18.12). See peculiar theory advanced by Frazer, *Folklore in the Old Testament*, II, 454.

61. *And Nadab and Abihu died*] Cf. 3.4; Lev. 10.1 ff.

62. *twenty and three thousand*] An increase over the first census (3.39) of one thousand, and an actual increase of 700 (see note to 3.39). This small increase (see ibn Ezra) may be accounted for by the losses that the Levites suffered in consequence of the Rebellion of Korah (Hertz).

63   These are they that were numbered by Moses and
Eleazar the priest, who numbered the children of Israel
64 in the plains of Moab by the Jordan at Jericho. But
among these there was not a man of them that were numbered by Moses and Aaron the priest, who numbered the
65 children of Israel in the wilderness of Sinai. For the LORD
had said of them: 'They shall surely die in the wilderness.'
And there was not left a man of them, save Caleb the son
of Jephunneh, and Joshua the son of Nun.

63-65. SUMMARY.

A concluding paragraph, emphasizing the fact that all those included
in the present census, with the exception of Caleb and Joshua, were
not reckoned among those included in the first census, since those all
died in the wilderness.

64. *But among these*]   The Israelites, but not the Levites (Rambam,
ibn Ezra). According to the Rabbis, the curse pronounced upon the
Israelites in consequence of the incident of the spies, that they should
all die in the wilderness (14.29), did not apply to the tribe of Levi
(B.B. 121a).

CHAPTER 27.

1-11. CASE OF ZELOPHEHAD'S DAUGHTERS
AND LAW OF INHERITANCE.

Zelophehad, the son of Hepher, of the tribe of Manasseh, died in the
wilderness, leaving five daughters, but no sons. According to ancient
practice, landed property was inherited by sons only, and if applied
in this case, the portion of Zelophehad in the promised land would be
entirely eliminated. The daughters of Zelophehad appear before Moses
and ask that they be made the heirs of their father. Moses regards
their claim as just, but has no precedent to guide him. He therefore
presents the case before God with the result that a series of inheritance

Then drew near the daughters of Zelophehad, the son **27**
of Hepher, the son of Gilead, the son of Machir, the son
of Manasseh, of the families of Manasseh the son of Joseph;
and these are the names of his daughters: Mahlah, Noah,
and Hoglah, and Milcah, and Tirzah. And they stood 2
before Moses, and before Eleazar the priest, and before
the princes and all the congregation, at the door of the
tent of meeting, saying: 'Our father died in the wilderness, 3
and he was not among the company of them that gathered
themselves together against the LORD in the company of
Korah, but he died in his own sin; and he had no sons.

laws are promulgated, in which the right of daughters in the inheritance of their father's estate, where there are no sons, is established.
A man's natural heirs are his sons, but if he has no sons his daughters
become his heirs. If he has neither sons nor daughters, his brothers
inherit him, and in the absence of brothers, his father's brothers
become his heirs. If the father also had no brothers, the inheritance
passes to the next of kin. Ch. 36 further qualifies the law by which
daughters are given the right of inheritance, by making it obligatory
upon them to marry within their own tribes, so that the land should
not be removed from one tribe to another, a principle which is the
basis of several other regulations in the Bible (comp. Josh. 17.3–6,
where it is recorded how this new law was carried out in this particular
case).

1. *the daughters of Zelophehad*]   Comp. 26.33.

of the families]   Of one of the families of Manasseh (cf. Sifre 133).

2. *at the door of the tent of meeting*]   Where cases of law were heard
and adjudicated (Sifre 133).

3. *and he was not among the company*]   They apparently thought
that those who associated themselves with Korah in his rebellion
forfeited their inheritance (ibn Ezra, Ramban). The sin of Korah
being in the nature of treason was looked upon as most heinous and
thus excluded those who were guilty of it from the right of obtaining
a share in the promised land.

he died in his own sin]   The sin which was common to all Israel,

4 Why should the name of our father be done away from
among his family, because he had no son? Give unto us
5 a possession among the brethren of our father.' And
6 Moses brought their cause before the LORD. And the
7 LORD spoke unto Moses, saying: 'The daughters of Zelophehad speak right: thou shalt surely give them a possession of an inheritance among their father's brethren; and

for which they were condemned to die in the wilderness (Luzzatto).
Some take this phrase together with the following: He died without
sons because of his sins (Judah Halevi, quoted with approval by ibn
Ezra and Ramban; comp. Ehrlich, who gives the same rendering).
Herxheimer says: He died as a result of the sin (natural sin) of Adam,
which brought death into the world. Some of the Rabbis identify
Zelophehad with the man who was found gathering wood on the Sabbath, and for this he was punished with death (15.22 ff.), while others
are of the opinion that he was one of those who attempted to force
a passage to the mountains of the Amorites (14.44, 45; Shab. 96b, 97a;
Sifre Zuta ad loc.).

4. *because he had no son*] Implying that they would have had no
claim if there had been a son (cf. Job 42.15, where daughters are given
inheritance even when there were sons). Their plea is apparently not
so much for themselves as for the perpetuation of the name of their
father. In the case of the Levirate marriage (Deut. 25.6; comp. B.B.
119b), it is provided that when there is no son, a brother of the deceased
should marry his widow, so that "his name be not blotted out of Israel."
The daughters of Zelophehad demand that this principle might be
preserved here by allowing them to become the heirs of their father.

5. *brought their cause before the Lord*] A similar procedure is recorded in the case of the men who were ritually unclean at the time when the
paschal sacrifice was to be offered (9.8; cf. 15.34). The Rabbis say that
Moses was forced to acknowledge his ignorance in public as a punishment for his apparent arrogance when he said, upon the advice of
Jethro: "and the cause that is too hard for you, ye shall bring unto
me" (Deut. 1.17; Ex. 18.22; Sanh. 8b; Num. R. 21.12, 13).

thou shalt cause the inheritance of their father to pass
unto them. And thou shalt speak unto the children of 8
Israel, saying: If a man die, and have no son, then ye shall
cause his inheritance to pass unto his daughter. And if 9
he have no daughter, then ye shall give his inheritance
unto his brethren. And if he have no brethren, then ye 10
shall give his inheritance unto his father's brethren. And 11
if his father have no brethren, then ye shall give his inheritance unto his kinsman that is next to him of his family,
and he shall possess it. And it shall be unto the children
of Israel a statute of judgment, as the LORD commanded
Moses.'

7. *to pass unto them*] The expression "to cause an inheritance to
pass" (העבר נחלה) is used chiefly in connection with the unusual trans-
fer of property (v. 8), while ordinarily the word נתן, "to give", is used
(vv. 9, 10, 11; Rashi). The daughters of Zelophehad are later (ch. 36)
enjoined to marry only within their tribe so that their inheritance
might remain in the possession of the tribe.

8. *And thou shalt speak*] After the individual case has been dis-
posed of, a general law, based upon this precedent, is promulgated.

9. *unto his brethren*] According to the rabbinic elaboration of this
law, the father comes before any of his descendants, although not
mentioned here at all (B.B. 115a). The hereditary succession according to the Rabbis is in the following order: 1) sons and their descendants; 2) daughters and their descendants; 3) the father; 4) brothers
and their descendants; 5) sisters and their descendants; 6) the
father's father; 7) the father's brothers and their descendants; 8) the
father's sisters and their descendants; 9) the father's father's father,
and so on (Maim. *Yad, Nahalot,* 1.1–3; comp. Ramban; Hirsch).

11. *unto his kinsman*] Blood-relative on the father's side (Sifre
134; B.B. 109b). The Rabbis make this term apply to the husband
who is the legal heir of his wife (B.B. 111b).

12 And the LORD said unto Moses: 'Get thee up into this
mountain of Abarim, and behold the land which I have
13 given unto the children of Israel. And when thou hast
seen it, thou also shalt be gathered unto thy people, as
14 Aaron thy brother was gathered; because ye rebelled
against My commandment in the wilderness of Zin, in
the strife of the congregation, to sanctify Me at the waters
before their eyes.'—These are the waters of Meribath-
15 kadesh in the wilderness of Zin.—And Moses spoke unto
16 the LORD, saying: 'Let the LORD, the God of the spirits

12–23. MOSES PREPARED FOR HIS DEATH.
JOSHUA APPOINTED HIS SUCCESSOR.

Moses is told to go up on the mountain and view from there the
land of Canaan, since he will not be permitted to enter the promised
land. Moses pleads that a worthy successor to him be appointed, and
at the command of God Joshua is introduced to Eleazar and to the
leaders of the community as their future leader.

12. *this mountain of Abarim*]   Abarim is a mountainous district,
N. W. of Moab and just N. E. of the Dead Sea, opposite Jericho
(21.11). Pisgah and Nebo are two of the ridges of that mountain.
With few slight variations, vv. 12–14 are repeated in Deut. 32.48–52,
where (34.1 ff.) the execution of this command, omitted here, is also
recorded (cf. Ramban).

13. *And when thou hast seen it*]   A privilege extended to Moses to
view the land from a distance (Sifre 136; Luzzatto).

as Aaron thy brother]   In Mt. Hor (20.23–29; Deut. 32.50).

14. *ye rebelled against My commandment . . . . to sanctify Me*]   God's
commandment aimed at the sanctification of His name and by trans-
gressing it they caused a profanation of His name, which is regarded
as rebellion (see ibn Ezra; comp. note on 20.12).

These are]   This addition is not found in Deut. 32.51.

16. *the God of the spirits of all flesh*]   See note on 16.22. The Rabbis
interpret this phrase: God, who knows the inclinations of each person,
how varied their natures and characters are and how difficult it is to

of all flesh, set a man over the congregation, who may go 17
out before them, and who may come in before them, and
who may lead them out, and who may bring them in;
that the congregation of the LORD be not as sheep which
have no shepherd.' And the LORD said unto Moses: 'Take 18
thee Joshua the son of Nun, a man in whom is spirit, and
lay thy hand upon him; and set him before Eleazar the 19
priest, and before all the congregation; and give him a
charge in their sight. And thou shalt put of thy honour 20

manage them, should appoint a competent leader who will have the
patience and the insight to guide them properly (see Rashi, *Biur*).
Moses is resigned to his fate, but is eager to see the future of his people
secured by having a proper leader appointed to take his place (Sifre
138).

17. *who may go out....*] These are figures taken from military
(I Sam. 18.13; Rashi, ibn Ezra, Luzzatto) or shepherd life (Herxheimer),
meaning one who will be familiar with all the needs of the people and
endeavor to supply them.

as sheep which have no shepherd] Comp. I Kings 22.17.

18. *in whom is spirit*] The spirit of God (Gen. 41.38), or the spirit
of prophecy (Targum), or the spirit of wisdom (Deut. 34.9), able to
direct the affairs of the nation.

and lay thy hand upon him] As a symbol of transmission of office
and consecration. The custom of laying of hands on the head of a
person or of a sacrificial animal is frequently referred to in the Bible
(Gen. 48.14; Lev. 4.24; Num. 8.10; comp. Lev. 24.14) and has also
various significances. In most cases, the rite indicates a conferring
of a blessing or initiation into office. In later times, *Semikah* became
the name for the ordination of Rabbis and judges, although the practice of laying on of hands, implied in the term, was not always followed
(Ket. 112a; see *J. E.*, s. v. Semikah, Ordination).

19. *give him a charge*] Give him the commission in the presence of
the people. Literally the word means "command him", i. e. give him
explicit instructions (cf. Deut. 3.28; I Sam. 13.14; II Sam. 7.11).

20. *of thy honour*] A. V. "dignity"; Leeser, "greatness", but

upon him, that all the congregation of the children of
21 Israel may hearken. And he shall stand before Eleazar
the priest, who shall inquire for him by the judgment of
the Urim before the LORD; at his word shall they go out,
and at his word they shall come in, both he, and all the
children of Israel with him, even all the congregation.'
22 And Moses did as the LORD commanded him; and he took
Joshua, and set him before Eleazar the priest, and before
23 all the congregation. And he laid his hands upon him,
and gave him a charge, as the LORD spoke by the hand of
Moses.

"majesty" would be the more accurate rendering. Moses is to transmit some of his majesty and glory to Joshua (comp. 11.17; Sifre 140),
so that the people should pay homage and respect to him.

21. *who shall inquire for him*] Eleazar will obtain revelations from
the Urim at the behest of Joshua (cf. I Sam. 22.10). Moses, to whom
God spoke face to face (12.8), had no need to consult the Urim, but
Joshua will have no direct communications from God, but will receive
his instructions from the High Priest, who in turn will receive them
from the Urim as occasion will demand it (cf. Josh. 20.1, the only
instance when God is represented as speaking directly to Joshua).
The Urim (usually found joined with Thummim, Deut. 33.8; Ezra
2.63) were apparently objects deposited in a bag or pouch (*Hoshen*),
which was worn by the High Priest on his breast (Ex. 28.30; Lev. 8.8).
Opinions differ as to the nature of these objects and the manner in
which they were used. It seems that they were used as lots for the
purpose of divination or for the decision of difficult cases (see Kennedy
in Hastings, *Dictionary of the Bible*, s. v.).

at his word] At the word of Eleazar interpreting the sign of the
Urim (Rashi, ibn Ezra).

even all the congregation] The leaders and elders of the people
(Yoma 73b).

22. The Samaritan version adds at the end of this verse: And he
said unto him, Thine eyes have seen, etc., as in Deut. 3.21 ff.

And the LORD spoke unto Moses, saying: Command ₂ **28** the children of Israel, and say unto them:

CHAPTER **28.**

28.1–30.1.   DAILY, SABBATH AND FESTIVAL PUBLIC SACRIFICES.

This section deals with the quality and kinds of the public sacrifices to be offered every day, Sabbaths, New Moons and festivals. Similar lists, but not quite as complete and also with some variations, are found in Lev. 23 and in Ezek. 45.18–46.15. The connection of this with the preceding section is not apparent and the Rabbis indulged in some homiletic speculations to account for the juxtaposition (Sifre 134). Some of the old Jewish commentators find the connection in the fact that after the appointment of Joshua, Moses was certain that he would not be permitted to enter Canaan and therefore established the form of the official and communal sacrifices, which should constitute the main form of worship in the sanctuary (ibn Ezra, Ramban). Joshua would attend to the military and civic affairs of the nation, while the religious worship to be carried out by the priests was to be regulated by the laws which are laid down here (cf. Malbim).

The offerings here prescribed consist of lambs, rams, bullocks and goats, the first three to be used as burnt-offerings while the goats were to be used as sin-offerings. All of these must be males and all have to be accompanied by the proper quantity of flour and the libations of wine and of oil, as prescribed in 15.1–16. It is to be noted that the offerings on Sabbaths and festivals are in addition to the daily offerings and the offerings on the New Year are in addition to the daily and the New Moon offerings. Thus, should the New Year happen to fall on a Sabbath, there would be offered: 1) the regular daily offering; 2) the regular Sabbath offering; 3) the regular New Moon offering; and 4) the special offerings for the New Year. The sacred number seven is very prominent in the number of animals to be offered. The following table, given by Gray (p. 406), will be helpful to a clearer understanding of the system followed in this section:

OCCASION	LAMBS	RAMS	BULLOCKS	GOATS
Each day	2	—	—	—
Each Sabbath	2	—	—	—
First of each month	7	1	2	1

My food which is presented unto Me for offerings made
by fire, of a sweet savour unto Me, shall ye observe to offer
3 unto Me in its due season. And thou shalt say unto them:

Occasion	Lambs	Rams	Bullocks	Goats
Each day of Passover	7	1	2	1
Feast of Weeks	7	1	2	1
New Year	7	1	1	1
Atonement Day	7	1	1	1
1st of Tabernacles	14	2	13	1
2nd of Tabernacles	14	2	12	1
3d of Tabernacles	14	2	11	1
4th of Tabernacles	14	2	10	1
5th of Tabernacles	14	2	9	1
6th of Tabernacles	14	2	8	1
7th of Tabernacles	14	2	7	1
8th of Tabernacles *Shemini 'Azeret*	7	1	1	1

2. *My food which is presented unto Me for offerings made by fire*]
Leeser has: "My offering, My bread for My sacrifice consumed by
fire" (cf. R. V.), i. e. My offering, namely My bread (Mendelssohn),
or My offering which is consumed by fire as if it were food (Herxheimer).
The expression "My food" as applied to sacrifices (Lev. 3.11, 16;
21.6) is a survival of an ancient notion among various peoples that
the deity actually consumed the offerings (cf. Judg. 9.13). Here it is
used as a technical expression, the origin of which has long been for-
gotten. Here it is "made by fire", i. e. the manner of offering is to
consign the sacrifice to the flames, by which a "sweet savour" is emit-
ted, which is symbolically regarded as divine food (comp. Targum,
"to be acceptable with favor").

in its due season] Referring to all the sacrifices subsequently mentioned, in all of which the element of time was regarded most essential
(ibn Ezra; Sifre 142; Sifre Zuta ad loc.; Pes. 66a).

3–8. Daily Public Sacrifice.

There were two public offerings every day, one in the morning and
one at dusk, both of the same quantity and kind (Ex. 29.38–42). A
whole treatise of the Mishna (Tamid) is devoted to the discussion of

This is the offering made by fire which ye shall bring unto the LORD: he-lambs of the first year without blemish, two day by day, for a continual burnt-offering. The one 4 lamb shalt thou offer in the morning, and the other lamb shalt thou offer at dusk; and the tenth part of an ephah 5 of fine flour for a meal-offering, mingled with the fourth part of a hin of beaten oil. It is a continual burnt-offering, 6 which was offered in mount Sinai, for a sweet savour, an offering made by fire unto the LORD. And the drink- 7 offering thereof shall be the fourth part of a hin for the

the details of these offerings. The cessation of the daily offerings is mentioned as one of the calamities that occurred on the seventeenth day of Tammuz (Meg. Ta'an. 4.6; comp. Dan. 8.11–13; 11.31; 12.11).

3. *which ye shall bring*] Out of the communal treasury (cf. Neh. 10.33–34; Sifre Zuta; Jos. *Ant.*, iii.10.1).

for a continual burnt-offering] The expression תמיד is probably used here in a technical sense, an abbreviated form of קרבן תמיד, the name of the daily sacrifice. The Rabbis interpret the expression ליום (towards the day, the position of the sun), as indicating that the morning sacrifice is to be slaughtered in the N. W. corner and the evening sacrifice in the N. E. corner of the altar (Tam. 4.1; Yoma 62a; comp. Sifre 142, where the opposite is given, and see Horovitz's note there and to Sifre Zuta).

4. *at dusk*] See note on 9.3.

5. *Ephah*] See note on 15.4.

beaten] Oil made by beating or pounding the olives in a mortar. This kind of oil was regarded especially fine and costly (Ex. 27.20; Lev. 24.2).

6. *which was offered in mount Sinai*] R. V. has "ordained", Leeser has "prepared", referring back to the initiation of the priests (Ex. 29.38–42). According to rabbinic tradition, no sacrifices were offered by the Israelites in the wilderness after they left mount Sinai (ibn Ezra; Sifre 143; Hag. 6a).

one lamb; in the holy place shalt thou pour out a drink-
8 offering of strong drink unto the LORD. And the other
lamb shalt thou present at dusk; as the meal-offering of
the morning, and as the drink-offering thereof, thou shalt
present it, an offering made by fire, of a sweet savour
unto the LORD.

9 And on the sabbath day two he-lambs of the first year
without blemish, and two tenth parts of an ephah of fine
flour for a meal-offering, mingled with oil, and the drink-
10 offering thereof. This is the burnt-offering of every sabbath,
beside the continual burnt-offering, and the drink-offering
thereof.

7. *in the holy place*] On the altar (see note on 15.5). Targ. Jon.
has "in a holy vessel".

strong drink] Undiluted wine (see note on 6.3; comp. Sifre 143;
Rashi, Ramban).

9–10. SABBATH PUBLIC SACRIFICE.

The special offering brought on the Sabbath, in addition to the
daily offering, was called *Musaf* (additional) and was offered some
time between the morning and afternoon daily offerings (Sifre 144;
Yoma 33a). It consisted of two lambs, the same quantity as the daily
offering, except that here the two lambs were offered at the same
time, while in the daily offering one was brought in the morning and
the other at dusk. In the Synagogue, a special service has been added
on Sabbaths, New Moons and festivals, known as Musaf, commemo-
rating this additional sacrifice.

10. *of every sabbath*] Leeser is more literal: "the Sabbath offering
of every Sabbath". It is suggested that the first שבת here is to be
rendered not Sabbath, but week, hence the translation would be "the
weekly offering on its Sabbath", and similarly in v. 14, "the monthly
offering on its New Moon" (Gray, quoting Marti to Isa. 66.23). The
Rabbis deduce from this phrase that if for any reason the Sabbath
offering was not brought, it cannot be complemented on another Sabbath (Sifre 144).

And in your new moons ye shall present a burnt-offering 11
unto the Lord: two young bullocks, and one ram, seven
he-lambs of the first year without blemish; and three 12
tenth parts of an ephah of fine flour for a meal-offering,
mingled with oil, for each bullock; and two tenth parts of
fine flour for a meal-offering, mingled with oil, for the one
ram; and a several tenth part of fine flour mingled with 13
oil for a meal-offering unto every lamb; for a burnt-offering
of a sweet savour, an offering made by fire unto the Lord.
And their drink-offerings shall be half a hin of wine for 14
a bullock, and the third part of a hin for the ram, and the
fourth part of a hin for a lamb. This is the burnt-offering
of every new moon throughout the months of the year.
And one he-goat for a sin-offering unto the Lord; it shall 15

11–15. NEW MOON PUBLIC SACRIFICE.

The celebration of the New Moon as a festival is not mentioned
anywhere in the Pentateuch, although from references found in other
books of the Bible it appears that it was celebrated as a festival, when
people even abstained from labor (I Sam. 20.4 ff.; II Kings 4.23; Isa.
1.13; Hos. 2.13; Amos 8.5). It was probably observed as a secular
holiday from most ancient times (Sforno, comp. Luzzatto). The sacrifices required here to be brought on the New Moon equal in number
those of some of the more important festivals (cf. Ezek. 46.6, 7) and
from the references given above it appears that it was celebrated as
a regular holiday (see also 10.10).

15.   *a sin-offering unto the Lord*]   The sin-offering for the New Moon
and for the festivals is explained by the Rabbis to serve as an atonement
for any possible defilement of the sanctuary, or in relation to the sacrifices (Shab. 1.4). The expression "unto the Lord" is explained variously by the Rabbis (ib. 9a). The talmudic legend has it that this was
really an atonement for God for making the moon smaller than the
sun, both of them having been originally made of the same size (Gen.
1.16; Hul. 60b).

be offered beside the continual burnt-offering, and the drink-offering thereof.

16 And in the first month, on the fourteenth day of the
17 month, is the LORD'S passover. And on the fifteenth day of this month shall be a feast; seven days shall unleavened
18 bread be eaten. In the first day shall be a holy convoca-
19 tion; ye shall do no manner of servile work; but ye shall present an offering made by fire, a burnt-offering unto the LORD: two young bullocks, and one ram, and seven he-lambs of the first year; they shall be unto you without
20 blemish; and their meal-offering, fine flour mingled with oil; three tenth parts shall ye offer for a bullock, and two
21 tenth parts for the ram; a several tenth part shalt thou
22 offer for every lamb of the seven lambs; and one he-goat
23 for a sin-offering, to make atonement for you. Ye shall offer these beside the burnt-offering of the morning, which

16–25. PASSOVER PUBLIC SACRIFICES.

The offerings to be brought on the seven days of the Passover festival are of the same kind and quantity as on the New Moon. In Lev. 23.5–8, the fact that sacrifices are to be offered on these days is mentioned, but the specific offerings are not indicated, while in Ezek. 45.23 a more elaborate sacrifice is prescribed for these days.

16. *on the fourteenth day of the month*] At sunset (Lev. 23.5), when the paschal lamb is offered and is eaten later during the evening of the fifteenth (ibn Ezra).

the Lord's passover] Leeser has: "the passover-lamb (must be offered) unto the Lord".

18. *a holy convocation*] A gathering of the people for religious purposes in honor of the festival.

servile work] Laborious work (BDB, 715a), any business or occupation that requires special exertion. However, food needed for the festival may be prepared, even though it entail labor.

is for a continual burnt-offering. After this manner ye 24
shall offer daily, for seven days, the food of the offering
made by fire, of a sweet savour unto the LORD; it shall be
offered beside the continual burnt-offering, and the drink-
offering thereof. And on the seventh day ye shall have a 25
holy convocation; ye shall do no manner of servile work.

Also in the day of the first-fruits, when ye bring a new 26
meal-offering unto the LORD in your feast of weeks, ye
shall have a holy convocation: ye shall do no manner of
servile work; but ye shall present a burnt-offering for a 27

24. *After this manner*] The same number of sacrifices and the
same measure of meal-offerings and libations are to be offered on each
of the seven days, in contradistinction to the feast of Tabernacles
when the number of bullocks varied each day (Sifre 147).

26–31. FEAST OF WEEKS PUBLIC SACRIFICES.

On the Feast of Weeks the offerings are the same as on Passover.
In Lev. 23.18–21, it is prescribed that the sacrifices on this festival
should be offered in connection with an offering of two loaves of bread
and that they should consist of seven lambs, one bullock, two rams
and one goat for a sin-offering and two other lambs for a peace-offering.
It is the opinion of the Rabbis that the offerings enumerated here
were *in addition* to those mentioned in Lev. (Sifre 149; Men. 4.2–3;
comp. Hoffmann, *Leviticus*, II, 220–223). In Ezek. this festival is
entirely omitted.

26. *Also in the day of the first-fruits*] Pentecost, the feast on which
the ripening of the wheat is celebrated (Ex. 34.22), and when the
first-fruits were brought to the Temple (Lev. 23.17, 20).

a new meal-offering] A meal-offering prepared from the new wheat
as explained in Lev. 23.16–17.

in your feast of weeks] The usual name for Pentecost (Ex. 34.22;
Deut. 16.10, 16; II Chron. 8.13), the word חג being omitted here.
Leeser has: "after your weeks are out" (comp. Targ. Jon. and Vulg.),
referring to the counting of seven weeks from the celebration of the
ripening of the barley on the second day of Passover (Deut. 16.9).

sweet savour unto the LORD: two young bullocks, one
28 ram, seven he-lambs of the first year; and their meal-
offering, fine flour mingled with oil, three tenth parts for
29 each bullock, two tenth parts for the one ram, a several
30 tenth part for every lamb of the seven lambs; one he-goat,
31 to make atonement for you. Beside the continual burnt-
offering, and the meal-offering thereof, ye shall offer
them—they shall be unto you without blemish—and
their drink-offerings.

29   And in the seventh month, on the first day of the month,
ye shall have a holy convocation: ye shall do no manner
of servile work; it is a day of blowing the horn unto you.
2 And ye shall prepare a burnt-offering for a sweet savour
unto the LORD: one young bullock, one ram, seven he-
3 lambs of the first year without blemish; and their meal-
offering, fine flour mingled with oil, three tenth parts for

31. *without blemish*] Referring back to v. 27, where the phrase
belongs (cf. v. 19). The Rabbis make this phrase apply also to the
libations (Sifre 149; Men. 8.7; 87a).

CHAPTER 29.

1–6. NEW YEAR PUBLIC SACRIFICES.

The special offering to be brought on the first day of the seventh
month, the day of the blowing of the trumpet, is practically the same
as that offered on the festivals mentioned before, except that here one
bullock is offered instead ot two.

1. *a day of blowing the horn*] The horns were blown on all
festivals and New Moons, when the sacrifices were offered (10.10),
but on the first day of the seventh month (New Year) a different note
(תרועה) was sounded (cf. Lev. 23.24, "a memorial proclaimed with
the blast of horns").

the bullock, two tenth parts for the ram, and one tenth ₄
part for every lamb of the seven lambs; and one he-goat ₅
for a sin-offering, to make atonement for you; beside the ₆
burnt-offering of the new moon, and the meal-offering
thereof, and the continual burnt-offering and the meal-
offering thereof, and their drink-offerings, according unto
their ordinance, for a sweet savour, an offering made by
fire unto the LORD.

And on the tenth day of this seventh month ye shall ₇
have a holy convocation; and ye shall afflict your souls;
ye shall do no manner of work; but ye shall present a ₈
burnt-offering unto the LORD for a sweet savour: one
young bullock, one ram, seven he-lambs of the first year;
they shall be unto you without blemish; and their meal- ₉
offering, fine flour mingled with oil, three tenth parts for
the bullock, two tenth parts for the one ram, a several ₁₀
tenth part for every lamb of the seven lambs; one he-goat ₁₁
for a sin-offering; beside the sin-offering of atonement,

7–11. DAY OF ATONEMENT PUBLIC SACRIFICES.

On the tenth day of the seventh month, the Day of Atonement, the
special offering is the same as on the New Year. This is in addition
to the other sacrifices brought on the Day of Atonement as prescribed
in Lev. 16.

7. *ye shall afflict your souls*] By abstaining from food and drink
(cf. Isa. 58.3, 5; Ps. 35.13).

no manner of work] Not only laborious work, forbidden on other
holidays (28.18; 29.1, 12), but also all kinds of labor, just as on the
Sabbath (Lev. 23.3).

11. *the sin-offering of atonement*] Referring to the description
given in Lev. 16.

and the continual burnt-offering, and the meal-offering thereof, and their drink-offerings.

12   And on the fifteenth day of the seventh month ye shall have a holy convocation: ye shall do no manner of servile work, and ye shall keep a feast unto the LORD seven days; 13 and ye shall present a burnt-offering, an offering made by fire, of a sweet savour unto the LORD: thirteen young bullocks, two rams, fourteen he-lambs of the first year; 14 they shall be without blemish; and their meal-offering, fine flour mingled with oil, three tenth parts for every bullock of the thirteen bullocks, two tenth parts for each 15 ram of the two rams, and a several tenth part for every 16 lamb of the fourteen lambs; and one he-goat for a sin-offering; beside the continual burnt-offering, the meal-offering thereof, and the drink-offering thereof.

12–34. TABERNACLES PUBLIC SACRIFICES.

The special offerings to be brought on the seven days of the Feast of Tabernacles are by far more numerous than those offered on any other festival. The peculiar feature here is that the number of bullocks to be offered is diminished every day, beginning with 13 on the first day and ending wlth 7 on the seventh. The number of lambs and rams is double that brought on any other festival. Ezekiel (45.25) prescribes the same quantity for Tabernacles as for Passover. The total number of offerings brought on this festival, as given here, is: 70 bullocks, 98 lambs, 14 rams and 7 goats. According to the Rabbis, the seventy bullocks were intended to serve as an atonement for the seventy nations of the world (Suk. 55b).

12. *ye shall keep a feast*] Usually called the Feast of Tabernacles (Lev. 23.24) or the Feast of Ingathering (Ex. 23.16), but also only Feast (*Hag*), as here (also I Kings. 8.12, comp. ib. 12.32), the chief pilgrim feast, characterized by rejoicing and merry-making.

And on the second day ye shall present twelve young 17
bullocks, two rams, fourteen he-lambs of the first year
without blemish; and their meal-offering and their drink- 18
offerings for the bullocks, for the rams, and for the lambs,
according to their number, after the ordinance; and one 19
he-goat for a sin-offering; beside the continual burnt-
offering, and the meal-offering thereof, and their drink-
offerings.

And on the third day eleven bullocks, two rams, fourteen 20
he-lambs of the first year without blemish; and their 21
meal-offering and their drink-offerings for the bullocks,
for the rams, and for the lambs, according to their number,
after the ordinance; and one he-goat for a sin-offering; 22
beside the continual burnt-offering, and the meal-offering
thereof, and the drink-offering thereof.

And on the fourth day ten bullocks, two rams, fourteen 23
he-lambs of the first year without blemish; their meal- 24
offering and their drink-offerings for the bullocks, for the
rams, and for the lambs, according to their number, after
the ordinance; and one he-goat for a sin-offering; beside 25
the continual burnt-offering, the meal-offering thereof,
and the drink-offering thereof.

And on the fifth day nine bullocks, two rams, fourteen 26
he-lambs of the first year without blemish; and their meal- 27
offering and their drink-offerings for the bullocks, for the
rams, and for the lambs, according to their number, after
the ordinance; and one he-goat for a sin-offering; beside 28
the continual burnt-offering, and the meal-offering thereof,
and the drink-offering thereof.

29 And on the sixth day eight bullocks, two rams, fourteen
30 he-lambs of the first year without blemish; and their
meal-offering and their drink-offerings for the bullocks,
for the rams, and for the lambs, according to their number,
31 after the ordinance; and one he-goat for a sin-offering;
beside the continual burnt-offering, the meal-offering
thereof, and the drink-offerings thereof.

32 And on the seventh day seven bullocks, two rams,
33 fourteen he-lambs of the first year without blemish; and
their meal-offering and their drink-offerings for the bullocks, for the rams and for the lambs, according to their
34 number, after the ordinance; and one he-goat for a sin-
offering; beside the continual burnt-offering, the meal-
offering thereof, and the drink-offering thereof.

35 On the eighth day ye shall have a solemn assembly:
36 ye shall do no manner of servile work; but ye shall present
a burnt-offering, an offering made by fire, of a sweet savour
unto the LORD: one bullock, one ram, seven he-lambs of
37 the first year without blemish; their meal-offering and
their drink-offerings for the bullock, for the ram, and for

29.35–30.1. EIGHTH DAY OF THE FEAST PUBLIC SACRIFICES.

The special sacrifices prescribed for the eighth day of the festival,
Shemini 'Azeret, are of the same quantity as those for the New Year and
the Day of Atonement. In conclusion it is pointed out that all these
offerings are in addition to any private offerings that one may wish to
bring on these days.

35. *a solemn assembly*] A popular assembly, convened for religious
purposes (II Kings 6.18; Isa. 1.13; Amos 5.21). The eighth day of
Tabernacles was celebrated as a special feast, with a distinct ritual
(Suk. 47a; comp. Rashi, quoting a famous homiletic simile).

the lambs, shall be according to their number, after the ordinance; and one he-goat for a sin-offering; beside the 38 continual burnt-offering, and the meal-offering thereof, and the drink-offering thereof.

These ye shall offer unto the LORD in your appointed 39 seasons, beside your vows, and your freewill-offerings, whether they be your burnt-offerings, or your meal-offerings, or your drink-offerings, or your peace-offerings.

And Moses told the children of Israel according to all **30** that the LORD commanded Moses.

39. *beside your vows, etc.*] All of which are individual offerings, which may also be brought during the festivals, if found more convenient, but which have no relation to the public offerings described above (Rashi).

CHAPTER 30.

30.1. This verse is the conclusion of the laws contained in chs. 28–29 (comp. Lev. 23.40). In R. V. this verse is counted as the last (40) verse of ch. 29.

2–17. ANNULMENT OF VOWS MADE BY WOMEN.

This section deals with the laws pertaining to vows made by women. Beginning with a general statement that one who makes a vow is bound to perform it, the law indicates some exceptions in the case of women making vows. An unmarried woman living in her father's house or a married woman living with her husband may have her vow annulled by her father or her husband, on the day when he hears of it. If he annuls it after that day, the vow is valid and the husband or father will bear the guilt in case she breaks the vow. A widow or a divorced woman is obliged to fulfill her vows just as the man is.

The inclusion of this section at this place has been a subject of speculation on the part of many commentators. Ibn Ezra surmises that this chapter really belongs after ch. 32, where the agreement made

2   And Moses spoke unto the heads of the tribes of the
children of Israel, saying:

This is the thing which the LORD hath commanded.
3 When a man voweth a vow unto the LORD, or sweareth an

with the tribes of Reuben and Gad is described. In that arrangement,
the tribes of Reuben and Gad made a definite promise to cross the
Jordan with the other tribes and to assist them in the conquest of
Canaan. Moses impressed upon them the importance of their promise,
which was in the form of a vow (cf. 32.24 and here v. 3), and then
proceeded to give further details of the law governing vows (see also
Ehrlich). Ramban connects this law with 29.39, where mention is
made of votive offerings, which led to the insertion of this section
dealing with vows of a personal character (comp. Rashbam, Herxheimer, Kahana). Other instances regarding vows are found in Lev.
5.4 ff. (regarding sacrifices prescribed for the breach of a vow unwittingly); Lev. 27.2 ff. (regarding votive offerings of persons, animals,
houses and fields); Num. 6.2 ff. (the case of the Nazir); Deut. 23.22–24
(a general statement to the effect that vows made must be kept, although one who makes no vows has no sin, comp. Eccl. 5.1–5).

2. *unto the heads of the tribes*] The phraseology here is rather
unusual, as we should expect it to begin in the regular way, "And God
spoke to Moses: Speak to the children of Israel". It is also very unusual
to have a law addressed to the heads of the tribes rather than to the
whole of Israel. Ramban suggests that the laws of vows were not to
be made public and were given only to the representatives of the
people, in order not to encourage the people to make vows, especially
since they will know that there are ways of having vows annulled.
According to ibn Ezra's explanation (given in introd. note), "the heads
of the tribes" here refers to the tribes of Reuben and Gad. The Rabbis
deduce from this phrase that permission is granted to a learned man
to annul any vow that an individual might have made in haste (Ned.
22b). This right is not explicitly mentioned here, but was extensively
made use of by the Rabbis (See *Yoreh De'ah*, 248, for the details of
this privilege).

3. *When a man*] Excluding a minor of either sex or a woman,
with regard to whose vows specific directions are given later (Sifre
153).

a vow unto the Lord] In a positive form, either to offer a sacrifice

oath to bind his soul with a bond, he shall not break his word; he shall do according to all that proceedeth out of his mouth. Also when a woman voweth a vow unto the 4 LORD, and bindeth herself by a bond, being in her father's house, in her youth, and her father heareth her vow, or 5 her bond wherewith she hath bound her soul, and her

or to make a donation to the sanctuary. The phrase may also include any kind of vow of an individual and secular character, in the making of which the name of God was mentioned (ibn Ezra).

to bind his soul with a bond] This refers to a negative obligation, not to do certain things, for example, abstaining from food and drink for a certain period, as in the case of the Nazirite (comp. *Biur*).

he shall not break his word] Leeser's "profane his word" is more literal. To break a vow is equal to an act of profanation of God's name, since vows usually contained the name of God in their formulas (cf. Ezek. 39.7).

all that proceedeth out of his mouth] It is the utterance of the vow that constitutes the obligation, and mere thought or intention is not binding. On the other hand, if he intended to say one thing and by mistake said something else, the vow is not valid, the principle being that the intention and the utterance must coincide (Sheb. 26a; Ter. 3.8; *Yoreh De'ah*, 210).

4. *being in her father's house*] Under his jurisdiction, i. e. before her marriage.

in her youth] Not a minor, whose vows are not valid (note on v. 3), but one of marriageable age, though still young. Women in ancient Israel were married at a very early age, so that mature un- married women were uncommon and no provision is made for them here. According to the Rabbis, "in her youth" refers to a maiden who is between eleven years and one day and twelve years and one day old, and who, on examination, is found to be able to appreciate the significance of a vow (Sifre 153).

5. *and her father heareth her vow*] Not that he was necessarily present at the time when the vow was made, but that he comes to hear of it later (see v. 8).

father holdeth his peace at her, then all her vows shall
stand, and every bond wherewith she hath bound her soul
6 shall stand. But if her father disallow her in the day that
he heareth, none of her vows, or of her bonds wherewith
she hath bound her soul, shall stand; and the LORD will
7 forgive her, because her father disallowed her. And if
she be married to a husband, while her vows are upon her,
or the clear utterance of her lips, wherewith she hath
8 bound her soul; and her husband hear it, whatsoever day
it be that he heareth it, and hold his peace at her; then
her vows shall stand, and her bonds wherewith she hath
9 bound her soul shall stand. But if her husband disallow

holdeth his peace at her] Leeser has: "be silent to her", i. e. says
nothing, whereby the vow becomes confirmed by him and binding
upon her.

6. *disallow her*] Expresses his opposition and disapproval.

in the day that he heareth] But after that day his disapproval has
no effect and the vow is binding upon her.

the Lord will forgive her] If she breaks her vow, since it was annulled
by her father (Sifre 153).

7. *while her vows are upon her*] Vows which she made before her
marriage, while in her father's house, which her father did not disallow. The Rabbis apply the present law to the case of a girl who
made a vow while she was in her father's house, and her father did
not disallow it, not having heard of it, and then she became betrothed
(ארוסה), but is still living with her father. In this case both her father
and her betrothed husband have to annul her vow if it is to become
void (Sifre 153).

the clear utterance of her lips] R. V. has "the rash utterance",
thoughtless speech, which, however, did not relieve one of the
obligation imposed by the vow (cf. Lev. 5.4; BDB).

8. *hear it*] Hear of it, since he could not hear it when it was made.

whatsoever day it be] This rendering is more in agreement with the
construction of the Hebrew text than that of R. V. and Leeser, "on
the day that he hear it".

her in the day that he heareth it, then he shall make void her vow which is upon her, and the clear utterance of her lips, wherewith she hath bound her soul; and the LORD will forgive her. But the vow of a widow, or of her that is 10 divorced, even every thing wherewith she hath bound her soul, shall stand against her. And if a woman vowed in 11 her husband's house, or bound her soul by a bond with an oath, and her husband heard it, and held his peace at 12 her, and disallowed her not, then all her vows shall stand, and every bond wherewith she bound her soul shall stand. But if her husband make them null and void in the day 13 that he heareth them, then whatsoever proceeded out of her lips, whether it were her vows, or the bond of her soul, shall not stand: her husband hath made them void; and the LORD will forgive her. Every vow, and every binding 14 oath to afflict the soul, her husband may let it stand, or

10. *shall stand against her*] Are valid, even though she returned to her father's house after her husband's death or after she obtained her divorce, while still in her twelfth year. In the case of the daughter of a priest, under similar conditions, the law permits her to partake of the priestly food (Lev. 22.13).

11. *And if a woman vowed in her husband's house*] Referring back to v. 9. If she did not have on her any vows at the time of marriage, but made a vow afterwards, her husband has a right to disallow such a vow. Ibn Ezra makes this refer to v. 10, saying that if the widow or divorced woman made a vow while in her husband's house and her husband did not disallow it, her vow is valid. But if he disallowed it at the time and the vow became void, and after that he died or divorced her, her former vow does not come into effect again, but remains inoperative and she is not obliged to fulfill it. While this interpretation is more in harmony with the arrangement of the verse here, it is contrary to the traditional interpretation (Ned. 89a; comp. *Biur*).

14. *to afflict the soul*] Denoting some form of abstinence, usually

15 her husband may make it void. But if her husband altogether hold his peace at her from day to day, then he
causeth all her vows to stand, or all her bonds, which are
upon her; he hath let them stand, because he held his
16 peace at her in the day that he heard them. But if he
shall make them null and void after that he hath heard
17 them, then he shall bear her iniquity. These are the
statutes, which the LORD commanded Moses, between
a man and his wife, between a father and his daughter,
being in her youth, in her father's house.

from food or drink (see note on 29.7). According to the Rabbis, vows of
abstinence are the only kind that the husband may disallow (Ned.
11.1; Sifre 155).

16. *null and void*] And then later compels her to break her vow,
she is not responsible, but he shall bear the guilt of her sin (cf. note
on 18.23), since she does it in obedience to his will (ibn Ezra). The
same would apply also to the father (v. 17, comp. Ramban).

17. *between a man and his wife*] Of whatever age she be; while
the next clause, "between a father and his daughter", has to be qualified by the following phrase.

CHAPTER 31.

1–54. THE WAR WITH THE MIDIANITES.

The last act of Moses was to execute vengeance on the Midianites
in accordance with the divine command (25.15–17). The Midianites
are represented as having, at the suggestion of Balaam, instigated the
Israelites to sin and to worship Baal-peor through their women, and
although the Moabites were associated with them in the plot, they
are regarded only as the instruments used by the Midianites for carrying out their scheme. Moses was therefore ordered to avenge Israel
and God on the Midianites by engaging them in a battle, which assumed
a religious character, and therefore Phinehas, the priest, and not
Joshua, was placed in command. A small army of 12,000 men, 1,000

And the Lord spoke unto Moses, saying: 'Avenge the 2 **31** children of Israel of the Midianites; afterward shalt thou

of each tribe, is mustered in and the attack is made. The Midianite army is entirely exterminated, the five kings of Midian, together with Balaam, are slain, while the Israelites meet with no casualty. The victorious army returns to Moses and Eleazar with the spoils and the captive women and children, but Moses is angered because they brought the women with them, since it was they who were the cause of Israel's sin and of the plague that followed it. He then orders them to slay all the women and all the male children, but permits them to keep the virgins alive. He then orders them to go through a process of purification because of their contact with the dead and promulgates several laws at the same time regarding the purification of objects that have become defiled. The spoils taken in the war are divided into two equal parts, one half to be given to those who took part in the war and the other half to those who remained in the camp. The warriors were to give 1/500 to the priests, while those who remained at camp were to give 1/50 to the Levites. This order is carried out and its execution is described in great detail. The officers of the army make a special offering to the Lord of some gold objects which they took as spoils and this contribution was placed in the tabernacle as a memorial before the Lord.

While the war itself is dismissed in a few verses and no details are given of the place of the battle and other points of the encounter, the laws about purification from the uncleanness through contact with the dead are given in a very elaborate manner (vv. 19–24), and the laws about the correct division of the spoils are also described in considerable detail and with many repetitions (25–54). This makes it appear as if the purpose of the chronicler here was not so much to tell the incident as to use it for the purpose of establishing certain laws for the future guidance of the people (comp. Wiener, *Essays in Pentateuch Criticism*, 169–171; Gray, 417–420).

2. *Avenge the children of Israel of the Midianites*] Leeser's rendering: "Execute the vengeance of the children of Israel on the Midianites", is more explicit. This is in fulfillment of the command in 25.15–17. The plague that consumed 24,000 of the Israelites (25.9), which came in consequence of the wiles of the Midianites, shall now be avenged on them.

3 be gathered unto thy people.' And Moses spoke unto the people, saying: 'Arm ye men from among you for the war, that they may go against Midian, to execute the 4 LORD'S vengeance on Midian. Of every tribe a thousand, throughout all the tribes of Israel, shall ye send to the 5 war.' So there were delivered, out of the thousands of Israel, a thousand of every tribe, twelve thousand armed 6 for war. And Moses sent them, a thousand of every tribe, to the war, them and Phinehas the son of Eleazar the

3. *Arm ye men from among you*] Equip them with ammunition, so that they may be ready for battle (comp. Ehrlich, who renders the word החלצו as a denominative of חלוץ, "form a vanguard"; see BDB).

that they may go] Lit. "they shall be against" (comp. II Sam. 11.23).

the Lord's vengeance] The vengeance commanded by the Lord, or vengeance in behalf of the Lord, since the Midianites were the cause of Israel's turning away from the worship of God (ibn Ezra, comp. Luzzatto).

4. *Of every tribe a thousand*] Only part of the army was mustered in for that purpose (comp. Judg. 21.10; II Sam. 17.1).

5. *So there were delivered*] Probably to Moses. The term used here may denote compulsory conscription (Ehrlich). The rabbinic homilists took the word in a similar sense, and used it homiletically. The Israelites understood that the death of Moses depended upon the destruction of the Midianites (v. 2), and if this could be delayed the death of Moses would be postponed. They therefore refused to go to battle, hoping thereby to prolong the life of Moses, and had to be forced into conscription (Sifre 157). LXX has here "they were counted", possibly after a reading וַיִּסָּפְרוּ (BDB).

thousands] Possibly "families", see p. 14.

6. *and Phinehas*] Who had already displayed his zeal in this cause by killing the Midianite woman together with Zimri (25.7). The reason why Phinehas and not Eleazar was sent was probably to avoid the possible defilement of the high-priest (see note on 17.2).

priest, to the war, with the holy vessels and the trumpets
for the alarm in his hand. And they warred against Midian, 7
as the LORD commanded Moses; and they slew every
male. And they slew the kings of Midian with the rest 8
of their slain: Evi, and Rekem, and Zur, and Hur, and
Reba, the five kings of Midian; Balaam also the son of

with the holy vessels] It is not certain what was included here among
the holy vessels. Some understand by it the ark (Sifre 157; ibn Ezra),
others the ark and the plate of gold from the high-priest's miter (Rashi),
while others again take the phrase to refer to the Urim and Thummim
(Num. R. 22.4; Tan. Mattot 6; Luzzatto). It is possible to construe
this phrase as being in apposition to trumpets (Keil), or to make it
refer to the holy vestments (Dillmann). A. V. has "the holy instruments", R. V. "the vessels of the sanctuary".

and the trumpets] See 10.1 ff.

in his hand] In his charge, under his control (Sifre 157; Rashi).

7. *every male*] It would appear from this, if taken literally, that
the Midianites were entirely exterminated in this war. We find, however, that the Midianites played an important part during the period
of the Judges (Judg. chs. 6–8) and references to them are also found
elsewhere (I Kings 11.18; Isa. 60.6). It is not possible to confine this
phrase to the army, since women and children are also included, unless
we assume that the army was annihilated and the men who remained
in the villages all fled, leaving their women and children, who were
later taken captive by the conquering Israelites (vv. 9–10). The more
likely explanation is that there were several branches of the same
tribe, one branch of which only was destroyed in this war (comp.
supra, note on 22.4).

8. *the kings of Midian*] In Josh. 13.21, where this incident is
briefly referred to and the kings given in the same order, they are
designated not as kings but as the "chiefs of Midian" and the "princes
of Sihon" (cf. I Sam. 6.4).

Balaam] Also associated with the five kings in Josh. 13.22,
but there he is described as "the soothsayer". Balaam is here represented as having remained in this part of the country, although in
24.25 he is said to have returned to his home in Aram. It is possible
that he came back again to Midian for some purpose (ibn Ezra).

9 Beor they slew with the sword. And the children of Israel
took captive the women of Midian and their little ones;
and all their cattle, and all their flocks, and all their goods,
10 they took for a prey. And all their cities in the places
wherein they dwelt, and all their encampments, they
11 burnt with fire. And they took all the spoil, and all the
12 prey, both of man and of beast. And they brought the
captives, and the prey, and the spoil, unto Moses, and
unto Eleazar the priest, and unto the congregation of
the children of Israel, unto the camp, unto the plains of
Moab, which are by the Jordan at Jericho.
13 And Moses, and Eleazar the priest, and all the princes
of the congregation, went forth to meet them without
14 the camp. And Moses was wroth with the officers of the
host, the captains of thousands and the captains of hun-
15 dreds, who came from the service of the war. And Moses

10. *their cities in the places wherein they dwelt*] At that time. The
Midianites were a nomad tribe and had no towns of their own. It is
suggested that these towns originally belonged to Moab and had been
captured by the Amorites under Sihon, who allotted some of them to
his vassals, among whom were the Midianite chiefs (Josh. 13.21; see
note on v. 8). This explains why in Josh. the conquest of the Midianites is associated with the conquest of Sihon (Keil).

encampments] Circular encampments of nomad tribes (Gen. 25.16),
perhaps surrounded by stone fences (Kahana).

13. *without the camp*] Since the warriors were not allowed to
enter the camp until they became purified from the defilement caused
by their contact with the dead (v. 19), Moses and the leaders had to
go outside the camp to meet them.

14. *with the officers of the host*] But not with Phinehas, who was
not the military leader of the expedition, but attached to the army as
a priest (v. 6), a spiritual adviser, who may have had no control or
even knowledge of what the soldiers did (Luzzatto, comp. Ramban).

said unto them: 'Have ye saved all the women alive?
Behold, these caused the children of Israel, through the 16
counsel of Balaam, to revolt so as to break faith with the
LORD in the matter of Peor, and so the plague was among
the congregation of the LORD. Now therefore kill every 17
male among the little ones, and kill every woman that
hath known man by lying with him. But all the women 18
children, that have not known man by lying with him,
keep alive for yourselves. And encamp ye without the 19
camp seven days; whosoever hath killed any person,

16. *through the counsel of Balaam*] The reference is not mentioned
in the story of Balaam as we have it, but tradition has preserved the
story that Balaam advised the Midianites to entice the Israelites, by
means of their women, to the worship of Baal-peor so that God's
anger might be aroused against them (see note on 25.1).

to revolt so as to break faith] R. V. has "to commit trespass", while
Leeser adds "gross", possibly following the reading למעל מעל (Lev.
5.21; comp. Targum, Luzzatto).

in the matter of Peor] Referring to 25.1–5.

17. *that hath known man*] Or is of the age "to know man", i. e.
of marriageable age (Sifre 157; Yeb. 60a; cf. Judg. 21.11). All males
are to be slain in order to secure the extinction of the tribe, and all
women are to be slain because of the sin of Baal-peor. This ruthless
command, which appears to us now as most inhuman, was the regular
procedure in warfare in ancient times.

19–24. PURIFICATION OF THE WARRIORS.

All the warriors who have become unclean because of their contact
with dead bodies, as well as all the objects that have thus become
unclean, have to undergo a process of purification before they may be
admitted into the camp again.

19. *without the camp*] The part of the camp where the tabernacle
was situated.

and whosoever hath touched any slain, purify yourselves
on the third day and on the seventh day, ye and your
20 captives. And as to every garment, and all that is made
of skin, and all work of goats' hair, and all things made
of wood, ye shall purify.'

purify yourselves] With the water mingled with the ashes of the
red heifer, as described in 19.12 ff.

and your captives] According to rabbinic tradition, non-Israelites
need not go through the prescribed process of purification (Sifre 157),
and the meaning here is that the captives should purify their garments
so that they may not contaminate the Israelites who come in contact
with them (Ramban, Luzzatto).

20. *ye shall purify*] Disregarding the Hithpael (תתחטאו), which
would make it reflexive. R. V. has "as to .... ye shall purify yourselves", i. e. you shall purify yourselves in respect to these garments
(comp. ibn Ezra). Leeser has "shall ye purify unto yourselves", which
is rather difficult. The law here provides that all garments, wood-
work and coverings that have come in contact with a dead body become unclean (Lev. 11.32) and have to go through a process of purification before they can be used again.

21–24. Eleazar explains the laws in greater detail to the military
leaders. While in ordinary cases of ritual cleanliness the only means
of purification is by placing the object in running water, or by having
the ashes of the red heifer mingled with water sprinkled upon it, in
this case the order was that all metal objects which can stand the fire
shall be purified through fire (Luzzatto). The Rabbis, however,
explain the order of Eleazar to refer not to ritual purification, but to
the cleansing of vessels used for food from the absorption in them of
forbidden food. Thus, articles used in fire, that is in cooking, boiling
or frying, as pots and pans, should be placed in fire until they become
white hot; other articles, such as dishes, spoons, should be placed in
boiling water, while articles used with cold food only, such as glasses,
need only be soaked in water to become fit for use by an Israelite.
This is in addition to the purification these vessels have to undergo
in order to remove from them the ritual impurity caused by contact
with a dead body (Rashi, Ramban).

And Eleazar the priest said unto the men of war that 21
went to the battle: 'This is the statute of the law which
the LORD hath commanded Moses: Howbeit the gold, 22
and the silver, the brass, the iron, the tin, and the lead,
every thing that may abide the fire, ye shall make to go 23
through the fire, and it shall be clean; nevertheless it
shall be purified with the water of sprinkling; and all
that abideth not the fire ye shall make to go through the
water. And ye shall wash your clothes on the seventh 24
day, and ye shall be clean, and afterward ye may come
into the camp.'

23. *that may abide the fire*] Leeser has: "that cometh into the
fire", i. e. the use of which was in fire. The object should be purified
by the same means as it was used (Rashi).

the water of sprinkling] The water in which the ashes of the red
heifer are mixed (19.9, 13, 20, 21). Besides this process necessary to
purify the object from its ritual uncleanness, it should also go through
the other process of purification which removes from it any forbidden
food that it may have absorbed before.

ye shall make to go through the water] Apart from the immersion necessary for their ritual purification, they are to be soaked in water to
remove any particle of forbidden food that may have remained in
them (Ramban, cf. Rashi).

24. *And ye shall wash your clothes*] Cf. 19.19.

into the camp] Even the part where the tabernacle was (cf. note
on 5.2–4).

25–54. DIVISION OF THE SPOILS OF WAR.

The principle is here laid down that those who remained behind
should share equally in the booty with the warriors. This practice
is mentioned also in I Sam. 30.24 ff. in the case of David's army. Here,
however, the additional provision is made that the warriors as well
as those who remained behind should set aside part of their respective
shares of the booty for the priests and the Levites.

25-26   And the LORD spoke unto Moses, saying: 'Take the
sum of the prey that was taken, both of man and of beast,
thou, and Eleazar the priest, and the heads of the fathers'
27 houses of the congregation; and divide the prey into two
parts: between the men skilled in war, that went out to
28 battle, and all the congregation; and levy a tribute unto
the LORD of the men of war that went out to battle: one
soul of five hundred, both of the persons, and of the beeves,
29 and of the asses, and of the flocks; take it of their half,
and give it unto Eleazar the priest, as a portion set apart
30 for the LORD. And of the children of Israel's half, thou
shalt take one drawn out of every fifty, of the persons,
of the beeves, of the asses, and of the flocks, even of all
the cattle, and give them unto the Levites, that keep the
31 charge of the tabernacle of the LORD.' And Moses and
Eleazar the priest did as the LORD commanded Moses.

28. *levy a tribute unto the Lord*] The men who went out to battle
are to give of their share 1/500 to the priests, while the men who remained in the camp are to give 1/50 of their share to the Levites.
The Koran prescribes a religious tribute of 1/5 (Sura 8.42, quoted by
Gray; comp. Torrey, *The Jewish Foundation of Islam*, N. Y., 1933,
p. 143, who endeavors to find the source of the quantity of the Islamic
tax in Jewish tradition).

beeves] Archaic pl. of beef, used for live animals.

30. *And of the children of Israel's half*] I. e. of the half given to
those who remained in the camp.

one drawn out of every fifty] The same proportion as that of the
number of men who went to war (12,000) to the whole of Israel (600,
000, Abarbanel; comp. Ehrlich to v. 28, who seems to be confused in
his arithmetic and does not refer to Abarbanel).

unto the Levites] Who were not included in the number of Israelites and therefore did not receive their share of the booty (cf. 18.25 ff.
regarding the tithes, where the Levites who received 1/10 were told
to give of this 1/10 to the priests).

Now the prey, over and above the booty which the men 32
of war took, was six hundred thousand and seventy thousand and five thousand sheep, and threescore and twelve 33
thousand beeves, and threescore and one thousand asses, 34
and thirty and two thousand persons in all, of the women 35
that had not known man by lying with him. And the 36
half, which was the portion of them that went out to war,
was in number three hundred thousand and thirty thousand and seven thousand and five hundred sheep. And 37
the LORD's tribute of the sheep was six hundred and
threescore and fifteen. And the beeves were thirty and 38
six thousand, of which the LORD's tribute was threescore
and twelve. And the asses were thirty thousand and five 39
hundred, of which the LORD's tribute was threescore and
one. And the persons were sixteen thousand, of whom 40
the LORD's tribute was thirty and two persons. And 41
Moses gave the tribute, which was set apart for the LORD,
unto Eleazar the priest, as the LORD commanded Moses.
And of the children of Israel's half, which Moses divided 42
off from the men that warred—now the congregation's 43
half was three hundred thousand and thirty thousand

32. *over and above the booty*]   The division was only with regard to
the captured female children and cattle, but not the plunder of other
objects which the soldiers took for themselves (v. 53). Leeser has
"being the rest of the spoil", meaning perhaps what was left of the
booty, some of which might have been used for food by the soldiers,
or some of the clothing and other articles might have been worn out
through use (Gray, McNeile).

40. *the Lord's tribute*]   Probably put to menial tasks in connection
with the sanctuary.

44 and seven thousand and five hundred sheep, and thirty
45 and six thousand beeves, and thirty thousand and five
46-47 hundred asses, and sixteen thousand persons—even of
the children of Israel's half, Moses took one drawn out
of every fifty, both of man and of beast, and gave them
unto the Levites, that kept the charge of the tabernacle
of the LORD; as the LORD commanded Moses.

48   And the officers that were over the thousands of the
host, the captains of thousands, and the captains of hun-
49 dreds, came near unto Moses; and they said unto Moses:
'Thy servants have taken the sum of the men of war that
are under our charge, and there lacketh not one man of
50 us. And we have brought the LORD's offering, what every
man hath gotten, of jewels of gold, armlets, and bracelets,
signet-rings, ear-rings, and girdles, to make atonement

50. *the Lord's offering*] In thankful recognition that not even
one man of the Israelites was hurt during the expedition. This was
a freewill-offering on the part of the officers of the army out of the
booty which they were entitled to keep for themselves.

of jewels of gold] Leeser has "vessels of gold", possibly regarding
this term as generic and the following as specific. In the case of Gideon's
war with the Midianites, there is also mentioned booty of gold objects
(Judg. 8.24–26), gold ornaments being worn by nomad tribes on their
persons more frequently than by peoples of settled communities.

to make atonement] Various interpretations have been suggested
with regard to the meaning of this atonement. Rashbam, quoting
his father, says that they required atonement for their sin which they
committed in counting the people (v. 49), pointing to a similar expression used in Ex. 30.11–16, when the people were counted at the command of God. Another suggestion is that the officers felt remorse
over the general slaughter which they caused among the Midianites,
while none of their own people was hurt, for which they wished to
offer an atonement (Ehrlich).

for our souls before the LORD.' And Moses and Eleazar 51
the priest took the gold of them, even all wrought jewels.
And all the gold of the gift that they set apart for the 52
LORD, of the captains of thousands, and of the captains
of hundreds, was sixteen thousand seven hundred and
fifty shekels.—For the men of war had taken booty, every 53
man for himself.—And Moses and Eleazar the priest 54
took the gold of the captains of thousands and of hundreds,
and brought it into the tent of meeting, for a memorial
for the children of Israel before the LORD.

51. *all wrought jewels*] Leeser has "all kinds of wrought articles",
i. e. articles prepared by artists. Ibn Ezra takes the expression to mean
that all these articles were perfect and that there were not among
them any spoiled or broken vessels.

53. *For the men of war*] The common soldiers also obtained
articles of value which they retained for themselves. This is a parenthetic sentence interrupting the sequence between vv. 52 and 54,
implying that the ordinary soldiers felt no need for offering an atonement, and kept the booty for themselves.

54. *for a memorial*] Cf. Ex. 30.16. Either the gold objects themselves were preserved as a memorial, or they were turned into objects
that were used in the tabernacle (Ramban).

CHAPTER 32.

1–42. REUBEN, GAD AND PART OF MANASSEH PERMITTED TO SETTLE EAST OF JORDAN.

The tribes of Reuben and Gad, possessed of many flocks, request
Moses to permit them to settle on the land east of the Jordan, in the
province of Gilead, which was rich in pasture lands. Moses is angered
at this request, believing that this would hinder the people in their
contemplated expedition to take possession of the land of Canaan,
west of the Jordan, and he expresses his indignation at this apparently
selfish request. The tribes of Reuben and Gad, however, explain that

32   Now the children of Reuben and the children of Gad
had a very great multitude of cattle; and when they saw
the land of Jazer, and the land of Gilead, that, behold, the

they are ready to proceed with the rest of the people to Canaan to
assist in the conquest of the land, but they wish to obtain permission
to build homes for their women and children, to whom they will return
only after the whole land west of the Jordan is in the possession of
the Israelites. Moses agrees to the proposition and instructs Eleazar
and Joshua to give the land conquered from Sihon and Og to the
tribes of Reuben and Gad, on condition that they fulfill their promise.
Should they fail in this, they are to be forced to settle with the others
in Canaan. The tribes of Reuben and Gad then rebuild several cities,
where they propose to leave their families and their cattle while they
are away fighting with the other tribes. Several families in the tribe
of Manasseh also capture some districts in Gilead and settle there
(cf. Josh. 17.14–18).

The same incident, with slight variations, is also found in Deut.
3.12–20 and referred to in a number of other places (Deut. 4.43; 29.7;
Josh. 12.6; 13.29, 31; 14.3; 18.7 and ch. 22).

1. *the children of Reuben and the children of Gad*] This order is
found in all the passages in which this story is referred to, but in this
chapter only here, while throughout the rest of the chapter Gad is
mentioned first. This is explained on the ground that everywhere the
order of seniority is followed, but here the plea came mainly from the
Gadites, who were the richer and more populous (comp. Deut. 33.6
with 20–21; Ramban, ibn Ezra).

the land of Jazer] The land round about Jazer, a city on the eastern
boundary of Gilead which, together with its "daughter cities", i. e.
the villages grouped round about it, was captured from the Amorites
(21.32).

the land of Gilead] The name Gilead is sometimes given to the
whole stretch of country lying between the Arnon and the Jarmuk,
the whole territory west of the Jordan occupied by the Israelites
(Josh. 22.9, 13, 22), but here it is used in a more restricted sense, referring to the land south of the river Jabbok, whose modern name is
"the Belka" (see note on v. 39, where the reference is to the land north
of the Jabbok).

place was a place for cattle, the children of Gad and the 2
children of Reuben came and spoke unto Moses, and to
Eleazar the priest, and unto the princes of the congregation,
saying: 'Ataroth, and Dibon, and Jazer, and Nimrah, and 3
Heshbon, and Elealeh, and Sebam, and Nebo, and Beon,
the land which the LORD smote before the congregation 4
of Israel, is a land for cattle, and thy servants have cattle.'
And they said: 'If we have found favour in thy sight, let 5
this land be given unto thy servants for a possession;
bring us not over the Jordan.' And Moses said unto the 6
children of Gad and to the children of Reuben: 'Shall

a place for cattle] Fertile pasture land, suitable for raising cattle
(Cant. 4.1; 6.3; Micah 7.14; comp. Smith, *Historical Geography of
Palestine*, p. 522 ff.).

3. All the names mentioned here, with several additions, are mentioned again in vv. 34–38 (also in Isa. 15 and 16 and Jer. 48, as belonging to Moab), and all of them have been identified with some degree
of accuracy. Ataroth is probably the modern Jebel Attarus, about
8 miles N. N. W. of Dibbon. Dibon, also called Dibon-gad (33.45),
is identified with the modern Dibbon, where the famous Moabite
stone was discovered. It was included in the territory conquered by
Sihon from the Moabites (21.26, 30). For Jazer see note on v. 1.
Nimrah, or Beth-nimrah (v. 36), is about 6 miles east of the Jordan,
almost opposite Jericho, the modern Tel Nimrin. For Heshbon see
note on 21.25. Elealeh is probably the modern el 'Al, a village N. E. of
Heshbon, now in ruins. Sebam, also called Sibmah (v. 38), was a town
near Heshbon. Nebo was probably a town near Mt. Nebo, about
5 miles S. W. of Heshbon. Beon, probably the same as Baal-meon
(v. 38; or Beth-meon, Jer. 48.23; or Beth-baal-meon, Josh. 13.17), is
identified with modern Ma'in. (Targum gives renderings for these
various names in homiletic interpretation of events that were supposed
to have occurred there; see Adler).

4. *the Lord smote*] In the destruction of Sihon and Og (ch. 21),
in whose possession these towns were (Targum adds here "its inhabitants").

7 your brethren go to the war, and shall ye sit here? And
wherefore will ye turn away the heart of the children of
Israel from going over into the land which the Lord hath
8 given them? Thus did your fathers, when I sent them
9 from Kadesh-barnea to see the land. For when they went
up unto the valley of Eshcol, and saw the land, they turned
away the heart of the children of Israel, that they should
not go into the land which the Lord had given them.
10 And the Lord's anger was kindled in that day, and He
11 swore, saying: Surely none of the men that came up out
of Egypt, from twenty years old and upward, shall see
the land which I swore unto Abraham, unto Isaac, and
unto Jacob; because they have not wholly followed Me;
12 save Caleb the son of Jephunneh the Kenizzite, and Joshua
the son of Nun; because they have wholly followed the
13 Lord. And the Lord's anger was kindled against Israel,
and He made them wander to and fro in the wilderness
forty years, until all the generation, that had done evil in

7. *wherefore will ye turn away*] R. V. has "discourage" (cf. ibn
Ezra). The people will be discouraged when they see you remain here,
either because they will think that you were afraid of the people of
Canaan and therefore preferred to remain here, which may weaken
also their ardor, or because they will be afraid that without your help
they will not be able to accomplish the conquest of the land.

8. *Thus did your fathers*] Referring to the incident of the spies,
chs. 13, 14.

11. *Surely none*] Cf. note on 14.23.

followed Me] They have not trusted Me (14.24).

12. *the Kenizzite*] The name of the family, a branch of the tribe
of Judah (13.6; 34.19), to which Caleb (Josh. 14.6, 14) and his brother
Othniel (Josh. 15.17) belonged.

the sight of the LORD, was consumed. And, behold, ye 14
are risen up in your fathers' stead, a brood of sinful men,
to augment yet the fierce anger of the LORD toward Israel.
For if ye turn away from after Him, He will yet again 15
leave them in the wilderness; and so ye will destroy all
this people.'

And they came near unto him, and said: 'We will build 16
sheepfolds here for our cattle, and cities for our little ones;
but we ourselves will be ready armed to go before the 17
children of Israel, until we have brought them unto their
place; and our little ones shall dwell in the fortified cities

14. *a brood of sinful men*] A contemptuous term for the children
of the sinful men who died in the wilderness for their sin. Targum has
"the disciples of sinful men" (comp. *Biur*); R. V. "an increase of sinful men"; Leeser "a new race of sinful men".

15. *and so ye will destroy*] If you repeat the sinful act of your
fathers, you may expect a similar fate, namely that you will have to
remain in the wilderness and because of you also all the other tribes,
as was the case before, and thus you will bring destruction upon this
whole people.

16. *sheepfolds here for our cattle, and cities for our little ones*] Sheepfolds
were made of stones piled up in the form of a wall or hedge, although
sometimes they were made of wooden stakes. The order is reversed
in v. 24. The Rabbis use this in a homiletic way. The people, anxious
about their possessions, mention cattle first, but Moses tells them to
think first of their families and then of their wealth, and they follow
his advice (v. 26; Num. R. 22.8).

17. *will be ready armed*] The word חשׁם comes from a root meaning
"to hasten", hence the lit. rendering would be, "will arm ourselves
hastening", which is rather peculiar. Some read here חמשׁים (cf. Ex.
13.18), meaning armed (see BDB 301b). Ehrlich takes נחלץ to mean
"we shall act as the vanguard", by selecting the strongest and the
bravest among us to go at the head of the army (cf. Josh. 6.7, 9, 13).

in the fortified cities] Which we shall now build for them, so that
they may be secure against a possible attack of an enemy.

18 because of the inhabitants of the land. We will not return
unto our houses, until the children of Israel have inherited
19 every man his inheritance. For we will not inherit with
them on the other side of the Jordan, and forward, because
our inheritance is fallen to us on this side of the Jordan
eastward.'

20　　And Moses said unto them: 'If ye will do this thing:
if ye will arm yourselves to go before the LORD to the war,
21 and every armed man of you will pass over the Jordan
before the LORD, until He hath driven out His enemies
22 from before Him, and the land be subdued before the
LORD, and ye return afterward; then ye shall be clear
before the LORD, and before Israel, and this land shall be
23 unto you for a possession before the LORD. But if ye will
not do so, behold, ye have sinned against the LORD; and
24 know ye your sin which will find you. Build you cities

19. *because our inheritance is fallen to us*] This is rather strange,
since this was the very thing for which they now ask. The suggestion
is therefore made that the word באה should be rendered literally, "is
coming to us", in the sense of appropriateness because of their need
of the pasture land (Ramban; comp. Ehrlich to Gen. 43.23). Leeser,
following Mendelssohn, has "when our inheritance", i. e. they renounce
their portion in the land of Canaan if this land which they desire will
be given to them.

20. *before the Lord*] Targum has here and in vv. 21 and 22 "before
God's people", so as to avoid anthropomorphism. The idea underlying
the expression is that God passes before the people in battle, symbol-
ized by the presence of the ark (ibn Ezra).

23. *and know ye your sin which will find you*] The consequence
of your sin. Sin is here personified (cf. Gen. 4.7), executing its own
punishment and finding its victim. LXX has "and ye will know your
sin when the evil will befall you".

24. *Build you cities*] Comp. note on v. 16.

for your little ones, and folds for your sheep; and do that which hath proceeded out of your mouth.'

And the children of Gad and the children of Reuben 25 spoke unto Moses, saying: 'Thy servants will do as my lord commandeth. Our little ones, our wives, our flocks, 26 and all our cattle, shall be there in the cities of Gilead; but thy servants will pass over, every man that is armed 27 for war, before the LORD to battle, as my lord saith.'

So Moses gave charge concerning them to Eleazar the 28 priest, and to Joshua the son of Nun, and to the heads of the fathers' houses of the tribes of the children of Israel. And Moses said unto them: 'If the children of Gad and 29 the children of Reuben will pass with you over the Jordan, every man that is armed to battle, before the LORD, and the land shall be subdued before you, then ye shall give them the land of Gilead for a possession; but if they will 30 not pass over with you armed, they shall have possessions among you in the land of Canaan.' And the children of 31

and do that which hath proceeded out of your mouth] See 30.2 and introd. note to ch. 30.

28. *So Moses gave charge concerning them*] Knowing that he would not enter Canaan, Moses made the compact public in a definite and explicit manner and gave the order to those who would have charge of the distribution of the land after the conquest (cf. Josh. 14.1).

30. *they shall have possessions among you*] If they do not keep their part of the agreement, they shall not be allowed to remain in Gilead, but shall be forced to go with you to Canaan and receive their portion there (ibn Ezra).

31. The Gadites and Reubenites repeat now in public, in the presence of Eleazar, Joshua and the heads of the tribes (v. 28), what they said to Moses before.

Gad and the children of Reuben answered, saying: 'As
32 the LORD hath said unto thy servants, so will we do. We
will pass over armed before the LORD into the land of
Canaan, and the possession of our inheritance shall remain
with us beyond the Jordan.'

33 And Moses gave unto them, even to the children of
Gad, and to the children of Reuben, and unto the half-tribe
of Manasseh the son of Joseph, the kingdom of Sihon king
of the Amorites, and the kingdom of Og king of Bashan,
the land, according to the cities thereof with their borders,
34 even the cities of the land round about. And the children
35 of Gad built Dibon, and Ataroth, and Aroer; and Atroth-

---

32. *shall remain with us*] The land that we now take possesion
of shall remain our inheritance, our portion in Canaan.

33. *the half-tribe of Manasseh*] This clause is here introduced for
the first time, although elsewhere the half-tribe of Manasseh is usually
associated with the Reubenites and Gadites as those who settled on
the land east of the Jordan. Its sudden introduction here caused some
modern scholars to suspect it as an interpolation. The old Jewish
commentators are of the opinion that the "half-tribe" here means
not half but part of the tribe, for of the eight clans of the tribe of
Manasseh only two settled east of the Jordan, while the other six
settled in Canaan (Josh. 17.1 ff.). Since they were small in number,
they were not included in the negotiations (ibn Ezra, Ramban). It
is also possible to regard this clause as anticipatory of vv. 39–42, where
it is recorded that certain families of Manasseh captured some towns
in Gilead, which they were allowed to retain for themselves (Luzzatto).

34. *built*] I. e. rebuilt the towns which had been destroyed during
the war. For the identification of some of these towns see note on
v. 3.

Aroer] Probably the Aroer which lay east of Rabbah in the north,
since another city by that name, lying south of the above on the northern bank of the Arnon and closer to Dibon and Ataroth, is described
as being in the territory of the Reubenites (Josh. 13.16, 25). It is, how-

shophan, and Jazer, and Jogbehah; and Beth-nimrah, and 36
Beth-haran; fortified cities, and folds for sheep. And the 37
children of Reuben built Heshbon, and Elealeh, and Kiriathaim; and Nebo, and Baal-meon—their names being 38
changed—and Sibmah; and gave their names unto the

ever, possible that some of these cities changed hands in different
periods of Jewish history.

35. *Atroth-shophan*]   Not identified, but probably close to Attarus.
Jogbehah]   Identified with modern Ajbehat, about 6 miles N. N. W.
from Amman.

36. *Beth-nimrah*]   The fuller name for Nimrah of v. 3.
Beth-haran]   Probably close to Beth-nimrin (see Josh. 13.27, Beth-
haram), identified by some with Tel er-Rameh, a few miles south of
Nimrin.

37. *Kiriathaim*]   Identified by some with Kureiyat, about 3 miles
S. E. of Attarus and quite a distance from Heshbon and El 'Al.

38. *Baal-meon*]   See note on Beon, v. 3.
their names being changed]   Because the names Nebo and Baal-
meon were given after the names of Moabite deities (Isa. 46.1). The
changed names, however, are not given here and apparently the old
names were restored after these cities were later reconquered by the
Moabites (Isa. 15.2; Jer. 48.22; Ezek. 25.9; see Ramban, Ehrlich).
LXX renders "surrounded by a wall", indicating possibly a different
reading (comp. Delitzsch, p. 143).

and gave their names]   Meaning that they gave new names to the
cities which they rebuilt. R. V. has "other names"; Mendelssohn,
also Leeser, has: "and they gave the former names", probably following
Ramban, who suggests that the names of these cities were changed
by Sihon when he captured them from the Moabites and that the
Israelites restored their former names (cf. Luzzatto).

39–42.   CAPTURE OF SOME DISTRICTS BY CLANS OF MANASSEH.

This section describes the expeditions of certain clans of the tribe
of Manasseh who, apparently on their own initiative, captured certain
districts in the country east of the Jordan, after the compact entered
into between Moses and the tribes of Reuben and Gad. They were
permitted by Moses to retain these districts and were therefore included

39 cities which they builded. And the children of Machir the
son of Manasseh went to Gilead, and took it, and dispos-
40 sessed the Amorites that were therein. And Moses gave
Gilead unto Machir the son of Manasseh; and he dwelt
41 therein. And Jair the son of Manasseh went and took the
42 villages thereof, and called them Havvoth-jair. And
Nobah went and took Kenath, and the villages thereof,
and called it Nobah, after his own name.

with the Reubenites and Gadites as those who settled on the land
east of the Jordan (cf. note on v. 33; comp. Gray, 437–439, for a complete discussion of the critical theory regarding this section, especially
the quotation from Budde, who endeavors to restore what he considers
the original text of this story).

39. *the children of Machir*] The clans of his family. In v. 40, also
in Deut. 3.15, Machir alone is mentioned.

to Gilead] Probably the northern part of Gilead, since the southern
part was given to Reuben and Gad (see note on v. 1).

41. *And Jair the son of Manasseh*] According to I Chron. 2.21,
22, Jair was the son of Sagub, the son of Hezron, of the tribe of Judah,
who married the daughter of Machir, so that Jair was a descendant
of Manasseh only on his mother's side (cf. 26.29, where it appears
that Machir was the only son of Manasseh). A Jair of Gilead is mentioned as one of the Judges, whose sons are represented as being in
possession of a district in Gilead, known as Havvoth-jair (Judg. 10.3,
4). Whether there is any relation between these two individuals cannot
be established. In order to harmonize the narrative in I Chron. 2.21,
22, in which it is implied that a descendant of Judah received a share
among the Manassites, which is against the law of the transference
of property (36.7), ibn Ezra suggests that this law was in operation
only in Canaan but not east of the Jordan.

Havvoth-jair] Tent-villages of Jair, a name which may have clung
to them even after they became settled towns. The number of these
villages is variously given (23 in I Chron. 2.23; 30 in Judg. 10.4).

42. *And Nobah*] No description of this Nobah is given here,
although from the context it would appear that this also refers to one
of the clans of Manasseh (Ramban).

Kenath] In I Chron. 2.23, Kenath is mentioned together with

Havvoth-jair, and in Judg. 8.11, Nobah is mentioned together with Jogbehah. Some identify Kenath with the modern Kanawat, which lies on the western slope of Jebel Hauran, marking the extreme northeastern limit of Manasseh's territory. According to this, the Nobah in Judges must be a different town, while the present town was known as Kenath and its new name, Nobah, failed to establish itself (Rashi, Ramban; Ruth R. 5.5, based on omission of the *mappik* from the ה in לה in the masoretic text).

CHAPTER 33.

1–49. ITINERARY OF THE ISRAELITES IN THE WILDERNESS.

This section contains a recapitulation of the itinerary of the Israelites in the wilderness. The catalogue includes the names of places where they encamped for a longer or shorter stay, and in some instances incidents that occurred in connection with some of these places are referred to. The Rabbis illustrate this by the following simile: A king took his son who was ill to a distant place to be cured. On his return, with the son entirely cured, the king points out to him the various places which they had passed through and recalls certain occurrences that happened there. The list was written by Moses at the command of God as a record for future generations (Num. R. 23.3; Tan., Masse'e, 2).

In all there are 42 stations (including Rameses) mentioned here, from Egypt to the Jordan, in the plains of Moab opposite Jericho. From Rameses to the wilderness of Sinai (vv. 5–15), 12 stations are given, all of which, with the exception of Dophkah and Alush, are also mentioned in Exodus. This journey took one year (10.11). From the wilderness of Sinai to the wilderness of Zin (vv. 16–36), which is Kadesh, 21 stations are enumerated, some of which are also mentioned elsewhere, but most of them are not referred to anywhere else. This is supposed to have been the route of their wanderings during the 38 years in the wilderness. In some of these places they may have remained only a short while and in others the stay may have been for a number of years. From Kadesh to the plains of Moab (vv. 37–49), 9 stations are mentioned, all of which, with the exception of Zalmonah, are also given elsewhere. This journey was supposed to have been covered in the course of the 40th year of their wanderings. Many of

33   These are the stages of the children of Israel, by which
they went forth out of the land of Egypt by their hosts
2 under the hand of Moses and Aaron. And Moses wrote
their goings forth, stage by stage, by the commandment
of the LORD; and these are their stages at their goings
3 forth. And they journeyed from Rameses in the first
month, on the fifteenth day of the first month; on the
morrow after the passover the children of Israel went out
4 with a high hand in the sight of all the Egyptians, while
the Egyptians were burying them that the LORD had

the names given here have not been identified, although the chief
points of the route are clear and agree in the main with other accounts
of the journey.

1. *by which they went forth*] Leeser's rendering (following Targum,
Vulgate) "who went forth", making the relative refer to the children
of Israel, is perhaps better.

2. *their goings forth, stage by stage*] This rendering is much happier
than R. V., "their goings out (or Leeser's "their departures") according
to their journeys". The word מסע is taken here to denote a station or
a stage in the journey.

by the commandment of the Lord] The journeys and the stages
were in accordance with the command of God (cf. 9.23; ibn Ezra), or
the phrase may refer to Moses' writing them down by divine order
(Ramban).

3. *Rameses*] The starting point of the journey (Gen. 47.11),
the district in Egypt where the Israelites were settled and where the
city of Rameses was built by them (Ex. 1.11)

on the morrow after the passover] After the offering of the paschal
lamb which took place on the afternoon of the 14th of Nisan. Targum
omits here the word "the morrow" (see Adler and comp. Kid. 37b,
Tos. s. v. ממחרת).

with a high hand] Openly, without fear (cf. 15.30).

4. *while the Egyptians were burying*] The contrast is striking.
The Israelites going out fearlessly and joyfully while the Egyptians,
their oppressors, are busy burying their first-born who died in the
plague during the night (cf. Ex. 12.12).

smitten among them, even all their first-born; upon their gods also the LORD executed judgments. And the children 5 of Israel journeyed from Rameses, and pitched in Succoth. And they journeyed from Succoth, and pitched in Etham, 6 which is in the edge of the wilderness. And they journeyed 7 from Etham, and turned back unto Pi-hahiroth, which is before Baal-zephon; and they pitched before Migdol. And they journeyed from Pene-hahiroth, and passed 8 through the midst of the sea into the wilderness; and they went three days' journey in the wilderness of Etham, and pitched in Marah. And they journeyed from Marah, and 9 came unto Elim; and in Elim were twelve springs of water, and threescore and ten palm-trees; and they pitched there. And they journeyed from Elim, and pitched by the Red 10 Sea. And they journeyed from the Red Sea, and pitched 11 in the wilderness of Sin. And they journeyed from the 12 wilderness of Sin, and pitched in Dophkah. And they 13

5. *And the children of Israel journeyed*] Repeated from v. 3, because of the lengthy interruption.

Succoth] Ex. 12.37.

6. *Etham*] Ex. 13.20.

7. *before Migdol*] I. e. at Pi-hahiroth, between Migdol and the sea (Ex. 14.2).

8. *Pene-hahiroth*] The same as Pi-hahiroth (Targum and most ancient versions, comp. ibn Ezra).

the wilderness of Etham] In Ex. 15.22, this place is called the wilderness of Shur.

Marah] Ex. 15.23.

9. *Elim*] Ex. 15.27.

10. *by the Red Sea*] This station is not mentioned in Exodus.

11. *the wilderness of Sin*] Described in Ex. 16.1 as lying between Elim and Sinai.

14 journeyed from Dophkah, and pitched in Alush. And they
journeyed from Alush, and pitched in Rephidim, where
15 was no water for the people to drink. And they journeyed
from Rephidim, and pitched in the wilderness of Sinai.
16 And they journeyed from the wilderness of Sinai, and
17 pitched in Kibroth-hattaavah. And they journeyed from
18 Kibroth-hattaavah, and pitched in Hazeroth. And they
19 journeyed from Hazeroth, and pitched in Rithmah. And
they journeyed from Rithmah, and pitched in Rimmon-
20 perez. And they journeyed from Rimmon-perez, and
21 pitched in Libnah. And they journeyed from Libnah,
22 and pitched in Rissah. And they journeyed from Rissah,
23 and pitched in Kehelah. And they journeyed from Kehelah,
24 and pitched in mount Shepher. And they journeyed from
25 mount Shepher, and pitched in Haradah. And they jour-
26 neyed from Haradah, and pitched in Makheloth. And
they journeyed from Makheloth, and pitched in Tahath.

12. Dophkah and Alush (v. 13) are mentioned here only and the
places have not been identified.

14. *Rephidim*] Ex. 17.1. The reference here to the lack of water
is strange, in view of the omission of the battle with the Amalekites
at Rephidim (Ex. 17.9), the giving of the manna in the wilderness of
Sin (Ex. 16.4 ff.) and the revelation at Mount Sinai (Ex. 19.2 ff.).
This may perhaps be accounted for by the fact that these events were
of such outstanding importance that they would be remembered even
without a reference being made to them (comp. Ramban).

16. *Kibroth-hattaavah*] 11.34 ff.

17. *Hazeroth*] 11.35; 12.16; Deut. 1.1.

18-29. The 12 names mentioned here do not occur again and their
identification is very uncertain, although attempts have been made
to identify some of them (see Gray, 446).

And they journeyed from Tahath, and pitched in Terah. 27
And they journeyed from Terah, and pitched in Mithkah. 28
And they journeyed from Mithkah, and pitched in Hash- 29
monah. And they journeyed from Hashmonah, and 30
pitched in Moseroth. And they journeyed from Moseroth, 31
and pitched in Bene-jaakan. And they journeyed from 32
Bene-jaakan, and pitched in Hor-haggidgad. And they 33
journeyed from Hor-haggidgad, and pitched in Jotbah.
And they journeyed from Jotbah, and pitched in Abronah. 34
And they journeyed from Abronah, and pitched in Ezion- 35
geber. And they journeyed from Ezion-geber, and pitched 36
in the wilderness of Zin—the same is Kadesh. And they 37
journeyed from Kadesh, and pitched in mount Hor, in the
edge of the land of Edom.—And Aaron the priest went up 38

30–34. These four names: Moseroth, Bene-jaakan, Hor-haggidgad
and Jotbah are mentioned again in different order and with variations in spelling in Deut. 10.6, 7 (see Driver ad loc.).

35. *Abronah*] Not mentioned anywhere else.

Ezion-geber] Also mentioned in Deut. 2.8; I Kings 9.26, where it
is described as lying near Elath, at the head of the Red Sea (the Gulf
of Akabah) in the land of Edom. From there to Kadesh is quite a long
distance, about 70 miles, and there may have been several stages
between these two points not indicated here. Ezion-geber has been
identified with the modern Ain el-Gudyan, about 15 miles north of
the Gulf of Akabah (Wooley & Lawrence, *The Wilderness of Zin*, pp. 32,
46, 87, London, 1936).

36. *the wilderness of Zin*] Often mentioned (13.21; 20.1; 27.14;
34.3; Deut. 32.51; Josh. 15.1).

the same is Kadesh] The Kadesh which is in the wilderness of Zin
(cf. note on 13.21; LXX adds here a phrase which identifies it with
the wilderness of Paran, south of the wilderness of Zin).

into mount Hor at the commandment of the LORD, and
died there, in the fortieth year after the children of Israel
were come out of the land of Egypt, in the fifth month,
39 on the first day of the month. And Aaron was a hundred
and twenty and three years old when he died in mount
40 Hor. And the Canaanite, the king of Arad, who dwelt in
the South in the land of Canaan, heard of the coming of
41 the children of Israel.—And they journeyed from mount
42 Hor, and pitched in Zalmonah. And they journeyed from
43 Zalmonah, and pitched in Punon. And they journeyed
44 from Punon, and pitched in Oboth. And they journeyed
from Oboth, and pitched in Ije-abarim, in the border of
45 Moab. And they journeyed from Ijim, and pitched in
46 Dibon-gad. And they journeyed from Dibon-gad, and
47 pitched in Almon-diblathaim. And they journeyed from
Almon-diblathaim, and pitched in the mountains of

38. The death of Aaron is recorded here as having occurred at
Mount Hor (as also 20.22; but comp. Deut. 10.6). The date is given
as the first day of the fifth month and his age as 123 (cf. Ex. 7.7).

40. *And the Canaanite . . . heard*] Only a reference here to the
incident mentioned in 21.1–3.

41. *Zalmonah*] Not found elsewhere, but Zalmon is found as the
name of a mountain (Judg. 9.48; Ps. 68.15).

42. *Punon*] Perhaps identical with Pinon, an Edomite city (Gen.
36.41; I Chron. 1.52).

44. For Oboth and Ije-abarim see 21.10, 11 and note.

45. *Dibon-gad*] See 21.30; 32.3, 34 and notes.

46. *Almon-diblathaim*] Not found again, except as Bath-dibla-
thaim in Jer. 48.22.

47. *mountains of Abarim*] See note on 27.12.

Abarim, in front of Nebo. And they journeyed from the 48
mountains of Abarim, and pitched in the plains of Moab
by the Jordan at Jericho. And they pitched by the Jordan, 49
from Beth-jeshimoth even unto Abel-shittim in the plains
of Moab.

And the LORD spoke unto Moses in the plains of Moab 50
by the Jordan at Jericho, saying: 'Speak unto the children 51
of Israel, and say unto them: When ye pass over the Jordan into the land of Canaan, then ye shall drive out all 52
the inhabitants of the land from before you, and destroy

Nebo] See note on 32.3.

49. *Beth-jeshimoth*] Mentioned also in Josh. 12.3; 13.20; Ezek.
25.9, and identified with the modern es-Suweime.

Abel-shittim] Probably the same as Shittim (see note on 25.1;
Micah 6.5). The distance between these two places is about 5 miles,
described here as the extent of the Israelitish camp in the plains of
Moab. According to rabbinic tradition, the extent of the camp was
3 *Parsahs* (parasang, Persian mile, equal to about 5.5 kilometers or
3.4 miles) or 12 Mils in length, a Mil being about 2000 Hebrew yards
(a Roman mile, about 1.5 kilometers; Yoma 75a; 'Er. 55b).

50–56.   CANAANITES TO BE DRIVEN OUT OF THE LAND
AND THEIR GODS DESTROYED.

This is the first of a series of legal enactments relating to the conquest of Canaan and the distribution of the land, with which this book
concludes. This first section enjoins the driving out of the natives
from Canaan and the extermination of their gods, and also includes
a repetition of the law regarding the division of the land.

52. *then ye shall drive out*] Dispossess. The word ירש has the
meaning of inherit, take possession, and also of dispossess, drive out
(BDB).

all their figured stones, and destroy all their molten images,
53 and demolish all their high places. And ye shall drive out
the inhabitants of the land, and dwell therein; for unto
54 you have I given the land to possess it. And ye shall inherit
the land by lot according to your families—to the more
ye shall give the more inheritance, and to the fewer thou
shalt give the less inheritance; wheresoever the lot falleth
to any man, that shall be his; according to the tribes of

figured stones] Stones on which figures are carved, which are used
for idolatrous purposes (cf. Lev. 26.1; see *Biur*, where the fanciful
suggestion is made that the word *mosaic* as applied to inlaid work is
a corruption of this word משכית). Leeser translates this word by "sta-
tues"; Targum paraphrases: "their houses of worship". The word,
although found several times in the Bible, is of uncertain meaning,
but is probably connected with a root meaning "to look at", and thus
objects to be looked at, attracting attention.

molten images] Images made of metal melted to represent certain
figures which the gods were conceived to have (cf. I Sam. 6.5, 11;
Ezek. 23.14; Ex. 34.17; Lev. 19.4).

high places] Elevated places were favored as places of worship
and hills were usually selected whereon to erect sanctuaries and altars.
This Canaanitish custom was later followed by the Hebrews who worshiped their God also on such *Bamot* (high places), which are constantly referred to in the Bible. The effort to wean the people away
from this custom proved unavailing until the period of Josiah, and
even then they were not entirely abolished (see Jer. 17.3). The reference here may be to artificial mounds used for worship or to the altars
and sanctuaries erected on the high places.

53. *And ye shall drive out the inhabitants of the land*] "The inhabi-
tants of" is not in the Hebrew text and has to be supplied (comp.
Targum, LXX). R. V. has "ye shall take possession of the land"
(Ramban, Malbim).

54. *ye shall inherit*] Cf. note on 26.54.

according to the tribes] The division was by lot according to the
tribes, and again according to the clans within the tribe, and then

your fathers shall ye inherit. But if ye will not drive out 55
the inhabitants of the land from before you, then shall
those that ye let remain of them be as thorns in your eyes,
and as pricks in your sides, and they shall harass you in
the land wherein ye dwell. And it shall come to pass, that 56
as I thought to do unto them, so will I do unto you.'

according to the individual families within the clan (see Ramban to
26.55).

55.   *as thorns in your eyes, and as pricks in your sides*]   Figures of
speech denoting that they will be to you a source of constant annoyance
and trouble (cf. Josh. 23.13). Elsewhere, the figure used with regard
to the Canaanites left in the land is that they will be as snares (Ex.
23.33; 34.12; Deut. 7.16) enticing you to worship their gods and to
follow in their ways (cf. Ramban).

wherein ye dwell]   Even though you are the masters of the land and
they are subject to you, they will cause you trouble (comp. the attractive theory advanced by Sulzberger, *The Status of Labor in Ancient
Israel*, p. 17 ff., as to the relation between the Canaanites who remained
in the land and their masters, the Israelites).

CHAPTER 34.

1–15.   THE BOUNDARIES OF CANAAN.

A description is given here of the boundaries of Palestine, the land
west of the Jordan, which was to become the possession of the nine
and a half tribes. Beginning with the south-eastern boundary, the
description proceeds westward, then northward, then eastward,
returning to the south-east, whence it started. The actual boundaries
of the promised land were much more extensive (cf. Gen. 15.18; Deut.
11.24). The land within the boundaries here described is the land of
Canaan proper, which was divided among the tribes and which is
practically identical with the future ideal land to be divided among
the twelve tribes after their return from the Babylonian exile, as out-
lined by Ezekiel (47.13–20). The only boundaries here that are clear

34 2 And the LORD spoke unto Moses, saying: 'Command the children of Israel, and say unto them: When ye come into the land of Canaan, this shall be the land that shall fall unto you for an inheritance, even the land of Canaan 3 according to the borders thereof. Thus your south side shall be from the wilderness of Zin close by the side of Edom, and your south border shall begin at the end of 4 the Salt Sea eastward; and your border shall turn about

and certain are the eastern, the Jordan, and the western, the Mediterranean, while the northern and southern boundaries are not very definite, since many of the places mentioned have not been identified with certainty. While the territory here delimited is said to be the land that shall be divided among the nine and a half tribes, parts of it may not have come into the possession of Israel until a late time, so that the description may be somewhat ideal in character. This is especially true with regard to the western boundary, since the Israelites had no territory on the coast of the Mediterranean until very late, when Jaffa was captured by the Maccabean Jonathan and later by his brother Simon (in 148 and 142 B.C.E. respectively). These boundaries are used by the Rabbis with regard to the application of those laws which are operative only in Palestine (Rashi). See Isaacs, *The True Boundaries of the Holy Land*, Chicago, 1917, for a detailed discussion of these verses and for instructive maps.

2. *that shall fall unto you*] The expression "fall" is used here because of the method of distributing the land by lot, which was *cast*.

3–5. The southern boundary begins in the wilderness of Zin, from the Dead Sea, along the border of Edom, to the Mediterranean, going south through the Mount of Akrabbim, then further south to Kadesh-barnea, then westward to Hazar-addar and Azmon, then still further west to the Brook of Egypt, the Wadi el-Arish, to the Mediterranean.

3. *from the wilderness of Zin*] The place whence the spies were sent (13.21). The boundary of the tribe of Judah (Josh. 15.1 ff.), which is practically the southern boundary of Canaan, is similarly described.

at the end of the Salt Sea] More fully in Josh. 15.2, "from the bay that looketh southward".

southward of the ascent of Akrabbim, and pass along to
Zin; and the goings out thereof shall be southward of
Kadesh-barnea; and it shall go forth to Hazar-addar, and
pass along to Azmon; and the border shall turn about 5
from Azmon unto the Brook of Egypt, and the goings out
thereof shall be at the Sea. And for the western border, 6
ye shall have the Great Sea for a border; this shall be your
west border. And this shall be your north border: from 7

4. *the ascent of Akrabbim*] Lit. the Pass of the Scorpions. The
exact place has not been identified, but must be sought in one of the
northern passes of the Wadi el-Fikreh (cf. Josh. 15.3).

the goings out thereof] The end of the boundary to the south of
Kadesh-barnea, whence it starts again in a northwesterly direction.
The two places, Hazar-addar and Azmon, are quite unknown (in
Josh. 15.3 other names are given), but the direction is definite.

5. *the Brook of Egypt*] Generally identified with the Wadi el-
Arish, which rises in the middle of the Sinaitic peninsula and flows
northward, emptying into the Mediterranean. The name, Brook of
Egypt, was given to it because it was regarded as the boundary line
between Palestine and Egypt, although more recently the name has
been associated with that of Muzur or Mizrim, the name of a north
Arabic country, through which the Wadi flows.

6. The western bondary is given here as the Mediterranean Sea,
but no definite delimitations as to the place north and south of the
sea border (comp. Isaacs, ch. II). See introductory note to this section.

for a border] As if it were written לִנְבוּל. R. V. has "and the border
thereof", perhaps including the adjacent district (see Gray, 458, quoting Haupt, who proposes a reading וּנְבוּלוֹ, "and the adjacent region"),
or islands near the coast line (Git. 8a).

7–9. The northern boundary starts at Mt. Hor on the Mediterranean, passes by the entrance of Hamath, running eastward as far
as Hazar-enan. It is difficult to determine definitely this boundary
line, since the names mentioned here have not been identified.

the Great Sea ye shall mark out your line unto mount Hor;
8 from mount Hor ye shall mark out a line unto the entrance
to Hamath; and the goings out of the border shall be at
9 Zedad; and the border shall go forth to Ziphron, and the
goings out thereof shall be at Hazar-enan; this shall be
10 your north border. And ye shall mark out your line for
11 the east border from Hazar-enan to Shepham; and the
border shall go down from Shepham to Riblah, on the
east side of Ain; and the border shall go down, and shall
strike upon the slope of the sea of Chinnereth eastward;

7. *mount Hor*] Not to be confused with the place by the same
name in Edom where Aaron died (29.22). It has been identified by
some with Jebel Akkar in the Lebanon range (BDB; see Git. 8a).

8. *the entrance to Hamath*] The southern boundary of the district
of Hamath which is about 115 miles north of Damascus, often used
to describe the northern limit of Canaan (13.21; Josh. 13.5).

Zedad] This as well as Ziphron and Hazar-enan in v. 9 have not
been identified, although many conjectures have been offered (cf.
Ezek. 47.15–17). The northern boundary, like the southern, is not a
straight line, but goes N. W. and then S. E., forming a sharp angle
at "the entrance of Hamath" (see Gray, 459–460).

10–12. The eastern boundary begins at Hazar-enan, passing
through two unknown places (Shepham and Riblah), reaching to the
Sea of Chinnereth (the Lake of Galilee), then going down to the Jordan
and coming back to the southeastern point of the Dead Sea, whence
the description of the boundaries started. In general terms, the boundaries of Canaan are: the wilderness to the south, the Mediterranean
to the west, the Lebanon to the north and the Jordan to the east.

11. *Riblah*] There is a Riblah in the land of Hamath, mentioned
in connection with Nebuchadnezzar's expedition against Palestine
(II Kings 23.32; 25.21; Jer. 39.5), but this cannot be meant here, since
it must have been farther north. For various conjectures regarding
this name see Gray, 461.

and shall strike] Meaning "reach" (Targum) or "meet", an unusual
signification of the word (comp. פגע, which also has this double meaning).

the slope of the sea of Chinnereth] lit. the shoulder, referring to the

and the border shall go down to the Jordan, and the goings 12
out thereof shall be at the Salt Sea; this shall be your land
according to the borders thereof round about.'

And Moses commanded the children of Israel, saying: 13
'This is the land wherein ye shall receive inheritance by
lot, which the LORD hath commanded to give unto the
nine tribes, and to the half-tribe; for the tribe of the child- 14
ren of Reuben according to their fathers' houses, and the
tribe of the children of Gad according to their fathers'
houses, have received, and the half-tribe of Manasseh
have received, their inheritance; the two tribes and the 15
half-tribe have received their inheritance beyond the Jordan at Jericho eastward, toward the sunrising.'

mountain slope N. E. of Lake Gennesaret, which was near the town
of Chinnereth (Josh. 19.35), known in the New Testament as the
Lake or Sea of Galilee.

13–15. In obedience to the divine command (v. 2), Moses directs
the Israelites to divide among themselves the land thus described,
the land of Canaan proper, which is to be the inheritance of the nine
and a half tribes, since the Reubenites, the Gadites and half of the
tribe of Manasseh have already received their portion on the eastern
side of the Jordan.

16–29. NAMES OF PRINCES OF TRIBES WHO WILL ASSIST JOSHUA
AND ELEAZAR IN ALLOTTING THE LAND.

Besides Joshua and Eleazar, who will take the place of Moses and
Aaron, ten additional chiefs are appointed, one from each tribe, to
superintend the proper division of the land. No representatives are
appointed for Reuben and Gad, since they were not interested in the
matter. The order followed here is that of the geographical positions
occupied by the tribes in Canaan from South to North, except that
Judah is mentioned before Simeon and Manasseh before Ephraim
(see Luzzatto's explanation of the omission of the word נשיא in the

16-17　　And the LORD spoke unto Moses, saying: 'These are
the names of the men that shall take possession of the
land for you: Eleazar the priest, and Joshua the son of
18 Nun. And ye shall take one prince of every tribe, to take
19 possession of the land. And these are the names of the
men: of the tribe of Judah, Caleb the son of Jephunneh.
20 And of the tribe of the children of Simeon, Shemuel the
21 son of Ammihud. Of the tribe of Benjamin, Elidad the
22 son of Chislon. And of the tribe of the children of Dan a
23 prince, Bukki the son of Jogli. Of the children of Joseph:
of the tribe of the children of Manasseh a prince, Hanniel
24 the son of Ephod; and of the tribe of the children of Eph-
25 raim a prince, Kemuel the son of Shiphtan. And of the
tribe of the children of Zebulun a prince, Elizaphan the
26 son of Parnach. And of the tribe of the children of Issachar
27 a prince, Paltiel the son of Azzan. And of the tribe of the
children of Asher a prince, Ahihud the son of Shelomi.
28 And of the tribe of the children of Naphtali a prince,
29 Pedahel the son of Ammihud. These are they whom the
LORD commanded to divide the inheritance unto the
children of Israel in the land of Canaan.'

case of the first three tribes). The names mentioned here are entirely
different from those in the previous lists of princes (1.5 ff.; 13.4 ff.),
with the exception of Caleb who alone, together with Joshua, remained
alive of those who came out of Egypt (14.26–30; 36–38).

　　17. *that shall take possession of the land for you*]　R. V. has: "divide
the land unto you for an inheritance"; Leeser has: "that shall parcel
out".

　　29. *to divide the inheritance*]　After each took possession of the
tribal territory in the name of his tribe, he was to distribute it among
the families of his tribe (Rashi, Luzzatto).

And the LORD spoke unto Moses in the plains of Moab **35**
by the Jordan at Jericho, saying: 'Command the children 2
of Israel, that they give unto the Levites of the inheritance

CHAPTER **35.**

1–8. THE TOWNS ASSIGNED TO THE LEVITES.

The Levites were not given a portion in the land, but were to be
scattered among the various tribes to serve as the religious guides of
the people (Gen. 49.7; Lev. 10.11; Deut. 31.9–13; 33.10). Moses now
commands the Israelites when they enter Canaan to set aside 48 towns
in the various districts of the land, where the Levites might settle.
Each town is to have a plot of land of 2000 cubits on each side of the
town, to be used by them as pasture ground for their cattle. Six of
these towns should also serve as "cities of refuge".

In Josh. 21, the manner in which this law was carried out is related
in detail. According to the description given there, the Levites received
nine cities in the territories of Judah and Simeon, three in that of
Naphtali and four each in the territories of the other tribes, so that
they received 38 cities on the west side and 10 on the east side of the
Jordan. The 13 towns in the territories of Judah, Simeon and Benjamin
were given to the priestly families, while the other Kohathite families
received 10 from Ephraim, Dan and western Manasseh. The Gershonites received 13 towns from Issachar, Asher, Naphtali and eastern
Manasseh and the Merarites 12 from Reuben, Gad and Zebulun.
References to this distribution of land among the Levitical families
are found also in Lev. 25.32, 34; Josh. 14.4; I Chron. 13.2; II Chron.
11.14; 31.15, 19 and probably also in Ezra 2.70; Neh. 7.73; 11.3, 20,
36. Ezekiel (48.8–14) suggests a somewhat different arrangement for
land to be allotted to the priests and the Levites in the future ideal
state.

Modern Bible critics have raised a doubt whether this law was ever
carried out in practice, in spite of the many references to it in other
books of the Bible. Many of them consider this a purely ideal and
imaginary description of a desirable allotment, which was never carried
out and which would have been almost impossible to carry out in the
manner here described. The main reason for their doubt is the fact
that in a number of texts, especially in Deut., the Levites are classed

of their possession cities to dwell in; and open land round
3 about the cities shall ye give unto the Levites. And the
cities shall they have to dwell in; and their open land shall
be for their cattle, and for their substance, and for all their
4 beasts. And the open land about the cities, which ye shall

with the stranger, the widow and the orphan, apparently landless
people, who are commended to the charity of the Israelites, while in
Num. 18 certain definite portions have been set aside for the support
of the Levites and the priests out of the produce of the field, and the
reason there definitely given is because they have no portion in the
land. This, however, does not necessarily preclude the arrangement
that certain towns should be placed at their disposal, where they might
settle their families and their cattle. Even with this allotment and
with the dues received by them, many of the Levites would still have
been poor and dependent on charity. According to this arrangement,
the whole territory assigned to the Levites would be about 15½ square
miles, a very small proportion of the entire area of Palestine (about
6000 square miles). That there were certain towns which were known
as priest-towns is proved by several references (Anathoth, Josh. 21.18;
I Kings 2.26; Jer. 1.1; 32.6; Nob, I Sam. 21.2; 22.19; Beth-el, I Sam.
10.3; Judg. 20.18; II Kings 17.28; Shiloh, I Sam. 1.3 ff.). The exact
distribution of the towns and the measurements of the open land as
given here may not have been carried out, but there is no reason to
doubt the fact that certain definite localities were set aside by each
tribe for the priests and the Levites, where they might find homes for
their families.

2. *cities to dwell in*] While the phrase does not necessarily imply
ownership, it does not exclude it, and in other places it appears that
these cities were meant to be owned by the Levites (Lev. 25.32–34;
but comp. Keil, 258–259).

open land] Common land, probably meaning pasture land, place
of driving (גרש "to drive") cattle (BDB). R. V. renders: "suburbs".

3. *their substance*] Although the word is used to include all kinds
of goods or property, it is used here specifically for flocks (cf. Gen. 13.6).

all their beasts] Leeser, following Mendelssohn, renders "their
requirements" (comp. Sforno, who makes the following distinction

give unto the Levites, shall be from the wall of the city
and outward a thousand cubits round about. And ye shall 5
measure without the city for the east side two thousand
cubits, and for the south side two thousand cubits, and

among these terms: *cattle*, including large cattle, beasts of burden;
substance, including small cattle; and *beasts*, including fowls, birds,
beehives, etc., comp. Ned. 81a).

5. *two thousand cubits*] The contradiction between this and v. 4,
where only 1000 cubits is mentioned, has given rise to a great deal of
speculation among commentators. LXX reads 2000 in both verses.
If we assume that 1000 cubits were left on each side of the city, thus
making a perfect square of 2000 cubits of the city and its open places,
then the city would remain without any dimensions, reduced to a point.
The suggestion has been made by Keil that the dimensions of the
open land were 2000 cubits plus the dimensions of the city on each
side. While this would solve the problem, it is not implied in the text.
Rashi, following the interpretation of R. Eliezer b. Jose ('Er. 56b and
Rashi ad loc., giving diagrams), says that the open space was 1000
cubits and that beyond that another 1000 cubits were to be added for
gardens and orchards. Maimonides (*Shemitah*, 12.2), following another
authority (Sotah 27a), says that the open space was 1000 cubits, and
beyond that 2000 additional cubits were to be set aside for gardens
and orchards, so that there would be a space of 3000 cubits round
about. Ramban suggests that the whole space, including the town,
was to be 2000 cubits square. The town itself was to be 1000 cubits
square and on each side of the town 500 cubits of open land, so that
there would be 1000 cubits of open land on both sides of the town, from
east to west and from north to south, 500 on each side. Luzzatto,
after discussing the various explanations offered, makes the following
suggestion: The open space was 1000 cubits within the city wall
and 1000 cubits outside of it, making together 2000 cubits, without
affecting the size of the city itself, which varied greatly. A novel
theory has been advanced by Saalschütz (*Das mosaische Recht*, 100 ff.),
who regards the city as a circle and the open space as an outer circle.
From the city wall to the outer circle was a thousand cubits and then
a prolongation of another 1000 cubits beyond the outer circle in four
directions, the whole plan being a geometrical star, consisting of four

for the west side two thousand cubits, and for the north
side two thousand cubits, the city being in the midst.
6 This shall be to them the open land about the cities. And
the cities which ye shall give unto the Levites, they shall
be the six cities of refuge, which ye shall give for the manslayer to flee thither; and beside them ye shall give forty
7 and two cities. All the cities which ye shall give to the
Levites shall be forty and eight cities: them shall ye give
8 with the open land about them. And concerning the cities
which ye shall give of the possession of the children of
Israel, from the many ye shall take many, and from the

triangles inscribed in a circle (comp. Ehrlich, who suggests that cubit
in v. 4 is the *holy* cubit, which was double the size of the ordinary cubit
of. v. 5).

6. *six cities of refuge*] Three on the west side and three on the
east side of the Jordan (v. 14; Josh. 20.7, 8).

8. *from the many ye shall take many*] This was not carried out very
carefully if we understand by these terms many in population, since
Naphtali, which was more numerous than either Ephraim or Gad,
assigned only three cities, while the other two gave four cities each.
The suggestion is therefore made that this does not refer to the population of the respective tribes but to the extent and quality of their
territories, as is indicated by the expression "according to its inheritance" (Ramban; Leeser has "that hath many", and Mendelssohn is
still more explicit: "that possesses much land").

9–34. THE CITIES OF REFUGE.

The purpose of the cities of refuge, alluded to in v. 6, is now described in great detail. They were intended to protect one who had
killed a man accidentally, from the vengeance of the murdered
man's family. Various illustrations are offered here to make clear
the distinction between murder and manslaughter. The murderer
only is to suffer the death penalty, while the one guilty of accidental
homicide, whose innocence of any criminal intent has been established

few ye shall take few; each tribe according to its inheritance
which it inheriteth shall give of its cities unto the Levites.'

And the LORD spoke unto Moses, saying: 'Speak unto 9-10
the children of Israel, and say unto them: When ye pass
over the Jordan into the land of Canaan, then ye shall 11
appoint you cities to be cities of refuge for you, that the

by a constituted authority, should be given the protection of the cities
of refuge, so that he might not fall a prey to the vengeance of the
relatives of the dead person.

According to primitive notions, murder could be avenged only by
the blood of the murderer, or by the blood of a member of his family.
In some cases, the murderer could redeem himself by the payment
of a ransom (*Kofer*). This ancient custom is here modified in several
important points. In the first place, distinction is made between
intentional and unintentional homicide. Not all killing is murder, and
the duty of the "avenger" is limited to cases of willful murder only.
The officials of the state must first determine whether the murder was
deliberate or not. Secondly, the murderer only is to be killed, and no
one else is responsible for the crime committed by another. Then
again, the murderer cannot escape punishment by the payment of
a ransom. If one man killed another, he was immediately exposed to
the danger of being killed by any of the murdered man's relatives
(*Goel*). He was then given the privilege of fleeing to any one of these
cities of refuge, within the walls of which the avenger might not enter.
A regular trial was conducted, and if it was found that the murder was
willful and intentional, the murderer was handed over to the *Goel* for
execution. If, however, it was found that the murder was unintentional, the protection of the cities of refuge was given to the slayer.
He must not leave the city of refuge before the death of the high-priest.
If he goes beyond the city limits before that time, he exposes himself
to the danger of being slain by the *Goel* (comp. Sulzberger, *The Ancient
Hebrew Law of Homicide*, Philadelphia, 1915).

11. *then ye shall appoint*] Select suitable places (Sifre; Rashi;
comp. ibn Ezra, who considers והקריתם a denominative verb from קריה
a city, meaning to build; comp. Josh. 20.7, ויקדשו, "set apart", so LXX).

cities of refuge] The word מקלט is used in the Bible only in connection with this law. In rabbinic Hebrew, the verb קלט means to receive

manslayer that killeth any person through error may flee
12 thither. And the cities shall be unto you for refuge from
the avenger, that the manslayer die not, until he stand
13 before the congregation for judgment. And as to the
cities which ye shall give, there shall be for you six cities
14 of refuge. Ye shall give three cities beyond the Jordan,

or contain. The elders of the city "shall take him into the city unto
them, and give him a place" (Josh. 20.4).

12. *from the avenger*] A shortened form of the avenger of blood
(*Goel ha-Dam*; vv. 19, 21). The word גאל means to redeem, hence to
act as one's kinsman, either in marrying the kinsman's widow (Ruth
3.13), or redeeming a kinsman from bondage (Lev. 25.48, 49), or
redeeming the kinsman's field (Lev. 25.25). In the present instance,
the *Goel* or *Goel ha-Dam* acts in a similar capacity, he is not so much
an avenger as a redeemer, one who redeems the loss sustained by the
family.

the congregation] The representatives of the congregation where
the homicide took place (cf. Deut. 19.12).

for judgment] To determine whether the killing was deliberate or
accidental.

13. *six cities of refuge*] According to the Rabbis, all the 48 Levitical cities were cities of refuge, only that in the case of the six designated as such the inhabitants were obliged to house the manslayer
gratis, while in the other 42, the elders of the congregation might
demand a fee for housing him (Mak. 9b, 11a).

14. The two and a half tribes east of the Jordan were provided
with as many cities of refuge as the nine and a half tribes settled in
Canaan, possibly because the distances were very great in the eastern
part, which was more sparsely populated (Ramban), or because there
existed a more primitive state of society, where homicides were more
frequent (Rashi, after Mak. 9a; cf. Hos. 6.8). In Deut. 19.9, provision
is made for additional three cities of refuge in Canaan (cf. Maim.,
Rozeah, 8.4). The names of the cities that were selected for that purpose are given in Josh. 20.7, 8, and their positions indicate that provision was made to cover the south, center and north of the land on
both sides of the Jordan.

and three cities shall ye give in the land of Canaan; they shall be cities of refuge. For the children of Israel, and 15 for the stranger and for the settler among them, shall these six cities be for refuge, that every one that killeth any person through error may flee thither. But if he smote 16 him with an instrument of iron, so that he died, he is a murderer; the murderer shall surely be put to death. And 17 if he smote him with a stone in the hand, whereby a man may die, and he died, he is a murderer; the murderer shall surely be put to death. Or if he smote him with a weapon 18 of wood in the hand, whereby a man may die, and he died,

15. *for the stranger*] See note on 15.14.

for the settler] "A person, not of Hebrew birth, who was attached to a Hebrew family in some more permanent way than the day-laborer" (Gray). In Josh. 20.9, the stranger only is mentioned (see Sulzberger, *Status of Labor*, 73).

16–23. Several examples are offered here to show the distinction between accidental homicide and deliberate murder. The evidence of intention must be present in order to establish a case of murder, either by the instrument used or by the relation that existed between the manslayer and his victim (cf. Ex. 21.12–14; Deut. 19.4 ff.).

16. *an instrument of iron*] Which is likely to kill. The slayer cannot claim ignorance of the fact that the instrument would cause death, since intention was present (cf. Rashi). If one strikes another with an iron instrument, he cannot be regarded as an unintentional manslayer, since he should know that an iron is likely to cause death.

17. *a stone in the hand*] Large enough to fill one's hand (Sifre, 160), or that can be thrown by the hand. Leeser, following Targum, has: "which one can take in the hand", even though not very large, but sufficient to kill a man (cf. Sanh. 76b, where it is established that an iron, even small, is likely to cause death, but in the case of a stone or a wooden instrument it must be of a size to cause death).

18. *a weapon of wood in the hand*] Such as a cane (cf. Ezek. 39.9), but heavy enough to cause death. In these three cases, the motive is not considered, as long as the weapon used was such as would cause death.

he is a murderer; the murderer shall surely be put to death.
19 The avenger of blood shall himself put the murderer to
death; when he meeteth him, he shall put him to death.
20 And if he thrust him of hatred, or hurled at him any thing,
21 lying in wait, so that he died; or in enmity smote him with
his hand, that he died; he that smote him shall surely be
put to death: he is a murderer; the avenger of blood shall
22 put the murderer to death when he meeteth him. But if
he thrust him suddenly without enmity, or hurled upon
23 him any thing without lying in wait, or with any stone,
whereby a man may die, seeing him not, and cast it upon
him, so that he died, and he was not his enemy, neither
24 sought his harm; then the congregation shall judge between
the smiter and the avenger of blood according to these
25 ordinances; and the congregation shall deliver the man-

19. *when he meeteth him*] Also wherever he meets him, even
within the city of refuge (Rashi, following Mak. 12a; Sanh. 45b).
Targum paraphrases: "when he is declared guilty by a court, he shall
kill him", with reference to v. 24 ff.

20. *thrust him of hatred*] Pushed him down, or threw something
at him, or smote him with his hand. In all these cases there is implied
malicious intent or premeditated action (lying in wait), even though
the object cast is not of the kind that would ordinarily be employed
by a murderer.

22–23. These cases are just the opposite of those enumerated in
vv. 20–21, where the accidental or unintentional nature of the act can
be established.

24. *the congregation*] Either where the homicide occurred or where
the manslayer lived. In Josh. 20.4, the manslayer relates his case to
the elders of the city of refuge on his arrival there and then they allot
to him a place in the city. This is probably intended as an additional
precaution after he was already found to be innocent of the crime by
the congregation of his own community (ib. v. 9; but comp. Gray, 475).

according to these ordinances] The examples given in vv. 16–23.

slayer out of the hand of the avenger of blood, and the
congregation shall restore him to his city of refuge, whither
he was fled; and he shall dwell therein until the death of
the high priest, who was anointed with the holy oil. But 26
if the manslayer shall at any time go beyond the border
of his city of refuge, whither he fleeth; and the avenger of 27
blood find him without the border of his city of refuge,
and the avenger of blood slay the manslayer; there shall
be no bloodguiltiness for him; because he must remain in 28
his city of refuge until the death of the high priest; but
after the death of the high priest the manslayer may
return into the land of his possession. And these things 29
shall be for a statute of judgment unto you throughout
your generations in all your dwellings. Whoso killeth 30

25. *shall restore him*] The meaning here apparently is that after
he fled to the city of refuge, the manslayer was taken to his own city
to be tried and if found not guilty of intentional murder, he was sent
back to the city of refuge.

until the death of the high priest] The priest atones for the sins of
the individual. The high priest has still greater power, for he atones
for the sins of the community on the Day of Atonement. The death
of the high priest was to be regarded as a complete atonement for all
the sins of Israel (Luzzatto, Keil). Maimonides (*Guide for the Per-
plexed*, III, 40) suggests that the death of such a high personage as
the high priest was likely to produce a saddening and sobering effect
upon the whole community, so as to make each one forget individual
grievances (comp. Ehrlich, McNeile, Gray, for other explanations of
this provision).

27. *no bloodguiltiness*] The *Goel* is not guilty of murder, since the
manslayer left the city of refuge which offered him protection (see
Mak. 7a).

29. *a statute of judgment*] Cf. note on 27.11.

any person, the murderer shall be slain at the mouth of
witnesses; but one witness shall not testify against any
31 person that he die. Moreover ye shall take no ransom for
the life of a murderer, that is guilty of death; but he shall
32 surely be put to death. And ye shall take no ransom for
him that is fled to his city of refuge, that he should come
again to dwell in the land, until the death of the priest.
33 So ye shall not pollute the land wherein ye are; for blood,
it polluteth the land; and no expiation can be made for
the land for the blood that is shed therein, but by the
34 blood of him that shed it. And thou shalt not defile the
land which ye inhabit, in the midst of which I dwell; for
I the LORD dwell in the midst of the children of Israel.'

30. *at the mouth of witnesses*] Even a murderer shall not be put
to death unless there are (at least two, Deut. 9.15) witnesses testifying
to the crime (Deut. 17.6).

32. Just as the murderer cannot free himself from punishment
by the payment of a ransom, so also the unintentional homicide cannot
avoid exile to the city of refuge by the payment of a ransom. There
is only one instance when ransom was permitted in the case of homicide,
namely when one's ox gored someone to death. In that case the owner
of the ox might redeem himself with a ransom (Ex. 21.29, 30). The
payment of a ransom, equivalent to the market value of the person
slain, was a widespread custom among ancient peoples. The Koran
(Sura 2, 173 ff.) permits a ransom even in the case of willful murder.

that he should come again] So that he might return to his home before
the death of the high priest.

ye shall not pollute the land] This expression is used in connection
with murder (here and in Ps. 106.38) and with adultery (Jer. 3.1, 2,
9; cf. Isa. 24.5), the two elemental breaches in the organization of a
state. The land is represented as becoming polluted by such crimes,
and God will not dwell in a land that is polluted (Sifre 161). Such
pollution can be expiated only by the blood of the one who caused it
(cf. Gen. 9.5).

And the heads of the fathers' houses of the family of **36**
the children of Gilead, the son of Machir, the son of Manasseh, of the families of the sons of Joseph, came near,
and spoke before Moses, and before the princes, the heads
of the fathers' houses of the children of Israel; and they 2
said: 'The LORD commanded my lord to give the land
for inheritance by lot to the children of Israel; and my
lord was commanded by the LORD to give the inheritance
of Zelophehad our brother unto his daughters. And if they 3
be married to any of the sons of the other tribes of the

CHAPTER **36.**

1–13. HEIRESSES MUST MARRY WITHIN THEIR TRIBES.

In consequence of the case of the daughters of Zelophehad (27.1–11),
whose father died without male issue, the law of hereditary succession
was promulgated, by which daughters are recognized as heirs, when
there are no sons. The members of the tribe of Manasseh, to which
Zelophehad belonged, now seek for another ruling in order to prevent
the possession being removed from the tribal allotment, should the
daughters of Zelophehad marry outside of the tribe. A law was con-
sequently passed that they must marry members of their own tribe
only, so as to keep the tribal land intact.

1. *the heads of the fathers' houses*] "Houses" is not in the Heb.
text, but supplied here from the context (cf. 17.18). Although Machir
is represented as having settled in Gilead, on the eastern side of the
Jordan (32.29, 40; Josh. 17.1), and the portion of the daughters of
Zelophehad is described as being in Canaan (Josh. 17.4), still the
representatives of the tribe were anxious to obtain a ruling from Moses
which would safeguard the integrity of the tribal land, whether situated east or west of the Jordan.

before Moses] LXX adds: "and before Eleazar the priest", as in
27.2.

2. *and my lord was commanded*] Cf. 27.2 ff.

children of Israel, then will their inheritance be taken
away from the inheritance of our fathers, and will be
added to the inheritance of the tribe whereunto they shall
belong; so will it be taken away from the lot of our inherit-
4 ance. And when the jubilee of the children of Israel shall
be, then will their inheritance be added unto the inheritance
of the tribe whereunto they shall belong; so will their
inheritance be taken away from the inheritance of the
5 tribe of our fathers.' And Moses commanded the children
of Israel according to the word of the LORD, saying: 'The
6 tribe of the sons of Joseph speaketh right. This is the
thing which the LORD hath commanded concerning the
daughters of Zelophehad, saying: Let them be married
to whom they think best; only into the family of the tribe
7 of their father shall they be married. So shall no inheritance of the children of Israel remove from tribe to tribe;
for the children of Israel shall cleave every one to the
8 inheritance of the tribe of his fathers. And every daughter,

3. *so will it be taken away*] If they marry members of other tribes,
their children, who will follow their father's pedigree, will inherit
them and thus a portion of the land of Manasseh will be held by members of other tribes.

4. *And when the jubilee*] Even when the jubilee year comes around,
this land will not be restored to the tribal possession, since only land
that is sold is restored in the jubilee year to the original owner, but
not land that is inherited (Lev. 25.10 ff., ibn Ezra).

5. *The tribe of the sons of Joseph*] Phraseology similar to that of
27.7.

6. *to whom they think best*] Within their tribe they should have
free choice, but they must not marry outside their tribe.

8. *And every daughter*] The law is now made general to apply to
all cases where daughters become the heiresses of their father's estate.

that possesseth an inheritance in any tribe of the children
of Israel, shall be wife unto one of the family of the tribe
of her father, that the children of Israel may possess every
man the inheritance of his fathers. So shall no inheritance 9
remove from one tribe to another tribe; for the tribes of
the children of Israel shall cleave each one to its own
inheritance.' Even as the LORD commanded Moses, so 10
did the daughters of Zelophehad. For Mahlah, Tirzah, 11
and Hoglah, and Milcah, and Noah, the daughters of
Zelophehad, were married unto their father's brothers'
sons. They were married into the families of the sons of 12
Manasseh the son of Joseph, and their inheritance remained in the tribe of the family of their father.

The Rabbis limited the application of this law to the period of the
wilderness, before the division of the land (B.B. 120a, 121a; comp.
ibn Ezra).

9. *So shall no inheritance remove*] A repetition of v. 7 to apply to
all cases of that kind. Ramban suggests that the repetition here refers
to cases where daughters had intermarried with members of other
tribes and then became heiresses through the death of their brothers.
In that case the land which they inherit shall not, after their death,
be handed over to their next of kin in regular succession, but should
go back to the next of kin in their own tribe.

11. The names of the daughters of Zelophehad are given here in
a slightly different order from that followed in 27.1 and Josh. 17.3.
It has been suggested that there the order was according to their age,
while here the chronological order of their marriages is followed (ibn
Ezra; Rashi to B.B. 120a).

their father's brothers' sons] Leeser has "uncles". The word דוד
usually means a paternal uncle, but it may also mean a relative, a
kinsman, so that this phrase may indicate simply that they married
their relatives, members of their tribe.

12. *in the tribe of the family of their father*] Not necessarily in the
family of their father, but in the tribe to which the family belonged,

13   These are the commandments and the ordinances,
which the Lord commanded by the hand of Moses unto
the children of Israel in the plains of Moab by the Jordan
at Jericho.

as some of them may have married distant relatives, who belonged to
different families of the tribe of Manasseh (see Sforno, Malbim).

13.   This verse is a subscription to the series of laws promulgated
during the stay of the Israelites in the plains of Moab, beginning
with ch. 22 (comp. Lev. 27.34, where a similar subscription is given
to the laws promulgated at Sinai).

INDEX

AARON, sons of, the priests, 21.
———, and Miriam, jealous of Moses, 119 ff.
———, sin of, at Meribah, 211 ff.
———, death of, 218 ff., 342.
Abarim, 224, 257, 296, 342, 343.
Abel-shittim, 234, 275, 342.
Abidan, 5, 19, 76, 99.
Abiezer, 285.
Abihail, 28.
Abihu, 21, 22, 291.
Abihud, 350.
Abila, 275.
Abiram, see Dathan.
Abronah, 341.
Absalom, a Nazirite, 58.
Adultery, law of, 46.
Agag, 266.
Aharah, 286.
Ahiezer, 5, 20, 76, 100.
Ahira, 5, 20, 77, 100.
Ahiram, 286.
Ain, 348.
Ain el Guderat, 210.
Ain el Gudyan, 341.
Ain el Hudereth, 119.
Ain Kadeis, 210.
Ajbehat, 335.
Akabah, Gulf of, 2, 117, 119, 239, 341.
Akrabbim, Mount of, 346, 347.
Almon-diblathaim, 342.
Altar, bronze covering of, 179 ff.
Alush, 340.

Amalek, 134, 144, 145, 266, 271.
Amen, 54.
Ammiel, 129.
Ammihud, 5, 19, 75, 99, 350.
Amminadab, 5, 17, 72, 98.
Ammishaddai, 5, 20, 76, 100.
Ammon, 229, 230.
Amorites, 135, 229, 230, 233, 238.
Amram, 26, 27, 291.
Anak, sons of, 127, 131, 136.
Angel of God, 216, 247, 249.
Ar, 226, 231.
Arad, 150, 220, 342.
Aram, Aram-naharaim,2 40, 254.
Arba' Kanfot, 163.
Ard, 287.
Areli, 284.
Arish, el, 210.
Ark, coverings of, 34.
———, movements of, 92, 102, 103, 104.
———, rod placed in front of, 184.
Arnon, river, 225, 226, 231, 328.
Arod, 284.
Aroer, 225, 334.
Ashbel, 286.
Ashes of purification, 204, 205, 207.
Asriel, 285.
Ass, Balaam's, 246 ff.
Assyria, prophecy on, 273.
Ataroth, 329, 334.

✦

The text of this book was set in the composing rooms of the Press of the JEWISH PUBLICATION SOCIETY OF AMERICA on the monotype in Binny Old Style. The basis of this useful letter was a type cut in Scotland, and it was first put on the Monotype Machine in 1908.

———

The paper is Spring Grove English finish book paper, cream white, mat finish, made by the P. H. Glatfelter Company, Spring Grove, Penna., especially for this edition.

———

Electrotyped, printed and bound by the Haddon Craftsmen, Incorporated, Camden, New Jersey.

✦

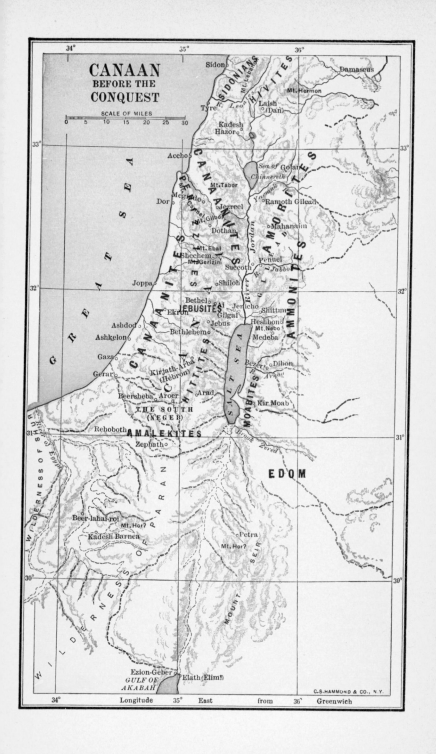

CANAAN
BEFORE THE
CONQUEST

SCALE OF MILES
0   5   10   15   20   25   30

GREAT SEA

WILDERNESS OF SHUR

WILDERNESS OF PARAN

MOUNT SEIR

GULF OF AKABAH

Sidon
Tyre
R. Leon
Kadesh
Accho
Dor
Megiddo
Mt. Tabor
Mt. Carmel
Jezreel
Gilboa
Dothan
Mt. Ebal
Shechem
Mt. Gerizim
Succoth
Shiloh
Joppa
Bethel
Ai
Ekron
Jericho
Gilgal
Jebus
Bethlehem
Ashdod
Ashkelon
Gaza
Kirjath-Arba
(Hebron)
Gerar
Beersheba
Aroer
Arad
THE SOUTH
(NEGEB)
Rehoboth
Zephath
Beer-lahai-roi
Mt. Hor?
Kadesh Barnea
Petra
Mt. Hor?
Ezion-Geber
Elath (Elim?)

Damascus
Mt. Lebanon
Mt. Hermon
Laish (Dan)
Hazor
Sea of Galilee
Chinnereth
Yarmuk
Ramoth Gilead
Mahanaim
Penuel
Jabbok
Shittim
Heshbon
Mt. Nebo
Medeba
Bezer
Dibon
R. Arnon
Kir Moab
Brook Zered

SIDONIANS
HIVITES
CANAANITES
AMORITES
GILEAD
JEBUSITES
HITTITES
AMMONITES
MOABITES
AMALEKITES
EDOM

Jordan River
SALT SEA

Longitude   35°   East   from   36°   Greenwich

34°   35°   36°

C.S. HAMMOND & CO., N.Y.

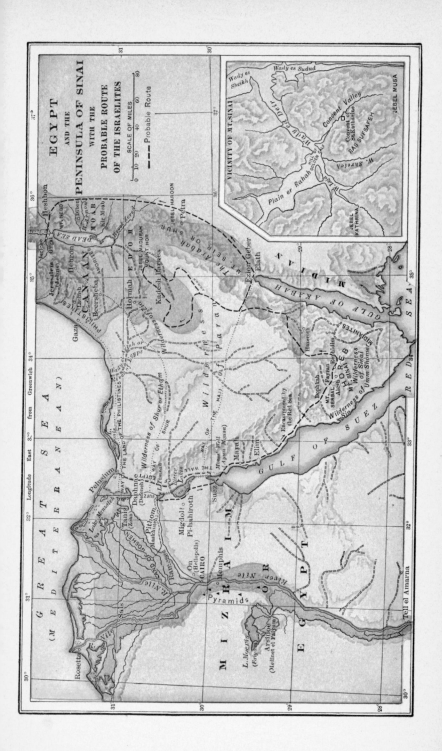

EGYPT
AND THE
PENINSULA OF SINAI
WITH THE
PROBABLE ROUTE
OF THE ISRAELITES

SCALE OF MILES
0 10 20   40   60   80

— — — Probable Route

VICINITY OF MT. SINAI

Wady es Sheikh
Wady es Sudud
Djebel ez Deir
Convent Valley
Convent of St. Katharine
RAS SUFSAFEH
JEBEL MUSA
Plain er Rahah
W. Shreich
JEBEL KATHARINA

G R E A T   S E A
(M E D I T E R R A N E A N)

Longitude East 32° from Greenwich 34°

Rosetta
Nile
Tanis (Zoan)
Lake Menzaleh
Pelusium
Daphnae (Defneh)
THE WAY OF THE LAND OF THE PHILISTINES
Pithom (Patumus?)
Rameses
On (Heliopolis) CAIRO
Memphis
Pyramids
River Nile
Arsinoe (Medinet el Faiyum)
L. Moeris (Birqeh)

M I Z R A I M   O R   E G Y P T

L A N D   O F   G O S H E N

Migdol
Pi-hahiroth
Suez
Marah
Elim
Wilderness of Shur or Etham
THE WAY OF THE WILDERNESS OF SHUR
Wady el Arish or Wady of Egypt

G U L F   O F   S U E Z

Wilderness of Sin
MT. SERBAL
Dophkah
Rephidim
Wilderness of Sinai
Wilderness of Umm Shomer
HOREB or SINAI
Hazeroth

Gaza
PHILISTINES
Beersheba
Hebron
Jerusalem (Salem)
Zaanaim
Tamaib
Hormah
Kadesh Barnea
Wilderness of Zin
Wilderness of Paran
THE ARABAH or THE HAJJ ROUTE
JEBEL MADURAH
MOUNT HOR
JEBEL HAROUN
Petra

C A N A A N

E D O M

Mt. Nebo
Jordan R.
Heshbon
Dibon
Aroer
Kir Moab
M O A B

Ezion Geber
Elath

Mts. Seir or Shur

G U L F   O F   A K A B A H

M I D I A N
MIDIANITES

R E D   S E A

Tell el Amarna